COMPLETE POEMS

BOOKS BY JIM HARRISON

JIM HARRISON
COMPLETE POEMS

Edited by Joseph Bednarik

COPPER CANYON PRESS
PORT TOWNSEND, WASHINGTON

Spanish-language poems in *Saving Daylight* not attributed to Pablo Neruda are by
Jaime Harrison Walgren, with assistance from William Barillas and María Chiggia.

Copper Canyon Press is in residence at Fort Worden State Park
in Port Townsend, Washington, under the auspices of Centrum.
Centrum is a gathering place for artists and creative thinkers from
around the world, students of all ages and backgrounds, and audiences
seeking extraordinary cultural enrichment.

LIBRARY OF CONGRESS CATALOGING-IN-PUBLICATION DATA
Names: Harrison, Jim, 1937–2016, author. | Bednarik, Joseph, 1964– editor.
Title: Jim Harrison : complete poems / edited by Joseph Bednarik.
Other titles: Poems
Description: Port Townsend, Washington : Copper Canyon Press, [2021] |
    Includes indexes. | Summary: "Contains every poem
    Harrison published over his fifty-year career, as well as a section of
    unpublished 'Last Poems.'"— Provided by publisher.
Identifiers: LCCN 2021025525 | ISBN 9781556595936 (cloth)
Subjects: LCGFT: Poetry.
Classification: LCC PS3558.A67 2021 | DDC 811/.54—dc23
LC record available at https://lccn.loc.gov/2021025525

COPPER CANYON PRESS
Post Office Box 271
Port Townsend, Washington 98368
www.coppercanyonpress.org

Dedicated to
Linda King Harrison
Jamie Harrison Potenberg
Anna Harrison Hjortsberg
Joyce Harrington Bahle

It's up to poets to revive the gods.

Jim Harrison

CONTENTS

IN SEARCH OF SMALL GODS

EDITOR'S NOTE: WHO HEARS?

Poetry, at its best, is the language your soul would speak
if you could teach your soul to speak.

Jim Harrison

Jim Harrison answered the call to become a poet when he was nineteen. Sixty years later he died at his writing desk, notebook opened to a fresh poem.

The holograph of that last poem is included as a coda in this volume—and watching that poem, line by line, you can practically see death enter Jim's office. Not to be interrupted, the poet kept his pen moving across the page because that was life's call. These are the final words Jim Harrison wrote on this earth: *God's body*—no end punctuation.

In an interview Jim described his call to poetry as "almost a metaphysical experience: I'm sitting on the roof of our house watching the moon rise over a big marsh and the birds of various species were crisscrossing the moon and I could see them clearly in silhouette. . . . You do take vows just like a priest or a Zen student takes vows. . . . That's your primary fidelity in life."

In that same interview, he said poetry "is something that you have to give your entire life to—and that includes *all* your life."

The book you are holding is the work of a lifetime.

Even when Jim Harrison's career led him to write novels and novellas, food columns and screenplays, the reading and the writing of poetry— and the good company of poets living and dead—were vital to what he called his "soul life." Fellow poets are everywhere throughout these pages. Harrison wrote letter-poems to Sergei Yesenin and Dan Gerber; co-wrote a "conversation in poetry" with Ted Kooser; dedicated books and poems to scores of poets, including Denise Levertov, who first championed Harrison's poetry; quotes Rilke, Rimbaud, Whitman, and

Dickinson; reads Su Tung-p'o at dawn; walks desert canyons with Ikkyū; and laments the hardships of Lorca, Mandelstam, and Vallejo.

Jim was profoundly moved when he discovered that Antonio Machado abandoned a satchel of unpublished poems to help carry his mother as they fled the Spanish Civil War. Machado and his mother died soon thereafter, and the fact that Machado's final poems have never been recovered deeply disturbed Harrison because, as he wrote in the literary journal *Brick,* they were "far more important to the world than the United Nations or internal combustion." In the final poem of *Dead Man's Float,* Jim's last book, he and Machado meet in an extraordinary location:

> Most of my life was spent
> building a bridge out over the sea
> though the sea was too wide.
> I'm proud of the bridge
> hanging in the pure sea air. Machado
> came for a visit and we sat on the
> end of the bridge, which was his idea.

Imagine those two poets—separated by time, geography, and language—dangling their feet over the edge of an unfinished bridge high above a sea that "roars and howls like / the animal it is." You *can* imagine this scene because a brilliant poet invited you to do so by creating the conditions *for* you to do so—and you accepted the invitation. Similar invitations are offered thousands of times in the ensuing pages, and you will find yourself present at other extraordinary locations, fully awake, breathing "the pure sea air," feeling the exhilaration of life's sheer edges.

In Jim Harrison's memoir, *Off to the Side,* the central section is titled "Seven Obsessions." Every memoirist would do well to follow Harrison's lead and train their attention on personal obsessions, where life's primary colors are brightest. Here are Jim's stated obsessions:

- The Road
- Hunting, Fishing (and Dogs)
- Private Religion
- Nature and Natives
- Alcohol
- Stripping
- France

First, observe that this is a list of *ten* obsessions, suggesting that numbers were never Jim Harrison's strong suit. And given his reputation as a gourmand, we could reasonably add "Good Food," and with nearly forty books published over his lifetime, "Writing." So let's amend the list and agree that Jim Harrison had (at least) twelve obsessions.

And because these subjects are *obsessions,* readers of *Jim Harrison: Complete Poems* can expect to find each and all throughout these pages. An enterprising scholar could create an "obsessions index," using these twelve categories. And just for the record, during the production phase of this book, I discovered that the most frequently used words in *Complete Poems* are *bird, dog, time, love, river, god.*

If this obsessions index ever gets created, hundreds of entries will be listed in the Private Religion section, including the sequence "After Ikkyū," the late poem "Notes on the Sacred Art of Log Sitting," and this passage from "Returning to Earth":

> I admit that yesterday I built an exploratory altar.
> Who can squash his delight in incomprehension?
> So on a piece of old newspaper I put an earthworm
> on a maple leaf, the remains of a bluebird after
> the cat was finished—head and feet, some dog hair,
> shavings from when we trimmed the horses' hooves,
> a snakeskin, a stalk of ragweed, a gourd,
> a lemon, a cedar splinter, a nonsymbolic doorknob,
> a bumblebee with his juice sucked out by a wasp.
> Before this altar I invented a doggerel mantra
> it is this   it is this   it is this

A card with the phrase *Make it vivid* was tacked to the wall above Jim's writing desk. Combine the doggerel mantra *it is this* with *Make it vivid* and the results are a poet who, according to *Publishers Weekly,* does "absolutely brilliant and outrageous things with language." The same review also called the poet "an untrammeled renegade genius," and *Jim Harrison: Complete Poems* is living proof of that bold honor.

—

Jim Harrison: Complete Poems contains all the poems Jim Harrison published during his lifetime, as well as a section of previously unpublished material, "Last Poems." When a book of this breadth and depth is compiled, hundreds of editorial questions and wonderments arise. While we consulted all of Jim's original poetry publications in journals, magazines, and books, we viewed *The Shape of the Journey: New and Collected Poems* (1998) as the definitive source text for Jim's first eight poetry titles. All subsequent poetry books were also published by Copper Canyon Press, so we consulted the press's manuscript archive and correspondence files to inform and guide editorial decisions. From this point forward, we regard *Jim Harrison: Complete Poems* as the definitive text.

Along with direct access to primary source material, this book greatly benefits from the extraordinary care and attention of managing editor John Pierce, proofreader Alison Lockhart, production assistant Claretta Holsey, and copyeditor David Caligiuri who, when returning the first round of copyedited pages, wrote in a letter, "This *Complete* is an adventure, and I thank you for including me." (Mr. Caligiuri, it should be noted, fiercely copyedited every Jim Harrison book that Copper Canyon published.)

Jim Harrison called his poems "flowers for the void." He once told me that he received the koan *Who hears?* from his Zen teacher. What a profound and provocative question for a poet—and now for readers.

Joseph Bednarik
Port Townsend, Washington

EVERYTHING ON EARTH IS TRUE

Terry Tempest Williams

> These simple rules to live within—a black
> pen at night, a gold pen in daylight. . . .
> He crumples as paper but rises daily from the dead.

The book you now hold in your hands is the physical evidence of a
life well lived by a man, named Jim Harrison, who was in love with the
world. He was a man of big appetites not only for good food and fine
wines but also for tasting, smelling, hearing, feeling, and seeing what
Nature, both human and wild, had to show him about living and dying
and locating a sliver of light in so much darkness. Writing poems was
Harrison's spiritual practice—following that line of light—walking
the path of poetry in crepuscular hours when wolves howl and ravens
fly. *Jim Harrison: Complete Poems* is a pilgrimage through a dedicated life
of a writer who dared "to give up again this human shape" and see
beyond our own solipsism and human exceptionalism. "On your walks
in the backcountry get to where you're going, then walk like a heron or
sandhill crane. They don't miss a thing." He exhorts us: "Listen to the
alarm."

In "After Ikkyū" he writes:

> Everywhere I go I study the scars on earth's face,
> including rivers and lakes. I'm not playing God
> but assessing intent. In the Patagonia Mountains
> you think, "small mines, pathetic deaths." In Cabeza Prieta
> men boiled in their own blood, ground temperature 170°F.
> Contrails of earthen scar-tissue stink of sulfur.
> Gold & copper to buy the horse that died, the woman who left.

Harrison acknowledges in the same book the sentience of other
species and their comprehension of truths:

> I confess that here and there in my life
> there is a vision of a great brown toad

leaking words of love and doom through his skin,
excrescences that would kill anyone, given time,
his words tinged as they are with the shapes
of death, one drumbeat, a heartbeat, the skins
of gods a rug spread beneath our feet.

We are nothing without metamorphosis. We are changelings on a changing Earth.

Jim Harrison marked the transformations in the landscapes he called home, from the Upper Peninsula of Michigan to the Sonoran Desert of Arizona to the Northern Rockies on the edge of Yellowstone in Livingston, Montana. His poems are checkpoints on the map of his soul.

"It doesn't really matter if these poems are thought of as slightly soiled dharma gates or just plain poems. They'll live or die by their own specific density, flowers for the void," he writes. "To write a poem you must first create a pen that will write what you want to say. For better or worse, this is the work of a lifetime."

In 1945, Jim Harrison lost the use of his left eye. He was eight years old. In an interview he said, "I probably wouldn't have been a poet if I hadn't lost my left eye when I was a boy. A neighbor girl shoved a broken bottle in my face during a quarrel. Afterward, I retreated to the natural world and never really came back."

I believe him. The fact that the broken glass that took his eye was part of a "laboratory beaker" makes this a story of alchemy. With half his vision gone, his ongoing fear that he could lose his other eye, becoming blind to the world, inspired him to pay fierce attention to the Garden of Earthly Delights reminiscent of Hieronymus Bosch's own alchemical vision: the iconic triptych of heaven and hell and the garden of sensual pleasures that resides between the two panels. In Harrison's passionate play with language and his own erotic life of the senses, he enlists what Virginia Woolf calls "the divine specific"—essential to any writer who moves through their days with wonder, inquiry, and imagination.

If we read Jim Harrison's *Complete Poems* as a query into a more conscious way of being, then we can begin to believe "the solstice says 'everything on earth is True.'" Harrison tells us insight begins in that place of standing on the precipice of darkness and light. Being human means being stretched between the known and the unknown: the longest day of summer is also a move toward winter, the longest night in winter is a turn toward brighter days. We bow to time and the cycles of change that are beyond our control. Light will come. Darkness will come. We are held in the numinous hours of grace before dawn and after dusk.

—

> To have reverence for life
> you must have reverence for death.

I first met Jim in 1989. I was at work on a book called *Refuge,* which is about the rise of Great Salt Lake and the death of my mother from ovarian cancer. Our friend Doug Peacock phoned to say he and Harrison were driving through Salt Lake City en route to Tucson. Peacock asked whether it was okay if they spent the night at our house in Emigration Canyon. Of course we said yes. I put away my manuscript where no one would see it.

What I remember is how nervous my husband, Brooke, and I were to have Jim Harrison stay with us. His reputation was as a hard-drinking, food-loving, lecherous, literate, Midwesterner-turned-Westerner wild man. They arrived. He was jolly and unnerving, his left eye looking beyond you while his right eye focused intensely on every word spoken. He was kind and gracious and terrifyingly astute in all manner of his perceptions. Our first conversation was an interrogation into who we were and what we cared about. The men talked about bears and trout while drinking a bottle of Bandol, brought along as a house gift. We gave Jim our bedroom out of respect. Peacock slept outdoors while Brooke and I slept on the floor of our study, down the hall from the bedroom. Sleeping lightly, I noticed that the light in Jim's bedroom was on most of the night.

In the morning, Jim emerged with a huge smile on his face. "Well, Tempest, I found your manuscript in your underwear drawer and read the whole damn thing. It's about the two things I love the most—Death and Birds."

I didn't know which was more horrifying: that Jim Harrison had gone through my underwear drawer or that he had read my manuscript. During a long breakfast on the patio, I shared with him the letter I had just received from my editor who had matter-of-factly said that my book had "failed on every level." And that if I still wanted to continue with the project, I should try again, beginning with page 494—that left six pages he approved of in a 500-page manuscript.

"They're fucking with your imagination," Jim said. "Write the book you want to write." He paused. "Write the book you *have* to write."

I did.

Jim taught me that "Nature withholds and hides from us until we try to learn her languages."

This was the first of many conversations—always about birds, a love we continued to share, especially when Jim was writing his novella "The Beige Dolorosa," his fictional project to rename all the birds of North America.

Once, arriving at his home in Patagonia, Arizona, we were greeted by a hastily painted sign nailed to the fence: "The Fucking Bird Is Dead!"

Turns out, a blue mockingbird had been sighted in a particular thicket exactly where Jim was living and writing through the winter. Enthusiastic birders put it on the Rare Bird Alert sponsored by the American Birding Association. Busloads of birders were now coming to his window to see this "rare vagrant" that he sharply reminded them was endemic to Mexico, only eighteen miles away. Word got out the writer had a shotgun; adding the blue mockingbird to one's life list might not be worth the risk.

Contrast this behavior with Harrison's lovely instructions, "Notes on the Sacred Art of Log Sitting," and you witness the weather system of a tightly refined nervous system:

Approach the log cautiously with proper reverence as if you were entering a French cathedral or the bedroom of your lover.

If it's over 60 degrees, inspect the lower sides of the log for Mohave rattlesnakes.

Now examine the log closely for the most comfortable place to sit, usually away from the sun.

Sit down.

Empty your mind of everything except what is in front of you—the natural landscape of the canyon.

Dismiss or allow to slide away any aspect of your grand or pathetic life.

Breathe softly.

Avoid a doze.

Internalize what you see in the canyon: the oaks and mesquites, the rumpled and grassy earth, hawks flying by, a few songbirds.

Stay put for forty-five minutes to an hour.

When you get up bow nine times to the log.

Three logs a day is generally my maximum.

And then, these last lines:

I can readily imagine buying a small ranch I'd call "The Log Ranch." I'd truck in thirty-three logs and arrange them on the property like the Stations of the Cross. This could soothe me during my limited time in the twenty-first century, which has been very coarse indeed.

This is just one of the reasons why I loved Jim Harrison. He was alive, charismatic, and good-humored, a large spirit you felt privileged to know, because you had to keep up with him if you had any self-respect as an intellectually engaged human being. He was predictable and unpredictable at once—loving at times, cranky and cruel, at times, taking liberties not his to take; and he took those liberties, repeatedly, with women, with friends, and I imagine with family.

He crossed a line with me one night, as we were about to go onstage at the Herbst Theatre. I was young and intimidated to be in conversation with him at the prestigious City Arts & Lectures series in San Francisco. He was known, I was not. Standing in the wings of the theater, we listened to the introductions. We were about to walk onstage when Jim, standing behind me, licked my ear and whispered a vulgarity. Call it trash-talking your opponent before a sporting event; call it harassment. It knocked me off-center and scrambled my mind. I lost my focus and didn't speak while Jim and the interviewer talked brilliantly. I finally reclaimed my composure with only minutes left in the hour.

On that night, Jim Harrison created a revolution in me, a recovered memory of when women were birds. We can fly away or fight. I found my voice by having lost it. It was a defining moment for me. Powerful men fuck with your imagination. Jim Harrison fucked with mine. I later wrote him a letter. "You spoke. I became mute. Every woman in that audience recognized my silence as their own." He wrote me back and apologized. We never spoke about it again.

Like most of us who are writers, Jim could be self-absorbed—until he wasn't, and that was usually when his heart broke over what becomes lost and cannot be retrieved:

> Where's my medicine bag? It's either hidden
> or doesn't exist. Inside are memories of earth:
> corn pollen, a bear claw, an umbilical cord.
> If they exist they help me ride the dark
> heavens of this life. Such fragile wings.

Jim Harrison was a poet writing from the future as much as the past. "To see behind the clarity of my glass / the birth of new creatures / suffused with light." His line-breaks allow us to enter his poetry with a double vision—the blind eye turned inward and the bright eye focused outward, which is the way Jim met the world in darkness and light.

I remember taking Jim and Peter Matthiessen on a walk in the Tetons to see a venerable goshawk on her nest in an aspen grove. Harrison was taken by the ruby-colored eye flashing on the side of her face as she guarded her young. Matthiessen remained quiet but never took his eyes off hers. We stayed briefly so as not to disturb her and warrant her legendary wrath. Both Jim and Peter were thrilled by her majesty perched above them. I watched each man quietly bow, paying his respect to this feathered god. Here were two of America's great writers, sons of wild Earth who chose to use their sizable gifts of perception and influence on behalf of the natural world.

Nature fed and fueled their literary ambitions with an uncommon humility, which saved them from being consumed by their public personas and falling into the fatal mistake of believing their own myths. Awe replaced arrogance.

Later at lunch, I listened to Jim and Peter bare their souls about their struggles with clinical depression, a fact not unusual to creatives. *Darkness is always there, it only stands revealed.* I witnessed the vulnerability of these men, witnesses and scribes to an unjust world. Pain brought forth their ink. There is a price to opening one's heart to Beauty.

In "I Believe" Harrison writes:

> I believe in . . . the Chihuahuan ravens that follow
> me on long walks. The rattler escaping the cold hose,
> the fluttering unknown gods that I nearly see
> from the left corner of my blind eye, struggling
> to stay alive in a world that grinds them underfoot.

How are we to stay upright at this time, poised as we are to lose so much? Where do we find the strength to remain attentive to what threatens to kill us in this era of climate collapse? I believe Jim Harrison shows us the way by being present in joy and wonder, in grief and despair, and most importantly, partaking fully in the day-to-day pleasures of a living world on this beautiful, broken planet we call home, regardless of what is coming.

Here are five lines I love, from "Returning to Earth":

> I want to have my life
> in cloud shapes, water shapes, wind shapes,
> crow call, marsh hawk swooping over grass and weed tips.
> Let the scavenger take what he finds.
> Let the predator love his prey.

From beginning to end, this single volume of *Complete Poems* is a book of prayers—born of Harrison's Christian background that underwent a natural metamorphosis more spiritually aligned with Zen Buddhism. Some of the prayer-poems are polished, some are rough, others feel unfinished, written while on one's knees or in prostrations, impatient and unresolved; a few are banal, a few indulgent, with many others sighting gratitudes "that hold our 10,000 generations of mothers in the clouds waiting for us to fall back into their arms again."

Most of these poems I read repeatedly as eloquent petitions to earth and moon and sun, testaments to "rushing, turbulent water and light, convinced by animals / and rivers that nature only leads us to herself."

I knew Jim as a man who loved his family—a family of women: his wife, Linda, and his daughters, Jamie and Anna, beautiful women, smart women, women who understood this "untrammeled renegade genius" and held him to account as Nature did.

In his last poems, Jim Harrison had the strong sense "that severe weather is coming." As we begin to emerge out of this pandemic, the closing lines from his poem "Quarantine" caught my attention. It offers us instructions:

> There is no time to fool around, the gods said.
> They blew my poem with the wind to
> the top of Antelope Butte. I can't walk there
> with my cane. Some gods have been dead
> a thousand years and need our magic
> and music to come back to life.
> We owe it to them. They got us started.

If writing poetry was Jim Harrison's spiritual practice, then reading his poetry can be a spiritual experience. We can follow his conscious admonitions:

Wake up.

Listen to the gods. / They're shouting in your ear every second.

We disemboweled the earth and die without lungs.

But birds / lead us outside where we belong.

Only the most extreme heat makes us malleable.

—

On March 26, 2016, I learned of Jim's death. I grieved his passing and celebrated his life. He was among the great ones—an elevated soul in all his unruliness who favored his senses and courted the wild on the page and in the world. His was a storied life that loomed large, and we are the beneficiaries. "Such a powerful wounded poet—wrote as if he had to sing with a cut throat . . . and he did have to sing," said Jorie Graham.

I lamented that Jim and I had not had one last conversation. But spending much of this year reading and rereading Copper Canyon Press's landmark edition of *Jim Harrison: Complete Poems,* I savored the weight of his wisdom and buoyancy of spirit just as I did when we were together. I realized how contemporary his poetry remains. When he writes of his "tears of doubt," my own tears stream down my cheeks as I wonder what will survive and what will perish in this moment of extinction and climate chaos.

For me, this passage in "After Ikkyū" has become a koan to what still exists:

Way up a sandy draw in the foothills
of the Whetstone Mountains I found cougar
tracks so fresh, damp sand was still
trickling in from the edges. For some reason

I knelt and sniffed them, quite sure
I was being watched by a living rock
in the vast, heat-blurred landscape.

Unbidden hope reached me like rain in the desert. How prescient Harrison's body of work continues to be in allowing us to feel the full range of what it means to be human, even in drought. "Despite gravity we're fragile as shadows," he writes in *Saving Daylight*. I am grateful for Jim's disciplined pen that wrote what he wanted to say. Jim Harrison's life-force as a writer grounded in place will continue to provoke and inspire readers for generations.

The spirit is here. Are you?

Our conversation is ongoing.

Castle Valley, Utah
June 1, 2021

COMPLETE POEMS

PLAIN SONG

1965

to Linda

POEM

Form is the woods: the beast,
a bobcat padding through red sumac,
the pheasant in brake or goldenrod
that he stalks—both rise to the flush,
the brief low flutter and catch in air;
and trees, rich green, the moving of boughs
and the separate leaf, yield
to conclusions they do not care about
or watch—the dead, frayed bird,
the beautiful plumage,
the spoor of feathers
and slight, pink bones.

SKETCH FOR A JOB-APPLICATION BLANK

My left eye is blind and jogs like
a milky sparrow in its socket;
my nose is large and never flares
in anger, the front teeth, bucked,
but not in lechery—I sucked
my thumb until the age of twelve.
O my youth was happy and I was never lonely
though my friends called me "pig eye"
and the teachers thought me loony.

> (When I bruised, my psyche kept intact:
> I fell from horses, and once a cow but never
> pigs—a neighbor lost a hand to a sow.)

But I had some fears:
the salesman of eyes,
his case was full of fishy baubles,
against black velvet, jeweled gore,
the great cocked hoof of a Belgian mare,
a nest of milk snakes by the water trough,
electric fences,
my uncle's hounds,
the pump arm of an oil well,
the chop and whir of a combine in the sun.

From my ancestors, the Swedes,
I suppose I inherit the love of rainy woods,
kegs of herring and neat whiskey—
I remember long nights of pinochle,
the bulge of Redman in my grandpa's cheek;
the rug smelled of manure and kerosene.
They laughed loudly and didn't speak for days.

(But on the other side, from the German Mennonites,
    their rag-smoke prayers and porky daughters
    I got intolerance, and aimless diligence.)

In '51 during a revival I was saved:
I prayed on a cold register for hours
and woke up lame. I was baptized
by immersion in the tank at Williamston—
the rusty water stung my eyes.
I left off the old things of the flesh
but not for long—one night beside a pond
she dried my feet with her yellow hair.
    O actual event dead quotient
    cross become green
I still love Jubal but pity Hagar.

(Now self is the first sacrament
    who loves not the misery and taint
    of the present tense is lost.
    I strain for a lunar arrogance.
                Light macerates
                the lamp infects
    warmth, more warmth, I cry.)

DAVID

He is young. The father is dead.
Outside, a cold November night,
the mourners' cars are parked upon the lawn;
beneath the porch light three
brothers talk to three sons
and shiver without knowing it.
His mind's all black thickets
and blood; he knows
flesh slips quietly off the bone,
he knows no last looks,
that among the profusion of flowers
the lid is closed to hide
what no one could bear—
that metal rends the flesh,
he knows beneath the white-pointed
creatures, stars,
that in the distant talk of brothers,
the father is dead.

EXERCISE

Hear this touch: grass parts
for the snake,
in furrows
soil curves around itself,
a rock topples into a lake,
roused organs,
fur against cloth,
arms unfold,
at the edge of a clearing
fire selects new wood.

A SEQUENCE OF WOMEN

I

I've known her too long:
we devour as two mirrors,
opposed,
swallow each other a thousand
times at midpoints,
lost in the black center
of the other.

II

She sits on the bed,
breasts slack,
watching a curl of dust
float through a ray of sun,
drift down to a corner.
So brief this meeting
with a strange child—
Do I want to be remembered?
Only as a mare might know
the body of her rider,
the pressure of legs
unlike any other.

III

The girl who was once my mistress
is dead now, I learn, in childbirth.
I thought that long ago women ceased
dying this way.

To set records straight, our enmity
relaxes, I wrote a verse for her—
to dole her by pieces, ring finger
and lock of hair.

But I'm a poor Midas to turn her golden,
to make a Helen, grand whore, of this graceless
girl; the sparrow that died was only
a sparrow:

Though in the dark, she doesn't sleep.
On cushions, embraced by silk, no lover
comes to her. In the first light when birds
stir she does not stir or sing. Oh eyes can't
focus to this dark.

NORTHERN MICHIGAN

On this back road the land
has the juice taken out of it:

stump fences surround nothing
worth their tearing down

by a deserted filling station
a Veedol sign, the rusted hulk

of a Frazer, "live bait"
on battered tin.

        A barn
with half a tobacco ad
owns the greenness of a manure
pile

a half-moon on a privy door
a rope swinging from an elm. A

collapsed henhouse, a pump
with the handle up

the orchard with wild tangled branches.

        —

In the far corner of the pasture,
in the shadow of the woodlot
a herd of twenty deer:
              three bucks
are showing off—
they jump in turn across the fence,
flanks arch and twist to get higher

in the twilight
as the last light filters
through the woods.

TREE

Tree,
arrows are made from you
a guitar
tables which hold food
the walls of this house;
your function is dictated
in the shape of the wood
from the sawyer who cradles
you in iron tongs, the touch
the teeth of steel—
but this is speech
and comes from the throat:
your mouth or countless mouths
are those leaves I look at now
with silver bellies and dark backs
that draw in sun, the air,
that transpire and breathe for you—
they are of no use to us
except as shade, the greenness
we expect, but to you they are life
and compressed into blackness,
after a century and inch of soil,
they make you your food.

RETURNING AT NIGHT

Returning at night

there's a catalpa moth
in the barberry

on the table the flowers
left alone turned black

in the root cellar
the potato sprouts
creeping through the door
glisten white and tubular
in the third phase
of the moon.

APOLOGY

I don't weigh an hour
in consecutive breaths—
my sleeves are short,
my elbows reveal thin wires
attached to a skull
that rattles when it wants
to sing; but sometimes
when a good rain falls
and there is heat enough
some fine clean grass
even flowers
grow up through the weeds
in this boneyard.

LOST

When hunting I became lost,
I walked for hours.
All the ridges looked the same—
the snow had a thick crust
but not enough to hold my weight.
I crossed my path twice.
It began to get dark, my sweat
turned cold, when between two huge
charred pine stumps I thought I saw
myself. I raised my rifle to shoot
this ghost but then my father spoke.

"SHE"

       She
who is this other
without masks, pitiless?
A bald eye in a dump,
a third-rail type who loves
the touch of flesh,
the bare thigh in a cafeteria
crying mercy to the stone?
Unlyric, she coils and strikes
for the sake of striking.

"I'VE HAD ENOUGH TONIGHT."

I've had enough tonight.
My small room is cavernous,
I hang like a bat from rafters
while below me hymns are sung—
three figures move in a circle of light,
dark trinity at whose touch
paper becomes stone
words float like cells
unite in reverse of nature.

Let me sleep.
My body shakes,
a gourd in the hand of some giant child.

"ONCE I STOOD ALL NIGHT"

Once I stood all night
beside a road with only the metallic
rattling of a sign to keep me company.

In the first light of dawn I read
        DANGER
        CURVE
and in a ditch of weeds
along a barbed-wire fence
there were three black crosses.

FAIR/BOY CHRISTIAN TAKES A BREAK

This other speaks of bones, blood-wet
and limber, the rock in bodies. He takes
me to the slaughterhouse, where lying
sprawled, as a giant coil of rope,
the bowels of cattle. At the county fair
we pay an extra quarter to see the her-
maphrodite. We watch the secret air tube
blow up the skirts of the farm girls,
tanned to the knees then strangely white.
We eat spareribs and pickled eggs,
the horses tear the ground to pull a load
of stone; in a burning tent we see
Fantasia do her Love Dance with the
Spaniard—they glisten with sweat, their
limbs knot together while below them farm
boys twitter like birds. Then the breasts
of a huge Negress rotate to a march in
opposing directions, and everyone stamps
and cheers, the udders shine in blurring
speed. Out of the tent we pass produce
stalls, some hung with ribbons, squash
and potatoes stacked in pyramids. A buck-
toothed girl cuts her honorable-mention
cake; when she leans to get me water
from a milk pail her breasts are chaste.
Through the evening I sit in the car (the
other is gone) while my father watches
the harness race, the 4-h talent show.
I think of St. Paul's Epistles and pray
the removal of what my troubled eyes have seen.

MORNING

The mirror tastes him
breath clouds
hands pressed against glass

in yellow morning light
a jay
flutters in unaccustomed
silence
from bush to limb of elm

a cow at breakfast
pauses
her jaws lax in momentary stillness

far off a milk truck
rattles
on the section road

light low mist
floats
over the buckwheat
through the orchard

the neighbor's dogs bark
then four roosters announce
day.

GARDEN

Standing at the window at night
my shadow is the length of the garden—
I move a huge arm and
cause plants to spring up,
tomatoes to ripen.
My head is as large
as a strawberry bed and I can
cup two bales of straw in one hand.
I take pride in this strength,
fed by light and darkness,
wielded against my father's garden—
a lord of shadows.

HORSE

A
quarter horse, no rider
canters through the pasture

thistles raise soft purple burrs
her flanks are shiny in the sun

I whistle and she runs
almost sideways toward me

the oats in my hand are sweets to her:

dun mane furling in its breeze,
her neck
corseted with muscle,
wet teeth friendly against my hand—
how can I believe
you ran under a low maple limb
to knock me off?

KINSHIP

Great-uncle Wilhelm, Mennonite, patriarch,
eater of blood sausage, leeks,
headcheese, salt pork,
you are led into church
by that wisp you plundered for nine children.
Your brain has sugared now,
your white beard is limp,
you talk of acres of corn
where there is only snow.
Your sister, a witch, old as a stump,
says you are punished now for the unspeakable
sin that barred you from the table for seven years.
They feed you cake to hasten your death.
Your land is divided.
Curse them but don't die.

FEBRUARY SUITE

Song,
angry bush
with the thrust of your roots
deep in this icy ground,
is there a polar sun?

—

Month of the frozen
goat—
La Roberta says cultivate
new friends,
          profit will
be yours with patience.
Not that stars are crossed
or light to be restored—
we die from want of velocity.

And you, longest of months
with your false springs,
you don't help or care about helping,
so splendidly ignorant of us.
Today icicles fell
but they will build downward again.

—

Who has a "fate"?
This fig tree
talks
about bad weather.

—

Here is a man drunk—
in the glass
his blurred innocence renewed.

—

The Great Leitzel
before falling to her death
did 249 flanges on the Roman rings—
her wrist was often raw
and bloody
but she kept it hidden.

—

He remembers Memorial Day—
the mother's hymn to Generals.
The American Legion fires blanks
out over the lassitude of the cemetery
in memory of sons who broke
like lightbulbs in a hoarse cry
of dust.

—

Now
behind bone
in the perfect dark
the dream of animals.

—

To remember
the soft bellies of fish
the furred animals that were part of your youth
not for their novelty
but as fellow creatures.

—

I look at the rifles
in their rack upon the wall:
though I know the Wars
only as history
some cellar in Europe might still
owe some of its moistness to blood.

      —

With my head on the table
I write,
my arm outstretched, in another field
of richer grain.

      —

A red-haired doll stares
at me from a highchair,
her small pink limbs twisted about
her neck.
I salute the postures of women.

      —

This hammer of joy,
this is no fist
but a wonderment got by cunning.

      —

The first thunderstorm
of March came last night
and when I awoke the snow had passed
away, the brown grass
lay matted and pubic.

Between the snow and grass,
somewhere into the ground with the rain
a long year has gone.

TRAVERSE CITY ZOO

Once I saw a wolf tread a circle in his cage
amid the stench of monkeys, the noise of musty
jungle birds. We threw him bits of doughy
bread but he didn't see us, padding on through
some imagined forest, his nose on blood.
We began to move on in boredom when he jumped
against the bars, snarled, then howled
in rage that long shrill howl that must remind
us of another life. Children screamed and ran,
their parents passing them in terror—the summer
day became hard and brittle. I stooped there
and watched his anger until the keeper
came with a Flash Gordon gun and shot him full
of dope. He grew smaller and sputtered into sleep.

REVERIE

He thinks of the dead. But they
appear as dead—beef-colored and torn.

There is a great dull music
in the ocean that lapses into seascape.

The girl bends slowly
from the waist. Then stoops.

In high school Brutus
died upon a rubber knife.

Lift the smock. The sun-
light stripes her back. A *fado* wails.

In an alley in Cambridge. Beneath
a party's noise. Bottle caps stuck to them.

FOX FARM

In the pasture a shire
whose broad muscles once
drew a hayrake,
a plough,
can't hold the weight of his great
head and neck—
he will be fed to the foxes.

And the Clydesdales and saddle nags
that stray along the fence
with limps and sagging bellies,
with rheumy eyes (one
has no tail).

But the foxes
not having known field
or woods,
bred, born in long rows of hutches,
will die to adorn some
woman's neck.

"THE PAINTING ON THE WALL"

The painting on the wall,
the smooth fat thigh of a girl
drives me from my room—
so lovely she is
that I look for her sisters
in the streets but find none.

TICKET

To those who stalk terminals
in the glaze of tears of light.

Sir Violet, food-stooped but nimble
asks me for a light, for my dork
with a whorelike glance.
He takes me for a student—
"Why education's the ticket to the future."
I answer with a Bronx cheer
and he shrugs and walks away.

Old queen of a dry country,
these soiled tiles,
the air that groans of buses
and wailing Negro children,
uncourtly stew bums,
orange rinds,
your garden of love
is a weedpatch.

NIGHTMARE

Through the blinds
a white arm caresses a vase of zinnias

beneath the skin
of a pond the laughter of an eye

in the loft
the hot straw suffocates
the rafters become snakes

through the mow door
three deer in a cool pasture
nibbling at the grass
mercurous in the moon.

CREDO, AFTER E.P.

Go, my songs
to the young and insolent,
speak the love of final things—
do not betray me
as a dancer, drunk,
is dumb to his clumsiness.

DUSK

Dusk over the lake,
clouds floating
heat lightning
a nightmare behind branches;
from the swamp
the odor of cedar and fern,
the long circular
wail of the loon—
the plump bird aches for fish
for night to come down.

Then it becomes so dark
and still
that I shatter the moon with an oar.

LISLE'S RIVER

Dust followed our car like a dry brown cloud.
At the river we swam, then in the canoe passed
downstream toward Manton; the current carried us
through cedar swamps, hot fields of marsh grass
where deer watched us and the killdeer shrieked.
We were at home in a thing that passes.
And that night, camped on a bluff, we ate eggs
and ham and three small trout; we drank too much
whiskey and pushed a burning stump down the bank—
it cast hurling shadows, leaves silvered and darkened,
the crash and hiss woke up a thousand birds.

Now, tell me, other than lying between some woman's legs,
what joy have you had since, that equaled this?

THREE NIGHT SONGS

I

He waits to happen with the clear
reality of what he thinks about—
to be a child who wakes beautifully,
a man always in the state of waking
to a new room, or at night, waking
to a strange room with snow outside,
and the moon beyond glass,
in a net of branches,
so bright and clear and cold.

II

Moving in liquid dark,
night's water,
a flat stone sinking,
wobbling toward bottom;
and not to wait there for morning,
to see the sun up through the water,
but to freeze until another glacier comes.

III

The mask riddles itself,
there's heat through the eye slits,
a noise of breathing,
the plaster around the mouth is wet;
and the dark takes no effort,
dark against deeper dark,
the mask dissembles,
a music comes to the point of horror.

CARDINAL

That great tree covered with snow
until its branches droop,
the oak, that keeps its leaves through winter
(in spring a bud breaks the stem),
has in its utmost branch
a cardinal,
who brushing snow aside, pauses for an instant
then plummets toward earth
until just above a drift he opens his wings
and brakes, fluttering
in a cloud of snow he pushed aside.

BELLEVUE

John in the desert
mixed honey with blood.
Three white birds surround me
and my voice is in my feet—
How beautiful with shoes, O Redeemer.
From a lightbulb a drop of blood emerges
and floats
softly down toward my head,
the room whines O Redeemer,
this is my baptism.

"THIS IS COLD SALT"

This is cold salt
a pulled tooth
the freshly set bone:
the girl who left my bed this morning,
who smiled last night as her slip
floated to the floor,
my Roselita,
today up on Amsterdam Avenue
I saw her with her Manuelo.

JOHN SEVERIN WALGREN, 1874-1962

Trees die of thirst or cold
or when the limit's reached;
in the hole in the elm
the wood is soft and punky—
it smells of the water of a vase
after the flowers are dumped.

You were so old we could not weep;
only the blood of the young,
those torn off earth in a night's sickness,
the daughter lying beside you
who became nothing so long ago—
she moves us to terror.

NEW LITURGY

Sanctus deus
praise be the skull among flowers
and ornamental war.

Sanctus deus
praise be my skull among flowers
black sun
red moon
cold metal of death.

Sanctus deus
white skull
bitter flowers
praise be the fruit no child eats
full of blood
dry as death.

MALEDICTION

Man's not a singing animal,
his tongue hangs from a wall—
        pinch the stone
        to make a moan
        from the throat
        a single note
        breaks the air
        so bare and harsh
        birds die.

He's crab-necked from cold,
song splits his voice
like a lake's ice cracking.
His heart's a rock,
a metronome, a clock,
a foghorn drone of murder.

God, curse this self-maimed beast,
the least of creatures,
    rivet his stone with worms.

WORD DRUNK

I think of the twenty thousand poems of Li Po
and wonder, do words follow me or I them—
a word drunk?
I do not care about fine phrases,
the whoring after honor,
the stipend, the gift, the grant—
but I would feed on an essence
until it yields to me my own dumb form—
the weight raw, void of intent;
to see behind the clarity of my glass
the birth of new creatures
suffused with light.

YOUNG BULL

This bronze ring punctures
the flesh of your nose,
the wound is fresh
and you nuzzle the itch
against a fence post.
Your testicles are fat and heavy
and sway when you shake off flies;
the chickens scratch about your feet
but you do not notice them.

Through lunch I pitied
you from the kitchen window—
the heat, pained fluid of August—
but when I came with cold water
and feed, you bellowed and heaved
against the slats wanting to murder me.

PARK AT NIGHT

Unwearied
the coo and choke
of doves
the march of stone
an hour before dawn.

Trees caged to the waist
wet statues
the trickling of water—
in the fountain
floating across the lamp
a leaf
some cellophane.

"NOT CASIDA, CANZONE—"

Not casida, canzone—
sentience in another's mouth,
and O song transfusor
not bird, beast, air or sun—
another's mouth.

Her weight anchors the bed
in a square of light across the street—
there's no dancing in this yellow
square of light.
Hot August night
I would move you far
to music.

GOING BACK

How long, stone, did it take
to get that fat?

The rain made the furrow a rut
and then among the mint and nettles
you make your appearance.

Sink again, you might cover bones.

HITCHHIKING

Awake:
the white hand of
my benefactor
drums on the seat
between us.
The world had become orange
in the rearview mirror
of a '55 Pontiac.
The road was covered with bugs
and mist coiled around
great house-sized rocks
and in the distance buried them.
Village. Passed three limp
gas stations then one
whose windows exploded with fire.
My mouth was filled with plastic cups.
Final item:
breakfast, nurtured
by a miraculous hatred.

SOUND

At dawn I squat on the garage
with snuff under a lip
to sweeten the roofing nails—
my shoes and pant cuffs
are wet with dew.
In the orchard the peach trees
sway with the loud
weight of birds, green fruit, yellow haze.
And my hammer—the cold head taps,
then swings its first full arc;
the sound echoes against the barn,
muffled in the loft,
and out the other side, then lost
in the noise of the birds
as they burst from the trees.

DEAD DEER

Amid pale green milkweed, wild clover,
a rotted deer
curled, shaglike,
after a winter so cold
the trees split open.
I think she couldn't keep up with
the others (they had no place
to go) and her food,
frozen grass and twigs,
wouldn't carry her weight.

Now from bony sockets,
she stares out on this
cruel luxuriance.

LI HO

Li Ho of the province of Honan
      (not to be confused with the god Li Po
      of Kansu or Szechwan
      who made twenty thousand verses),
Li Ho, whose mother said,
"My son daily vomits up his heart,"
mounts his horse and rides
to where a temple lies as lace among foliage.
His youth is bargained
for some poems in his saddlebag—
his beard is gray. Leaning
against the flank of his horse he considers
the flight of birds
but his hands are heavy. (Take this cup,
he thinks, fill it, I want to drink again.)
Deep in his throat, but perhaps it is a bird,
he hears a child cry.

COMPLAINT

Song, I am unused to you—
When you come
your voice is behind trees
calling another by my name.

So little of me comes out to you
I cannot hold your weight—
I bury you in sleep
or pour more wine, or lost in another's
music, I forget that you ever spoke.

If you come again, come with
Elias! Elias! Elias!
If only once the summons were a roar,
a pillar of light,
I would not betray you.

RETURN

The sun's warm against the slats of the granary,
a puddle of ice in the shadow of the steps;
a bluetick hound lopes
across the winter wheat—
fresh green, cold green.
The windmill, long out of use,
screeches and twists in the wind.
A spring day too loud for talk
when bones tire of their flesh
and want something better.

LOCATIONS

1968

to Herbert Weisinger

WALKING

Walking back on a chill morning past Kilmer's Lake
into the first broad gully, down its trough
and over a ridge of poplar, scrub oak, and into
a larger gully, walking into the slow fresh warmth
of midmorning to Spider Lake where I drank
at a small spring remembered from ten years back;
walking northwest two miles where another gully
opened, seeing a stump on a knoll where my father
stood one deer season, and tiring of sleet and cold
burned a pine stump, the snow gathering fire-orange
on a dull day; walking past charred stumps blackened
by the '81 fire to a great hollow stump near a basswood
swale—I sat within it on a November morning
watching deer browse beyond my young range of shotgun
and slug, chest beating hard for killing—
into the edge of a swale waist-high with ferns,
seeing the quick movement of a blue racer,
and thick curl of the snake against a birch log,
a pale blue with nothing of the sky in it,
a fleshy blue, blue of knotted veins in an arm;
walking to Savage's Lake where I ate my bread
and cheese, drank cool lake water, and slept for a while,
dreaming of fire, snake and fish and women in white
linen walking, pinkish warm limbs beneath white linen;
then walking, walking homeward toward Well's Lake,
brain at boil now with heat, afternoon glistening
in yellow heat, dead dun-brown grass, windless,
with all distant things shimmering, grasshoppers, birds
dulled to quietness; walking a log road near a cedar swamp
looking cool with green darkness and whine of mosquitoes,
crow's caw overhead, Cooper's hawk floating singly
in mateless haze; walking dumbly, footsore, cutting

into evening through sumac and blackberry brambles,
onto the lake road, feet sliding in the gravel,
whippoorwills, night birds wakening, stumbling to lake
shore, shedding clothes on sweet moss; walking
into syrupy August moonless dark, water cold, pushing
lily pads aside, walking out into the lake with feet
springing on mucky bottom until the water flows overhead;
sinking again to walk on the bottom then buoyed up,
walking on the surface, moving through beds of reeds,
snakes and frogs moving, to the far edge of the lake
then walking upward over the basswood and alders, the field
of sharp stubble and hay bales, toward the woods,
floating over the bushy crests of hardwoods and tips
of pine, barely touching in miles of rolling heavy dark,
coming to the larger water, there walking along the troughs
of waves folding in upon themselves; walking to an island,
small, narrow, sandy, sparsely wooded, in the middle
of the island in a clump of cedars a small spring
which I enter, sliding far down into a deep cool
dark endless weight of water.

SUITE TO FATHERS

for Denise Levertov

I

I think that night's our balance,
our counterweight—a blind woman
we turn to for nothing but dark.

—

In Val-Mont I see a slab of parchment,
a black quill pen in stone.
In a sculptor's garden
there was a head made from stone,
large as a room, the eyes neatly hooded
staring out with a crazed somnolence
fond of walled gardens.

—

The countesses arch like cats in châteaux.
They wake up as countesses and usually sleep with counts.
Nevertheless he writes them painful letters,
thinking of Eleanor of Aquitaine, Gaspara Stampa.
With Kappus he calls forth the stone in the rose.

—

In Egypt the dhows sweep the Nile
with ancient sails. I am in Egypt,
he thinks, this Baltic jew—it is hot,
how can I make bricks with no straw?
His own country rich with her food and slaughter,
fit only for sheep and generals.

—

He thinks of the coffin of the East,
of the tiers of dead in Venice,
those countless singulars.
At lunch, the baked apple too sweet with kirsch
becomes the tongues of convent girls at gossip,
under the drum and shadow of pigeons
the girl at promenade has almond in her hair.

      —

From Duino, beneath the mist,
the green is so dark and green it cannot bear itself.
In the night, from black paper
I cut the silhouette of this exiled god,
finding him as the bones of a fish in stone.

      II

In the cemetery the grass is pale,
fake green as if dumped from Easter baskets,
from overturned clay and the deeper marl
which sits in wet gray heaps by the creek.
There are no frogs, death drains there.
Landscape of glass, perhaps Christ
will quarry you after the worms.
The newspaper says caskets float in leaky vaults.
Above me, I feel paper birds.
The sun is a brass bell.
This is not earth I walk across
but the pages of some giant magazine.

      —

Come song,
allow me some eloquence,
good people die.

—

The June after you died
I dove down into a lake,
the water turned to cold, then colder,
and ached against my ears.
I swam under a sunken log then paused,
letting my back rub against it,
like some huge fish with rib cage
and soft belly open to the bottom.
I saw the light shimmering far above
but did not want to rise.

—

It was so far up from the dark—
once it was night three days,
after that four, then six and over again.
The nest was torn from the tree,
the tree from the ground,
the ground itself sinking torn.
I envied the dead their sleep of rot.
I was a fable to myself,
a speech to become meat.

III
Once in Nevada I sat on a boulder at twilight—
I had no ride and wanted to avoid the snakes.
I watched the full moon rise a fleshy red
out of the mountains, out of a distant sandstorm.
I thought then if I might travel deep enough
I might embrace the dead as equals,
not in their separate stillness as dead, but in music
one with another's harmonies.
The moon became paler,
rising, floating upward in her arc
and I with her, intermingled in her whiteness,
until at dawn again she bloodied
herself with earth.

      ―

In the beginning I trusted in spirits,
slight things, those of the dead in procession,
the household gods in mild delirium
with their sweet round music and modest feasts.
Now I listen only to that hard black core,
a ball harsh as coal, rending for light
far back in my own sour brain.

      ―

The tongue knots itself
a cramped fist of music,
the oracle a white-walled room of bone
that darkens now with a greater dark;
and the brain a glacier of blood,
inching forward, sliding, the bottom
silt covered but sweet,
becoming a river now

laving the skull with coolness—
the leaves on her surface
dipping against the bone.

—

Voyager, the self the voyage—
dark, let me open your lids.
Night stares down with her great bruised eye.

SUITE TO APPLENESS

I

If you love me drink this discolored wine,
tanning at the edge with the sourness of flowers—
their heads, soldiers', floating as flowers,
heads, necks, owned by gravity now as war
owned them and made them move to law;
and the water is heavier than war, the heads
bobbing freely there with each new wave lap.

—

And if your arm offends you, cut it off.
Then the leg by walking, tear out the eye,
the trunk, body be eyeless, armless, bodiless.
And if your brain offends you . . .
If Christ offends you, tear him out,
or if the earth offends you, skin her
back in rolls, nailed to dry
on barnside, an animal skin in sunlight;
or the earth that girl's head,
throwing herself from the asylum roof,
head and earth whirling earthward.

—

Or if we reoccur with death our humus, heat,
as growths or even mushrooms; on my belly
I sight for them at dead-leaf line—
no better way—thinking there that I hear
the incredible itch of things to grow,
Spring, soon to be billion-jetted.

—

Earth in the boy's hand, the girl's head,
standing against the granary; earth a green
apple he picked to throw at starlings,
plucked from among green underleaves,
silver leaf bellies burred with fine white hairs;
the apple hurled, hurtling greenly with wet solidity,
earth spinning in upon herself,
shedding her brains and whales and oceans,
her mountains strewn and crushed.

II

In the Quonset shed unloading the fertilizer,
each bag weighing eighty pounds,
muscles ache, lungs choke with heat and nitrogen;
then climbing the ladder of the water tank
to see in the orchard the brightness of apples,
sinking clothed into the icy water, feet thunking
iron bottom, a circle of hot yellow light above.

—

The old tree, a McIntosh:
sixty-eight bushel last year,
with seventy-three bushel the year before that,
sitting up within it on a smooth branch,
avoiding the hoe, invisible to the ground,
buoyed up by apples, brain still shocked,
warped, shaved into curls of paper,
a wasps' globe of gray paper—
lamina of oil and clouds—
now drawing in greenness, the apples
swelling to heaviness on a hot August afternoon;
to sing, singing, voice cracks at second sing,
paper throat, brain unmoist for singing.

—

Cranking the pump to loud life,
the wheel three turns to the left,
six hundred feet of pipe lying in the field;
the ground beneath begins shaking, bumping
with the force of coming water, sprinklers whirl,
the ground darkening with spray of flung water.

⸺

After the harvest of cabbage the cabbage roots,
an acre of them and the discarded outer leaves,
scaly pale green roots against black soil,
to be forked into piles with the tomato vines;
a warm week later throwing them onto the wagon,
inside the piles the vines and leaves have rotted,
losing shape, into a thick green slime and jelly.

III

Or in the orchard that night
in July: the apple trees too thick
with branches, unpruned, abandoned,
to bear good fruit—the limbs
moving slightly in still air with my drunkenness;
a cloud passed over the moon
sweeping the orchard with a shadow—
the shadow moving thickly across the darkening field,
a moving lustrous dark, toward a darker woodlot.

⸺

Then the night exploded with crows—
an owl or raccoon disturbed a nest—
I saw them far off above the trees,
small pieces of black in the moonlight
in shrill fury circling with caw caw caw,
skin prickling with its rawness

brain swirling with their circling
in recoil moving backward, crushing
the fallen apples with my feet,
the field moving then as the folds
of a body with their caw caw caw.
Young crows opened by owl's beak,
raccoon's claws and teeth,
night opened, brain broken as with a hammer
by weight of blackness and crows,
crushed apples and drunkenness.

—

Or Christ bless torn Christ, crows,
the lives of their young
torn from the darkness,
apples and the dead webbed branches
choking the fruit;
night and earth herself
a drunken hammer, the girl's head,
all things bruised or crushed
as an apple.

THE SIGN

I

There are no magic numbers or magic lives.
He dreams of Sagittarius in a thicket,
dogs yipe at his hooves, the eye of the archer
seaward, his gaze toward impossible things—
bird to be fish, archer and horse a whale
or dolphin; then rears up, canters
away from the shore across a wide field
of fern and honeysuckle brambles
to a woods where he nibbles at small
fresh leeks coming up among dead leaves.

—

Strange creature to be thought of,
welded in the skull as unicorn,
hooves, bow, quiver of arrows and beard;
that girl sitting at cliff edge
or beside a brook, how does he take her?
He lifts her up to kiss her,
and at night standing by a stream,
heavy mist up to his flanks,
mist curling and floating through his legs,
a chill comes over him;
she in restless sleep in a small stone cottage.

—

Between the scorpion and goat,
three signs—
winter in Cancer and this love of snow.

—

And contempt for all signs, the nine
spokes of the sun, the imagined belt
of dark or girdle in which night
mantles herself. The stars guide
no one save those at sea
or in the wilderness; avoid what stinks
or causes pain, hate death and cruelty
to any living thing.
You do not need the stars for that.

      II
But often at night something asks
the brain to ride, run riderless;
plumed night swirling, brain riding itself
through blackness, crazed with motion,
footless against the earth,
perhaps hooves imagined in lunacy;
through swamps feared even in daytime
at gallop, crashing through poplar
thickets, tamarack, pools of green slime,
withers splattered with mud, breathing
deep in an open marsh in the center of
the great swamp, then running again
toward a knoll of cedar where deer feed,
pausing, stringing the bow, chasing
the deer for miles, crossing a blacktop road
where the hooves clatter.

     —

On a May night walking home from a tavern
through a village with only three streetlights,
a slip of moon and still air moist with scent of first grass;
to look into the blackness by the roadside,

and in all directions, village, forest,
and field covered with it:
        eighteen miles of black to Traverse City
        thirteen miles of black to Buckley
        nineteen miles of black to Karlin
        twelve miles of black to Walton Junction

     —

And infinite black above;
earth herself a heavy whirling ball of pitch.
If the brain expands to cover these distances . . .
stumbling to the porch where the cat
has left an injured snake that hisses with the brain,
the brain rearing up to shed the black
and the snake coiled bleeding at its center.

     III

Not centaur nor archer but man,
man standing exhausted at night
beneath a night sky so deep and measureless,
head thrown back he sees his constellation,
his brain fleshes it and draws the lines
which begin to ripple then glimmer,
heave and twist, assume color, rear up,
the head high, the chest and torso gleaming,
beard glistening, flanks strapped with muscle,
hooves stomping in place, stomping night's floor,
rearing again, fading, then regaining terror,
the bow in hand, a strung bow, and arrow fitted,
drawn back, the arrow molten-tipped.
Slay. He only still "slays."
And when the arrow reaches earth I'll die.

     —

But in morning light, already shrill and hot
by ten, digging a well pit, the sandy earth crumbles
and traps the legs, binding them to earth; then digging
again, driving a shallow well with a sledge,
the well-tip shaded as an arrowhead, sledge hitting
steel with metallic ring and scream; the pump head
and arm bound to pipe, sitting in damp sand
with legs around the pipe pumping the first water
onto my chest and head—head swollen with pain
of last night's sign and leavings of whiskey.

On another morning, the frost as a sheet
of white stubbled silk soon to melt into greenness,
partridge thumping ground with wings to call their mates,
near a river, thick and turbulent and brown—
a great buck deer, startled
from a thicket, a stag of a thousand stories,
how easily his spread antlers trace a back and bow
not unlike your own, then the arc of him
bounding away into his green clear music.

WAR SUITE

I

The wars: we're drawn to them
as if in fever, we sleepwalk to them,
wake up in full stride of nightmare,
blood slippery, mouth deep in their gore.

—

Even in *Gilgamesh,* the darker bodies
strewn over stone battlements,
dry skin against rough stone, the sand
sifting through rock face, swollen flesh
covered with it, sand against blackening lips,
flesh covered with it, the bodies
bloating in the heat, then hidden,
then covered; or at an oasis, beneath
still palms, a viper floats toward water,
her soft belly flattened of its weight, tongue
flicking at water beside the faces of the dead,
their faces, chests, pressed to earth, bodies
also flattened, lax with their weight,
now surely groundlings, and the moon
swollen in the night, the sheen
of it on lax bodies and on the water.

—

Now in Aquitaine, this man is no less dead
for being noble, a knight with a clang
and rasp to his shield and hammer;
air thick with horses,
earth fixed under their moving feet
but bodies falling, sweat and blood

under armor, death blows, sweet knight's
blood flowing, horses screaming, horses
now riderless drinking at a brook, mouths sore
with bits, sweat drying gray on flanks,
noses dripping cool water, nibbling
grass through bits, patches of grass
with the blood still red and wet on them.

II

I sing sixty-seven wars; the war now,
the war for Rapunzel, earth cannot use
her hair, the war of drowning hair
drifting upward as it descends,
the lover holding his cock like
a switchblade, war of
apples and pears beating against the earth,
earth tearing a hole in sky, air to hold
the light it has gathered, river bending
until its back is broken, death a black
carp to swim in our innards.

Grand wars; the final auk poised
on her ice floe, the wolf shot
from a helicopter; that shrill god
in her choir loft among damp wine-colored
crumpled robes, face against a dusty
window, staring out at a black pond
and the floor of a woodlot
covered with ferns—if that wasp
on the pane stings her . . .
cancer to kill child, child to kill cancer,
nail to enter the wood, the Virgin
to flutter in the air above Rome like a Piper Cub,

giraffe's neck to grow after greener leaves,
bullet to enter an eye, bullet
to escape the skull, bullet to fall
to earth, eye to look for its skull,
skull to burst, belly to find its cage or ribs.

—

Face down in the pool, his great fatty
heart wants to keep beating; tongue pressed
to rug in a chemical hallway; on a country
road, caught by flashbulb headlights,
he wishes suddenly to be stronger than a car.

III
The elephant to couple in peace,
the porpoise to be free of the microphone;
this page to know a master, a future,
a page with the flesh melodious,
to bring her up through the page, paper-shrouded,
from whatever depth she lies,
dulling her gift, bringing her to song
and not to life.

—

This death mask to harden before
the face escapes, life passes
down through the neck—the sculptor
turns hearing it rub against the door.

—

Mind to stay free of madness, of war;
war all howling and stiff-necked dead,
night of mind punctuated with moans and stars,
black smoke moiling, puling mind striped as a zebra,
ass in air madly stalking her lion.

      —

Fire to eat tar, tar to drip,
hare to beat hound
grouse to avoid shot
trout to shake fly
chest to draw breath
breath to force song,
a song to be heard,
remembered and sung.

      —

To come to an opening in a field
without pausing, to move there in a full circle of light;
but night's out there not even behind the glass—
there's nothing to keep her out or in;
to walk backward to her, to step
off her edge or become her edge,
to swell and roll in her darkness,
a landlocked sea moving free—
dark and clear within her continent.

AMERICAN GIRL

I

Not a new poem for Helen,
if they were heaped . . .
but she never wanted a poem,
she whose affections the moment aimed.
And not to sing a new Helen into being
with *t'adores*, anachronistic gymnastics,
to be diligent in praise of her
only to be struck down by her.
Sing then, if song,
after bitter retreat,
on your knees,
as anyone who would love.
My senses led me here
and I had no wit to do otherwise.
Who breathes. Has looked upon. Alone.
In the darkness. Remembers.

—

Better to sit as a boy did in a still
cool attic in fall, tomatoes left to ripen
in autumn light on newspapers,
sucking his honeyed thumb, the forbidden
magazine across the lap and only
the mind's own nakedness for company;
the lovely photo, almost damp,
as supple and pink to the eye,
a hot country of body
but unknown and distant,
perhaps futureless.

—

A child once thought the dead were buried
to bear children: in the morning from his loft
in the fumes of wood smoke and bacon
he watches them dress, their bathing suits drying
by the stove. The water will fill them up.

      II

He dreams of Egypt in Sunday School,
the maidens of Ur-of-Chaldea, Bathsheba bathing
on her rooftop, the young virgin brought
to David to warm his hollow bones. And the horror
of Sodom and Gomorrah, Lot's frenzy
with his daughters; women railed against
in Habakkuk and Jeremiah, Isaiah's feverish
wife and Christ and the woman at the well—
to look in lust is to do without doing;
eyes follow the teacher's rump as she leaves the room.

     —

At sixteen his first whore, youngish
and acrid, sharing with her a yellow room
and a fifth of blackberry brandy;
first frightened with only his shoes on,
then calmed, then pleased, speechlessly
preening and arrogant. They became
blackberry brandy but never sweetly again—
vile in Laramie before dawn through
a darkened bar and up the long backstairs,
on Commerce St. in Grand Rapids shrieking
with gin. He craved some distant cousin
in Sweden he'd never seen, incestuously,
in some flower-strewn woods near the water.

     —

After a New Year's and his first French meal,
enchantée of course pursing her thick lips,
throwing one leg over the other
in the abandonment of sitting down,
throwing off room-length heat beneath layers
of nylon, stuffed with turbot and filet as she is,
splendidly in health, though her only apparent
exercise is screwing, "making the love,"
not gentle-like but as a Mack truck
noses a loading platform.

     III
The same "she" seen from a bus
or store window, often too young,
across the subway tracks in pure ozone,
the blond cheerleader with legs
bared to hundreds of eyes.
Always a fool before the coins—
I Ching forcing turmoil, the cauldron.
The fool has eyes and touch,
is mammalian. He lacks all odds,
ruts then is scathed. There's Helen
in a Greek nightclub, a hundred
years old and selling pistachios,
half a century away from any bed—
her face a shucked pecan.

—

Near the shore in a bed of reeds
he finally sees her for a moment,
the moon their only witness,
a single white eye;
her face is swirling in the dark,
changing faces a thousand times
then slipping back into black water.

─

But they are confections, put-together things
who will not stay in or go out but pause
on the edge of a room or wherever they are,
uncertain of what they are or whether they care.
So are they praised for what they aren't, young,
and blamed for what they haven't, a wilderness
of blood; pitiful creatures, calcined, watery,
with airbrushed bodies and brains.

─

I write this out of hard silence
to be rid of it. Not, as once, in love,
chin on breastbone as if the head
by its own dull weight would snap,
a green flower from a green stem.

LULLABY FOR A DAUGHTER

Go to sleep. Night is a coal pit
full of black water—
      night's a dark cloud
full of warm rain.

Go to sleep. Night is a flower
resting from bees—
      night's a green sea
swollen with fish.

Go to sleep. Night is a white moon
riding her mare—
      night's a bright sun
burned to black cinder.

Go to sleep,
night's come,
cat's day,
owl's day,
star's feast of praise,
moon to reign over
her sweet subject, dark.

SEQUENCE

1

The mad have black roots in their brains
around which vessels clot and embrace
each other as mating snakes.

The roots feed on the brain until the brain
is all root—now the brain is gray
and suffocates in its own folds.

The brain grows smaller and beats
against its cage of bone
like a small wet bird.

Let us pity the mad we see every day,
the bird is dying without air and water
and growing smaller,
the air is cold, her beak is sharp,
the beating shriller.

2

He loves her until
tomorrow or until 12:15 a.m.
when again he assumes the firedrake,
ricochets from the walls
in the exhaustion of kingship;
somewhere in his skull the Bible's leaves
seem turned by another's hand.

The pool table's green felt is earth,
ivory balls, people cracked toward leather holes.
Christ's blood is whiskey. Light is dark.
And light from a cave in whose furnace
three children continue their burning.

3

The dead haloed in gladiolus
and electric organs,
those impossible hurts, trepanations,
the left eye punctured with glass;
he'll go to Canada with his dog,
a truly loved and loving creature—
fish in the water, bear in his den.
Not fox shrinking before foxhound
snaps its neck, horse cowered before crop.

4

In the woods the low red bridge,
under it and above the flowing water,
spiders roost in girder's
rust and scale, flaking to touch.
Swift clear water. Soiled sand,
slippery green moss on rock face.
From the red bridge, years back
he dove into an eddy catching
the river's backward bend and swirl,
wishing not to swim on or in
as a duck and fish
but to be the water herself,
flowing then and still.

COLD AUGUST

The sun had shrunk to a dime,
passing behind the smallest
of clouds; the field was root
bare—shorthorns had grazed
it to leather. August's coldest
day when the green, unlike
its former self, returned to earth
as metal. Then from a swamp
I saw two large shadows floating
across the river, move up the sloping
bank, float swiftly as shadows against
the field toward where I stood.
I looked up as two great red-tailed
hawks passed overhead; for an instant
I felt as prey then wheeled to watch
them disappear in southward course.

NIGHT IN BOSTON

From the roof the night's the color
of a mollusk, stained with teeth and oil—
she wants to be rid of us and go to sea.

And the soot is the odor of brine
and imperishable sausages.

Beneath me from a window I hear "Blue Hawaii."
On Pontchartrain the Rex Club
dances on a houseboat in a storm—
a sot calms the water without wetting a foot.

I'd walk to Iceland, saluting trawlers.
I won't sell the rights to this miracle.

It was hot in Indiana.
The lovers sat on a porch swing, laughing;
a car passed on the gravel road,
red taillights bobbing over the ruts,
dust sweeping the house,
the scent of vetch from the pasture.

Out there the baleen nuzzles his iceberg,
monuments drown in the lava of birdshit.
I scuffle the cinders but the building doesn't shudder—
they've balanced it on a rock.
The Charles floats seaward, bored with history.

Night, cutting you open
I see you're full of sour air
like any rubber ball.

FEBRUARY SWANS

Of the hundred swans in West Bay
not one flies south in winter.
They breathe the dust of snow
swirling in flumes across the water,
white as their whiteness;
bones slighted by hunger
they move through the clots of ice,
heads looped low and tucked to the wind,
looking for fish in the deep greenness of water.

Now in the country, far from the Bay,
from a dark room I see a swan gliding
down the street, larger than a car, silent.
She'll need a fish the size of a human
to feed her hunger, so far from the water.
But there's nothing to eat between those snowbanks.
She looks toward my window. I think:
Go back to the Bay, beautiful thing,
it was thirty below last night.
We gaze at each other until my breath
has glazed the window with frost.

THIN ICE

Now this paste of ash and water;
water slipping over ice, greenish

brown water, white ice, November ice,
thin as glass, shot with air.

The kinglet, soundless, against the yellow
grapeleaves of the arbor, smallest of birds;

shrill day, the blowing, oily Atlantic off
Strong's Neck; the salt smell drifts, blown

through the newish Cape Cod homes.
On such days children fall down wells,

or drown falling through thin first ice,
or fall reaching after the last apple

the picker neglected, the tree leafless,
the apple spoiled anyway by frost; toad freezes,

snake's taken his hole; the cat makes much
shorter trips; dog's bark is louder.

The green has floated from earth, moved south,
or drifted upward at night, invisible to us.

Man walks, throwing off alone thin heat;
this cold's life, death's steamy mark and target.

NATURAL WORLD

1

The earth is almost round. The seas
are curved and hug the earth, both
ends are crowned with ice.

The great Blue Whale swims near
this ice, his heart is warm
and weighs two thousand pounds,
his tongue weighs twice as much;
he weighs one hundred fifty tons.

There are so few of him left
he often can't find a mate;
he drags his six-foot sex
through icy waters,
flukes spread crashing.
His brain is large enough
for a man to sleep in.

2

On Hawk Mountain in Pennsylvania
thousands upon thousands
upon thousands of hawks in migration
have been slaughtered for pleasure.
Drawn north or south in spring and fall:
merlin and kestrel, peregrine, gyrfalcon,
marsh hawk, red-tailed, sharp-tailed,
sharp-shinned, Swainson's hawk,
golden eagle and osprey
slaughtered for pleasure.

MOVING

Not those who have lived here and gone
but what they have left: a worn-out broom,
coat hangers, the legs of a doll,
errors of possession to remind us of ourselves;
but for drunkenness or prayers the walls
collapse in boredom, or any new ecstasy
could hold them up, any moan or caress
or pillow-muffled laugh;
leaving behind as a gift seven rooms of air
once thought cathedral, those imagined
beasts at windows,
her griefs hung from the ceiling for spectacle.

But finally here I am often there
in its vacant shabbiness,
standing back to a window in the dark,
carried by the house as history, a boat,
deeper into a year, into the shadow
of all that happened there.

WHITE

To move into it again, as it was,
     the cows rattling in black stalls,
lowing beneath the wind, the elm
     against the barn, thrashing
there as shadow, all loose boards
     creaking, the moon drawn,
pushed rolling white by wind
     and fat,
     bone white
     snow-and-flour white
     white white
moving into the puddle by the lilacs,
     whiter there, rippling white
beneath dark green twisting petals.
To be silvered by her as the barn,
the grass, the manure pile, the lilacs,
to look again at the reflection
     of her huge eye in water.

AFTER THE ANONYMOUS SWEDISH

Seventeenth century

Deep in the forest there is a pond,
small, shaded by a pine so tall
its shadow crosses her surface.
The water is cold and dark and clear,
let it preserve those who lie at the bottom
invisible to us in perpetual dark.
It is our heaven, this bottomless
water that will keep us forever still;
though hands might barely touch they'll never
wander up an arm in caress or lift a drink;
we'll lie with the swords and bones
of our fathers on a bed of silt and pine needles.
In our night we'll wait
for those who walk the green and turning earth,
our brothers, even the birds and deer,
who always float down to us
with alarmed and startled eyes.

DAWN WHISKEY

Mind follow the nose
this honey of whiskey
I smell through the throat of the bottle.

I hear a wren in the maple
and ten million crickets,
leaf rustle
behind the wren and crickets,
farther back a faint dog bark.

And the glass is cool,
a sweet cedar post that flames so briskly.
Sight bear this honey
through the shell curved around the brain,
your small soft globes
pouring in new light—
remember things that burn with gold
as this whiskey to my tongue.

BREAKTHROUGH

He contends with the other only to find
a third, both ride him like a pack,
a hump, in tertiary boldness a single
growth beneath the skin hugging the spine.

Let them embrace his shadow, forgotten
in haste—he runs through the woods,
the birches a white net, leaf skein
through which the stars and moon
pour down a sheet of light,
the lake three hundred acres of glass.

Naked he enters the water, swimming
beneath it, rising for breath
and moving under again and again.
They've followed. They watch.
The three stare at one another, two in frail
ghostliness, the third treading exhausted.
He sinks as they lope across the water,
and when he surfaces, they're standing
in the ringlet he left, meeting his arms
and holding, the dark line of the woods
visible through their bodies.
He forces his wind and sinks
toward bottom; fixed in still muck,
pike bump his legs.

LEGENDA

This song stays.
No new one carries us, bears
us so high, more swiftly.
And it has no place,
it changes as we change
death drawn to silence
at noon or in still night,
who knows another, wishes one.

None wishes night,
but only one night, one day,
sun and dark at final rest.
River at spring crest,
sky clear blue,
forest at June greenness,
delight of eye in brain fully flowering,
delight of air and light and breath.

A YEAR'S CHANGES

This nadir: the wet hole
in which a beast heaps twigs and bits
of hair, bark and tree skin,
both food and turds mix in the warm
dust its body makes.
In winter the dream of summer,
in summer the dream of sleep,
in spring feasting,
living dreams through the morning.
Fall, my cancer, pared to bone,
I lost my fur, my bite gone dull,
all edges, red and showing; now naked,
February painted with ice, preserve me
in wakefulness—I wait for the rain,
to see a red pine free of snow,
my body uncrabbed, unleashed,
my brain alive.

      —

In northern Manitoba
a man saw a great bald eagle—
hanging from its neck,
teeth locked in skin and feathers,
the bleached skull of a weasel.

      —

To sing not instinct or tact,
wisdom,
the song's full stop and death,
but audible things, things moving
at noon in full raw light;
a dog moving around

the tree with the shade—
shade and dog in motion—
alive at noon in full natural light.

       —

This nightflower, the size of a cat's head—
now moist and sentient—
let it hang there in the dark;
bare beauty asking nothing of us,
if we could graft you to us,
so singular and married to the instant.
But now rest picked, a trillium
never to repeat yourself. Soon enough
you'll know dead air, brief homage,
a sliver of glass in someone's brain.

       —

Homesick for a dark, clear black space
free of objects; to feel locked as wood
within a tree, a rock deep enough
in earth never to see the surface.

       —

Snow. There's no earth left under it.
It's too cold to breathe.
Teeth ache, trees crack, the air is bluish.
My breath goes straight up.
This woods is so quiet
that if it weren't for the buffer of trees
I could hear everything on earth.

       —

Only talk. Cloth after the pattern is cut,
discarded, spare wood barely kindling.

At night when the god in you trips,
hee-haws, barks and refuses to come
to tether. Stalk without quarry.
Yesterday I fired a rifle into the lake.

—

A cold spring dawn
near Parker Creek,
a doe bounding away through
shoulder-high fog
fairly floating,
soundless
as if she were running in a cloud.

—

That his death was disfigurement:
at impact when light passed
the cells yawned then froze in postures
unlike their former selves, teeth
stuck by the glue of their blood
to windshields, visors. And in the night,
a quiet snowy landscape, three bodies
slump, horribly rended.

—

Acacia Accidie Accipiter
flower boredom flight
gummy wet pale stemmed
barely above root level
and darkened by ferns;
but hawk
high now spots the car he shot
and left there,
swings low

in narrowing circles,
feeds.

—

My mouth stuffed up with snow,
nothing in me moves,
earth nudges all things this month.
I've outgrown this shell
I found in a sea of ice—
its drunken convolutions—
something should call me to another life.

—

Too cold for late May, snow flurries,
warblers tight in their trees, the air
with winter's clearness, dull
pearlish clear under clouds, clean
clear bite of wind, silver maple flexing
in the wind, wind rippling petals,
ripped from flowering crab,
pale pink against green firs, the body
chilled, blood unstirred, thick with frost:
body be snake,
self equal to ground heat,
be wind cold, earth heated,
bend with tree, whip with grass,
move free clean and bright clear.

—

Night draws on him until he's soft
and blackened, he waits for bones
sharp-edged as broken stone, rubble
in a deserted quarry, to defoliate,
come clean and bare

come clean and dry,
for salt,
he waits for salt.

    —

In the dark I think of the fire,
how hot the shed was when it burned,
the layers of tar paper and dry pine,
the fruit-like billows and blue embers,
the exhausted smell as of a creature
beginning to stink when it has no more to eat.

    —

The doe shot in the back
and just below the shoulder
has her heart and lungs blown out.
In the last crazed seconds she leaves
a circle of blood on the snow.
An hour later we eat
her still-warm liver for lunch,
fried in butter with onions.
In the evening we roast
her loins, and drink two gallons of wine,
reeling drunken and yelling on the snow.
Jon Jackson will eat venison for a month,
he has no job, food or money,
and his pump and well are frozen.

    —

June, sun high, nearly straight above,
all green things in short weak shadow;
clipping acres of pine for someone's
Christmas, forearms sore with trimming,
itching with heat—

drawing boughs away from a trunk
a branch confused with the thick
ugliness of a hognose snake.

—

Dogged days, dull, unflowering,
the mind petaled in cold wet dark;
outside the orange world is gray,
all things gray turned in upon
themselves in the globed eye of the seer—
gray seen.
But the orange world is orange to itself,
the war continues redly,
the moon is up in Asia,
the dark is only eight thousand miles deep.

—

At the edge of the swamp a thorn apple tree
beneath which partridge feed on red berries,
and an elm tipped over in a storm
opening a circle of earth formerly closed,
huge elm roots in a watery place, bare,
wet, as if there were some lid to let
secrets out or a place where the ground
herself begins, then grows outward
to surround the earth; the hole, a black
pool of quiet water, the white roots
of undergrowth. It appears bottomless,
an oracle I should worship at; I want
some part of me to be lost in it and return
again from its darkness, changing the creature,
or return to draw me back to a home.

LOCATIONS

I want this hardened arm to stop
dragging a cherished image.

Rimbaud

In the end you are tired of those places,
you're thirty, your only perfect three,
you'll never own another thing.
At night you caress them as if the tongue
turned inward could soothe, head lolling
in its nest of dark, the heart fibrotic,
inedible. Say that on some polar night
an Eskimo thinks of his igloo roof, the blocks
of ice sculptured to keep out air, as the roof
of his skull; all that he is, has seen,
is pictured there—thigh with the texture
of the moon, whale's tooth burnished from use
as nothing, fixtures of place, some delicate
as a young child's ear, close as snails to earth,
beneath the earth as earthworms, farther beneath
as molten rock, into the hollow, vaulted place,
pure heat and pure whiteness,
where earth's center dwells.

You were in Harar but only for a moment,
rifles jostling blue barrels against blue barrels
in the oxcart, a round crater, hot, brown,
a bowl of hell covered with dust.

The angels you sensed in your youth
smelled strongly as a rattlesnake
smells of rotten cucumber, the bear
rising in the glade of ferns of hot fur
and sweat, dry ashes pissed upon.

You squandered your time as a mirror,
you kept airplanes from crashing at your doorstep,
they lifted themselves heavily to avoid your sign,
fizzling like matches in the Atlantic.

You look at Betelgeuse for the splendor
of her name but she inflames another universe.
Our smallest of suns barely touches earth
in the Gobi, Sahara, Mojave, Mato Grosso.

Dumb salvages: there is a box made of wood,
cavernous, all good things are kept there,
and if the branches of ice that claw against the window
become hands, that is their business.

Yuma is an unbearable place.
The food has fire in it as
does the brazero's daughter
who serves the food in an orange dress
the color of a mussel's lip.
Outside it is hot as the crevasse
of her buttocks—perfect body temperature.
You have no idea where your body stops
and the heat begins.

On Lake Superior the undertow swallows
a child and no one notices until evening.
They often drown in the green water
of abandoned gravel pits,
or fall into earth where the crust is thin.

I have tried to stop the war.

You wanted to be a sculptor
creating a new shape that would exalt itself
as the shape of a ball or hand
or breast or dog or hoof,

paw print in snow, each cluster of grapes
vaguely different, bat's wing shaped
as half a leaf, a lake working
against its rim of ground.

You wear yellow this year for Christmas,
the color of Christ's wounds after three days,
the color of Nelse's jacket you wear when writing,
Nelse full of Guckenheimer, sloth, herring, tubercles.

There were sweet places to sleep: beds warmed
by women who get up to work or in the brush
beneath Coit Tower, on picnic tables in Fallon, Nevada,
and Hastings, Nebraska, surrounded by giant curs,
then dew that falls like fine ice upon your face
in a bean field near Stockton, near a waterfall
in the Huron Mountains, memorable sleeps
in the bus stations of San Jose and Toledo, Ohio.

At a roller rink on Chippewa Lake
the skaters move to calliope music.
You watch a motorboat putt by the dock,
they are trolling for bass at night
and for a moment the boat and the two men
are caught in the blue light of the rink,
then pass on slowly upon the black water.

Liquor has reduced you to thumbnails,
keratin, the scales of fish
your ancient relatives,
stranded in a rock pool.

O claritas, sweet suppleness
of breath,
love within a cloud that
blinds us
hear, speak, the world without.

Grove St., Gough St., Heber, Utah,
one in despair, two in disgust,
the third beneath the shadow
of a mountain wall, beyond
the roar of a diesel truck,
faintly the screech of lion.

Self-immolation,
the heaviest of dreams—
you become a charcoal rick
for Christ, for man himself.
They laugh with you as you disappear
lying as a black log upon the cement,
the fire doused by your own blood.

The thunderstorm moved across the lake
in a sheet of rain, the lightning
struck a strawpile, which burned in the night
with hot roars of energy
as in '48 when a jet plane crashed near town,
the pilot parachuting as a leaf through the red sky,
landing miles away, missing the fire.

There was one sun,
one cloud,
two horses running,
a leopard in chase;
only the one sun and a single cloud
a third across her face.
Above, the twelve moons of Jupiter
hissing in cold and darkness.

You worshiped the hindquarters
of beautiful women,
and the beautiful hindquarters of women
who were not beautiful;

the test was the hindquarters
as your father judged cattle.

He is standing behind a plow
in a yellow photograph,
a gangster hat to the back of his head,
in an undershirt with narrow straps,
reins over a shoulder waiting for the photo,
the horses with a foreleg raised,
waiting for the pull with impatience.

The cannon on the courthouse lawn was plugged,
useless against the japs.

In the dark barn
a stillborn calf on the straw,
rope to hooves, its mother bawling
pulled nearly to death.

You've never been across the ocean,
you swept the auditorium with a broom
after the travel lectures and dreamed of going
but the maps have become old, the brain
set on the Mackenzie River, even Greenland
where dentists stalk polar bears from Cessnas.

The wrecked train smelled of camphor,
a bird floating softly above the steam,
the door of the refrigerator car cracked open
and food begins to perish in the summer night.

You've become sure that every year
the sky descends a little,
but there is joy in this pressure,
joy bumping against the lid
like a demented fly, a bird breaking
its neck against a picture window

while outside new gods roll over
in the snow in billowy sleep.

The oil workers sit on the curb
in front of the Blue Moon Bar & Cafe,
their necks red from the sun,
pale white beneath the collars
or above the sleeves; in the distance
you hear the clumping of the wells.
And at a friend's house
there are aunts and uncles, supper plates
of red beans and pork, a guitar is taken
from the wall—in the music
the urge of homesickness, a peach not to be held
or a woman so lovely but not to be touched,
some former shabby home far south of here,
in a warmer place.

Cold cement, a little snow upon it.
Where are the small gods who bless cells?
There are only men. Once you were in a room
with a girl of honey-colored hair,
the yellow sun streamed down air of yellow straw.
You owe it to yourself to despise this place,
the walls sift black powder;
you owe yourself a particular cave.
You wait for her, a stone in loamy stillness,
who will arrive with less pitiful secrets
from sidereal reaches, from other planets of the mind,
who beneath the chamber music of gown and incense
will reflect the damp sweetness of a cave.

At that farm there were so many hogs,
in the center of the pen in the chilled air
he straddles the pig and slits its throat,
blood gushes forth too dark to be blood,

gutted, singed, and scraped into pinkness—
there are too many bowels, the organs
too large, pale sponges that are lungs,
the pink is too pink to understand.

This is earth I've fallen against,
there was no life before this;
                still icon
as if seen through mist,
cold liquid sun, blue falling
from the air,
                foam of ship's prow
cutting water, a green shore beyond
the rocks;
beyond, a green continent.

OUTLYER & GHAZALS

1971

for Pat Paton

OUTLYER

IN INTERIMS: OUTLYER

Let us open together the last bud of the future.
                                        Apollinaire

He Halts. He Haw. Plummets.
The snake in the river is belly-up
diamond head caught in crotch of branch,
length wavering yellow with force of water.
Who strangles as this taste of present?
Numen of walking and sleep, knees of snow
as the shark's backbone is gristle.
And if my sister hadn't died in an auto wreck
and had been taken by the injuns
I would have had something to do:
go into the mountains and get her back.

Miranda, I have proof that when people die
they become birds. And I've lost
my chance to go to sea or become a cowboy.
Age narrows me to this window and its
three-week snow. This is Russia and I a clerk.
Miranda throws herself from the window,
the icon clutched to her breasts,
into the snow, over and over.

A world of ruminants, cloven-hoofed,
sum it: is it less worthless for being "in front"?
There are the others, ignorant of us
to a man: says Johnson of Lowell who
wouldn't come to tea who's he sunbitch
and he know armaments and cattle like
a Renaissance prince knew love & daggers
and faintly knew of Dante, or Cecco.
It is a world that belongs to Kipling.

What will I die with in my hand?
A paintbrush (for houses), an M I 5
a hammer or ax, a book or gavel
                a candlestick
tiptoeing upstairs.
What will I hold or will I
be caught with this usual thing
that I want to be my heart but
it is my brain and I turn it
over and over and over.

Only miracles should apply,
we have stones enough—
they steal all the heat and trip
everyone even the wary.
Throw stones away.

And
a tricky way of saying something unnecessary
will not do.

The girl standing outside the bus station
in Muskegon, Michigan, hasn't noticed me.
I doubt she reads poetry or if she did
would like it at all or if she liked it
the affection would be casual and temporary.
She would anyway rather ride a horse
than read a poet, read a comic rather than
ride a poet. Sweetie, fifteen minutes
in that black alley bent over the garbage can
with me in the saddle would make
our affections equal. Let's be fair.

I love my dear daughter
her skin is so warm
and if I don't hurt her
she'll come to great harm.
I love my dog Missy
her skin is so warm,
I love all my friends
their skins are so warm,
my dear mother dead father
live sister dead sister
two brothers
their skins are so warm,
I love my lovely wife
her skin is most warm,
and I love my dear self
my skin is so warm,
I come to great harm.
I come to great harm.

I want to be told a children's story
that will stick.
I'm sorry I can't settle for less.
Some core of final delight.
In the funeral parlor my limbs
are so heavy I can't rise.
This isn't me in this nest of silk
but a relative bearing my face and name.
I still wanted to become a cowboy
or bring peace to the Middle East.
This isn't me. I saw Christ this summer
rising over the Absaroka Range.
Of course I was drunk.
I carry my vices to the wilderness.

That faintly blue person there among
the nasturtiums, among crooning relatives
and weeping wife, however, isn't me.

Where. We are born dead.
Our minds can taste this source
until that other death.
A long rain and we are children
and a long snow,
sleeping children in deep snow.

As in interims all journeys end
in three steps
with a mirrored door, beyond it a closet
and a closet wall.
And he wants to write poems to resurrect god,
to raise all buried things the eye
buries and the heart and brain, to
move wild laughter in the throat of death.

A new ax
a new ax
I'm going to play
with my new ax
sharp blue blade
handle of ash.
Then, exhausted, listen
to my new record, Johnny Cash.
Nine dollars in all,
two lovely things to play with
far better and more lasting
than a nine-dollar whore
or two bottles of whiskey.
A new ax and Johnny Cash

sharp blue blade and handle of ash
O the *stream of your blood*
runs as black as the coal.

Saw ghosts not faintly or wispish,
loud they were raising on burly arms
at midday, witches' Sunday in full light,
murder in delight, all former dark things
in noonlight, all light things love
we perform at night and fuck as war wounds
rub, and sigh as others sighed, blind
in delight to the world outside the window.

When I began to make false analogies
between animals & humans, then countries,
Russia is like America and America like Russia,
the universe is the world and the world
a university, the teacher is a crayfish,
the poem is a bird and a housefly, a pig
without a poke, a flame and an oilcan,
a woman who never menstruates, a woman
without glands who makes love by generalized
friction; then I went to the country
to think of precision, O the moon
is the width of a woman's thigh.

The Mexican girl about fourteen years old
in the 1923 *National Geographic* found in the attic
when we thought the chimney was on fire and I stood
on the roof with snow falling looking down into
the black hole where the fire roared at the bottom.
The girl: lying in the Rio Grande in a thin
wet shift, water covering back between breasts
and buttocks but then isolate the buttocks
in the muddy water, two graceful melons from the deep
in the Rio Grande, to ride them up to the river's source

or down to the sea, it wouldn't matter, or I would
carry her like a pack into some fastness like
the Sawtooth Mountains. The melon butter of her
in water, myself in the cloudy brown water
as a fish beneath her.

All falseness flows: you would rust
in jerks, hobbles; they, dewlaps,
sniff eglantine and in mint-cleared voices
not from dark but in puddles over cement,
an inch-deep of watery mud: all falseness
flows; comes now, where should it rest?
Merlin, as Merlin, *le cri de Merlin,*
whose shores are never watched, as women
have no more than one mouth staring
at the ground; repeat now, from what cloud
or clouds or country, countries in dim sleep,
pure song, mouthless, as if a church buried
beneath the sea—one bell tower standing
and one bell; staring for whom at ground's length,
elbows in ground, stare at me now: she grows
from the tree half-vine and half-woman
and haunts all my nights, as music can
that uses our tendons as chords, bowels to hurtle
her gifts; myths as Arcturus, Aldebaran
pictured as colored in with blood,
her eyes were bees and in her hair ice
seemed to glisten, drawn up as plants, the snake
wrapped around the crucifix knows, glass knows,
and O song, meal is made of us not even for small gods
who wait in the morning; dark pushes with no
to and fro, over and under, we who serve her
as canticles for who falls deeper, *breaks away,*
knows praise other than our own: sing.

Merely land and heavily drawn away from the sea
long before us, green has begun, every crevasse, kelp,
bird dung, froth of sea, foam over granite, wet
sea rose and roar of Baltic: who went from continent
to island, as wolves or elk would at night,
sea ice as salted glass, slight lid, mirror over
dark; as Odin least of all gods, with pine smell
of dark and animals crossed in winter
with whales butting shores,
dressed without heat in skins; said Christ who came
late, nothing to be found here, lovers of wood
not stone, north goes over and down, farthest from sun,
aloud in distance white wolf, whiter bear
with red mouth; they can eat flesh and nothing else.

     white winter

     white snow

     black trees

     green boughs

     over us

Arctic sun, one wildflower in profusion,
grass is blue, sterile fishless lake in rock
and northern lights shimmering, crackling.
As a child in mourning, mourned for, knows
how short and bittersweet, not less for saying again,
the child singing knows, near death, it is so alive,
brief and sweet, earth scarcely known, small
songs made of her, how large as hawk or tree,
only a stone lives beyond sweet things:
so that the sea raises herself not swallows
but pushed by wind and moon destroys them;
only dark gives light, Apollo, Christ,
only a blue and knotted earth broken by green
as high above gods see us in our sleeping end.

We know no other, curled as we are here,
sleep over earth, tongues, fog, thunder, wars.
Christ raises. Islands from the sea, see people come.
Clear your speech, it is all that we have,
aloud and here and now.

TRADER

I traded a girl
two apples for an orange.
I hate citrus
but she was beautiful.
As lovers we were rotten—
this was before the sexual revolution—
and we only necked and pawed,
"Don't write below the lines!"
But now she's traded
that child's red mitten
I only touched
for a stovepipe hat,
four children,
and a milkman husband.
Soon I learn there will be no milkmen
and she'll want to trade again.
Stop. I won't take a giant Marianas
trench for two red apples.
You've had your orange
now lie in it.

HOSPITAL

Someone is screaming almost in Morse
code, three longs, a short, three
longs again. Man, woman, or animal?

Pale-blue room. How many have died
here and will I with my ears drummed
to pain with three longs, one short, three longs?

It's never a yelp, it starts
far back in the throat
with three longs, a short, three longs.

All beasts everywhere listen to this.
It must be music to the gods—
three longs, one short, three longs.

I don't know who it is,
a beautiful woman with a lion's lungs
screaming three longs, one short, three longs?

COWGIRL

The boots were on the couch and had
manure on their heels and tips.

The cowgirl with vermilion udders and ears
that tasted of cream pulled on her jeans.

The saddle is not sore and the crotch with
its directionless brain is pounded by hammers.

Less like flowers than grease fittings women
win us to a life of holes, their negative space.

I don't know you and won't. You look at my hairline
while I work, conscious of history, in a bottomless lake.

Thighs that are indecently strong and have won the West,
I'll go back home where women are pliant as marshmallows.

DRINKING SONG

I want to die in the saddle. An enemy of civilization
I want to walk around in the woods, fish and drink.

I'm going to be a child about it and I can't help it, I was
born this way and it makes me very happy to fish and drink.

I left when it was still dark and walked on the path to the
river, the Yellow Dog, where I spent the day fishing and drinking.

After she left me and I quit my job and wept for a year and
all my poems were born dead, I decided I would only fish and drink.

Water will never leave earth and whiskey is good for the brain.
What else am I supposed to do in these last days but fish and drink?

In the river was a trout, and I was on the bank, my heart in my
chest, clouds above, she was in NY forever and I, fishing and drinking.

SHE AGAIN

No trips to Egypt this week—
heart goes gagurble, gouts blood
here and "thar" with alcohol in it
to stun you: Out there
        just waking
with someone else or alone
with the room raining and windows
open, an osprey perched on the bedpost,
scree deafens, morning's gold light;
you won't come back, my heart bores
you now, too many knots of scar tissue;
I cannot hold I grasp, airless knuckles,
all birds, light, your song & hair
slip through. I see your back through
the window, forever banished,
and the dark figure in the corner,
another lover.

AWAKE

Limp with night fears: hellebore, wolfsbane,
Marlowe is daggered, fire, volts, African vipers,
the grizzly the horses sensed, the rattlesnake
by the mailbox—how he struck at thrown rocks,
black water, framed by police, wanton wife,
I'm a bad poet broke and broken at thirty-two,
a renter, shot by mistake, airplanes and trains,
half-mast hard-ons, a poisoned earth, sun will
go out, car break down in a blizzard,
my animals die, fistfights, alcohol, caskets,
the hammerhead gliding under the boat near
Loggerhead Key, my soul, my heart, my brain,
my life so interminably struck with an ax
as wet wood splits bluntly, mauled into
sections for burning.

GHAZALS

NOTES ON THE GHAZALS

Poems are always better than a bloody turkey foot in the mailbox.
Few would disagree. Robert Creeley once said, partly reconstituting
Olson, "Form is never more than an extension of content." True and
sage. We choose what suits us and will not fairly wear what doesn't fit.
Don't try to bury a horse in a human coffin, no matter how much you
loved the horse, or stick some mute, lovely butterfly or luna moth in a
damp cavern. I hate to use the word, but form must be an "organic"
revelation of content or the poem, however otherwise lively, will strike
us false or merely tricky, an exercise in wit, crochet, pale embroidery.

   The ghazal is an antique form dating from the thirteenth century and
practiced by hundreds of poets since in languages as varied as Urdu,
Arabic, Pashto, Turkish, Persian, German, French, and Spanish. Even
Goethe and Schlegel wrote ghazals. Among my own contemporaries,
Adrienne Rich has been especially successful with the form. I have
not adhered to the strictness of metrics and structure of the ancient
practitioners, with the exception of using a minimum of five couplets.
The couplets are not related by reason or logic and their only continuity
is made by a metaphorical jump. Ghazals are essentially lyrics and I
have worked with whatever aspect of our life now that seemed to want
to enter my field of vision. Crude, holy, natural, political, sexual. After
several years spent with longer forms I've tried to regain some of the
spontaneity of the dance, the song unencumbered by any philosophical
apparatus, faithful only to its own music.

J.H.

I

Unbind my hair, she says. The night is white and warm,
the snow on the mountains absorbing the moon.

We have to get there before the music begins, scattered,
elliptical, needing to be drawn together and sung.

They have dark green voices and listening, there are birds,
coal shovels, the glazed hysteria of the soon-to-be-dead.

I suspect Jesus *will* return and the surprise will be
fatal. I'll ride the equator on a whale, a giraffe on land.

Even stone when inscribed bears the ecstatic. Pressed to
some new wall, ungiving, the screams become thinner.

Let us have the tambourine and guitars and forests, fruit,
and a new sun to guide us, a holy book, tracked in new blood.

II

I load my own shells and have a suitcase of pressed
cardboard. Naturally I'm poor and picturesque.

My father is dead and doesn't care if his vault leaks,
that his casket is cheap, his son a poet and a liar.

All the honest farmers in my family's past are watching
me through the barn slats, from the corncrib and hogpen.

Ghosts demand more than wives & teachers. I'll make a
"V" of my two books and plow a furrow in the garden.

And I want to judge the poetry table at the County Fair.
A new form, poems stacked in pyramids like prize potatoes.

This county agent of poetry will tell poets, "More potash
& nitrogen, the rows are crooked and the field limp, depleted."

III

The alfalfa was sweet and damp in fields where shepherds
lay once and rams strutted and Indians left signs of war.

He harnesses the horses drawing the wagon of wheat toward
the road, ground froze, an inch of sifting snow around their feet.

She forks the hay into the mow, in winter is a hired girl
in town and is always tired when she gets up for school.

Asleep again between peach rows, drunk at midmorning and something
conclusive is needed, a tooth pulled, a fistfight, a girl.

Would any god come down from where and end a small war between
two walls of bone, brain veering, bucking in fatal velocity?

IV

Near a brown river with carp no doubt pressing their
round pursed mouths to the river's bed. Tails upward.

Watching him behind his heifer, standing on a milk
stool, flies buzzing and sister cows swishing tails.

In the tree house the separate nickels placed in her hand.
Skirt rises, her dog yelps below and can't climb ladders.

River and barn and tree. Field where wheat is scarcely high
enough to hide, in light rain knees on pebbles and March mud.

In the brain with Elinor and Sonia, Deirdre of course
in dull flare of peat and Magdalen fresh from the troops.

I want to be old, and old, young. With these few bodies at
my side in a creel with fresh ferns & flowers over them.

V

Yes yes yes it was the year of the tall ships
and the sea owned more and larger fish.

Antiquarians know that London's gutters were
pissed into openly and daggers worn by whores.

Smart's Jeoffry had distant relatives roaming
the docks hungry for garbage at dawn. Any garbage.

O Keats in Grasmere, walking, walking. Tom
is dead and this lover is loverless, loving.

Wordsworth stoops, laughs only once a month and then
in private, mourns a daughter on another shore.

But Keats's heart, Keats in Italy, Keats's heart
Keats how I love thee, I love thee John Keats.

VI

Now changed. None come to Carthage. No cauldrons, all love
comes without oily sacraments. Skin breathes cooler air.

And light was there and two cliff swallows hung and swooped
for flies, audible heat from the field where steers fed.

I'm going to Stonehenge to recant, or from the manure pile
behind this shed I'm going to admit to a cow that I've lied.

He writes with a putty knife and goo, at night the North Star
hangs on the mountain peak like a Christmas ornament.

On the table the frozen rattlesnake thaws, the perfect club!
The perfect crime! Soon now to be skinned for my hatband.

VII

Says he, "Ah Edward I too have a dark past of manual labor."
But now Trivium Charontis seem to want me for Mars.

If her thighs weigh 21 pounds apiece what do her lips weigh?
Do that trick where you touch your toes. Do that right now.

The bold U.S.A. cowpoke in Bozeman, Montana, hates hippies,
cuts off their hair, makes $200 a month, room and board.

We want the sow bear that killed Clark's sheep to go away.
She has two cubs but must die for her terrible appetite.

Girl-of-my-dreams if you'll be mine I'll give up poetry
and be your index finger, lapdog, donkey, obvious unicorn.

VIII

The color of a poppy and bruised, the subalpine green that
ascends the mountainside from where the eagle looked at sheep.

Her sappy brain fleers, is part of the satin shirt (Western) she
wears, chartreuse with red scarf. Poeet he says with two *ee*s!

The bull we frighten by waving our hats bellows, his pecker
lengthens touching the grass, he wheels, foam from the mouth.

How do we shoot those things that don't even know they're animals
grazing and stalking in the high meadow: puma elk grizzly deer.

When he pulled the trigger the deer bucked like a horse, spine
broken, grew pink in circles, became a lover kissing him goodnight.

IX

He said the grizzly sat eating the sheep and when the bullet
struck tore the sheep in two, fell over backward dead.

With her mouth warm or cold she remains a welcome mat, a hole
shot through it many years ago in Ohio. Hump. Hemp treaded.

Is there an acre left to be allotted to each man & beast so
they might regard each other on hands and knees behind fences?

The sun straight above was white and aluminum and the trout
on the river bottom watched his feet slip clumsily on the rocks.

I want an obscene epitaph, one that will disgust the Memorial
Day crowds so that they'll indignantly topple my gravestone.

X

Praise me at Durkheim Fair where I've never been, hurling
grenade wursts at those who killed my uncle back in 1944.

Nothing is forgiven. The hurt child is thirty-one years old
and the girl in the pale blue dress walks out with another.

Where love lies. In the crawl space under the back porch
thinking of the aunt seen shedding her black bathing suit.

That girl was rended by the rapist. I'll send her a healing
sonnet in heaven. Forgive us. Forgive us. Forgive us.

The moon I saw through her legs beneath the cherry tree had
no footprints on it and a thigh easily blocked out its light.

Lauren Hutton has replaced Norma Jean, Ava Gardner, Lee Remick
and Vanessa Redgrave in my Calvinist fantasies. Don't go away.

XI

The brain opens the hand which touches that spot, clinically
soft, a member raises from his chair and insists upon his rights.

In some eye bank a cornea is frozen in liquid nitrogen. One day
my love I'll see your body from the left side of my face.

Half the team, a Belgian mare, was huge though weak. She died
convulsively from the 80-volt prod, still harnessed to her mate.

Alvin C. shot the last wolf in the Judith Basin after a four-year
hunt, raising a new breed of hounds to help. Dressed out 90 lbs.

When it rains I want to go north into the taiga, and before I
freeze in arid cold watch the reindeer watch the northern lights.

XII

Says Borges in *Ficciones,* "I'm in hell. I'm dead," and the dark
is glandular and swells about my feet concealing the ground.

Let us love the sun, little children but it is around too
much to notice and has no visible phases to care about.

Two pounds of steak eaten in deference to a tequila hangover.
His sign is that of a pig, a thousand-pound Hampshire boar.

Some would say her face looked homely with that thing sticking
out of it as if to feed her. Not I, said Wynken, not I.

The child is fully clothed but sits in the puddle madly
slapping the warm water on which the sun ripples and churns.

XIII

The night is thin and watery; fish in the air
and moonglint off her necklace of human teeth.

Bring O bring back my Bonnie and I'll return yours
with interest and exhaustion. I'm stuck between those legs.

Dangers of drugs: out in the swamp's middle he's stoned
and a bear hound mammothly threatens. Dazed with fright.

Marcia I won't go to Paris—too free with your body—
it's mine it's mine it's mine not just everyone's.

Now in this natal month Christ must be in some distant
nebula. O come down right now and be with us.

In the hole he fell in, a well pit, yellow jackets stung
him to death. Within minutes death can come by bees.

XIV

That heartless finch, botulinal. An official wheeze passes through
the screen door into the night, the vision of her finally dead.

I've decided here in Chico, Montana, that Nixon isn't president
and that that nasty item, Agnew, is retired to a hamster farm.

And that those mountains hold no people but geologists
spying on each other, and beasts spying on the geologists.

Mule deer die from curiosity—what can that thing be
wandering around with a stick, forgotten from last year?

Some tourists confuse me for an actual cowboy, ecstasy in
deceit, no longer a poet but a bona fide paper buckaroo.

I offer a twenty-one-gun salute to the caress as the blackflies buzz
around me and the rotting elk hides. The true source of the stink.

XV

Why did this sheep die? The legs are thin, stomach hugely
bloated. The girl cries and kicks her legs on the sofa.

The new marvels of language don't come up from the depths
but from the transparent layer, the soiled skin of things.

In London for puissant literary reasons he sits with the other
lost ones at a Soho striptease show. An endless oyster bar.

We'll need miracles of art and reason to raise these years
which are tombstones carved out of soap by the world's senators.

We'll have to move out at dawn and the dew is only a military
metaphor for the generally felt hidden-behind-bushes sorrow.

XVI

It is an hour before dawn and even prophets sleep
on their beds of gravel. Dreams of fish & hemlines.

The scissors moves across the paper and through
the beard. It doesn't know enough or when to stop.

The bear tires of his bicycle but he's strapped on
with straps of silver and gold straps inlaid with scalps.

We are imperturbable as deer whose ancestors saw the last
man and passed on the sweet knowledge by shitting on graves.

Let us arrange to meet sometime in transit, we'll all take
the same train perhaps, Cendrars's Express or the defunct Wabash.

Her swoon was officially interminable with unconvincing
geometric convulsions, no doubt her civic theater experience.

XVII

O Atlanta, roseate dawn, the clodhoppers, hillbillies, rednecks,
drunken dreams of murdering Blacks; the gin mills still.

Our fried chicken and Key lime pie and rickets. To drain all
your swamps and touch a match, Seminoles forbidden drink.

Save the dogs everywhere. In France by actual count, Count
Blah Blah shot 885 pheasants in one day, his personal record.

There was a story of a lost child who remained lost & starved
to death hiding in a hollow log from both animals and searchers.

Cuba is off there beyond the Tortugas, forever invisible; Isle
of Pines where Crane wept, collecting tons of starfish and eels.

Her love was committed to horses and poets weighing less than
150 lbs. I weigh 200 and was not allowed into her Blue Fuck Room.

XVIII

I told the dark-haired girl to come down out of the apple
tree and take her medicine. In a dream I told her so.

We're going to have to do something about the night. The tissue
won't restore itself in the dark. I feel safe only at noon.

Waking. Out by the shed, their home, the Chicano cherry pickers
sing hymns on a hot morning, three guitars and a concertina.

We don't need dime-store surrealists buying objects to write
about or all this up-against-the-wall nonsense in *Art News*.

Even in the wilderness, in Hell Roaring Creek Basin, in this
grizzly kingdom, I fear stepping into a hidden missile silo.

My friend has become crippled, back wrenched into an "S" like
my brain. We'll go to Judah to wait for the Apocalypse.

XIX

We were much saddened by Bill Knott's death.
When he reemerged as a hospital orderly we were encouraged.

Sad thoughts of different cuts of meat and how I own no
cattle and am not a rancher with a freezer full of prime beef.

A pure plump dove sits on the wire as if two wings emerged
from a russet pear, head tucked into the sleeping fruit.

Your new romance is full of nails hidden from the saw's teeth,
a board under which a coral snake waits for a child's hand.

I don't want to die in a foreign land and was only in one
once, England, where I felt near death in the Cotswolds.

The cattle walked in the shallow water and birds flew
behind them to feed on the disturbed insects.

XX

Some sort of rag of pure language, no dictums but a bell
sound over clear water, beginning day no. 245 of a good year.

The faces made out of leaves and hidden within them, faces
that don't want to be discovered or given names by anyone.

There was a virgin out walking the night during the plague when
the wolves entered Avila for carrion. The first took her neck.

The ninth month when everything is expected of me and nothing
can be told—September when I sit and watch the summer die.

She knelt while I looked out the car window at a mountain
(Emigrant Peak). We need girls and mountains frequently.

If I can clean up my brain, perhaps a stick of dynamite will
be needed, the Sibyl will return as an undiscovered lover.

XXI

He sings from the bottom of a well but she can hear him up
through the oat straw, toads, boards, three entwined snakes.

It quiets the cattle they say mythically as who alive has
tried it, their blank stares, cows digesting song. Rumen.

Her long hissing glides at the roller-skating rink, skates
to calves to thighs to ass in blue satin and organ music.

How could you be sane if 250,000 came to the Isle of Wight
to hear your songs near the sea and they looked like an ocean?

Darling companion. We'll listen until it threatens and walls
fall to trumpet sounds or not and this true drug lifts us up.

That noise that came to us out in the dark, grizzly, leviathan,
drags the dead horse away to hollow swelling growls.

XXII

Maps. Maps. Maps. Venezuela, Keewanaw, Iceland open up
unfolding and when I get to them they'll look like maps.

New pilgrims everywhere won't visit tombs, need living
monuments to live again. But there are only tombs to visit.

They left her in the rain tied to the water with cobwebs,
stars stuck like burrs to her hair. I found her by her wailing.

It's obvious I'll never go to Petersburg and Akhmadulina
has married another in scorn of my worship of her picture.

You're not fooling yourself—if you weren't a coward you'd be
another target in Chicago, tremulous bull's-eye for hog fever.

XXIII

I imagined her dead, killed by some local maniac who
crept upon the house with snowmobile at low throttle.

Alcohol that lets me play out hates and loves and fights;
in each bottle is a woman, the betrayer and the slain.

I insist on a one-to-one relationship with nature.
If Thursday I'm a frog it will have to be my business.

You are well. You grow taller. Friends think I've bought you
stilts but it is I shrinking, up past my knees in marl.

She said take out the garbage. I trot through a field with the
sack in my teeth. At the dump I pause to snarl at a rat.

XXIV

This amber light floating strangely upward in the woods—nearly
dark now with a warlock hooting through the tips of trees.

If I were to be murdered here as an Enemy of the State you would
have to bury me under that woodpile for want of a shovel.

She was near the window and beyond her breasts I could see
the burdock, nettles, goldenrod in a field beyond the orchard.

We'll have to abandon this place and live out of the car again.
You'll nurse the baby while we're stuck in the snow out of gas.

The ice had entered the wood. It was twenty below and the beech
easy to split. I lived in a lean-to covered with deerskins.

I have been emptied of poison and returned home dried
out with a dirty bill of health and screaming for new wine.

XXV

O happy day! Said *overpowered,* had by it all and transfixed
and unforgetting other times that refused to swirl and flow.

The calendar above my head made of unnatural numbers, day
lasted five days and I expect a splendid year's worth of dawn.

Rain pumps. Juliet in her tower and Gaspara Stampa again and
that girl lolling in the hammock with a fruit smell about her.

Under tag alder, beneath the ferns, crawling to know animals
for hours, how it looks to them down in this lightless place.

The girl out in the snows in the Laurentians saves her money
for Montreal and I am to meet her in a few years by "accident."

Magdalen comes in a waking dream and refuses to cover me,
crying out for ice, release from time, for a cool spring.

XXVI

What will I do with seven billion cubic feet of clouds
in my head? I want to be wise and dispense it for quarters.

All these push-ups are making me a muscular fatman. Love would
make me lean and burning. Love. Sorry the elevator's full.

She was zeroed in on by creeps and forgot my meaningful glances
from the door. But then I'm walleyed and wear used capes.

She was built entirely of makeup, greasepaint all the way through
like a billiard ball is a billiard ball beneath its hard skin.

We'll have to leave this place in favor of where the sun
is cold when seen at all, bones rust, it rains all day.

The cat is mine and so is the dog. You take the orchard,
house and car and parents. I'm going to Greenland at dawn.

XXVII

I want a sign, a heraldic bird, or even an angel at midnight
or a plane ticket to Alexandria, a room full of good dreams.

This won't do; farmlife with chickens clucking in the barnyard,
lambs, cows, vicious horses kicking when I bite their necks.

The woman carved of ice was commissioned by certain unknown
parties and lasted into a March thaw, tits turning to water.

Phone call. That strange cowboy who pinned a button to the boy's
fly near the jukebox—well last night he shot his mom.

Arrested, taken in as it were for having a purple fundament,
a brain full of grotesqueries, a mouth exploding with red lies.

Hops a plane to NYC riding on the wing through a thunderstorm,
a parade, a suite at the Plaza, a new silver-plated revolver.

XXVIII

In the hotel room (far above the city) I said I bet you
can't crawl around the room like a dog hoho. But she could!

All our cities are lewd and slippery, most of all San Francisco
where people fuck in the fog wearing coarse wool.

And in Los Angeles the dry heat makes women burn so that
lubricants are fired in large doses from machine guns.

We'll settle the city question by walking deeply into forests
and in reasonably vestal groves eat animal meat and love.

I'm afraid nothing can be helped and all letters must be
returned unopened. Poetry must die so poems will live again.

Mines: there were no cities of golden-haired women down there
but rats, raccoon bones, snake skeletons and dark. Black dark.

XXIX

For my horse, Brotherinlaw, who had no character
breaking into panic at first grizzly scent.

Stuff this up your ass New York City you hissing
clip joint and plaster-mouthed child killer.

In Washington they eat bean soup and there's
bean soup on the streets and in the mouths of monuments.

The bull in the grove of lodgepole pines, a champion
broke his prick against a cow and is now worthless.

For that woman whose mouth has paper burns
a fresh trout, salt, honey, and healing music.

XXX

I am walked on a leash by my dog and am water
only to be crossed by a bridge. Dog and bridge.

An ear not owned by a face, an egg without a yolk
and my mother without a rooster. Not to have been.

London has no bees and it is bee time. No hounds
in the orchard, no small craft warnings or sailing ships.

In how many poems through how many innocent branches
has the moon peeked without being round.

This song is for New York City who peeled me like
an apple, the fat off the lamb, raw and coreless.

XXXI

I couldn't walk across that bridge in Hannibal
at night. I was carried in a Nash Ambassador.

On Gough Street the cars went overhead. I counted
two thousand or more one night before I slept.

She hit him in the face with her high-heeled shoe
as he scrambled around the floor getting away.

What am I going to do about the mist and the canning
factory in San Jose where I loaded green beans all night?

Billions of green beans in the Hanging Gardens off Green
Street falling softly on our heads, the dread dope again.

XXXII

All those girls dead in the war from misplaced or aimed
bombs, or victims of the conquerors, some eventually happy.

My friends, he said after midnight, you all live badly.
Dog's teeth grew longer and wife in bed became a lizard.

Goddamn the dark and its shrill violet hysteria.
I want to be finally sane and bow to all sentient creatures.

I'll name all the things I know new and old and you may
select from the list and remember the list but forget me.

It was cold and windy and the moon blew white fish across
the surface where phosphorescent tarpon swam below.

Ice in the air and the man just around the corner has a gun
and that nurse threw a tumor at you from the hospital window.

XXXIII

That her left foot is smaller if only slightly
than her right and when bare cloven down to the arch.

Lovers when they are up and down and think they are whirling
look like a pink tractor tire from the ceiling.

Drag the wooden girl to the fire but don't throw
her in as would the Great Diana of Asia.

Oh the price, the price price. Oh the toll, the toll toll.
Oh the cost, the cost cost. Of her he thought.

To dogs and fire, Bengal tiger, gorilla, Miura bull
throw those who hate thee, let my love be perfect.

I will lift her up out of Montana where her hoof
bruised my thigh. I planted apple trees all day.

XXXIV

When she walked on her hands and knees in the Arab
chamber the fly rod, flies, the river became extinct.

When I fall out of the sky upon you again I'll
feather at the last moment and come in feet first.

There are rotted apples in the clover beneath the fog
and mice invisibly beneath the apples eat them.

There is not enough music. The modal chord I carried
around for weeks is lost for want of an instrument.

In the eye of the turtle and the goldfish and the dog
I see myself upside down clawing the floor.

XXXV

When she dried herself on the dock a drop of water
followed gravity to her secret place with its time lock.

I've been sacrificed to, given up for, had flowers
left on my pillow by unknown hands. The last is a lie.

How could she cheat on me with that African? Let's refer
back to the lore of the locker room & shabby albino secrets.

O the shame of another's wife especially a friend's.
Even a peek is criminal. That greener grass is brown.

Your love for me lasted no longer than my savings for Yurp.
I couldn't bear all those photos of McQueen on your dresser.

Love strikes me any time. The druggist's daughter, the 4-H
girl riding her blue-ribbon horse at canter at the fair.

XXXVI

A scenario: I'm the Star, Lauren, Faye, Ali, little stars,
we tour America in a '59 Dodge, they read my smoldering poems.

I climbed the chute and lowered myself onto the Brahma bull,
we jump the fence trampling crowds, ford rivers, are happy.

All fantasies of a life of love and laughter where I hold your
hand and watch suffering take the very first boat out of port.

The child lost his only quarter at the fair but under the grandstand
he finds a tunnel where all cowshit goes when it dies.

His epitaph: he could dive to the bottom or he paddled in black
water or bruised by flotsam he drowned in his own watery sign.

In the morning the sky was red as were his eyes and his brain
and he rolled over in the grass soaked with dew and said no.

XXXVII

Who could knock at this door left open, repeat
this after me and fold it over as an endless sheet.

I love or I am a pig which perhaps I should be,
a poisoned ham in the dining room of Congress.

Not to kill but to infect with mercy. You are known
finally by what magazines you read in whose toilet.

I'll never be a cocksman or even a butterfly. The one
because I am the other, and the other, the other one.

This is the one song sung loud though in code: I love.
A lunepig shot with fatal poison, butterfly, no one.

XXXVIII

Once and for all to hear, I'm not going to shoot anybody
for any revolution. I'm told it hurts terribly to be shot.

Think that there are miniature pools of whiskey in your flesh
and small deposits of drugs and nicotine encysted in fat.

Beautiful enchanted women (or girls). Would you take your
places by my side, or do you want to fuck up your lives elsewhere?

The veteran said it was "wall-to-wall death" as the men had
been eating lunch, the mortar had hit, the shack blown to pieces.

We'll pick the first violets and mushrooms together & loiter
idyllically in the woods. I'll grow goat feet & prance around.

Master, master, he says, where can I find a house & living
for my family, without blowing my whole life on nonsense?

XXXIX

If you laid out all the limbs from the Civil War hospital
in Washington they would encircle the White House seven times.

Alaska cost two cents per acre net and when Seward
slept lightly he talked to his wife about ice.

My heart is Grant's for his bottle a day and his
foul mouth, his wife that weighed over five hundred pounds.

A hundred years later Walt Whitman often still
walks the length of the Potomac and *on* the water.

A child now sees it as a place for funerals and bags
of components beneath the senators' heads.

XL

If you were less of a vowel or had a full stop in your
brain. A cat's toy, a mouse stuffed with cotton.

It seems we must reject the ovoid for the sphere,
the sphere for the box, the box for the eye of the needle.

And the world for the senate for the circus
for the war for a fair for a carnival. The hobbyhorse.

The attic for a drawer and the drawer for a shell.
The shell for the final arena of water.

That fish with teeth longer than its body is ours
and the giant squid who scars the whale with sucker marks.

XLI

Song for Nat King Cole and the dog who ate the baby
from the carriage as if the carriage were a bowl.

A leafy peace & wormless earth we want, no wires,
connections, struts or props, only guitars and flutes.

The song of a man with a dirty-minded wife—there is
smoke from her pit which is the pit of a peach.

I wrenched my back horribly chopping down a tree—quiff,
quim, queeritus, peter hoister, pray for torn backs.

The crickets are chirping tonight and an ant crosses
the sleeping body of a snake to get to the other side.

I love the inventions of men, the pea sheller, the cherry
picker, the hay baler, the gun and throne and grenade.

XLII

New music might, that sucks men down in howls
at sea, please us if trapped in the inner ear.

When rising I knew there was a cock in that dream
where it shouldn't have been I confess I confess.

Say there this elbow tips glass upward, heat rolls
down in burns, say hallow this life hid under liquid.

Late in the morning Jesus ate his second breakfast,
walked out at five years, drove his first nail into a tree.

Say the monkey's jaw torn open by howling, say after
the drowned man's discovered scowling under the harbor's ice.

XLIII

Ghazal in fear there might not be another
to talk into fine white ash after another blooms.

He dies from it over and over; Duncan has
his own earth to walk through. Let us borrow it.

Mary is Spanish and from her heart comes forth
a pietà of withered leather, all bawling bulls.

Stand in the wine of it, the clear cool gold
of this morning and let your lips open now.

The fish on the beach that the blackbirds eat
smell from here as dead men might after war.

XLIV

That's a dark trough we'd hide in. Said his
sleep without *frisson* in a meadow beyond Jupiter.

It is no baronet of earth to stretch to—flags
planted will be only flags where no wind is.

Hang me rather there or the prez's jowl on a stick
when we piss on the moon as a wolf does NNW of Kobuk.

I'll be south on the Bitterroot while you're up there
and when you land I'll fire a solitary shot at moonface.

I wish you ill's ills, a heavy thumb & slow hands
and may you strike hard enough to see nothing at all.

XLV

What in coils works with riddle's logic, Riemann's
time a cluster of grapes moved and moving, convolute?

As nothing is separate from Empire the signs change
and move, now drawn outward, not "about" but "in."

The stars were only stars. If I looked up then it was
to see my nose flaring on another's face.

Ouspensky says, from one corner the mind looking for
herself may go to another then another as I went.

And in literal void, dazzling dark, who takes
who where? We are happened upon and are found at home.

XLVI

O she buzzed in my ear "I love you" and I dug at
the tickle with a forefinger with which I *knew* her.

At the post office I was given the official FBI
Eldridge Cleaver poster—"Guess he ain't around here."

The escaping turkey vulture vomits his load of rotten
fawn for quick flight. The lesson is obvious & literary.

We are not going to rise again. Simple as that.
We are not going to rise again. Simple as that.

I say it from marrow depth I miss my tomcat gone now from
us three months. He was a fellow creature and I loved him.

XLVII

The clouds swirling low past the house and
beneath the treetops and upstairs windows, tin thunder.

On the hill you can see far out at sea a black ship
burying seven hundred yards of public grief.

The fish that swam this morning in the river swims
through the rain in the orchard over the tips of grass.

Spec. Forces Sgt. Clyde Smith says those fucking
VC won't come out in the open and fight. O.K. Corral.

This brain has an abscess which drinks whiskey
turning the blood white and milky and thin.

The white dog with three legs dug a deep
hole near the pear tree and hid herself.

XLVIII

Dog, the lightning frightened us, dark house and both of us
silvered by it. Now we'll have three months of wind and cold.

Safe. From miracles and clouds, cut off from you and your
earthly city, parades of rats, froth, and skull tympanums.

The breathing in the thicket behind the beech tree was a deer
that hadn't heard me, a doe. I had hoped for a pretty girl.

Flickers gathering, swallows already gone. I'm going south
to the Yucatán or Costa Rica and foment foment and fish.

In the Sudan grass waving, roots white cords, utterly hidden
and only the hounds could find me assuming someone would look.

The sun shines coldly. I aim my shotgun at a ship at sea
and say nothing. The dog barks at the ship and countless waves.

XLIX

After the "invitation" by the preacher she collapsed in the
aisle and swallowed her tongue. It came back out when pried.

No fire falls and the world is wet not to speak of gray and
heat resistant. This winter the snow will stay forever.

The dead cherry trees diseased with leaf rot were piled and
soaked with fuel oil, flames shooting upward into the rain.

Rouse your soul to frenzy said Pasternak. Icons built
of flesh with enough heat to save a life from water.

A new sign won't be given and the old ones you forgot won't
return again until the moment before you die, unneeded then.

Fuse is wet, match won't light it and nothing will. Heat comes
out of the center, radiates faintly and no paper will burn.

L

A boot called Botte Sauvage renders rattlers harmless but they
cost too much; the poet bitten to death for want of boots.

I'm told that black corduroy offers protection from moonburn
and that if you rub yourself with a skunk, women will stay away.

There is a hiding place among the relics of the fifties, poets
hiding in the trunks of Hudson Hornets off the Merritt Parkway.

They said she was in Rome with her husband, a sculptor, but
I'm not fooled. At the Excelsior I'll expose her as a whore.

Down in the canyon the survivors were wailing in the overturned
car but it was dark, the cliffs steep, so we drove on to the bar.

She wants affection but is dressed in aluminum siding and her
edges are jagged; when cold, the skin peels off the tongue at touch.

LI

Who could put anything together that would stay in one place
as remorseless as that cabin hidden in the maple grove.

In Nevada the whores are less clean and fresh than in
Montana, and do not grow more beautiful with use.

The car went only seventeen miles before the motor burned up
and I sat in the grass thinking I had been taken and was sad.

This toothache means my body is wearing out, new monkey glands
for ears in the future, dog teeth, a pink transplanted body.

She is growing old. Of course with the peach, apple, plum,
you can eat around the bruised parts but still the core is black.

Windermere and Derwent Water are exhausted with their own
charm and want everyone to go back to their snot-nosed slums.

LII

I was lucky enough to have invented a liquid heart
by drinking a full gallon of DNA stolen from a lab.

To discover eleven more dollars than you thought you
had and the wild freedom in the tavern that follows.

He's writing mood music for the dead again and ought to have
his ass kicked though it is bruised too much already by his sport.

Both serpent becoming dragon and the twelve moons lost
at sea, worshiped items, rifts no longer needed by us.

Hot Mickey Mouse jazz and the mice jigging up the path
to the beehive castle, all with the bleached faces of congressmen.

LIII

These corners that stick out and catch on things
and I don't fill my body's clothes.

Euclid, walking in switchbacks, kite's tip, always
either *up* or *down* or both, triangular tongue & cunt.

Backing up to the rose tree to perceive which of its
points touch where. I'll soon be rid of you.

There are no small people who hitch rides on snakes
or ancient people with signs. I am here now.

That I will be suicided by myself or that lids close over
and over simply because they once were open.

We'll ask you to leave this room and brick up the door
and all the doors in the hallway until you go outside.

LIV

Aieeee was said in a blip the size of an ostrich egg,
blood pressures to a faint, humming heart flutters.

I can't die in this theater—the movie, *Point Blank,*
god's cheap abuse of irony. But the picture is fading.

This dry and yellow heat where each chicken's
scratch uproots a cloud and hay bursts into flame.

The horse is enraged with flies and rolls over
in the red dirt until he is a giant liver.

From the mailman's undulant car and through the lilacs
the baseball game. The kitchen window is white with noon.

LV

The child crawls in widening circles, backs to the wall
as a dog would. The lights grow dim, his mother talks.

Swag: a hot night and the clouds running low were brains and I
above them with the moon saw down through a glass skull.

And O god I think I want to sleep within some tree
or on a warmer planet beneath a march of asteroids.

He saw the lady in the Empire dress raise it to sit bare
along the black tree branch where she sang a ditty of nature.

They are packing up in the lamplight, moving out again
for the West this time sure only of inevitable miracles.

No mail delights me as much as this—written with plum juice
on red paper and announcing the rebirth of three dead species.

LVI

God I am cold and want to go to sleep for a long time
and only wake up when the sun shines and dogs laugh.

I passed away in my sleep from general grief and a seven-
year hangover. Fat angels wrapped me in traditional mauve.

A local Indian maiden of sixteen told the judge to go
fuck himself, got thirty days, died of appendicitis in jail.

I molded all the hashish to look like deer & rabbit turds
and spread them in the woods for rest stops when I walk.

Please consider the case closed. Otis Redding died in a
firestorm and we want to put him together again somehow.

LVII

I thought it was night but found out the windows were painted
black and a bluebird bigger than a child's head was singing.

When we get out of Nam the pilot said we'll go down to S.A.
and kick the shit outta those commie greasers. Of course.

In sleepwalking all year long I grew cataracts, white-haired,
flesh fattened, texture of mushrooms, whistled notes at moon.

After seven hours of television and a quart of vodka he wept
over the National Anthem. O America Carcinoma the eagle dead.

Celebrate her with psalms and new songs—she'll be fifteen
tomorrow, a classic beauty who won't trouble her mind with poems.

I wanted to drag a few words out of silence then sleep and none
were what I truly wanted. So much silence and so many words.

LVIII

These losses are final—you walked out of the grape arbor
and are never to be seen again and you aren't aware of it.

I set off after the grail seven years ago but like a spiral
from above these circles narrow, tighten into a single point.

Let's forgive her for her Chinese-checker brain and the pills
that charge it electrically. She's pulled the switch too often.

After the country dance in the yellow Buick Dynaflow with
leather seats we thought Ferlin Husky was singing to us.

A bottle of Corbys won you. A decade later on hearing
I was a poet you laughed. You are permanently coarsened.

Catherine near the lake is a tale I'm telling—a whiff
of lilac and a girl bleeds through her eyes like a pigeon.

LIX

On the fourteenth Sunday after Pentecost I rose early
and went fishing where I saw an osprey eat a bass in a tree.

We are not all guilty for anything. Let all stupefied
Calvinists take pleasure in sweet dirty pictures and gin.

As an active farmer I'm concerned. Apollinaire fertilizer
won't feed the pigs or chickens. Year of my seventh failure.

When we awoke the music was faint and a golden light came
through the window, one fly buzzed, she whispered another's name.

Let me announce I'm not against homosexuality. Now that the air
is clear on this issue you can talk freely Donny Darkeyes.

A home with a heated garage where dad can tinker with his
poetry on a workbench and mom glazes the steamed froth for lunch.

LX

She called from Sundance, Wyoming, and said the posse had
forced her into obscene acts in the motel. Bob was dead.

The horse kicked the man off his feet and the man rolled
screaming in the dirt. The red-haired girl watched it all.

I've proclaimed June Carter queen-of-song as she makes me
tremble, tears form, chills come. I go to the tavern and drink.

The father ran away and was found near a highway underpass
near Fallon, Nevada, where he looked for shelter from the rain.

My friend the poet is out there in the West being terrified,
he wants to come home and eat well in New York City.

Daddy is dead and late one night won't appear on the porch
in his hunting clothes as I've long wanted him to. He's dead.

LXI

Wondering what this new light is, before he died he walked
across the kitchen and said, "My stomach is very cold."

And this haze, yellowish, covers all this morning, meadow,
orchard, woods. Something bad is happening somewhere to her.

I was ashamed of her Appalachian vulgarity and vaguely askew
teeth, her bad grammar, her wanting to screw more often than I.

It was May wine and the night liquid with dark and fog when
we stopped the car and loved to the sound of frogs in the swamp.

I'm bringing to a stop all my befouled nostalgia about childhood.
My eye was gored out, there was a war and my nickname was *pig*.

There was an old house that smelled of kerosene and apples
and we hugged in a dark attic, not knowing how to continue.

LXII

He climbed the ladder looking over the wall at the party
given for poets by the Prince of China. Fun was had by all.

A certain gracelessness entered his walk and gestures. A tumor
the size of a chickpea grew into a pink balloon in his brain.

I won't die in Paris or Jerusalem as planned but by electrocution
when I climb up the windmill to unscrew the shorted yard lights.

Samadhi. When I slept in the woods I awoke before dawn
and drank brandy and listened to the birds until the moon disappeared.

When she married she turned from a beautiful girl into a
useless sow with mud on her breasts and choruses of oinks.

O the bard is sure he loves the moon. And the inanimate moon
loves him back with silences, and moonbeams made of chalk.

LXIII

O well, it was the night of the terrible jackhammer
and she put my exhausted pelt in the closet for a souvenir.

Baalim. Why can only one in seven be saved from them
and live again? They never come in fire but in perfect cold.

Sepulchral pussy. Annabel Lee of the snows—the night's
too long this time of year to sleep through. Dark edges.

All these songs may be sung to the kazoo and I am not
ashamed, add mongrel's bark, and the music of duck and pig.

Mab has returned as a giantess. She's out there: bombs in
fist and false laurel, dressed antigreen in black metal.

From this vantage point I can only think of you in the
barnyard, one-tenth ounce panties and it's a good vision.

LXIV

That the housefly is guided in flight by a fly brain diminishes
me—there was a time when I didn't own such thoughts.

You admit then you wouldn't love me if I were a dog or rabbit,
was legless with truly bad skin. I have no defense. Same to you.

Poetry (that afternoon, of course) came flying through the
treetops, a shuddering pink bird, beshitting itself in flight.

When we were in love in 1956 I thought I would give up Keats
and be in the UAW and you would spend Friday's check wisely.

Hard rock, acid rock, goofballs, hash, haven't altered my love
for woodcock and grouse. It is the other way around, Mom.

I resigned. Walked down the steps. Got on the Greyhound bus
and went home only to find it wasn't what I remembered at all.

LXV

There was a peculiar faint light from low in the east
and a leaf skein that scattered it on the ground where I lay.

I fell into the hidden mine shaft in Keewanaw, emerging
in a year with teeth and eyes of burnished copper, black skin.

What will become of her, what will become of her now that
she's sold into slavery to an Air Force lieutenant?

I spent the night prophesying to the huge black rock
in the river around which the current boiled and slid.

We'll have to put a stop to this dying everywhere of young
men. It's not working out and they won't come back.

Those poems you wrote won't raise the dead or stir the
living or open the young girl's lips to jubilance.

LETTERS TO YESENIN

1973

for J.D.

1

to D.G.

This matted and glossy photo of Yesenin
bought at a Leningrad newsstand—permanently
tilted on my desk: he doesn't stare at me
he stares at nothing; the difference between
a plane crash and a noose adds up to nothing.
And what can I do with heroes with my brain fixed
on so few of them? Again nothing. Regard his flat
magazine eyes with my half-cocked own, both
of us seeing nothing. In the vodka was nothing
and Isadora was nothing, the pistol waved
in New York was nothing, and that plank bridge
near your village home in Ryazan covered seven feet
of nothing, the clumsy noose that swung the tilted
body was nothing but a noose, a law of gravity
this seeking for the ground, a few feet of nothing
between shoes and the floor a light-year away.
So this is a song of Yesenin's noose that came
to nothing, but did a good job as we say back home
where there's nothing but snow. But I stood under
your balcony in St. Petersburg, yes St. Petersburg!
a crazed tourist with so much nothing in my heart
it wanted to implode. And I walked down to the Neva
embankment with a fine sleet falling and there was
finally something, a great river vastly flowing, flat
as your eyes; something to marry to my nothing heart
other than the poems you hurled into nothing those
years before the articulate noose.

2

to Rose

I don't have any medals. I feel their lack
of weight on my chest. Years ago I was ambitious.
But now it is clear that nothing will happen.
All those poems that made me soar along a foot
from the ground are not so much forgotten as never
read in the first place. They rolled like moons
of light into a puddle and were drowned. Not even
the puddle can be located now. Yet I am encouraged
by the way you hanged yourself, telling me that such
things don't matter. You, the fabulous poet of
Mother Russia. But still, even now, schoolgirls
hold your dead heart, your poems, in their laps
on hot August afternoons by the river while they wait
for their boyfriends to get out of work or their
lovers to return from the army, their dead pets to
return to life again. To be called to supper. You
have a new life on their laps and can scent their
lavender scent, the cloud of hair that falls
over you, feel their feet trailing in the river,
or hidden in a purse walk the Neva again. Best of all
you are used badly like a bouquet of flowers to make
them shed their dresses in apartments. See those
steam pipes running along the ceiling. The rope.

3

I wanted to feel exalted so I picked up
Doctor Zhivago again. But the newspaper was there
with the horrors of the Olympics, those dead and
perpetually martyred sons of David. I want to present
all Israelis with .357 magnums so that they are
never to be martyred again. I wanted to be exalted
so I picked up *Doctor Zhivago* again but the TV was on
with a movie about the sufferings of convicts in
the early history of Australia. But then the movie
was over and the level of the bourbon bottle was dropping
and I still wanted to be exalted lying there with
the book on my chest. I recalled Moscow but I could
not place dear Yuri, only you Yesenin, seeing the Kremlin
glitter and ripple like Asia. And when drunk you appeared
as some Bakst stage drawing, a slain Tartar. But that is
all ballet. And what a dance you had kicking your legs from
the rope—We all change our minds, Berryman said in Minnesota
halfway down the river. Villon said of the rope that my neck
will feel the weight of my ass. But I wanted to feel exalted
again and read the poems at the end of *Doctor Zhivago* and
just barely made it. Suicide. Beauty takes my courage
away this cold autumn evening. My year-old daughter's red
robe hangs from the doorknob shouting *Stop.*

4

I am four years older than you but scarcely an unwobbling
pivot. It was no fun sitting around being famous, was it?
I'll never have to learn that lesson. You find a page torn
out of a book and read it feeling that here you might find
the mystery of print in such phrases as "summer was on the
way" or "Gertrude regarded him somewhat quizzically." Your
Sagane was a fraud. Love poems to girls you never met living
in a country you never visited. I've been everywhere to no
particular purpose. And am well past love but not love poems.
I wanted to fall in love on the coast of Ecuador but the girls
were itsy-bitsy and showers are not prominent in that area.
Unlike Killarney where I also didn't fall in love the girls
had good teeth. As in the movies the Latin girls proved to be
spitfires with an endemic shanker problem. I didn't fall in love
in Palm Beach or Paris. Or London. Or Leningrad. I wanted to fall
in love at the ballet but my seat was too far back to see faces
clearly. At Sadko a pretty girl was sitting with a general
and did not exchange my glance. In Normandy I fell in love but
had colitis and couldn't concentrate. She had a way of not paying
any attention to me that could not be misunderstood. That is
a year's love story. Except Key West where absolutely nothing
happened with romantic overtones. Now you might understand why
I drink and grow fat. When I reach three hundred pounds there
will be no more love problems, only fat problems. Then I will
write reams of love poems. And if she pats my back a cubic yard
of fat will jiggle. Last night I drank a hundred-proof quart
and looked at a photo of my sister. Ten years dead. Show me a
single wound on earth that love has healed. I fed my dying dog
a pound of beef and buried her happy in the barnyard.

5

Lustra. Officially the cold comes from Manitoba;
yesterday at sixty knots. So that the waves mounted
the breakwater. The first snow. The farmers and carpenters
in the tavern with red, windburned faces. I am in there
playing the pinball machine watching all those delicious
lights flutter, the bells ring. I am halfway through
a bottle of vodka and am happy to hear Manitoba
howling outside. Home for dinner I ask my baby daughter
if she loves me but she is too young to talk. She cares
most about eating as I care most about drinking. Our wants
are simple as they say. Still when I wake from my nap
the universe is dissolved in grief again. The baby is sleeping
and I have no one to talk my language. My breath is shallow
and my temples pound. Vodka. Last October in Moscow I taught
a group of East Germans to sing "Fuck Nixon," and we were
quite happy until the bar closed. At the newsstand I saw a
picture of Bella Akhmadulina and wept. Vodka. You would have
liked her verses. The doorman drew near, alarmed. Outside
the KGB floated through the snow like arctic bats.
Maybe I belong there. They won't let me print my verses. On the
night train to Leningrad I will confess everything to someone.
All my books are remaindered and out of print. My face in
the mirror asks me who I am and says I don't know. But stop
this whining. I am alive and a hundred thousand acres of birches
around my house wave in the wind. They are women standing
on their heads. Their leaves on the ground today are small
saucers of snow from which I drink with endless thirst.

6

Fruit and butter. She smelled like the skin of an apple.
The sun was hot and I felt an unbounded sickness with earth.
A single October day began to last a year. You can't fuck
your life away, I thought. But you can! Listening in Nepal
to those peahens scream in the evening. Then, through the glade,
lordly he enters, his ass a ten-foot fan, a painting by a crazed
old master. Look, they are human. Heads the size of two knuckles.
But returning to her buttery appleness and autumn, my dead friend.
We cannot give our lives over to women. Kneeling there under that
vulgar sugar maple tree I couldn't breathe and with a hundred
variations of red above me and against my mouth. She said I'm
going away to Oregon perhaps. I said that I'm going myself to
California where I hear they sleep out every night. So that
ended that and the fan was tucked neatly and the peahens' screams
were heard no more in the land and old ladies and old men slept
soundly again and threw away their cotton earplugs and the earth
of course was soaked with salt and August passed without a single
ear of corn. Of course this was only one neighborhood. Universality
is disgusting. But you had your own truly insurmountable horrors
with that dancer, lacking all wisdom as you did. Your critic said
you were "often revolted by your sensuality." He means
all of that endless fucking of course. Tsk tsk. Put one measure
against another and how rarely they fuse, and how almost never is
there any fire and how often there is only boredom and a craving
for cigarettes, a sandwich, or a drink. Particularly a drink.
I am drunk because I no longer can love. I make love and I'm
writing on a blackboard. Once it was a toteboard, a gun handle
until I myself became a notch. And a notch, to be obvious, is a
nothing. This all must pass as a monk's tale, a future lie.

7

Death thou comest when I had thee least in mind, said Everyman
years ago in England. Can't get around much anymore. So it's
really a terrible surprise unless like you we commit suicide.
I worry some that the rope didn't break your neck, but that
you dangled there strangling from your body's weight. Such
physics can mean a rather important matter of three or four
minutes. Then I would guess there was a moment of black peacefulness
then you were hurtling in space like a mortar. Who can say
if a carcass smiles, if the baggage is happy at full rest. The
child drowns in a predictable puddle or inside the plastic bag
from which you just took your tuxedo. The evening is certainly
ruined and we can go on from there but that too is predictable.
I want to know. I have no explanations for myself but if someone
told me that my sister wasn't with Jesus they would get an
ass-kicking. There's a fascinating tumor called a melanoma
that apparently draws pigment from surrounding tissue until
it's black as coal. That fatal lump of coal tucked against the
spine. And of all things on earth a bullet can hit human
flesh is one of the least resistant. It's late autumn and this
is an official autumnal mood, a fully sanctioned event in which
one may feel the thrill of victory and the agony of defeat. But
as poets we would prefer to have a star fall on us (that meteor
got me in the gizzard!), or lightning strike us and not while we're
playing golf but perhaps in a wheat field while we're making
love in a thunderstorm, or a tornado take us away outside of
Mingo, Kansas, like Judy Garland unfortunately. Or a rainbow
suffocate us. Or skewered dueling the mighty forces of anti-
art. Maybe in sleep as a Gray Eminence. A painless sleep of course.
Or saving a girl from drowning who turns out to be a mermaid.

8

I cleaned the granary dust off your photo with my shirtsleeve.
Now that we are tidy we can wait for the host to descend
presumably from the sky as that seems to exhaust the alternatives.
You had a nice summer in the granary. I was out there with you
every day in June and July writing one of my six-week wonders,
another novel. Loud country music on the phonograph, wasps
and bees and birds and mice. The horses looked in the window
every hour or so, curious and rather stupid. Chief Joseph stared
down from the wall at both of us, a far nobler man than
we ever thought possible. We can't lead ourselves and he led
a thousand with a thousand horses a thousand miles. He was a god
and had three wives when one is usually more than enough for
a human. These past weeks I have been organizing myself into
my separate pieces. I have the limberness of a man twice my age
and this is as good a time as any to turn around. Joseph was
very understanding, incidentally, when the cavalry shot so many
of the women and children. It was to be expected. Earth is
full of precedents. They hang around like underground trees
waiting for their chance. The fish swam around four years solid
in preparation for August the seventh, 1972, when I took his life
and ate his body. Just as we may see our own ghosts next to
us whose shapes we will someday flesh out. All of this suffering
to become a ghost. Yours held a rope, manila, straight from
the tropics. But we don't reduce such glories to a mudbath.
The ghost giggles at genuflections. You can't buy him a drink.
Out in a clearing in the woods the other day I got up on a
stump and did a little dance for mine. We know the most fright-
ening time is noon. The evidence says I'm halfway there, such
wealth I can't give away, thirty-four years of seconds.

9

What if I own more paper clips than I'll ever use in this
lifetime? My other possessions are shabby: the house half-
painted, the car without a muffler, one dog with bad eyes
and the other dog a horny moron. Even the baby has a rash on
her neck but then we don't own humans. My good books were
stolen at parties long ago and two of the barn windows are
broken and the furnace is unreliable and field mice daily
feed on the wiring. But the new foal appears healthy though
unmanageable, crawling under the fence and chased by my wife
who is stricken by the flu, not to speak of my own body which
has long suffered the ravages of drink and various nervous
disorders that make me laugh and weep and caress my shotguns.
But paper clips. Rich in paper clips to sort my writings which
fill so many cartons under the bed. When I attach them I say
it's your job after all to keep this whole thing together. And
I used them once with a rubber band to fire holes into the
face of the president hanging on the office wall. We have freedom.
You couldn't do that to Brezhnev much less Stalin on whose
grave Mandelstam sits proudly in the form of the ultimate
crow, a peerless crow, a crow without comparison on earth.
But the paper clips are a small comfort like meeting someone
fatter than myself and we both wordlessly recognize the fact
or meeting someone my age who is more of a drunk, more savaged
and hag-ridden until they are no longer human and seeing
them on the street I wonder how their heads which are only
wounds balance on the top of their bodies. A manuscript of
a novel sits in front of me held together with twenty clips.
It is the paper equivalent of a duck and a company far away
has bought this perhaps beautiful duck and my time is free again.

It would surely be known for years after as the day I shot
a cow. Walking out of the house before dawn with the sky an icy
blackness and not one star or cockcrow or shiver of breeze, the rifle
barrel black and icy to the touch. I walked a mile in the dark
and a flushed grouse rose louder than any thunderclap. I entered
a neck of a woodlot I'd scouted and sat on a stump waiting for
a deer I intended to kill. But then I was dressed too warmly
and had a formidable hangover with maybe three hours of sleep so
I slept again seeing a tin open-fronted café in Anconcito down
on the coast of Ecuador and the eyes of a piglet staring at me as
I drank my mineral water dazed with the opium I had taken for
la turista. Crippled syphilitic children begging, one little boy
with a tooth as long as a forefinger, an ivory tusk which would
be pulled on maturity and threaded as an amulet ending up finally
in Moscow in a diplomatic pouch. The boy would explore with his
tongue the gum hole for this Russian gift. What did he know about
Russia. Then carrying a naked girl in the water on my shoulders
and her short hairs tickled the back of my neck with just the suggestion
of a firm grip behind them so if I had been stupid enough to turn
around I might have suffocated at eighteen and not written you
any letters. There were bristles against my neck and hot breath
in my hair. It must be a deer smelling my hair so I wheeled and shot.
But it was a cow and the muzzle blast was blue in the gray light.
She bawled horribly and ran in zigzags. I put her away with a shot
to the head. What will I do with this cow? It's a guernsey and she
won't be milked this morning. I knelt and stared into her huge eyeball,
her iris making a mirror so I combed my hair and thought about the
whole dreary mess. Then I walked backward through a muddy orchard
so I wouldn't be trailed, got in my car and drove to New York nonstop.

11

for Diane W.

No tranquil pills this year wanting to live peeled as they
described the nine throats of Cerberus. Those old greek names
keep popping up. You can tell we went to college and our sleep
is troubled. There are geographical equivalents for exotic tropes
of mind; living peeled was the Arizona Inn in Tucson talking with D.W.
about love and art with so much pain my ears rang and the breath
came short. And outside the fine desert air wasn't fine anymore:
the Indians became kachina dolls and a girl was tortured daily
for particular reasons. This other is our Akhmatova and often we want
to hide from her—seasoned as she is in so many hells. But why paint
her for one of the dead who knew her pungency of love, the unforgivable
low-tide smell of it, how few of us bear it for long before reducing
it to a civil act. You were odd for a poet attaching yourself
to a woman no less a poet than yourself. It still starts with
the dance. In the end she probably strangled you and maybe back
in Ryazan there was a far better bird with less extravagant plumage.
But to say I'm going to spend the day thinking wisely about
women is to say I'm going to write an indomitably great poem before
lunch or maybe rule the world by tomorrow dawn. And I couldn't
love one of those great SHES—it's far too late and they are far
too few to find anyway though that's a driveling excuse. I saw one
in a tree and on a roof. I saw one in a hammock and thigh-deep
in a pond. I saw one out in the desert and sitting under a willow
by the river. All past tense you notice and past haunting but not
past caring. What did she do to you and did you think of her when
your terrible shadow fell down the wall. I see that creature sitting
on the lawn in Louveciennes, the mistress of a superior secret. We
have both died from want of her, cut off well past our prime.

12

I was proud at four that my father called me Little Turd of Misery.
A special name somehow connected to all the cows and horses in
the perpetual mire of the barnyard. It has a resonance to it un-
known to president senator poet septic-tank cleaner critic butcher
hack or baker liberal or snot, rightist and faker and faggot and
cunt hound. A child was brought forth and he was named Little Turd
of Misery and like you was thrown into the lake to learn how to
swim, owned dogs that died stupidly but without grief. Why does
the dog chase his broken legs in a circle? He almost catches them
like we almost catch our unruly poems. And our fathers and uncles
had ordinary pursuits, hunted and fished, smelled of tobacco and
liquor, grew crops, made sauerkraut and wine, wept in the dark,
chased stray cows, mended fences, were hounded as they say by
creditors. Barns burned. Cabbages rotted. Corn died of drought
before its holy ears were formed, wheat flattened by hail and wind and
the soup grew only one potato and a piece of salt pork from its
center. Generations of slavery. All so we could fuck neurotically
and begin the day rather than end it drinking and dreaming of dead
dogs, swollen creeks with small bridges, ponds where cows are caught
and drown, sucked in by the muck. But the wary boy catches fish
there, steals a chicken for his dog's monthly birthday, learns
to smoke, sees his first dirty picture and sings his first dirty
song, goes away, becomes deaf with song, becomes blinded by love,
gets letters from home but never returns. And his nights become less black
and holy, less moon-blown and sweet. His brain burns away like
gray paraffin. He's tired. His parents are dead or he is dead
to his parents. He smells the smell of a horse. The room is
cold. He dims the light and builds a noose. It works too well.

13

All of those little five-dollar-a-week rooms smelling thick of
cigarette smoke and stale tea bags. The private bar of soap
smearing the dresser top, on the chair a box of cookies and a letter
from home. And what does he think he's doing and do we all begin our
voyage into Egypt this way? The endless bondage of words. That's why
you turned to those hooligan taverns and vodka, Crane to his
sailors in Red Hook. Four walls breathe in and out. The clothes on
the floor are a dirty shroud. The water is stale in its glass.
Just one pull on the bottle starts the morning faster. If you
don't rouse your soul you will surely die while others are having
lunch. Noon. You passed the point of retreat and took that dancer,
a goad, perhaps a goddess. The food got better anyhow and the
bottles. This is all called romantic by some without nostrils
tinctured by cocaine. No romance here, but a willingness to age
and die at the speed of sound. Outside there's a successful revolution
and you've been designated a parasite. Everywhere crushed women
are bearing officious anti-Semites. Stalin begins his diet of
iron shavings and blood. Murder swings with St. Basil's bell, a
thousand per gong free of charge. North on the Baltic Petrodvorets
is empty and inland, Pushkin is empty. Nabokov has sensibly flown
the shabby coop. But a hundred million serfs are free and own
more than the common bread; a red-tinged glory, neither fire nor
sun, a sheen without irony on the land. Who could care that you
wanted to die, that your politics changed daily, that your songs
turned to glass and were broken? No time to marry back in Ryazan,
buy a goat, three dogs, and fish for perch. The age gave you a
pistol and you gave it back, gave you two wives and you gave
them both back, gave you a rope to swing from which you used wisely.
You were good enough to write that last poem in blood.

Imagine being a dog and never knowing what you're doing. You're
simply *doing:* eating garbage, fawning, mounting in public with
terrible energy. But let's not be romantic. Those curs, however
sweet, don't have souls. For all of the horrors at least some of
us have better lives than dogs. Show me a dog that ever printed
a book of poems read by no one in particular before he died at
seventeen, old age for a dog. No dog ever equaled Rimbaud for
grace or greatness, for rum running, gun running, slave trading
and buggery. The current phrase, "anything that gets you off,"
includes dogs but they lack our catholicity. Still, Sergei, we never
wanted to be dogs. Maybe Indians or princes, Caesars or Mongolian
chieftains, women in expensive undergarments. But if women, lesbians
to satisfy our ordinary tastes for women. In a fantasy if you
become a woman you quickly are caressing your girlfriend. That
pervert. I never thought she would. Be like that. When she's away
from me. Back to consciousness, the room smells like a locker room.
Out the window it's barely May in Moscow and the girls have shed
their winter coats. One watches a group of fishermen. She has
green eyes and is recent from the bath. If you were close enough
which you'll never be you could catch her scent of lemon and
the clear softness of her nape where it meets her hair. She'll
probably die of flu next year or marry an engineer. The same
things really as far as you're concerned. And it's the same in this
country. A fine wife and farm, children, animals, three good reviews.
Then a foggy day in late March with dozens of crows in the air
and a girl on a horse passes you in the woods. Your dog barks.
The girl stops, laughing. She has green eyes. Your heart is off
and running. Your groin hopes. You pray not to see her again.

15

The soul of water. The most involved play. She wonders if she
is permitted to name the stars. Tell her no. This month, May,
is said to be "the month of tiny plant-sucking pests." So even
nature is said to war against us though those pests it seems are
only having lunch. So the old woman had named the stars above
her hut and wondered if god had perhaps given them other names that
she didn't know about. Her priest was always combing his hair
and shining his shoes. We were driven from the church, weren't we
Sergei? In hearses. But is this time for joking? Yes. Always.
We wonder if our fathers in heaven or hell watch when we are about
our lying and shameful acts. As if they up or down there weren't
sick enough of life without watching for eternity some faulty
version of it, no doubt on a kind of TV. Tune the next hour out
dad, I'm going to be bad. Six lines of coke and a moronic twitch.
Please don't watch. I can't help myself. I provide for my children.
They're delighted with the fish I catch. My wife smiles hourly.
She has her horses, dogs, cat, barn, garden. But in New York twenty
layers above the city some cloud or stratum of evil wants to enter
me and I'm certainly willing. Even on ground level in Key West.
Look she has no clothes on and I only wanted to be a friend and
maybe talk about art. Only a lamb. Of course this Little Boy Blue
act is tiresome and believed by no one on earth, heaven or hell.
So we've tried to name the stars and think we are forgiven in
advance. Rimbaud turned to Black or Arab boys remembering when he
was twelve and there was no evil. Only a helpless sensual wonder.
Pleasure gives. And takes. It is dark and hot and the brain is
howling with those senseless drugs. Mosquitoes land upon those
fields of sweat, the pool between her breasts. You want to be home
rocking your child in a sunny room. Now that it's over. But wait.

16

Today we've moved back to the granary again and I've anointed
the room with *Petrouchka*. Your story, I think. And music. That
ends with you floating far above in St. Petersburg's blue winter
air, shaking your fist among the fish and green horses, the dim-
inutive yellow sun and chicken playing the bass drum. Your
sawdust is spilled and you are forever borne by air. A simple story.
Another madman, Nijinsky, danced your part and you danced his.
None of us apparently is unique. Think of dying waving a fist full
of ballpoint pens that change into small snakes and that your
skull will be transposed into the cymbal it was always meant to be.
But shall we come down to earth? For years I have been too ready
to come down to earth. A good poet is only a sorcerer bored with
magic who has turned his attention elsewhere. O let us see wonders
that psilocybin never conceived of in her powdery head. Just now
I stepped on a leaf that blew in the door. There was a buzzing
and I thought it concealed a wasp, but the dead wasp turned out to be
a tiny bird, smaller than a hummingbird or june bug. Probably one
of a kind and I can tell no one because it would anger the swarm
of naturalists so vocal these days. I'll tuck the body in my hair
where it will remain forever a secret or tape it to the back of
your picture to give you more depth than any mirror on earth.
And another oddity: the record needle stuck just at the point
the trumpet blast announced the appearance of your ghost in the
form of Petrouchka. I will let it repeat itself a thousand times
through the afternoon until you stand beside the desk in your
costume. But I've no right to bring you back to life. We must
respect your affection for the rope. You knew the exact juncture
in your life when the act of dangling could be made a dance.

17

Behind my back I have returned to life with much more surprise
than conviction. All those months in the cold with neither
tears nor appetite no matter that I was in Nairobi or Arusha, Rome,
the fabled Paris flat and dry as a newsphoto. And lions looked
like lions in books. Only the rumbling sound of an elephant shooting
water into his stomach with a massive trunk made any sense. But I
thought you would have been pleased with the Galla women in Ethiopia
and walking the Colonnade near the Vendôme. I knew you had walked
there. Such a few signs of life. Life brings us down to earth he
thinks. Father of two at thirty-five can't seem to earn a living.
But whatever muse there is on earth is not concerned with groceries.
We like to believe that Getty couldn't buy a good line for a billion
dollars. When we first offered ourselves up to her when young and
in our waking dreams she promised nothing. Not certainly that we
could buy a bike for our daughter's birthday or eat good cuts of
beef instead of hamburger. She doesn't seem to care that our wine
is ordinary. She walks in and out the door without knocking. She takes
off her clothes and ruins the marriage bed. She out-and-out killed
you Sergei for no reason I can think of. And you might want to
kill her but she changes so fast whether into a song, a deer, a pig,
the girl sitting on the pier in a short dress. You want to fish
but you turn and there larger than any movie are two thighs and louder
than any howl they beckon you to the life they hold so gently. We
said that her eyes were bees and ice glistened in her hair. And we
know she can become a rope but then you're never sure as all rope
tends to resemble itself though it is common for it to rest in coils
like snakes. Or rope. But I must earn our living and can't think
about rope though I am to be allowed an occasional girl drawing up
her thighs on a pier. You might want her even in your ghostly form.

18

Thus the poet is a beached gypsy, the first porpoise to whom it
occurred to commit suicide. True, my friend, even porpoises have
learned your trick and for similar reasons: losing hundreds of
thousands of wives, sons, daughters, husbands to the tuna nets.
The seventh lover in a row disappears and it can't be endured.
There is some interesting evidence that Joplin was a porpoise and
simply decided to stop breathing at an unknown depth. Perhaps the
navy has her body and is exploring ways to turn it into a weapon.
Off Boca Grande a baby porpoise approached my boat. It was a girl
about the size of my two-year-old daughter who might for all I know
be a porpoise. Anyway she danced around the boat for an hour
while her mother kept a safer distance. I set the mother at ease by
singing my infamous theme song: "Death dupe dear dingle devil flower
bird dung girl," repeating seven times until the mother approached
and I leaned over the gunnel and we kissed. I was tempted to swim
off with them but remembered I had a date with someone who tripled
as a girl, cocaine dealer and duck though she chose to be the last,
alas, that evening. And as in all ancient stories I returned to the
spot but never found her or her little girl again. Even now mariners
passing the spot deep in the night can hear nothing. But enough
of porpoise love. And how they are known to beach themselves. I've
begun to doubt whether we ever would have been friends. Maybe. Not
that it's to the point—I know three one-eyed poets like myself
but am close to none of them. These letters might have kept me
alive—something to do you know as opposed to the nothing you chose.
Loud yeses don't convince. Nietzsche said you were a rope dancer
before you were born. I say yes before breakfast but to the smell
of bacon. Wise souls move through the dark only one step at a time.

Naturally we would prefer seven epiphanies a day and an earth
not so apparently devoid of angels. We become very tired with
pretending we like to earn a living, with the ordinary objects and
events of our lives. What a beautiful toothbrush. How wonderful
to work overtime. What a nice cold we have to go with the cold
crabbed spring. How fun to have no money at all. This thin soup
tastes great. I'm learning something every morning from cheap wine
hangovers. These rejection slips are making me a bigger person.
The mailbox is always so empty let's paint it pink. It's good for
my soul that she prefers to screw another. Our cat's right eyeball
became ulcerated and had to be pulled but she's the same old cat.
I can't pay my taxes and will be sent to prison but it will probably
be a good experience. That rattlesnake striking at dog and daughter
was interesting. How it writhed beautifully with its head cut
off and dog and daughter were tugging at it. How purging to lose
our last twenty dollars in a crap game. Seven come eleven indeed.
But what grand songs you made out of an awful life though you had
no faith that less was more, that there was some golden splendor
in humiliation. After all those poems you were declared a coward
and a parasite. Mayakovsky hissed in public over your corpse and
work only to take his own life a little while later. Meanwhile
back in America Crane had his Guggenheim year and technically jumped
ship. Had he been seven hundred feet tall he would have been ok.
I suspect you would have been the kind of friends you both needed
so badly. So many husbands have little time for their homosexual
friends. But we should never imagine we love this daily plate of shit.
The horses in the yard bite and chase each other. I'll make a carol
of my dream: carried in a litter by lovely women, a 20 lb. bag of cocaine,
angels shedding tunics in my path, all dead friends come to life again.

20

The mushrooms helped again: walking hangdoggedly to the granary
after the empty mailbox trip I saw across the barnyard at the base
of an elm stump a hundred feet away a group of white morels. How
many there were will be kept concealed for obvious reasons. While
I plucked them I considered each a letter from the outside world
to my little cul-de-sac, this valley: catching myself in this act
doing what I most despise, throwing myself in the laps of others.
Save my life. Help me. By return post. That sort of thing. So we
throw ourselves in the laps of others until certain famous laps
grow tired, vigorous laps whose movement is slowed by the freight
of all those cries. Then if you become famous after getting off
so many laps you can look at the beautiful women at your feet and
say I'll take that foot and that breast and that thigh and those lips
you have become so denatured and particular. They float and merge
their parts trying to come up with something that will please you.
Selecting the finest belly you write your name with a long thin
line of cocaine but she is perspiring and you can't properly snort
it off. Disappointments. The belly weeps but you dismiss her, sad
and frightened that your dreams have come to no end. Why cast Robert
Redford in your life story if all that he's going to do is sit there
and piss and moan at the typewriter for two hours in expensive
Eastman color? Not much will happen if you don't like to drink
champagne out of shoes. And sated with a half-dozen French meals a day
you long for those simple boiled potatoes your estranged wife made
so perfectly. The letters from your children are defiled in a stack
of fan mail and obscene photos. Your old dog and horse have been
given to kindly people and your wife will soon marry a jolly farmer.
No matter that your million-selling books are cast in bronze. On a
whim you fly to Palm Beach, jump on your yacht and set the automatic.
You fit a nylon hawser around your neck, hurl overboard, and after
the sharks have lunch your head skips in the noose like a marlin bait.

218 JIM HARRISON : COMPLETE POEMS

To answer some of the questions you might ask were you alive and
had we become friends but what do poets ask one another after long
absence? How have you been other than dead and how have I been
dying on earth without naming the average string of complaints which
is only worrying aloud, naming the dreaded motes that float around
the brain, those pink balloons calling themselves poverty, failure,
sickness, lust, and envy. To mention a very few. But you want part-
iculars, not the human condition or a letter to the editor on why
when I'm at my worst I think I've been fucked over. So here's this
Spring's news: now that the grass is taller I walk in some fear of
snakes. Feeling melancholy I watched my wife plant the garden row
on row while the baby tried to catch frogs. It's hard not to eat too
much when you deeply love food but I've limited myself to a half
gallon of Burgundy a day. On long walks my eyes are so sunk back
in my brain they see nothing, then move forward again toward the light
and see a high meadow turning pale green and swimming in the fog
with crows tracing perceptible and geometrical paths just above
the fog but audible. At the shore I cast for fish, some of them
large with deliquescing smelt and alewives in their bellies. Other
than marriage I haven't been in love for years; close calls over
the world I mentioned to you before, but it's not love if it isn't
a surprise. I look at women and know deeply they are from another
planet and sometimes even lightly touching a girl's arm I know
I am touching a lovely though alien creature. We don't get back
those days we don't caress, don't make love. If I could get you out
in the backcountry down in Key West and get some psilocybin into
you you would cut your legendary vodka consumption. Naturally I
still believe in miracles and the holy fate of the imagination. How
is it being dead and would I like it and should I put it off for a while?

These last few notes to you have been a bit somber like biographies
of artists written by joyless people so that the whole book is
a record of agony at thirty rather than thirty-three and a third.
You know the sound—Keeeaaattts wuzzz verrry unhappppppy abouttt
dyinnnng. So here are some of those off-the-wall extravagancies.
Dawn in Ecuador with mariachi music, dawn at Ngorongoro with elephants
far below in the crater swaggering through the marsh grass, dawn in
Moscow and snowing with gold minarets shouting that you have at last
reached Asia, dawn in Addis Ababa with a Muslim waver in the cool
air smelling of ginger and a lion roaring on the lawn, dawn in
bleary Paris with a roll tasting like zinc and a girl in a cellophane
blouse staring at you with four miraculous eyes, dawn in Normandy
with a conceivable princess breathing in the next room and horses
wandering across the moat beneath my window, dawn in Montana with
herons calling from the swamp, dawn in Key West wondering if it was
a woman or tarpon that left your bed before cockcrow, dawn at home
when your eyes are molten and the ghost of your dog chases the fox
across the pasture, dawn on the Escanaba with trout dimpling the
mist and the water with a dulcet roar, dawn in London when the party-
girl leaves your taxi to go home to Shakespeare, dawn in Leningrad
with the last linden leaves falling and you knocking at the door
for a drunken talk but I am asleep. Not to speak of the endless and
nearly unconscious water walks after midnight when even the stars
might descend another foot to get closer to earth. Heat. The wetness
of air. Couplings. Even the mosquitoes are lovely and seem to imitate
miniature birds. And a lion's cough is followed rhythmically by a
hyena's laugh to prove that nature loves symmetry. The Black girl
leaves the grand hotel for her implausibly shabby home. The poet
had dropped five sorts of drugs in his belly swill of alcohol and
has imagined his deathless lines commemorating your last Leningrad night.

23

I want to bother you with some recent nonsense; a classmate dropped
dead, his heart was attacked at thirty-three. At the crematory
they lowered his body by fire-resistant titanium cables reminding
one of the steak on a neglected barbecue grill, only more so. We're
not supposed to believe that the vase of ashes is the real him.
You can imagine the mighty roar of the gas jets, a train coming
closer, the soul of thunder. But this is only old hat, or old death,
whichever. "Pause here, son of sorrow, remember death," someone once
said. "We can't have all things here to please us, our little Sue Ann
is gone to Jesus," reads an Alabama gravestone. But maybe even Robert
Frost and Charles Olson don't know they are dead. That would include
you of course. It is no quantity, absolute zero, the air in a hole
minus its airiness, the vacuum from the passing bird or bullet, the
end of the stem where the peach was, the place above the ground
where the barn burned with such energy we plugged our ears. If not,
show yourself in ten minutes. Let's settle this issue because I feel
badly today: a sense that my teeth and body are rotting on the hoof.
I could avoid the whole thing with a few drinks—it's been over
eight hours—but I want to face it like Simon Magus or poor Faustus.
Nothing, however, presents itself other than that fading picture of
my sister with an engine in her lap, not a very encouraging item
to be sure. I took Anna who is two for her first swim today. We didn't
know we were going swimming so she wore a pink dress, standing in
the lake up to her waist in wonderment. The gaucheries of children,
the way they love birds and neon lights, kill snakes and eat sand.
But I decided I wanted to go swimming for the first time and wanted
to make love for the first time again. These thoughts can make you
unhappy. Perhaps if your old dog had been in the apartment that night
you wouldn't have done it. Everything's so fragile except ropes.

24

Dear friend. It rained long and hard after a hot week and when I
awoke the world was green and leafy again, or as J.D. says, everything
was new like a warm rain after a movie. And I said enough of death
and its obvious health hazards, it's a white-on-white jigsaw puzzle
in one piece. An hour with the doctor yesterday when he said my
blood pressure was so high I might explode as if I had just swallowed
an especially tasty grenade. I must warn my friends not to stand
too close. Blood can be poisonous; the Kikuyu in Kenya are often
infected when they burrow hacking away in the gut of an elephant.
Some don't come back. But doctors don't say such things, except
W.C. Williams. Just like your doctor when you were going batty, mine
said, "You must be distressed, you eat and drink and smoke far too
much. Cut out these things. The lab found lilacs and part of the
backbone of a garter snake or garter in your stool sample, and the
remnants of a hair ball. Do you chew your comb? We are checking to
see if it's your hair as there are possible criminal questions here.
Meanwhile get this thatch of expensive prescriptions filled and I
advise extensive psychiatric care. I heard your barking when I left
the room. How did you manage gout at your age?" My eyes misted
and I heard fiddle music and I looked up from page 86 in the June
Vogue where my old nemesis Lauren Hutton was staring at me in a
doctor's office in northern Michigan. This is Paul Bunyan country
Lauren. And how did I get gout? All of that fried salt and side
pork as a child. Humble fare. Quintuple heaps of caviar and decanters
of vodka at the Hotel Europa in Leningrad. *Tête de veau,* the brains,
tongue and cheeks of a calf. Side orders of *tripe à la mode de Caen*
sweetbreads with morels. Stewed kidneys and heart. Three-pound steaks
as snacks, five dozen oysters and three lobsters in Boston. A barrel
of nice gravy. Wild boar. Venison. Duck. Partridge. Pig's feet. But
you know, Sergei, I must eat these magical trifles to keep from
getting brainy and sad, to avoid leaving this physical world.

25

An afterthought to my previous note; we must closely watch any self-pity and whining. It simply isn't manly. Better by far to be a cowboy drinking rusty water, surviving on the maggots that unwittingly ate the pemmican in the saddlebags. I would be the Lone and I don't need no one said the cowpoke. Just a man and his horse against everything else on earth and horses are so dumb they run all day from flies never learning that flies are everywhere. Though in their violent motion they avoid the flies for a few moments. It's time again not to push a metaphor too far. But back again to the successful farmer who has his original hoe bronzed like baby shoes above the Formica mantelpiece—I earned what I got, nobody give me nothing he says. Pasternak said you probably didn't think death was the end of it all. Maybe you were only checking it out for something new to write about. We thieves of fire are capable of such arrogance when not otherwise occupied as real people pretending to be poet farmers, important writers, capable lovers, sports fops, regular guys, rock stars with tiny nonetheless appreciative audiences. But the self-pity and whining must stop. I forgot to add that at the doctor's an old woman called in to say that her legs had turned blue and she couldn't walk or hold her urine and she was alone. Try that one on. Thirty years ago I remember my mother singing *Hello Central, give me heaven, I think my daddy is there* about the usual little boy in a wartime situation. We forget about those actual people, certainly our ancestors and neighbors, who die in earnest. They called my dad, the county agent, and his friend a poor farmer was swinging like you only from a rafter in the barn from a hay rope. What to do with his strange children—their thin bodies, low brows and narrow eyes— who were my schoolmates. They're working in auto factories now and still voiceless. We are different in that we suffer and love, are bored, with our mouths open and must speak on occasion for those others.

26

Going in the bar last Sunday night I noticed that they were having
high-school graduation down the street. Caps and gowns. June and
mayflies fresh from the channel fluttering in the warm still air.
After a few drinks I felt jealous and wanted someone to say, "Best of
luck in your chosen field," or, "The road of life is ahead of you."
Remember your first trip to Moscow at nineteen? Everything was pos-
sible. You watched those noblewomen at the riding academy who would
soon be permanently unhorsed, something you were to have mixed
feelings about, what with the way poets suck up to and are attracted
to the aristocracy however gimcrack. And though the great Blok
welcomed you, you felt tentative, an unknown quantity, and remained
so for several years. But how quickly one goes from being unknown
and embarrassed to bored and arrogant, from being ignored to expecting
deference. From fleabag rooms to at least the Plaza. And the daydreams
and hustling, the fantasies and endless work that get you from one
to the other, only to discover that you really want to go home. Start
over with a new deck. But back home all the animals are dead, the
friends have disappeared and the fields gone to weed. The fish
have flown from the creeks and ponds and the birds have all drowned
or gone to China. No one knows you—they have little time for poetry
in the country, or in the city for that matter except for the minis-
trations of a few friends. Your name bobs up like a Halloween
apple and literature people have the vague feeling that they should read
you if they ever "catch up" on their reading. Once on a train I saw
a girl reading a book of mine but she was homely and I had a toothache
so I let the moment pass. What delicious notoriety. The journalist
said I looked like a bricklayer or beer salesman, not being fashion-
ably slender. But lately the sun shines through, the sweet release
of flinging these lines at the dead, almost like my baby Anna throw-
ing grain to the horses a mile away, in the far corner of the pasture.

27

I won my wings! I got all A's! We bought fresh fruit! The toilet
broke! Thus my life draws fuel ineluctably from triumph. Manic,
rainy June slides into July and I am carefully dressing myself in
primary colors for happiness. When the summer solstice has passed
you know you're finally safe again. That midnight surely dates
the year. "Look to your romantic interests and business investments,"
says the star hack in the newspapers. But what if you have neither?
Millions will be up to nothing. One of those pure empty days with
all the presence of a hole in the ground. The stars have stolen
twenty-four hours and vengeance is out of the question. But I'm
a three-peckered purple goat if you were tied to any planet by your
cord. That is mischief, an inferior magic; pulling the lining out
of a top hat. You merely rolled on the ground moaning trying to pull
that mask off but it had grown into your face. "Such a price the
gods exact for song to become what we sing," said someone. If it
aches that badly you have to take the head off, narrow the neck to
a third its normal size, a practice known as hanging by gift of the
state or as a do-it-yourself project. But what I wonder about is your
velocity: ten years from Ryazan to Leningrad. A little more than
a decade, two years into your fifth seven and on out like a proton
in an accelerator. You simply fell off the edge of the world while
most of us are given circles or, hopefully, spirals. The new
territory had a wall which you went over and on the other side there
was something we weren't permitted to see. Everyone suspects it's
nothing. Time will tell. But how you preyed on, longed for, those
first ten years. We'll have to refuse that, however its freshness
in your hands. Romantic. Fatal. We learn to see with the child's
delight again or perish. We hope it was your vision you lost,
that before those final minutes you didn't find out something new.

28

to Robert Duncan

O to use the word *wingèd* as in bird or victory or airplane for
the first time. Not for spirit though, yours or anyone else's
or the bird that flew errantly into the car radiator. Or for poems
that sink heavily to our stomachs like fried foods, the powerful
ones, visceral, as impure as the bodies they flaunt. Curious what
you paid for your cocaine to get wingèd. We know the price of
the poems, one body and soul net, one brain already tethered to the
dark, one ingenious leash never to hold a dog, two midwinter eyes
that lost their technicolor. Think what you missed. Mayakovsky's
pistol shot. The Siege of Leningrad. Crows feasting on all of those
frozen German eyes. Good Russian crows that earned a meal putting
up with all of that insufferable racket of war. Curious crows watching
midnight purges, wary of owls, and the girl in the green dress
on the ground before a line of soldiers. She and the crow exchange
pitiless glances. She flaps her arms but is not wingèd. Maybe
there is one ancient crow that remembers the Czarina's jeweled
sleigh, the ring of its small gold bells; and the sickly wingèd
horse in the cellar of the Winter Palace, product of a mad breeding
experiment for eventual escape, how it was dumped into the Neva
before the talons grew through the hooves, the marvel of it lost
in the uproar of those days, the proof of it in the bones somewhere
on the floor of the Baltic delta. But we all get lost in the course
of empire, which lacks the Brownian movement's stability. We count
on iron men to stick to their guns. Our governments are weapons
of exhaustion. Poems fly out of yellow windows at night with a stall
factor just under a foot, beneath our knees and the pre–Fourth of
July corn in the garden. At least at that level radar can't detect
them and they're safe from State interference. We know perfectly
well you flapped your arms madly, unwingèd but craving a little flight.

29

We're nearing the end of this homage that often resembles a
suicide note to a suicide. I didn't mean it that way but how
often our hands sneak up on our throats and catch us unaware.
What are you doing here we say. Don't squeeze so hard. The hands
inside the vodka bottle and on the accelerator, needles and coke-
sore noses. It's not very attractive, is it? But now there is rain
on the tin roof, the world outside is green and leafy with bluebirds
this morning dive-bombing drowning worms from a telephone wire,
the baby laughing as the dog eats the thirty-third snake of the
summer. And the bodies on the streets and beaches. Girl bottoms!
Holy. Tummies in the sun! Very probably holy. Peach evidence almost
struggling for air! A libidinal stew that calls us to life however
ancient and basal. May they plug their lovely ears with their big
toes. God surely loves them to make them look that way and can I
do less than He at least in this respect. As my humble country
father said in our first birds-and-bees talk so many years ago: "That
thing ain't just to pee through." This vulgarity saves us as
certainly as our chauvinism. Just now in midafternoon I wanted
a tumbler of wine but John Calvin said, "You got up at noon. No wine
until you get your work done. You haven't done your exercises to
suppress the gut the newspaper says women find most disgusting.
The fence isn't mended and the neighbor's cow keeps crawling through
in the night, stealing the fresh clover you are saving for Rachel
the mare when she drops her foal." So the wine bottle remains
corked and Calvin slips through the floorboards to the crawl space
where he spends all of his time hating his body. Would these concerns
have saved you? Two daughters and a wife. Children prop our rotting
bodies with cries of *earn earn earn*. On occasion we are kissed. So odd
in a single green month to go from the closest to so far from death.

30

The last and I'm shrinking from the coldness of your spirit: that
chill lurid air that surrounds great Lenin in his tomb as if we
had descended into a cloud to find on the catafalque a man who has
usurped nature, isn't dead any more than you or I are dead. Only
unlikely to meet and talk to our current forms. Today I couldn't
understand words so I scythed ragweed and goldenrod before it could
go to seed and multiply. I played with god imagining how to hold His
obvious scythe that caught you, so unlike the others, aware and
cooperative. Is He glad to help if we're willing? A boring question
since we're so able and ingenious. Sappho's sparrows are always
telling us that love will save us, some *other* will arrive to draw
us cool water, lie down with us in our private darkness and make
us well. I think not. What a fabulous lie. We've disposed of sparrows
and god, the death of color, those who are dominated by noon and
the vision of night flowing in your ears and eyes and down your
throat. But we didn't mean to arrive at conclusions. Fifty years are
only a moment between this granary and a hanged man half the earth
away. You are ten years younger than my grandmother Hulda who still
sings Lutheran hymns and watches the Muskegon River flow. In whatever
we do, we do damage to ourselves; and in those first images there
were always cowboys or cossacks fighting at night, murdered animals
and girls never to be touched; dozing with head on your dog's chest
you understand breath and believe in golden cities where you will
live forever. And that fatal expectancy—not comprehending that we
like our poems are flowers for the void. In those last days you
wondered why they turned their faces. Any common soul knew you
had consented to death, the only possible blasphemy. I write to
you like some half-witted, less courageous brother, unwilling to tease
those ghosts you slept with faithfully until they cast you out.

POSTSCRIPT

At 8:12 a.m. all of the watches in the world are being wound.
Which is not quite the same thing as all of the guitars on earth
being tuned at midnight. Or that all suicides come after the mail-
man when all hope is gone. Before the mailman, watches are wound,
windows looked through, shoes precisely tied, tooth care, the
attenuations of the hangover noted. Which is not the same as
the new moon after midnight or her bare feet stepping slowly toward
you and the snake easing himself from the ground for a meal.
The world is so necessary. Someone must execute stray dogs and
free the space they're taking up. I can see people walking down
Nevsky Prospekt winding their watches before you were discovered
too far above the ground, that mystical space that was somewhere
occupied by a stray dog or a girl in an asylum on her hands
and knees. A hanged face turns slowly from a plum to a lump of
coal. I'm winding my watch in antipathy. I see the cat racing
around the yard in a fantasy of threat. She's preparing for
eventualities. She prizes the only prize. But we aren't the cats
we once were thousands of years ago. You didn't die with the
dignity of an animal. Today you make me want to tie myself to
a tree, stake my feet to earth herself so I can't get away. It didn't
come as a burning bush or pillar of light but I've decided to stay.

INCIDENTS

A LAST GHAZAL

Anconcito. The fisheater. Men were standing on cork rafts
on the water, visible between great Pacific swells.

So in Ecuador you decide to forget her in St. George in
Normandy. Try not to think of a white horse for several days.

All of the lilacs in the yard lie when they take you back to your
youth. There are white hairs on your chin, you can't jump the fence.

What is this feeling that the police are ineluctably closing
in and you will miss many of your daughters' birthdays.

There are still flowers of evil that want to lead you to another
life. We have photographic evidence of this in color, black-and-white.

Asleep and in a dreaming state near death I feel the awkward girl
in my head say please not now, I haven't quite lived yet.

A DOMESTIC POEM FOR PORTIA

This is all it is.
These pictures cast up in front of me
with the mind's various energies.
Hence so many flies in this old granary.
I've become one of those blackened beef sides
hanging in a South American market so when I sing
to myself I dispel a black cloud around my mouth
and when Linda brings iced tea she thinks I'm only
a photo in the *National Geographic* and drinks the tea
herself, musing he's snuck off to the bar
and his five-year pool game.
This seems to be all it is.
Garcia sings *Brown-eyed women and red grenadine.*
Some mother-source of pleasure so that the guitar
mutes and revolves the vision of her as she rinses
her hair bending thigh-deep in the lake, her buttocks appear
to be struggling by themselves to get out of that bikini
with a faint glisten of sun at each cheek-top.
But when I talked to her she was thin in the head,
a magazine photo slipping through the air like
a stringless kite.
It's apparent now that this is all there is.
This shabby wicker chair, music, the three p.m.
glass of red wine as a reward for sitting still
as our parents once instructed us. "Sit still!"
I want my head to go visit friends, traveling they call it
and without airports. Then little Anna up to her neck
in the lake for the first time, the ancient lineage
of swimming revealing itself in her two-year-old fat
body, eyes sparkle with awe and delight in this natural
house of water. Hearing a screech I step to the porch
and see three hawks above the neighbor's pasture

chasing each other in battle or courtship.
This must be all there is.
At full rest with female-wet eyes becoming red wondering
falsely how in christ's name am I going to earn
enough to keep us up in the country where the air
is sweet and green, an immense kingdom of water nearby
and five animals looking to me for food, and two daughters
and a mother assuming my strength. I courageously fix
the fence, mulch the tomatoes, fertilize the pasture—
a nickel-plated farmer. Wake up in the middle
of the night frightened, thinking nearly two decades
ago I took my vows and never dreamed I'd be responsible
for so many souls. Eight of them whispering *provide*.
This could very well be all that there is.
And I'm not unhappy with it. A check in the mail that will
take us through another month. I see in the papers
I've earned us "lower class"! How strange. Waiting
for Rachel's foal to drop. That will make nine. Provide.
Count my big belly ten. But there's an odd grace in being
an ordinary artist. A single tradition clipping the heads
off so many centuries. Those two drunks a millennium ago on
a mountaintop in China—laughing over the beauty of the moment.
At peace despite their muddled brains. The male dog, a trifle
stupid, rushes through the door announcing absolutely nothing.
He has great confidence in me. I'm hanging on to nothing today and
with confidence, a sureness that the very air between our bodies,
the light of what we are, has to be enough.

MISSY, 1966–1971

I want to be worthy of this waking dream—
      floating   above
      the August landscape
in a coffin with my dog
who's just died from fibroid cancer.
Yes. We'll be up there and absorb
the light of stars and phosphorus
like the new army telescopic sights
and the light hanging captive
in clouds
and the light glittering upward
from the water
and porch lights
from the few trucks & cars
at 3 a.m.
and one lone airliner.
Grief holding us safe in a knot we'll float
over every mile we covered, birch clump, thorn apple,
wild cherry trees and aspen in search of grouse,
your singular white figure fixed then as Sirius the Dog Star.
I think this crazed boy striking
out at nothing
wants to join you
so homeward
bound.

FOUR MATRICES

1. HOME

New Matrices, all ice. Fixed here and solidly.
What was that song? My grave is hiding from me.
I'll go to that juniper thicket across
the road. Or stay here. Or go. Or stay.
A contessa. A girl on a roan horse behind
the goldenrod. The barn. The whiskey shelf.
Count options, false starts. And glooms of love,
the lover's next-room boredom. Juliet's in Verona.
Juliets are always in Verona after a few days.
Or trout and grouse, wading & walking after them.
Days of it. Dis. Dis. Dis. Dante called it,
this actual hell, this stillness. Lasting
how long? Waking is visionary. I'll awake but
to sleep again, new and bitter each new time.

2. COUNTING ARIZONA

Amphora in rocks. Kachina of fur and rust. The land
here seemed burned out & wasn't; just no lushness
of green, verdigris, leaves in sweet rot or swamps.
I don't belong and won't, perhaps only less foreign
than the natives. INDIANS: Zuni, Navajo, Jicarilla,
Papago, Mescalero Apache, Hopi. Aliens. That range is
owned by cone-nosed beetles, cattle, scorpion and snake
and the mines. A few deer, javelinas, quail, mountain thrush
and jackrabbit. Frightened. I count and point. Beware.
Just off the road's shoulder is wilderness and finally
Mexico and peopleless. And too much sun. I want to go home.

3. HOME

Cores. Knots. A vortex around which nothing swirls
or moves. Here then. Where I am now and can't seem
to move, some perfect cripple; a suspended brain.
It was cold, it is cold. It will be cold. And dry.
A root hits tablerock, curls upward, winds around
itself until it becomes a noose. Obvious! Obvious!
All the better. Simple things: just now a horse walked
past the window. I was naked when I carried the dying dog
to the couch. And weeping with alcohol and rock and
cold and stillness, horses and roots, unmoving brain.

4. THE SEA

Screw-gumption despite cold rain and clouds drifting below treetops.
Poor thing, strung up by false & falser delights; not lost,
a word that weighs nothing except *lost* to one's self, floating.
How light these imagined loves, floating too, from the head
in a night's sleep when the body's heat is nonmental.
It's a happy mage that walks through the world with his eyes
earthward using clouds only for a pick-me-up. The brain's not
a solid thing he thinks eating calf's brains. But butchers
are solid people. Somewhere between butcher and that unstable
weight is ballad, some song, though not moving to our obvious
harmonies. Count those waterbirds and beware, costumed as women;
part air and part water. But we are drawn to them as clumsy
rowboats sunk in fifty fathoms. After drifting the oceans for years.

NORTH AMERICAN IMAGE CYCLE

to Tom McGuane

The boy stood in the burning house. Set it up
that way, and with all windows open. I don't want
a roof. I want to fill all those spaces where we
never allow words to occur.

—

Crudities:
        implausible as this brilliantly cold
day in late June, barely forty. Two horses outside
the granary door, braced leaning into the wind
not even trying to figure it out.

And the great shattering cold waves
On Good Harbor Bay, the sea permanently bleak;
a squall line a hundred miles long, the island a dull
ugly green, and only one brief sweep of yellow light.

It is nearly against nature and that is why I love
it and would not trade it for all your princely heart.

—

The snail is beautiful, nearly Persian. Do we dwell in
or *on* beauty? The Belgian mare in my barn weighs 2300 lbs.
but thinks of herself oddly as woman, very feminine and shy
tossing her flaxen mane then rolling hugely & wantonly
in the snow. She takes the proffered apple not with her teeth
but delicately with her lips.

—

Phenomenon. Agonies. Mostly unshared. Dear Friends
the nightmare I recounted was pastel. I believed in numbers.
What is so crisp and intense as a number? Not our bodies

in their average frenzies. Fortunately the heart
doesn't melt as wax does at the sight of a kitten.
Place a kitten near a candle when bored.

—

In a dream I saw Spicer's body hanging from a hundred feet
of clothesline rope under the Golden Gate. Ask Weldon Kees
and Lew Welch to make contact, if alive or not. Crane's jump
in all things, a raincoat, borrowed. When I fish the Marquesas
every year I say to the passing fish, have you seen Crane's bones?
How deep and where do they lie and are they drawn together or
spread and are they peaceful on the bottom?

—

Are these horses less wonderful for my daughter having to shovel
horseshit an hour a day? The teacher would say someone has
to do it and go on to the social contract before a lunch of
cheese sandwiches, tomato soup and chalk dust à la mode.
But we are thinking of horses not teachers. And of the shovel
and the dreaded weight at the end that is less useful than
the much ruminated cow manure. Throw it out the door.
Sally, Nancy, Belle, Saud & Tramp watch with soft curious
horse eyes.

—

Oooooooo, he said to himself. That night of wonderment.
The head might explode from it. Certainly the heart beats
in circles like a Masarati cam. The insistence of physical
love and she didn't know her head was in an ashtray and
afterward didn't seem to care.

—

More mad dogs and fewer streetlights, Mr. Nixon. That advice
will cost you a hundred bucks, has been billed for that amount.
Date check after the first for tax reasons. The mad
dogs can be gotten from Spain, cheap. And everyone loves
to throw stones at streetlights.

＿

And my puppy is over her kidney infection, diagnosed
as chronic & fatal. Saved from the gas chamber. I salute
the technology of antibiotics. All dogs are in particular
as was Christopher Smart's cat Jeoffry. He said drunkenly
near dawn O let her sleep with us during her last days and
let her wounds become my own.

＿

First sighting:
She was up in the apple tree with one leg hanging
and the other drawn under her, sidesaddle on the branch.
Her face was bare of features and being an artist of sorts
I filled them in. It was deadly serious and I wanted
to ask someone what she was doing so nudely up in the apple
tree behind the barn, but had no one to ask and the mouth
I'd designed was too fresh on her face to open; so I stared
up and noticed she didn't lack the truly important features of
her sex but any desire was constrained by fear. So I sat
in the grass and dozed from what I'd been drinking that afternoon
waking to hear her sing no mantra but some ancient lute song,
and seeing her again as she dropped from the tree to my side
I thought her bare feet were cloven a bit too obviously.

＿

At four in the morning my body bumped against the ceiling.
Thank Jesus for ceilings or I would have been lost to earth,
rather, earth lost to me as she doesn't know me well.

—

Remember her cheers? How you loved the cheerleader far beyond
desperation. How you nearly threw yourself into Niagara Falls
unprotected by a rubber barrel on your high-school senior trip.
Now you have a permanent rubber barrel around you but you
no longer love the cheerleader.

—

He sang *I'm talking through a hat that isn't mine.* It's
Jackson Pollock's, given him by Pollock's brother, Charles,
and there is blood on the rim, his own not Pollock's. This talisman
was lost in a bar somewhere, anywhere in America, and is
worn now by a dump-picker who found it among the garbage.
Appropriate! As both of them, one so great and the other so
small, treated themselves like garbage. *sanctus detritus redivivus*

—

I felt myself floating toward the shadow of the dreamer I once
was. I said that I had become too old to dream and the androgynous
dreamer said let's marry anyway and be unhappy but joyous
in our dreams. There were poems before books on earth.

—

The stewardess said You're a poet?
When I think of a poet I think of someone sitting
around all day humming *Got a date with a daydream.*

—

This fat & sexless life.

—

I mourned Portia's unfair operation. Then the horse
ate her garden to ground level. The horse's name
happened to be Rex.

—

We must not think of our country as a ten-trillion-dollar
blowjob no matter how the idea tempts us.

—

Overheard story in Montana bar: She thought when she lost
her teeth we'd divorce and she cried a lot; so I said
to her we won't divorce but we'll marry someone else. The vaunted
simplicity of cowboys who are really cossacks—the horse
rhythms obviously affecting the brain chemistry. A slavic tribe
with ambivalent affection for guns & ewes, mares & drudgery.

—

He became humbler with his journalism, bought a porkpie hat
at Kresge's and wore an inoperable malachite pencil over
his left ear as his only visible rebellion.

—

The green green grass of home is owned by another now
and I'm not allowed on the property for my ounce of sentiment.

—

In the Montana whorehouse the madam yells "Burma"
through the door to the girl and her customer
when the time is up, circa twenty minutes for twenty
dollars, the value being established by Nixon's Price
Commission on infolding nightflowers, petaled creatures.

So the customer who is a language buff looks down
at his shoes, all that he's wearing, and thinks:
How did I get my pants off over my shoes? Has a genuine
miracle happened? Why do they use Burma as a signal
rather than Peking or Topeka or French fries? On the dresser
is a photo of the girl with a child, her son in a sailor
suit. Does he cry Burma in the night to get his mother
home? A tape cassette playing Wilson Pickett. Can my
future be traced on those stretch marks and if she were
wet would they form small rivers, minnows and all?
That twenty was hard-earned by art to be printed in New York
at $5.95 net. Will she buy him another sailor suit?
The room is hot. Perhaps during the C-minus transport
the house has been moved to Burma and outside is a green
hell with lianas masquerading as vipers and vice versa.
On a tray there is some dental floss, Moon Drop lotion
and a cordless vibrator, an aerosol can of Cupid's Quiver.
I really didn't want to go to Burma this afternoon, ma'am,
he thinks. I'll miss supper and fishing the evening hatch.

—

Second sighting:
She was up on the roof when I went up to check
the texture of the night and to generally be an ordinary
poet who muses about the Boston skyline from an Alston roof.
She was leaning in the shadows against the none-too-solid
cornice but had no fears of being aerial. Her sex was soft
as a small mound of coal dust, the material
of spiderwebs, a dove's head.

—

Start with seven for luck:
homo erectus, erect of course,
a compass, viper, wand or club,

gun, usual knife with any her or she
in repose for imagined punishment.
See him shudder, "throb" the books say,
quake, his flanks with a doggish bend.
Her eyes stare past his ear, they are
a green not found in nature and three
feet deep. Nothing need be forgiven.

———

Awake. A dab of numero uno in the smoking
pipe. The whole table in Montana loves
each other. They are relaxing from a long
day's sleep. The women are beautiful
and clean, the men young and ambitious.
They verge on taking over something not quite
comprehensible. The dance begins. Libidinous.
A horse's nose is pressed against the kitchen
window. It seems the very room wants to rise
up and screw but these are the sons and daughters
of an *entre* act, of Calvin, pre-Korean, middle Nam.
And their eyes are pink with hopeless energy.

———

He throws a fifty-lire piece in the fountain
and wants to tell his outrageous wish but they
won't listen. The wish won't count if you tell it
she says. He broods. The air is full of these goddamn
wops and their filthy pigeons. What good
is a wish that can't be told, that was wished
to anger those who won't hear it. Give me the single
raindrop that fell through the hole in the pagan
temple as my bride. Wishes must be phrased in old-time
languages, a sort of fatigued Episcopalian; here
and there it wasn't: that pinochle become the national

sport of the U.S.A.; that dysentery disappear straightaway
from earth; that the girl hidden in New York change
her silly predilection for her sisters, fall like
rain through the roof of a pagan temple on this gentle soul.

—

Grease density
Moon tup
Pink eye
Yellow book
Muddy horse (he fell in the pond)
Great big stomach from reading cookbooks
The child fell
The fly drank then backstroked on the skin of wine then perished
It is a true suntan because her ass is white
Red rock with green lichen
Green ground with red lichen
Since Bob jogs he snores less says his wife
Yes the hoopless barrel will break when filled
We fear the vicious Brazilian honeybee
Her eroticism is fungoid as in fungus
Some of us are aliens from god knows where
The midwest barren without good shellfish

—

The announcement said get to the high ground
but we were unable to move while the waters
crept up to the window, peeked in, then receded.
There was a fish near the mailbox, a lake trout
with two immature lamprey eels dangling from
their teethhold on the stomach.

—

For five days the moon was red from the dust storm.
It lost its novelty. Then on the sixth the moon
was pink and regained its novelty. On the seventh
it disappeared though reports from Perth, Australia,
established a white bladder-shaped object in the sky.

⁓

Third sighting:
Is she the black-crowned night heron
        our lady of the marshes
hidden at the far end of the lake
the verge of an enormous swamp
hearing her call amid stippled shadow ten thousand tree frogs
        the vision of eros as water bird

emerging from the green brush near midnight
stately wading legs

RETURNING TO EARTH

1977

for Guy & Anna

What forgotten reverie, what initiation,
it may be, separated wisdom from the
monastery and, creating Merlin,
joined it to passion?

W.B. Yeats, *A Vision*

RETURNING TO EARTH

She
pulls the sheet of this dance
across me
then runs, staking
the corners far out at sea.

—

So curious in the middle of America, the only "locus"
I know, to live and love at great distance. (Growing
up, everyone is willing to drive seventy miles to see
a really big grain elevator, ninety miles for a dance,
two hundred to look over a pair of Belgian mares
returning the next day for the purchase, three hundred
miles to see Hal Newhouser pitch in Detroit, eight
hundred miles to see the Grand Ole Opry, a thousand
miles to take the mongoloid kid to a Georgia faith healer.)
I hitched two thousand for my first glimpse of the Pacific.
When she first saw the Atlantic she said near Key Largo,
"I thought it would be bigger."

—

I widowed my small
collection of magic
until it poisoned itself with longing.
I have learned nothing.
I give orders to the rain.
I tried to catch the tempest in a gill net.
The stars seem a little closer lately.
I'm no longer afraid to die
but is this a guidepost of lunacy?
I intend to see the ten hundred million worlds Mañjushri
passed through before he failed to awaken the maiden.

Taking off and landing are the dangerous times.
I was commanded in a dream to dance.

—

O Faustus talks to himself,
talks to himself, talks to himself,
talks to himself, talks to himself,
Faustus talks to himself,
talks to himself.

—

Ikkyū's ten years near the whorehouses
shortens distances, is truly palpable;
and in ten years you will surely
get over your itch. Or not.

—

Don't waste yourself staring at the moon.
All of those moon-staring-rearview-mirror deaths!
Study the shadow of the horse turd in the grass.
There must be a difference between looking at a picture
of a bird and the actual bird (barn swallow)
fifteen feet from my nose on the shed eaves.
That cloud SSW looks like the underside
of a river in the sky.

—

O I'm lucky
got a car that starts almost every day
tho' I want a new yellow Chevy pickup
got two letters today
and I'd rather have three
have a lovely wife
but want all the pretty ones

got three white hawks in the barn
but want a Himalayan eagle
have a planet in the basement
but would prefer the moon in the granary
have the northern lights
but want the Southern Cross.

—

The stillness of this earth
which we pass through
with the precise speed of our dreams.

—

I'm getting very old. If I were a mutt
in dog years I'd be seven, not stray so far.
I am large. Tarpon my age are often large
but they are inescapably fish. A porpoise
my age was the King of New Guinea in 1343.
Perhaps I am the king of my dogs, cats, horses,
but I have dropped any notion of explaining
to them why I read so much. To be mysterious
is a prerogative of kingship. I discovered
lately that my subjects do not live a life,
but are life itself. They do not recognize
the pain of the schizophrenia of kingship.
To them I am pretty much a fellow creature.

—

So distances: yearns for Guayaquil and Petersburg,
the obvious Paris and Rome,
restraint in the Cotswolds, perfumes of Arusha,
Entebbe bristling with machine guns,
also Ecuadorian & Ethiopian airports,
border guards always whistling in boredom

and playing with machine guns;
all to count the flies on the lion's eyelids
and the lioness hobbling in deep grass
lacking one paw, to scan the marlin's caudal fin
cutting the Humboldt swell, an impossible scissors.

—

There must be a cricket named Zagreus
in the granary tucked under a roof beam,
under which my three-year-old daughter
boogies madly,
her first taste of the Grateful Dead;
she is well out of her mind.

—

Rain on the tin roof which covers a temple,
rain on my walking head which covers a temple,
rain covering my laugh shooting
toward the woods for no reason,
rain splattering in pasture's heat
raising cones of dust,
and off the horses' backs,
on oriole's nest in ash tree,
on my feet poking out the door,
testing the endurance of our actual pains,
biting hard against the sore tooth.

—

She's rolling in the bear fat
She's rolling in the sand
She's climbing a vine
She's boarding a jet
She flies into the distance wearing blue shoes

—

Having become the person I most feared in Childhood—
A DRUNKARD. They were pointed out to us
in our small town: oil workers, some poor farmers
(on Saturday marketing), a mechanic, a fired teacher.
They'd stumble when walking, sometimes yell
on the street at noon, wreck their old cars;
their wives would request special prayers in church,
and the children often came to school in winter
with no socks. We took up a collection to buy
the dump-picker's daughter shoes. Also my uncles
are prone to booze, also my father though it was well-
controlled, and now my fifteen-year war with the bottle
with whiskey removing me from the present
in a sweet, laughing haze, removing anger, anxiety,
instilling soft grandness, decorating ugliness
and reaffirming my questionable worth. SEE: Olson's
fingers touch his thumb, encircling the bottle—he
gulps deeply, talking through one night into the next
afternoon, talking, basking in Gorton's fishy odor.
So many of my brethren seem to die of busted guts.
Now there is a measured truce with maps and lines
drawn elegantly against the binge, concessions,
measurings, hesitant steps. My favorite two bars
are just north and barely south of the 45th parallel.

I no longer believe in the idea of magic,
christs, the self, metal buddhas, bibles.
A horse is only the space his horseness requires.
If I pissed in the woods would a tree see my ear
fall off and would the ear return to the body
on the morning of the third day? Do bo trees
ever remember the buddhas who've slept beneath them?
I admit that yesterday I built an exploratory altar.

Who can squash his delight in incomprehension?
So on a piece of old newspaper I put an earthworm
on a maple leaf, the remains of a bluebird after
the cat was finished—head and feet, some dog hair,
shavings from when we trimmed the horses' hooves,
a snakeskin, a stalk of ragweed, a gourd,
a lemon, a cedar splinter, a nonsymbolic doorknob,
a bumblebee with his juice sucked out by a wasp.
Before this altar I invented a doggerel mantra
it is this   it is this   it is this

     —

It is very hard to give birds advice.
They are already members of eternity.
In their genes they have both compass
and calendar. Their wing bones are hollow.
We are surprised by how light a dead bird is.

     —

But what am I penetrating?
Only that it seems nothing convinces
itself or anyone else reliably
of its presence. It is in the distance.

     —

No Persephone in my life,
Ariadne, Helen, Pocahontas,
Evangeline of the Book House
but others not less extraordinary who step
lightly into the dream life, refusing to leave:
girl in a green dress,
woman lolling in foot-deep Caribbean,
woman on balcony near Vatican,
girl floating across Copley Square in 1958,

mythologized woman in hut in 1951,
girl weeping in lilacs,
woman slapping my face,
girl smoking joint in bathtub looking at big toe,
slender woman eating three lobsters,
woman who blew out her heart with cocaine,
girl livid and deformed in dreams,
girl breaking the window in rage,
woman sick in hotel room,
heartless woman in photo—
not heartless but a photo.

—

My left eye is nearly blind.
No words have ever been read with it.
Not that the eye is virgin—thirty years ago
it was punctured by glass. In everything
it sees a pastel mist. The poster of Chief Joseph
could be King Kong, Hong Kong, a naked lady riding
a donkey into Salinas, Kansas. A war atrocity.
This eye is the perfect art critic. This eye
is a perfect lover saying bodies don't matter,
it is the voice. This eye can make a lightbulb
into the moon when it chooses. Once a year I open
it to the full moon out in the pasture and yell,
white light white light.

—

A half-dozen times a day
I climb through the electric fence
on my way and back to my study
in the barnyard. I have to be cautious.
I have learned my true dimensions,
how far my body sticks out from my brain.

—

We are each
the only world
we are going to get.

—

I don't want to die. It would certainly
inconvenience my wife and daughters.
I am sufficiently young that it would help
my publisher unpack his warehouse of books.
It would help me stop drinking and lose weight.
I could talk to Boris Pasternak.
He never saw the film.

—

Wanting to pull the particular nail
that will collapse the entire house
so that there is nothing there,
not even a foundation: a rubble heap,
no sign at all, just grass, weeds and trees
among which you cannot find a shard of masonry,
which like an arrowhead might suggest
an entire civilization.

—

She was lying back in the rowboat.
It was hot.
She tickled me with her toes.
She picked lily pads.
She watched mating dragonflies.
"How many fish below us?"
"O a hundred or so."
"It would be fun to fall in love with someone."
The rower continued his rowing.

—

Why be afraid of a process you're
already able to describe with precision?
To say you don't believe in it
is to say that you're *not.*
It doesn't care so why should you?
You've been given your body back
without a quarrel. See this vision
of your imagined body float toward you:
it disappears into you without a trace.
You feel full with a fullness again.
Your dimensions aren't scattered in dreams.

—

This fat pet bird I've kept so many years,
a crow with a malformed wing
tucked against its side, no doubt a vestigial fin:
I taught him early to drink from my whiskey
or wineglass in the shed but he prefers wine.
He flies only in circles of course
but when he drinks he flies in great
circles miles wide, preferring bad days
with low cold clouds looking like leper brains.
I barely hear his whimps & howls: O jesus
the pain O shit it hurts O god let it end.
He drags himself through air mostly landing
near a screen door slamming, a baby's cry,
a dog's bark, a forest fire, a sleeping coyote.
These fabulous memories of earth!

—

Not to live in fancy
these short hours: let shadows
fall from walls as shadows, nothing else.

New York is exactly
dead center
in New York.
Not to indulge this heartsickness as failure.
Did I write three songs or seven
or half-a-one, one line, phrases?
A single word
that might hang in the still, black air
for more than a few moments?
Then the laughter comes again.
We *sing it away.*
What short wicks
we fuel with our blood.

—

Disease!
My prostate beating & pulsing
down there like a frightened turkey's heart.

—

A cold day,
low ceiling.
A cloud the size
of a Greyhound bus
just hit the house.

—

Offenses this summer against Nature:
poured iced tea on a garter snake's head
as he or she dozed on the elm stump,
pissed on a bumblebee (inattentive),
kicked a thousand wasps to death in my slippers.
Favors done this summer for Nature:
let the mice keep their nest in the green station wagon,

let Rachel the mare breathe her hot damp horse breath
against my bare knee when she wanted to,
tried without success to get the song sparrow out
of the shed where she had trapped herself fluttering
along the cranny under the assumption that the way *out*
is always the way *up,* and her wings lie to her
with each separate beat against the ceiling saying
there is no way down and out,
there is no way down and out,
the open door back into the world.

     —

Coleridge's pet spider
he says is very intellectual,
spins webs of deceit
straight out of his big
hanging ass.

     —

Mandrill, *Mandrillus sphinx,*
crest, mane, beard, yellow, purple, green,
a large fierce, gregarious baboon—
has small wit but ties himself to a typewriter
with wolfish and bloody appetite.
He is just one, thousands will follow,
something true to be found among the countless
millions of typed pages. There's a picture
of him in Tibet though no mandrills have been known
to live there. He wants to be with his picture
though there's no way to get there. So he types.
So he dreams *lupanar lupanar lupanar*
brothels with steam and white dust, music
that describes undiscovered constellations
so precisely the astronomers of the next century

will know where to look. Peaches dripping light.
Lupanar. The female arriving in dreams is unique,
not another like her on earth; she's created for a moment.
It only happens one time. One time O one time.
He types. She's his only real food.
O *lupanar* of dreams.

—

Head bobbing right and left,
with no effort
and for the first time
I see all sides of the pillar at once,
the earth,   her body.

—

I can't jump
high anymore.

—

He tightens
pumps in blue cold air
gasoline
the electricity from summer storms
the seven-by-seven-foot
blue face of lightning
that shot down the gravel road
like a ghost rocket.

—

Saw the lord of crows
late at night in my living room;
don't know what true color of man—
black-white-red-yellow—
as he was hooded with the mask of a crow;

arms, legs, with primary feathers sewn to leather
downy black breast
silver bells at wrist
long feathered tail
dancing for a moment or two then disappearing.
Only in the morning did it occur to me
that it was a woman.

—

What sways us is not each other
but our dumb insistent pulse beating
I was I am I will I was
sometimes operatic, then in church
or barroom tenor, drunkenly, in prayer,
slowly in the confusion of dreams
but the same tripartite, the three
of being here trailing off into itself,
no finale any more than a beginning
until all of us lie buried
in the stupefying ache of caskets.

—

This earth of intentions.
Moonfucked, you can't eat or drink
or sleep at ten feet. Kneeling, love
is at nose tip. Or wound about
each other our eyes forget that they are eyes
and begin to see. You remember individual
fence posts, fish, trees, ankles,
from your tenth year.
Those savages lacking other immediate alternatives
screwed the ground to exhaustion.

—

Bad art: walking away untouched, unmoving,
barely tickled, *amused,* diverted killing time,
throwing salt on the grass. The grace of Yukio Mishima's
suicide intervening in the false harmony,
Kawabata decides to live longer, also a harmony.
In bad music, the cheapest and easiest way to get
out of it infers Clapton. Eros girdled in metal
and ozone. A man in a vacuum of images, stirring
his skull with his dick, sparing himself his future,
fancy bound, unparticular, unpeculiar, following
the strings of his dreaming to more dreaming
in a sump narcosis, never having given himself
over to his life, never owning an instant.

     —

Week's eating log:
whitefish poached with lemon, onion, wine, garlic;
Chulapa—pork roasted twelve hours with pinto beans,
red peppers, chili powder; grilled twenty-two pounds
of beef ribs for friends; a lamb leg pasted with Dijon
mustard, soy, garlic; Chinese pork ribs; *menudo*
just for Benny & me as no one else would eat it—
had to cook tripe five hours then mix with hominy
and peppers with chorizo tacos on the side;
copious fresh vegetables, Burgundy, Columbard, booze
with all of the above; at night fevered dreams
of her sumptuous butt, a Mercator projection,
the map of an enormous meal in my brain.
Still trying to lose weight.

     —

How strange to see a horse
stare
straight up.

—

Everything is a good idea at the time.
Staring with stupid longing at a picture, dumbstruck
as they used to call it, an instant's whimsy;
a body needlessly unlike any other's,
deserved by someone so monstrous
as Lucrezia Borgia: how do you come to terms
with it? thinks the American. You don't, *terms*
being a financial word not applicable
to bodies. Wisdom shies away, the packhorse
startled at the diamondback beneath the mesquite,
the beauty of threat. Now look at her as surely
as that other beast, the dead crow beneath the apple
tree so beautiful in its black glossiness
but without eyes, feet stiff and cool as the air.
I watched it for a year and owned its bleached
shinbone but gave it to someone who needed
the shinbone of a crow.

—

She says it's too hot,
the night's too short,
that I'm too drunk,
but it's not *too* anything, ever.

—

Living all my life with a totally normal-sized dick
(cf. the authorities: Van de Velde, Masters & Johnson)
neither hedgehog or horse, neither emu or elephant
(saw one in Kenya, the girls said O my goodness)
neither wharf rat, arrogant buck dinosaur,
prepotent swan, ground squirrel, Lauxmont Admiral
famous Holstein bull who sired 200,000 artificially.
I am saved from trying to punish anyone,

from confusing it with a gun, harpoon, cannon, sword,
cudgel, Louisville Slugger. It just sits there
in the dark, shy and friendly
like the new kid at school.

—

In our poetry we want to rub our nose hard
into whatever is before it; to purge
these dreams of pictures, photos, phantom people.
She offers a flex of butt, belly button, breasts,
slight puff of veneris, gap in teeth often capped,
grace of knees, high cheekbones and neck,
all the thickness of paper. The grandest illusion
as in ten thousand movies in all those hours
of dark, the only true sound the exploding
popcorn and the dairy fetor of butter. After the movie
a stack of magazines at the drugstore
to filter through, to be filtered through.

—

A choral piece for a dead dog:
how real the orchestra and hundred
voices on my lawn; pagan with the dog
on a high cedar platform to give the fire
its full marriage of air; the chorus
sings DOG a thousand times, dancing
in a circle. That would be a proper
dog funeral. By god. No dreams here
but a mighty shouting of *dog*.

—

Sunday night,
I'm lucky to have all of this vodka,
a gift of Stolichnaya.
And books. And a radio

playing WSM all the way from Nashville.
Four new pups in the bedroom.
The house snores. My tooth aches.
It is time to fry an egg.

—

Heard the foghorn out at sea,
saw horses' backs shiny with rain,
felt my belly jiggle as I walked
through the barnyard in a light rain
with my daughter's small red umbrella
to protect the not-very-precious manuscript,
tiptoeing barefoot in the tall wet grass
trying to avoid the snakes.

—

With all this rain
the pond is full.
The ducks are one week old
and already speak their language perfectly—
a soft nasal hiss.
With no instructions they skim bugs from the pond's
surface and look fearfully at me.

—

The minister whacks off as does the insurance man,
habitual golfer, sweet lady in her bower,
as do novelists, monks, nuns in nunneries,
maidens in dormitories, stallion against fence post,
goat against puzzled pig who does not cease feeding,
and so do senators, generals, wives during TV
game shows, movie stars and football players, students
to utter distraction, teachers, butchers, world leaders,
everyone except poets who fear the dreaded
growth of hair on the palms, blindness.

They know that even in an empty hotel room
in South Dakota that someone is watching.

—

With my dog
I watched a single crow
fly across the field.
We are each one.

—

Thirty feet up in the air
near the top of my novel I want a bird to sing
from the crown of the barn roof.
A hundred feet away there is a grove of trees,
maple and elm and ash,
placed quite accidentally before any of us were born.
Everyone remembers who planted the lilacs
forty years and three wars ago.

—

In the morning paper
the arsonist
who was also a paranoid schizophrenic,
a homosexual,
retarded,
an alcoholic
who lacerated his body with a penknife
and most significantly for the rest of us,
started fires where none were desired,
on whim.

—

Spent months regathering dreams lost in the diaspora,
all of the prism's colors, birds, animals, bodies,
getting them back within the skin

where they'd do no damage.
How difficult catching them armed
only with a butterfly-catcher's net,
a gun, airplane, an ice pick,
a chalice of rainwater, a green headless
buddha on loan from a veteran of foreign wars.

—

Saw that third eye in a dream
but couldn't remember if it looked
from a hole in a wall of ice,
or a hole in a floor of ice,
but it was an eye looking from a hole in ice.

—

Two white-faced cattle out in the dark-green pasture,
one in the shade of the woodlot,
one out in the hot sunlight,
eating slowly and staring at each other.

—

So exhausted after my walk from orchestrating
the moves of one billion August grasshoppers
plus fifty thousand butterflies
swimming at the heads
of fifty thousand wildflowers
red blue yellow orange
orange flowers the only things that rhyme with orange
the one rabbit in the pasture
one fly buzzing at the window
a single hot wind through the window
a man sitting at my desk resembling me.

—

He sneaks up on the temple slowly at noon.
He's so slow it seems like it's taking years.
Now his hands are on a pillar, the fingers
encircling it, with only the tips inside the gate.

—

After all of this long moist dreaming
I perceive how accurate the rooster's crow
is from down the road.

—

You can suffer and not even know you're suffering
because you've been suffering so long you can't remember
another life. You're actually a dead dog on a country road.
And a man gets used to his rotten foot.
After a while it's simply a rotten foot,
and his rotten ideas are even easier to get used to
because they don't hurt as much as a rotten foot.
The road from Belsen to Watergate paved
with perfectly comfortable ideas, ideas to sleep on
like a mattress stuffed with money and death,
an actual waterbed filled with liquid gold.
So our inept tuna cravings and Japan's (she imitates
our foulest features) cost an annual
250,000 particular dolphin deaths,
certainly as dear as people to themselves
or so the evidence says.

—

Near my lover's old frame house with a field
behind it, the grass is a brilliant gold.
Standing on the gravel road before the house
a great flock of blackbirds coming over so close
to my head I see them all individually,
eyes, crests, the feet drawn out in flight.

—

I owe the dentist nine hundred dollars.
This is more than I made on three
of my books of poems. But then I am gloriously
free. I can let my mouth rot and quit
writing poems. I could let the dentist
write the poems while I walked into the dark
with a tray of golden teeth I'd sculpt
for myself in the forms of shark's teeth,
lion's teeth, teeth of grizzly and python.
Watch me open my mouth as I wear these wondrous
teeth. The audience gross is exactly nine hundred!
The house lights dim. My lips part.
There is a glimpse of sun.

—

Abel always votes.
Cain usually thinks better of it
knowing not very deep in his heart
that no one deserves to be encouraged.
Abel has a good job & is a responsible screw,
but many intelligent women seem drawn
to Crazy Horse, a descendant of Cain,
even if he only gets off his buffalo pony
once a year to throw stones at the moon.
Of course these women marry Abel but at bars and parties
they are the first to turn to the opening door
to see who is coming in.

—

I was standing near the mow door
in the darkness, a party going on in the château.
She was there with her sister.
We kissed then lay down on fresh straw in a paddock.

An angry stallion jumped over on top of us.
I could see his outline clearly against the sky.
Why did we die so long ago.

—

How wind, cloud and water
blaspheme symmetry at every instant,
forms that can't be remembered and stored:
Grand Marais, Cape Ann at Eastern Point,
Lake Manyara from a cliff, Boca Grande's sharks
giving still water a moving shape—they are there
and there and there—the waterfall next to a girl
so obviously on a white horse, to mud
puddle cat avoids, back to Halibut Point,
Manitou convulsed in storms to thousand-mile
weed line in Sargasso Sea to brown violent confluence
of Orinoco and ocean off Devil's Gate; mixing wind,
cloud, water, the purest mathematics of their
description studied as glyphs, alchemists
everywhere working with humble gold, somewhere to begin,
having to keep eyes closed to wind, cloud, water.

—

Saw an ox. A black horse I recognized.
A procession of carts full of flowers
pulled by nothing. Asymmetrical planets.
Fish out of their element of water.
Simple music—a single note an hour.
How are we to hear it, if at all?
No music in statement, the lowest denominator
by which our fragments can't find each other.
But I can still hear the notes of April,
the strained, fragile notes of March:
convalescent, tentative, a weak drink

taken over and over in immense doses.
It is the body that is the suite entire,
brain firmly fused to the trunk, spine
more actual than mountains, brain moving
as a river, governed precisely by her energies.

—

Whippoorwill. Mourning dove. Hot morning rain
changing to a violent squall coming SSW out of the lake,
thunder enveloping itself then unfolding
as cloth in wind furls, holds back, furls again;
running nearly naked in shorts to my shed,
thunder rattling windows and walls,
acorns rattling against barn's tin roof;
the floor shudders, then stillness as squall passes,
as strange as a strong wind at summer twilight
when the air is yellow. Now cool still air.
Mourning dove.
Oriole.

—

O my darling sister
O she crossed over
she's crossed over
is planted now near her father
six feet under earth's skin—
their still point on this whirling earth
now and I think forever.

—

Now it is as close to you as the clothes you wear.
The clothes are attached to your body
by a cord that runs up your spine, out your neck
and through the earth, back up your spine.

At nineteen I began to degenerate,
slight smell of death in my gestures,
unbelieving, tentative, wailing . . .
so nineteen years have gone. It doesn't matter.
It might have taken fifty. Or never.
Now the barriers are dissolving, the stone fences
in shambles. I want to have my life
in cloud shapes, water shapes, wind shapes,
crow call, marsh hawk swooping over grass and weed tips.
Let the scavenger take what he finds.
Let the predator love his prey.

from SELECTED
& NEW POEMS

1982

to John & Rebecca

NOT WRITING MY NAME

In the snow, that is. The "J" could have been
three hundred yards into the high pasture
across the road. The same with the "I" which I intended
to dot by sprawling and flopping in a drift. The "M"
naturally would have required something more
than twelve hundred yards of hard walking as we
have two empty-bottomed isosceleses to deal with.
What star-crossed jock ego would churn through those
drifts to write a name invisible except to crows?
And the dog would have confused the crows the way
he first runs ahead, then crisscrosses my path.
It's too cold anyhow—ten below at noon though the sun
would tell me otherwise. And the wind whips coils
and wisps of snow across the hardened drifts and around
my feet like huge ghost snakes. These other signatures:
Vole tracks so light I have to kneel to trace his
circlings which are his name. Vole. And an unknown bird,
scarcely heavier than the vole, that lacks a left foot. Fox tracks
leading up a drift onto my favorite boulder where he swished
his tail, definitely peed, and left. The dog sniffs
the tracks, also pees but sparingly. He might need it later,
he saves his messages. For a moment mastodons float
through the trees, thunderhead colored, stuffing their maws
with branches. This place used to be Africa. Now it's so cold
there are blue shadows in my footprints, and a blue-shadow
dog runs next to my own, flat and rippling to the snow, less than
paper thick. I try to invoke a crow for company; none appears.
I have become the place the crow didn't appear.

FROG

First memory
of swimming underwater:
eggs of frogs hanging in diaphanous clumps
from green lily pad stems;
at night in the tent I heard
the father of it all booming
and croaking in the reeds.

ROOSTER

to Pat Ryan

I have to kill the rooster tomorrow. He's being an asshole,
having seriously wounded one of our two hens with his insistent banging.
You walk into the barn to feed the horses and pick up an egg
or two for breakfast and he jumps her proclaiming *she's mine she's mine.*
Her wing is torn and the primary feathers won't grow back.
Chickens have largely been denatured, you know. He has no part
in those delicious fresh eggs. He crows on in a vacuum. He is
utterly pointless. He's as dumb as a tapeworm and no one cares
if he lives or dies. There. I can kill him
with an easy mind. But I'm still not up to it. Maybe I can hire
a weasel or a barn rat to do the job, or throw him to Justine,
the dog, who would be glad to rend him except the neighbors
have chickens too, she'd get the habit and we would have a beloved shot
dog to bury. So he deserves to die, having no purpose. We'll
have stewed barnyard chicken, closer to eating a gamebird than
that tasteless supermarket chicken born and bred in a caged
darkness. Everything we eat is dead except an occasional oyster
or clam. Should I hire the neighbor boy to kill him? Will the
hens stop laying out of grief? Isn't his long wavering crow
magnificent? Isn't the worthless rooster the poet's bird brother?
No. He's just a rooster and the world has no place for him.
Should I wait for a full wintry moon, take him to the top of the
hill after dropping three hits of mescaline and strangle him?
Should I set him free for a fox meal? They're coming back now
after the mange nearly wiped them out. He's like a leaking roof
with drops falling on my chest. He's the Chinese torture in the barn.
He's lust mad. His crow penetrates walls. His head bobs in lunar
jerks. The hens shudder but are bored with the pain of eggs.
What can I do with him? Nothing isn't enough. In the morning
we will sit down together and talk it out. I will tell him he
doesn't matter and he will wag his head, strut, perhaps crow.

EPITHALAMIUM

for Peter and Maria

For the first time the wind
blew straight down from the heavens.
I was wandering around the barnyard
about three a.m. in full moonlight
when it started, flattening my hair
against my head; my dog cowered
between my knees, and the last leaves
of a cold November shot to the ground.
Then the wind slowed and went back to the north.
This happened last night and already at noon
my faith in it is passing.

A REDOLENCE FOR NIMS

O triple sob—turned forty
at midnight—body at dawn
booze-soddened but hopeful,
knowing that the only thing
to remember is dreams.
Dead clear zero, Sunday afternoon
in an attic of a closed resort
on Lake Michigan with one lone
duck riding the diminishing
swells of yesterday's storm
against the snowy cliffs of North Manitou:
Whom are we to love?
How many and what for?
My heart's gone to sea for years.
This is a prayer, plaint, wish,
howl of void beneath breastbone.
Dreams, soul chasers, bring
back my heart alive.

FOLLOWERS

Driving east on Buddha's birthday,
April 9, 1978, past my own birthplace
Grayling, Michigan, south 300 miles to Toledo,
then east again to New York for no reason—
belled heart swinging in grief for months
until I wanted to take my life in my hands;
three crows from home followed above
the car until the Delaware River where
they turned back: one stood all black
and lordly on a fresh pheasant killed
by a car: all this time
counting the mind, counting crows,
each day's ingredients
the same, barring rare
bad luck
good luck
dumb luck
all set in marble by the habitual,
locked as the day passes moment by moment:
say on the tracks the train can't
turn 90 degrees to the right because it's not
the nature of a train,
but we think a man can dive
in a pond, swim across it,
and climb a tree though few of us do.

MY FIRST DAY AS A PAINTER

Things to paint:
my dog (yellow),
nude women,
dead coyote with gray whiskers,
nude women,
a tree full of crows,
nude women,
the self in the mirror,
nude women,
a favorite cloud,
nude women,
a worn-out scalpel,
nude women,
dead friends,
nude women ages 14–80 (12–82),
call me wherever you are at noon
in the glory of noon light,
bring your dogs and birds,
everybody is welcome:
nude women spinning in godlike whirls
creating each other in endless
streams of human eggs!

WAITING

There are no calls from the outside.
Miracles are the perversity of literature.
We should know that by now.
Only that these never-revealed connections of things
lead us oddly on. Caesar's legions
entering Greenland's ice, the scout far in front
wanting to do battle where there are
no enemies,
never were any enemies.

NOON

Spring: despondency,
fall: despair,
onset of winter
a light rain in the heart
the pony tethered to the telephone
pole day after day until he's eaten
the circle, moved to another pole,
another circle: winter never deepens
but falls dead upon the ground,
body of the sky whirled
in gray gusts:
from Manitoba stretched brains
of north; heat for heart, head,
in smallest things—dry socks,
strange breasts, an ounce of sun
glittering above the blue shadows
of the barn.

BIRTHDAY

The masques of dream—monk in his
lineage—what does he wear to shield
himself? First shield made of a cloud,
second—a tree, third—a shadow; and
leading to the stretched coils of light
(how they want to gather us up
with our permission), three men.
Two dead tho' dead is supernumerary.
The cause is the effect.
He laughed like a lake would
but only once, never twice into the same
mystery. Not ever to stop but only
to drop the baggage, to shed the
thirty-ninth skin.

CLEAR WATER 3

Ah, yes. Fame never got anyone
off the hook, it seems. Some poignant
evidence to be offered here in McGuane.
There's a cutoff beyond which a certain
number of people know you exist for various
reasons, good or bad or with a notorious
indifference.   Said Spicer:
My vocabulary did this to me. Meaning
what he was, near death in an alcoholic ward.
Crane or Cavafy. Alcohol as biography
more surely than serial poems. I doubt it.
We are drawn to where we end like water
for reasons of character, volume, gravity,
the sound we make in passing/not all the sounds
we made in passing in one place—a book.
Each day's momentum of voice carrying
backward and forward to the limits, beginning
and end. We drink to enchant our voices,
to heal them, to soothe with laughter, to glide
awhile. My words kill, killed, me, my lord. Yes.

DŌGEN'S DREAM

What happens when the god of spring
meets spring? He thinks for a moment
of great whales traveling from the bottom
to the top of the earth, the day the voyage
began seven million years ago
when spring last changed its season.
He enters himself, emptiness
desiring emptiness. He sleeps
and his sleep is the dance of all the birds
on earth flying north.

WEEPING

for Dave Kelly from long ago

Six days of clouds since
I returned from Montana,
a state of mind out West.
A bleak afternoon in the granary killing flies and wasps.
Sitting on a *zafu* watching flies.
Two days ago a sandhill crane flew over
so low I could see an eyeball clearly cocked
toward my singular own.
As I drink I miss more flies.
I am searching out the ecstatic life
with flyswatter and wineglass in hand,
the sky above an inverted steel sink.
I am looking for weeping
which is a superior form of rest.
Can't there be dry weeping? Nope.
Dry weeping is like dry fucking
which most of us remember as unsatisfying.
Wet fucking is another story
but not the object here, though decidedly
more interesting than weeping.
I would frankly like to throw
myself around and have some real passion.
Some wet passion! to be sure.
At nineteen in 1957 on Grove Street in NY
I could weep about art, Hart Crane, my empty
stomach, homesickness for pheasants and goldenrod,
Yesenin's suicide, a red-haired girl with an improbable
butt, my dad planting the garden alone.
It was a year in which I wrung out pillowcases at dawn.
But this is the flip side of the record, a log
of the search for weeping. I've been dry

for a decade and it isn't panning out.
Like a Hollywood producer I sit by a pool
and hatch inane plots against the weeping imagination,
spinning wheels, treading water,
beating the mental bishop,
flogging the mental clam,
pulling the mental wire
like a cub scout in a lonely pup tent.
I'm told I laugh too much.
I laugh deeply at Johnny Carson monologues,
at my poetry, at health food & politics,
at the tragic poetry of others, at the weedy garden,
at my dog hitting the electric fence,
at women freeing themselves when I am in bondage,
at the thought of my death.
In fact I'm tickled pink with life.
I actually have a trick to weep but it's cheating.
I used it once when I was very drunk.
I thought of the deaths of my wife and daughters.
I threw myself to the floor weeping.
I wept horribly and shook, gnashed my teeth.
I must die before them.

THE CHATHAM GHAZAL

It is the lamp on the kitchen table
well after midnight saying nothing but light.

Here are a list of ten million measurements.
You may keep them. Or throw them away.

A strange warm day when November has forgotten
to be November. Birds form shrill clouds.

Phototropiques. We emerge upward from liquid.
See the invisible husks we've left behind called memories.

The press wonders how we drink so much poison and stay
alive. The antidote is chance, mobility, sleeplessness.

They've killed another cow. With the mountain of guts
I also bury all of the skins of thirty-seven years.

MARRIAGE GHAZAL

for Peter & Beck

Hammering & drifting. Sea wrack. Cast upon & cast out.
Who's here but shore? Where we stop is where shore is.

I saw the light beyond mountains turned umber by morning.
I walked by memory as if I had no legs. Or head.

In a bed of reeds I found my body and entered it,
taking my life upon myself, the soul made comfortable.

So the body's a nest for the soul and we set out inland,
the figure of a walker who only recognized the sea and moon.

And coming to the first town the body became a chorus—
O my god this is a place or thing and I'll stay awhile.

The body met a human with fur and the moon mounted her head
in an arc when she sat & they built a boat together.

MARCH WALK

I was walking because I wasn't upstairs sitting.
I could have been looking for pre-1900 gold coins
in the woods all afternoon. What a way to make a living!
The same mastodon was there only three hundred years from
where I last saw him. I felt the sabers on the saber tooth,
the hot wet breath on the back of my hand. Three deer
and a number of crows, how many will remain undisclosed:
It wasn't six and it wasn't thirty. There were four girls
ranging back to 1957. The one before that just arrived
upstairs. There was that long morose trip into the world
hanging onto my skin for a quarter of a mile, shed with some
difficulty. There was one dog, my own, and one grouse
not my own. A strong wind flowed over and through us like
dry water. I kissed a scar on a hip. I found a rotting
crab apple and a distant relative to quartz. You could spend
a lifetime and still not walk to an island. I met none of the
dead today having released them yesterday at three o'clock.
If you're going to make love to a woman you have to give
her some of your heart. Else don't. If I had found a gold coin
I might have left it there with my intermittent interest in
money. The dead snipe wasn't in the same place but the rocks
were. The apple tree was a good place to stand. Every late fall
the deer come there for dessert. They will stand for days
waiting for a single apple to tumble from the upmost limb.

THE WOMAN FROM SPIRITWOOD

Sleeping from Mandan to Jamestown,
waking near Spiritwood in the van,
shrinking in fever with the van
buffeted by wind so that it shudders,
the wind maybe fifty knots straight N by NW
out of Saskatchewan. Stopping for gas we see men
at the picnic tables cleaning the geese they've shot:
October first with the feathers carried off by the wind
into fields where buffalo once roamed, also
the Oglala & Miniconjou Sioux roamed in search
of buffalo and Crazy Horse on a horse that outlived him.
She comes out of the station, smiling, leaning into the wind.
She is so beautiful that an invisible hand reaches
into your rib cage and twists your heart one notch
counterclockwise. There is nowhere to go.
I've been everywhere and there's nowhere to go.
The talk is halting, slow until it becomes
the end of another part of the future.
I scratch gravel toward and from this wound,
seeing within the shadow that this shadow casts
how freedom must be there
before there can be freedom.

GATHERING APRIL

for Simic

Stuffing a crow call in one ear
and an unknown bird's in the other,
lying on the warm cellar door out of
the cool wind which I take small sparing
bites of with three toes still wet from the pond's
edge: April is so violent up here you hide
in corners or, when in the woods, in swales
and behind beech trees. Twenty years ago
this April I offered my stupid heart up to
this bloody voyage. It was near a marsh
on a long walk. You can't get rid of those
thousand pointless bottles of whiskey
that you brought along. Last night after
the poker game I read Obata's Li Po.
He was no less a fool but adding those
twenty thousand poems you come up
with a god. There are patents on all
the forms of cancer but still we praise
god from whom or which all blessings flow:
that an April exists, that a body lays itself
down on a warm cellar door and remembers, drinks
in birds and wind, whiskey, frog songs
from the marsh, the little dooms hiding
in the shadow of each fence post.

WALTER OF BATTERSEA

for Anjelica

I shall commit suicide or die
trying, Walter thought beside
the Thames—at low tide and very
feminine.

Picture him: a cold November day,
the world through a long lens; he's
in new blue pants and races the river
for thirty-three steps.

Walter won. Hands down. Then lost
again. Better to die trying! The sky
so bleak. God blows his nose above
the Chelsea Flour Mills.

What is he at forty, Nov. 9, 1978, so far
from home: grist for his own mill; all
things have become black-and-white
without hormonal surge.

And religious. He's forgiven god
for the one hundred ladies who turned him
down and took him up. O that song—
I asked her for water and she gave
me kerosene.

No visions of Albion, no visions at all,
in fact, the still point of the present winding
about itself, graceful, unsnarled. I am
here today and gone tomorrow.

How much is he here? Not quite with
all his heart and soul. Step lightly

or the earth revolves into a berserk
spin. Fall off or dance.

And choosing dance not god, at least
for the time being. Things aren't what
they seem but what they are—infinitely
inconsolable.

He knows it's irony that's least
valuable in this long deathwatch.
Irony scratching its tired ass. No trade-offs
with time and fortune.

It's indelicate to say things twice except
in prayer. The drunk repeats to keep
his grasp, a sort of prayer: the hysteria
of the mad, a verbless prayer.

Walter recrossed the bridge which was
only a bridge. He heard his footsteps
just barely behind him. The river is not
where it starts and ends.

AFTER READING TAKAHASHI

for Lucien, Peter, and Whalen

Nothing is the same to anyone.
Moscow is east of Nairobi
but thinks of herself as perpetually west.
The bird sees the top of my head,
an even trade for her feathered belly.
Our eyes staring through the nose bridge
never to see each other.
She is not I, I not her.
So what, you think, having little
notion of my concerns. O that dank
basement of "so what" known by all
though never quite the same way.
All of us drinking through a cold afternoon,
our eyes are on the mirror behind
the bottles, on the snow out the window
which the wind chases fruitlessly,
each in his separateness drinking,
talk noises coming out of our mouths.
In the corner a pretty girl plays pinball.
I have no language to talk to her.
I have come to the point in life when
I could be her father. This was never true before.
The bear hunter talked about the mountains.
We looked at them together out of the
tavern window in Emigrant, Montana.
He spent fifty years in the Absaroka mountains
hunting grizzly bears and, at one time, wolves.
We will never see the same mountains.
He knows them like his hands, his wife's
breasts and legs, his old dog sitting outside
in the pickup. I only see beautiful mountains

and say "beautiful mountains" to which he nods
graciously but they are a photo of China to me.
And all lessons are fatal: the great snowy owl
that flew in front of me so that
I ducked in the car; it will never happen again.
I've been warned by a snowy night, an owl,
the infinite black above and below me to look
at all creatures and things with a billion eyes,
not struggling with the single heartbeat
that is my life.

THE THEORY & PRACTICE OF RIVERS AND NEW POEMS

1989

THE THEORY & PRACTICE OF RIVERS

The rivers of my life:
moving looms of light,
anchored beneath the log
at night I can see the moon
up through the water
as shattered milk, the nudge
of fishes, belly and back
in turn grating against log
and bottom; and letting go, the current
lifts me up and out
into the dark, gathering motion,
drifting into an eddy
with a sideways swirl,
the sandbar cooler than the air:
to speak it clearly,
how the water goes
is how the earth is shaped.

It is not so much that I got
there from here, which is everyone's
story: but the shape
of the voyage, how it pushed
outward in every direction
until it stopped:
roots of plants and trees,
certain coral heads,
photos of splintered lightning,
blood vessels,
the shapes of creeks and rivers.

This is the ascent out of water:
there is no time but that
of convenience, time so that everything

won't happen at once; dark
doesn't fall—dark comes up
out of the earth, an exhalation.
It gathers itself close
to the ground, rising
to envelop us, as if the bottom
of the sea rose up to meet us.
Have you ever gone
to the bottom of the sea?

Mute unity of water.
I sculpted this girl
out of ice so beautifully
she was taken away.
How banal the swan song
which is a water song.
There never was a swan
who said good-bye. My raven
in the pine tree squawked his way
to death, falling from branch
to branch. To branch again.
To ground. The song, the muffle
of earth as the body falls,
feather against pine needles.

Near the estuary north of Guilford
my brother recites the Episcopalian
burial service over his dead daughter.
Gloria, as in *Gloria in Excelsis.*
I cannot bear this passion and courage;
my eyes turn toward the swamp
and sea, so blurred they'll never quite
clear themselves again. The inside of the eye,
vitreous humor, is the same pulp found
inside the squid. I can see Gloria

in the snow and in the water. She lives
in the snow and water and in my eyes.
This is a song for her.

Kokopele saved me this time:
flute song in soft dark
sound of water over rock,
the moon glitter rippling;
breath caught as my hunched
figure moved in a comic circle,
seven times around the cabin
through the woods in the dark.
Why did I decide to frighten myself?

Light snow in early May,
wolf prints in alluvial fan,
moving across the sandbar
in the river braided near its mouth
until the final twist; then the prints
move across drift ice in a dead
channel, and back into the swamp.

The closest I came to describing it:
it is early winter, mid-November
with light snow, the ground rock-hard
with frost. We are moving but I can't
seem to find my wife and two daughters.
I have left our old house and can't remember
how to find the new one.

The days are stacked against
what we think we are:
the story of the water babies
swimming up- and downstream
amid waterweed, twisting
with cherubic smiles in the current,

human and fish married.
Again! The girl I so painfully
sculpted out of ice
was taken away. She said:
"Goddamn the Lizard King,"
her night message and good-bye.
The days are stacked against
what we think we are:
near the raven rookery
inside the bend of river
with snowmelt and rain
flooding the bend; I've failed to stalk
these birds again and they flutter
and wheel above me with parental screams
saying, *Get out get out you bastard.*
The days are stacked against
what we think we are.
After a month of interior weeping
it occurred to me that in times like these
I have nothing to fall back on
except the sun and moon and earth.
I dress in camouflage and crawl
around swamps and forest, seeing
the bitch coyote five times but never
before she sees me. Her look
is curious, almost a smile.
The days are stacked against
what we think we are:
it is nearly impossible
to surprise ourselves.
I will never wake up
and be able to play the piano.
South fifteen miles, still

near the river, calling coyotes
with Dennis E: full moon in east,
northern lights in pale green swirl,
from the west an immense line squall
and thunderstorm approaching off Lake Superior.
Failing with his call he uses
the song of the loon to bring
an answer from the coyotes.
"They can't resist it," he says.
The days are stacked against
what we think we are.
Standing in the river up to my waist
the infant beaver peeks at me
from the flooded tag alder
and approaches though warned
by her mother whacking her tail.
About seven feet away she bobs
to dive, mooning me with her small
pink ass, rising again for another
look, then downward swimming
past my leg, still looking.
The days are finally stacked
against what we think we are:
how long can I stare at the river?
Three months in a row now
with no signs of stopping,
glancing to the right, an almost
embarrassed feeling that the river
will stop flowing and I can go home.
The days, at last, are stacked against
what we think we are.
Who in their most hallowed, sleepless
night with the moon seven feet

outside the window, the moon
that the river swallows, would wish
it otherwise?

On New Year's Eve I'm wrapped
in my habits, looking up to the TV
to see the red ball, the apple,
rise or fall, I forget which:
a poem on the cherry-wood table, a fire,
a blizzard, some whiskey, three
restless cats, and two sleeping dogs,
at home and making three gallons
of *menudo* for the revelers who'll
need it come tomorrow after amateur night:
about ten pounds of tripe, ancho,
molido, serrano, and chipotle pepper, cumin,
coriander, a few calves' or piglets' feet.
I don't wonder what is becoming
to the man already becoming.
I also added a half-quart of stock
left over from last night's *bollito misto*
wherein I poach for appropriate times:
fifteen pounds of veal bones to be discarded,
a beef brisket, a pork roast, Italian sausage,
a large barnyard hen, a pheasant, a guinea
hen, and for about thirty minutes until
rosy rare a whole filet, served with
three sauces: tomato coulis, piquante (anchovies & capers etc.)
and a rouille. Last week when my daughter
came home from NYC I made her venison
with truffles, also roast quail for Christmas
breakfast, also a wild turkey, some roast mallards & grouse,
also a cacciatore of rabbit & pheasant.
Oddly the best meal of the year
was in the cabin by the river:

a single fresh brook trout *au bleu*
with one boiled new potato and one
wild-leek vinaigrette. By the river
I try to keep alive, perhaps to write
more poems, though lately I think
of us all as lay-down comedians
who, when we finally tried to get up,
have found that our feet are mushy,
and what's more, no one cares
or bothers to read anymore those
sotto voce below-radar flights
from the empirical. But I am wrapped
in my habits. I must send my prayer
upward and downward. "Why do you write
poems?" the stewardess asked. "I guess
it's because every angel is terrible,
still though, alas, I invoke these almost
deadly birds of the soul,"
I cribbed from Rilke.

The travels on dry riverbeds: Salt River,
or nearly dry up Canyon de Chelly,
a half-foot of water—a skin over
the brown riverbed. The Navajo
family stuck with a load of dry
corn and crab apples. Only the woman
speaks English, the children at first shy
and frightened of my blind left eye
(some tribes attach importance to this—
strangely enough, this eye can see underwater).
We're up on the del Muerto fork and while
I'm kneeling in the water shoving rocks
under the axle I glance skyward
at an Anasazi cliff dwelling, the "ancient
ones" they're called. This morning

a young schizophrenic Navajo attacked
our truck with a club, his head seeming
to turn nearly all the way around as
an owl's. Finally the children smile
as the truck is pulled free. I am given
a hatful of the most delicious crab apples
in the world. I watch the first apple
core float west on the slender current,
my throat a knot of everything
I no longer understand.

Sitting on the bank, the water
stares back so deeply you can hear
it afterward when you wish. It is the water
of dreams, and for the nightwalker
who can almost walk on the water,
it is most of all the water of awakening,
passing with the speed of life
herself, drifting in circles in an eddy
joining the current again
as if the eddy were a few moments' sleep.

The story can't hesitate to stop.
I can't find a river in Los Angeles
except the cement one behind Sportsman's Lodge
on Ventura. There I feel my
high blood pressure like an electric tiara
around my head, a small comic cloud,
a miniature junkyard where my confused
desires, hopes, hates, and loves short circuit
in little puffs of hissing ozone. And the women
are hard green horses disappearing,
concealing themselves in buildings and tops
of wild palms in ambush.

A riverless city of redolent
and banal sobs, green girls
in trees, girls hard as basalt.
"My grandfather screwed me
when I was seven years old,"
she said, while I looked out
at the cement river flowing with dusty rain,
at three dogs playing in the cement river.
"He's dead now so there's no point
sweating it," she added.

Up in the Amazon River Basin
during a dark time Matthiessen built
a raft with a native, chewed some coca leaves,
boarded the raft and off they went on a river
not on any map, uncharted, wanting to see
the Great Mother of Snakes; a truncated
version of our voyage of seventy years—
actuarial average. To see green and live green,
moving on water sometimes clouded often clear.
Now our own pond is white with ice.
In the barnyard lying in the snow
I can hear the underground creek,
a creek without a name.

I forgot to tell you that while
I was away my heart broke
and I became not so much old, but older,
definably older within a few days.
This happened on a cold dawn in New Iberia
while I was feeding a frightened stray
dog a sack of pork rinds in the rain.

Three girls danced the "Cotton-Eyed Joe,"
almost sedate, erect, with relentless grace,

where did they come from
and where did they go
in ever-so-delicate circles?
And because of time, circles
that no longer close
or return to themselves.

I rode the gray horse
all day in the rain.
The fields became unmoving rivers,
the trees foreshortened.
I saw a girl in a white dress
standing half-hidden in the water
behind a maple tree.
I pretended not to notice
and made a long slow circle
behind a floating hedgetop
to catch her unawares.
She was gone but I had that prickly
fear someone was watching from a tree,
far up in a leaf-veil of green maple leaves.
Now the horse began swimming
toward higher ground, from where
I watched the tree until dark.

"Life, this vastly mysterious process
to which our culture inures us
lest we become useless citizens!
And is it terrible to be lonely and ill?"
she wrote. "Not at all, in fact, it is better
to be lonely when ill. To others, friends,
relatives, loved ones, death is our most
interesting, our most dramatic act.
Perhaps the best thing I've learned
from these apparently cursed and bedraggled

Indians I've studied all these years
is how to die. Last year I sat beside
a seven-year-old Hopi girl as she sang
her death song in a slight quavering
voice. Who among us whites, child
or adult, will sing while we die?"

On White Fish Bay, the motor broke down
in heavy seas. We chopped ice off the gunwales
quite happily as it was unlikely we'd survive
and it was something to do. Ted just sat there
out of the wind and spray, drinking whiskey.
"I been on the wagon for a year. If I'm going
to die by god at least I get to have a drink."

What is it to actually go outside the nest
we have built for ourselves, and earlier
our father's nest: to go into a forest
alone with our eyes open? It's different
when you don't know what's over the hill—
keep the river on your left, then you see
the river on your right. I have simply
forgotten left and right, even up and down,
whirl then sleep on a cloudy day to forget
direction. It is hard to learn how
to be lost after so much training.

In New York I clocked
seven tugboats on the East River
in less than a half hour;
then I went to a party
where very rich people
talked about their arches,
foot arches, not architectural arches.
Back at my post I dozed

and saw only one more tugboat
before I slept.

But in New York I also saw a big hole
of maddened pipes with all the direction
of the swastika and a few immigrants
figuring it all out with the impenetrable
good sense of those who do the actual
work of the world.

How did I forget that rich turbulent
river, so cold in the rumply brown folds
of spring; by August cool, clear, glittery
in the sunlight; umbrous as it dips
under the logjam. In May, the river
a roar beyond a thin wall of sleep, with
the world of snow still gliding in rivulets
down imperceptible slopes; in August
through the screened window against which
bugs and moths scratch so lightly,
as lightly as the river sounds.

How can I renew oaths
I can't quite remember?
In New Orleans I was light in body and soul
because of food poisoning, the bathroom gymnastics
of flesh against marble floor,
seeing the underside of the bathtub
for the first time since I was a child,
and the next day crossing Cajun bridges
in the Atchafalaya, where Blacks were thrown
to alligators I'm told, Black souls whirling
in brown water, whirling
in an immaculate crawfish
rosary.

In the water I can remember
women I didn't know: Adriana
dancing her way home at the end
of a rope, a cool Tuscany night,
the apple tree in bloom;
the moon which I checked
was not quite full, a half-moon,
the rest of the life abandoned to the dark.

I warned myself all night
but then halfway between my ears
I turned toward the heavens
and reached the top of my head.
From there I can go just about
anywhere I want and I've never
found my way back home.

This isn't the old song
of the suicidal house,
I forgot the tune about small
windows growing smaller, the door
neither big enough to enter
nor exit, the sinking hydraulic ceilings
and the attic full of wet cement.
I wanted to go to the Camargue,
to Corsica, to return to Costa Rica,
but I couldn't escape the suicidal house
until May when I drove
through the snow to reach the river.

On the bank by the spring creek
my shadow seemed to leap
up to gather me, or it leapt
up to gather me, not seeming so
but as a natural fact. Faulkner said

that the drowned man's shadow had watched
him from the river all the time.

Drowning in the bourgeois trough,
a *bourride* or gruel of money, drugs,
whiskey, hotels, the dream coasts,
ass in the air at the trough, drowning
in a river of pus, pus of civilization,
pus of cities, unholy river of shit,
of filth, shit of nightmares, shit
of skewed dreams and swallowed years.
The river pulls me out,
draws me elsewhere
and down to blue water,
green water,
black water.

How far between the Virgin
and the Garrison and back?
Why is it a hundred times farther to get back,
the return upriver in the dark?
It isn't innocence, but to win back breath,
body heat, the light that gathers around
a waking animal. Ten years ago I saw
the dancing Virgin in a basement
in New York, a whirl of hot color
from floor to ceiling, whirling in a dance.
At eighteen in New York
on Grove Street I discovered
red wine, garlic, Rimbaud,
and a red-haired girl. Livid colors
not known in farm country,
also Charlie Parker, Sonny Rollins,
the odors from restaurant vents,
thirty-five-cent Italian sausages

on MacDougal, and the Hudson River:
days of river-watching and trying
to get on a boat for the tropics and see
that Great Ocean river, the Gulf Stream.
Another fifteen years before I saw
the Ocean river and the sharks hanging
under the sargassum weed lines,
a blue river in green water,
and the sharks staring back, sinking
down listlessly into darker water;
the torpor of heat, a hundred low-tide
nights begging a forgetfulness
I haven't quite earned.

I forgot where I heard that poems
are designed to waken sleeping gods;
in our time they've taken on nearly
unrecognizable shapes as gods will do;
one is a dog, one is a scarecrow
that doesn't work—crows perch
on the wind-whipped sleeves,
one is a carpenter who doesn't become Jesus,
one is a girl who went to heaven
sixty years early. Gods die,
and not always out of choice,
like near-sighted cats jumping
between buildings seven stories up.
One god drew feathers out of my skin
so I could fly, a favor close to terror.
But this isn't a map of the gods.
When they live in rivers
it's because rivers have no equilibrium;
gods resent equilibrium when everything
that lives *moves;* boulders
are a war of atoms, and the dandelion

cracks upward through the blacktop road.
Seltzer's tropical beetle grew
from a larval lump in a man's arm,
emerging full grown, pincers waving.
On Mt. Cuchama there were so many
gods passing through I hid in a hole
in a rock, waking one by accident.
I fled with a tight ass and cold skin.
I could draw a map of this place
but they're never caught in the same location
twice. And their voices change from involuntary
screams to the singular wail of the loon,
possibly the wind that can howl down Wall St.
Gods have long abandoned the banality of war
though they were stirred by a hundred-year-old
guitarist I heard in Brazil, also the autistic child
at the piano. We'll be greeted at death
so why should I wait? Today I invoked
any available god back in the woods in the fog.
The world was white with last week's melting
blizzard, the fog drifting upward, then descending.
The only sound was a porcupine eating bark
off an old tree, and a rivulet beneath the snow.
Sometimes the obvious is true: the full
moon on her bare bottom by the river!
For the gay, the full moon on the lover's prick!
Gods laugh at the fiction of gender.
Water-gods, moon-gods, god-fever,
sun-gods, fire-gods, give this earth-diver
more songs before I die.

A "system" suggests the cutting off,
i.e., in channel morphology, the reduction,
the suppression of texture to simplify:
to understand a man, or woman, growing

old with eagerness you first consider
the sensuality of death, an unacknowledged
surprise to most. In nature the physiology
has heat and color, beast and tree
saying aloud the wonder of death;
to study rivers, including the postcard
waterfalls, is to adopt another life;
a limited life attaches itself to the endless
movement, the renowned underground
rivers of South America which I've felt
thundering far beneath my feet—to die
is to descend into such rivers and flow
along in the perfect dark. But above ground
I'm memorizing life, from the winter moon
to the sound of my exhaustion in March
when all the sodden plans have collapsed
and only daughters, the dogs and cats
keep one from disappearing at gunpoint.
I brought myself here and stare nose to nose
at the tolerant cat who laps whiskey
from my mustache. Life often shatters
in schizoid splinters. I will avoid
becoming the cold stone wall I am straddling.

I had forgot what it was I liked
about life. I hear if you own a chimpanzee
they cease at a point to be funny. Writers
and politicians share an embarrassed moment
when they are sure all problems will disappear
if you get the language right.
That's not all they share—in each other's
company they are like boys who have been
discovered at wiener-play in the toilet.
At worst, it's the gift of gab.
At best it's Martin Luther King and Rimbaud.

Bearing down hard on love and death
there is an equal and opposite reaction.
All these years they have split the pie,
leaving the topping for the preachers
who don't want folks to fuck or eat.
What kind of magic, or rite of fertility,
to transcend this shit-soaked stew?

The river is as far as I can move
from the world of numbers: I'm all
for full retreats, escapes, a 47 yr. old runaway.
"Gettin' too old to run away," I wrote
but not quite believing this option is gray.
I stare into the deepest pool of the river
which holds the mystery of a cellar to a child,
and think of those two-track roads that dwindle
into nothing in the forest. I have this feeling
of walking around for days with the wind
knocked out of me. In the cellar was a root
cellar where we stored potatoes, apples, carrots
and where a family of harmless blacksnakes lived.
In certain rivers there are pools a hundred
foot deep. In a swamp I must keep secret
there is a deep boiling spring around which
in the dog days of August large brook trout
swim and feed. An adult can speak dreams
to children saying that there is a spring
that goes down to the center of the earth.
Maybe there is. Next summer I'm designing
and building a small river about seventy-seven
foot long. It will flow both ways, in reverse
of nature. I will build a dam and blow it up.

The involuntary image that sweeps
into the mind, irresistible and without evident

cause as a dream or thunderstorm,
or rising to the surface from childhood,
the longest journey taken in a split second,
from there to now, without pause:
in the woods with Mary Cooper, my first love
wearing a violet scarf in May. We're
looking after her huge mongoloid aunt,
trailing after this woman who loves us
but so dimly perceives the world. We pick
and clean wild leeks for her. The creek
is wild and dangerous with the last
of the snowmelt. The child-woman
tries to enter the creek and we tackle her.
She's stronger, then slowly understands,
half-wet and muddy. She kisses me
while Mary laughs, then Mary kisses me
over and over. Now I see the pools
in the Mongol eyes that watch and smile
with delight and hear the roar of the creek,
smell the scent of leeks on her muddy lips.

This is an obscene koan set plumb
in the middle of the Occident:
the man with three hands lacks symmetry
but claps the loudest, the chicken
in circles on the sideless road, a plane
that takes off and can never land.
I am not quite alert enough to live.
The fallen nest and fire in the closet,
my world without guardrails, the electric
noose, the puddle that had no bottom.
The fish in underground rivers are white
and blind as the porpoises who live far up
the muddy Amazon. In New York and LA
you don't want to see, hear, smell,

and you only open your mouth in restaurants.
At night you touch people with rock-hard skins.
I'm trying to become alert enough to live.
Yesterday after the blizzard I hiked far back
in a new swamp and found an iceless
pond connected to the river by a small creek.
Against deep white snow and black trees
there was a sulfurous fumarole, rank and sharp
in cold air. The water bubbled up brown,
then spread in turquoise to deep black,
without the track of a single mammal to drink.
This was nature's own, a beauty too strong
for life; a place to drown not live.

On waking after the accident
I was presented with the "whole picture"
as they say, magnificently detailed,
a child's diorama of what life appears to be:
staring at the picture I became drowsy
with relief when I noticed a yellow
dot of light in the lower right-hand corner.
I unhooked the machines and tubes and crawled
to the picture, with an eyeball to the dot
of light, which turned out to be a miniature
tunnel at the end of which I could see
mountains and stars whirling and tumbling,
sheets of emotions, vertical rivers, upside-
down lakes, herds of unknown mammals, birds
shedding feathers and regrowing them instantly,
snakes with feathered heads eating their own
shed skins, fish swimming straight up,
the bottom of Isaiah's robe, live whales
on dry ground, lions drinking from a golden
bowl of milk, the rush of night,
and somewhere in this the murmur of gods—

a tree-rubbing-tree music, a sweet howl
of water and rock-grating-rock, fire
hissing from fissures, the moon settled
comfortably on the ground, beginning to roll.

KOBUN

Hotei didn't need a *zafu*,
saying that his ass was sufficient.
The head's a cloud anchor
that the feet must follow.
Travel light, he said,
or don't travel at all.

LOOKING FORWARD TO AGE

I will walk down to a marina
on a hot day and not go out to sea.

I will go to bed and get up early,
and carry too much cash in my wallet.

On Memorial Day I will visit the graves
of all those who died in my novels.

If I have become famous I'll wear a green
janitor's suit and row a wooden boat.

From a key ring on my belt will hang
thirty-three keys that open no doors.

Perhaps I'll take all of my grandchildren
to Disneyland in a camper but probably not.

One day standing in a river with my fly rod
I'll have the courage to admit my life.

In a one-room cabin at night I'll consign
photos, all tentative memories to the fire.

And you my loves, few as there have been, let's lie
and say it could never have been otherwise.

So that: we may glide off in peace, not howling
like orphans in this endless century of war.

HOMILY

These simple rules to live within—a black
pen at night, a gold pen in daylight,
avoid blue food and ten-ounce shots
of whiskey, don't point a gun at yourself,
don't snipe with the cri-cri-cri of a *becassine,*
don't use gas for starter fluid, don't read
dirty magazines in front of stewardesses—
it happens all the time; it's time to stop
cleaning your plate, forget the birthdays
of the dead, give all you can to the poor.
This might go on and on and will: who can
choose between the animal in the road
and the ditch? A magnum for lunch
is a little too much but not enough
for dinner. Polish the actual stars at night
as an invisible man pets a dog, an actual
man a memory-dog lost under
the morning glory trellis forty years ago.
Dance with yourself with all your heart
and soul, and occasionally others, but don't
eat all the berries birds eat or you'll die.
Kiss yourself in the mirror but don't fall in love
with photos of ladies in magazines. Don't fall
in love as if you were falling through
the floor in an abandoned house, or off
a dock at night, or down a crevasse
covered with false snow, a cow floundering
in quicksand while the other cows watch
without particular interest, backward
off a crumbling cornice. Don't fall in love
with two at once. From the ceiling you can see
this circle of three, though one might be elsewhere.

He is rended, he rends himself, he dances,
he whirls so hard everything he *is* flies off.
He crumples as paper but rises daily from the dead.

SOUTHERN CROSS

That hot desert beach in Ecuador,
with scarcely a splotch of vegetation
fronting as it does
a Pacific so immensely lush
it hurls lobsters on great flat
boulders where children brave fatal
waves to pick them up.
Turning from one to the other quickly,
it is incomprehensible: from wild, gray
sunblasted burro eating cactus to azure
immensity of ocean, from miniature
goat dead on infantile feet in sand
to imponderable roar of swells, equatorial sun;
music that squeezes the blood out of the heart
by midnight, and girls whose legs
glisten with sweat, their teeth white
as Canadian snow, legs pounding as plump
brown pistons, and night noises I've
never heard, though at the coolest period
in these latitudes, near the faintest
beginning of dawn, there was the cold
unmistakable machine gun, the harshest
chatter death can make. Only then do
I think of my very distant relative, Lorca,
that precocious skeleton, as he crumpled
earthward against brown pine needles;
and the sky, vaster than the Pacific,
whirled overhead, a sky without birds or clouds,
azul te quiero azul.

SULLIVAN POEM

March 5: first day without a fire.
Too early. Too early. Too early!
Take joy in the day
without consideration, the three
newly-brought-to-life bugs
who are not meant to know
what they are doing avoid each other
on windows stained
by a dozen storms.

We eat our father's food:
herring, beans, salt pork,
sauerkraut, pig hocks, salt cod.
I have said good-bye with one thousand
laments so that even the heart of the rose
becomes empty as my dog's rubber ball.
The dead are not meant to go,
but to trail off so that one can
see them on a distant hillock,
across the river, in dreams
from which one awakens nearly healed:
don't worry, it's fine to be dead,
they say; we were a little early
but could not help ourselves.
Everyone dies as the child they were,
and at the moment, this secret,
intricately concealed heart blooms
forth with the first song anyone
sang in the dark, "Now I lay me
down to sleep, I pray the Lord
my soul to keep . . ."

Now this oddly gentle winter, almost dulcet,
winds to a blurred close with trees full
of birds that belong farther south,
and people are missing something
to complain about; a violent March
is an unacknowledged prayer;
a rape of nature, a healing blizzard,
a very near disaster.

So this last lament:
as unknowable as the eye of the crow
staring down from the walnut tree,
blind as the Magellanic clouds,
as cold as that March mud puddle
at the foot of the granary steps,
unseeable as the birthright of the LA
whore's Nebraska childhood of lilacs
and cornfields and an unnamed prairie
bird that lived in a thicket
where she hid,
as treacherous as a pond's spring
ice to a child,
black as the scar of a half-peeled
birch tree,
the wrench of the beast's heart just
short of the waterhole,
as bell-clear as a gunshot at dawn,
is the ache of a father's death.

It is that, but far more:
as if we take a voyage out of life
as surely as we took a voyage in,
almost as frightened children
in a cellar's cold gray air;
or before memory—they put me on a boat

on this river, then I was lifted off;
in our hearts, it is always just after
dawn, and each bird's song is the first,
and that ever-so-slight breeze that touches
the tops of trees and ripples the lake
moves through our bodies as if we were gods.

HORSE

What if it were our privilege
to sculpt our dreams of animals?
But those shapes in the night
come and go too quickly to be held
in stone: but not to avoid these shapes
as if dreams were only a nighttime
pocket to be remembered and avoided.
Who can say in the depths of
his life and heart what beast
most stopped life, the animals
he watched, the animals he only touched
in dreams? Even our hearts don't beat
the way we want them to. What
can we know in that waking,
sleeping edge? We put down
my daughter's old horse, old and
arthritic, a home burial. By dawn with eye
half-open, I said to myself, is
he still running, is he still running
around, under the ground?

COBRA

What are these nightmares,
so wildly colored? We're in every
movie we see, even in our sleep.
Not that we can become what
we fear most but that we can't
resist ourselves. The grizzly
attack; after that divorce
and standing outside the school
with a rifle so they can't take my
daughter Anna. By god! Long ago
in Kenya where I examined the
grass closely before I sat down
to a poisonous lunch, I worried
about cobras. When going insane I worried
about cobra venom in Major Grey's Chutney.
Simple as that. Then in overnight sleep I became
a lordly cobra, feeling the pasture grass
at high noon glide beneath my
stomach. I watched the house with
my head arched above the weeds,
then slept in the cool dirt under the granary.

PORPOISE

Every year, when we're fly-fishing for tarpon
off Key West, Guy insists that porpoises
are good luck. But it's not so banal
as catching more fish or having a fashion
model fall out of the sky lightly on your head,
or at your feet depending on certain
preferences. It's what porpoises do to the ocean.
You see a school making love off Boca Grande,
the baby with his question mark staring
at us a few feet from the boat.
Porpoises dance for as long as they live.
You can do nothing for them.
They alter the universe.

THE BRAND NEW STATUE OF LIBERTY

to Lee Iacocca (another Michigan boy)

I was commissioned in a dream by Imanja,
also the Black Pope of Brazil, Tancred,
to design a seven-tiered necklace
of seven thousand skulls for the Statue of Liberty.
Of course from a distance they'll look
like pearls, but in November
when the strongest winds blow, the skulls
will rattle wildly, bone against metal,
a crack and chatter of bone against metal,
the true sound of history, this metal striking bone.
I'm not going to get heavy-handed—
a job is a job and I've leased a football
field for the summer, gathered a group of ladies
who are art lovers, leased in advance
a bull Sikorsky freight helicopter
to drop on the necklace: funding comes
from Ford Foundation, Rockefeller, the NEA.
There is one Jewish skull from Atlanta, two
from Mississippi, but this is basically
an indigenous cast except skulls from tribes
of Blacks who got a free ride over from Africa,
representative skulls from all the Indian
tribes, an assortment of grizzly, wolf,
coyote and buffalo skulls. But what beauty
when the morning summer sun glances
off these bony pates! And her great
iron lips quivering in a smile, almost a smirk
so that she'll drop the torch to fondle the jewels.

THE TIMES ATLAS

*For my mentor, long dead, Richard
Halliburton and his* Seven League Boots.

Today was the coldest day in the history
of the Midwest. Thank god for the moon
in this terrible storm.

There are areas far out at sea where
it rains a great deal. Camus said
it rained so hard even the sea was wet.

O god all our continents are only rifted
magma welled up from below. We don't
have a solid place to stand.

A little bullshit here as the Nile
is purportedly eighty miles longer
than the Amazon. I proclaim it a tie.

Pay out your 125 bucks and find out the world
isn't what you think it is but what
it is. We whirl so nothing falls off.
Eels, polar bears, bugs and men enjoy

the maker's design. No one really
leaves this place. O loveliness
of Caribbean sun off water under
trade wind's lilt.

Meanwhile the weather is no longer amusing.
Earth frightens me, the blizzard, house's
shudder, oceanic roar, the brittle night
that might leave so many dead.

NEW LOVE

With these dire portents
we'll learn the language
of knees, shoulder blades,
chins but not the first floor up,
shinbones, the incomprehensible
belly buttons of childhood,
heels and the soles of our feet,
spines and neckbones,
risqué photos of the tender
inside of elbows, tumescent fingers
draw the outlines of lost parts
on the wall; bottom and pubis
Delphic, unapproachable as Jupiter,
a memory worn as the first love
we knew, ourselves a test pattern
become obsession: this love
in the plague years—we used to kiss
a mirror to see if we were dead.
Now we relearn the future as we learned
to walk, as a baby grabs its toes,
tilts backward, rocking. Tonight I'll touch
your wrist and in a year perhaps grind
my blind eye's socket against your hipbone.
With all this death, behind our backs,
the moon has become the moon again.

WHAT HE SAID WHEN I WAS ELEVEN

August, a dense heat wave at the cabin
mixed with torrents of rain,
the two-tracks become miniature rivers.

In the Russian Orthodox Church
one does not talk to God, one sings.
This empty and sun-blasted land

has a voice rising in shimmers.
I did not sing in Moscow
but St. Basil's in Leningrad raised

a quiet tune. But now seven worlds
away I hang the *cazas-moscas*
from the ceiling and catch seven flies

in the first hour, buzzing madly
against the stickiness. I've never seen
the scissor-tailed flycatcher, a favorite

bird of my youth, the worn Audubon
card pinned to the wall. When I miss
flies three times with the swatter

they go free for good. Fair is fair.
There is too much nature pressing against
the window as if it were a green night;

and the river swirling in glazed turbulence
is less friendly than ever before.
Forty years ago she called, *Come home, come home,*

it's suppertime. I was fishing a fishless
cattle pond with a new three-dollar pole,
dreaming the dark blue ocean of pictures.

In the barn I threw down hay
while my Swede grandpa finished milking,
squirting the barn cat's mouth with an udder.

I kissed the wet nose of my favorite cow,
drank a dipper of fresh warm milk
and carried two pails to the house,

scraping the manure off my feet
in the pump shed. She poured the milk
in the cream separator and I began cranking.

At supper the oilcloth was decorated
with worn pink roses. We ate cold herring,
also the bluegills we had caught at daylight.

The fly-strip above the table idled in
the window's breeze, a new fly in its death buzz.
Grandpa said, "We are all flies."

That's what he said forty years ago.

ACTING

for J.N.

In the best sense,
becoming another
so that there is no trace left
of what we think is the self.
I am whoever.
It is not gesture
but the cortex of gesture,
not movement
but the soul of movement.
Look at the earth with your left eye
and at the sky with your right.
Worship contraries.
What makes us alike
is also what makes us different.
From Man to Jokester to Trickster
is a nudge toward the deep,
the incalculable abyss
you stare into so it will
stare back into you.
We are our consciousness
and it is the god in us
who struggles to be in everyone
in order to be ourselves.
When you see the chalked form
of the murdered man on the cement
throw yourself onto it and feel
the heat of the stone-hard fit.
This is the liquid poem,
the forefinger traced around both
the neck and the sun:
to be and be and be

as a creek turns corners
by grace of volume, heft of water,
speed by rate of drop,
even the contour of stone
changing day by day.
So that: when you wake in the night,
the freedom of the nightmare
turned to dream follows you
into morning, and there is no
skin on earth you cannot enter,
no beast or plant,
no man or woman
you may not flow through
and become.

MY FRIEND THE BEAR

Down in the bone myth of the cellar
of this farmhouse, behind the empty fruit jars
the whole wall swings open to the room
where I keep the bear. There's a tunnel
to the outside on the far wall that emerges
in the lilac grove in the backyard
but she rarely uses it, knowing there's no room
around here for a freewheeling bear.
She's not a dainty eater so once a day
I shovel shit while she lopes in playful circles.
Privately she likes religion—from the bedroom
I hear her incantatory moans and howls
below me—and April 23rd, when I open
the car trunk and whistle at midnight
and she shoots up the tunnel, almost airborne
when she meets the night. We head north
and her growls are less friendly as she scents
the forest-above-the-road smell. I release
her where I found her as an orphan three
years ago, bawling against the dead carcass
of her mother. I let her go at the head
of the gully leading down to the swamp,
jumping free of her snarls and roars.
But each October 9th, one day before bear season
she reappears at the cabin frightening
the bird dogs. We embrace ear to ear,
her huge head on my shoulder,
her breathing like god's.

CABIN POEM

I

The blond girl
with a polka heart:
one foot, then another,
then aerial
in a twisting jump,
chin upward
with a scream of such
splendor
I go back to my cabin,
and start a fire.

II

Art & life
drunk & sober
empty & full
guilt & grace
cabin & home
north & south
struggle & peace
after which we catch
a glimpse of stars,
the white glistening pelt
of the Milky Way,
hear the startled bear crashing
through the delta swamp below me.
In these troubled times
I go inside and start a fire.

III

I am the bird that hears the worm,
or, my cousin said, the pulse of a wound
that probes to the opposite side.
I have abandoned alcohol, cocaine,
the news, and outdoor prayer
as support systems.
How can you make a case for yourself
before an ocean of trees, or standing
waist-deep in the river? Or sitting
on the logjam with a pistol?
I reject oneness with bears.
She has two cubs and thinks she
owns the swamp I thought I bought.
I shoot once in the air to tell her
it's my turn at the logjam
for an hour's thought about nothing.
Perhaps that is oneness with bears.
I've decided to make up my mind
about nothing, to assume the water mask,
to finish my life disguised as a creek,
an eddy, joining at night the full,
sweet flow, to absorb the sky,
to swallow the heat and cold, the moon
and the stars, to swallow myself
in ceaseless flow.

RICH FOLKS, POOR FOLKS, AND NEITHER

I

Rich folks keep their teeth
until late in life,
and park their cars in heated garages.
They own kitsch statues of praying hands
that conceal seven pounds of solid gold,
knowing that burglars hedge at icons.
At the merest twinge they go to the dentist,
and their dogs' anuses are professionally
inspected for unsuspected diseases.
Rich folks dream of the perfect massage
that will bring secret, effortless orgasm,
and absolutely super and undiscovered
islands with first-rate hotels
where they will learn to windsurf
in five minutes. They buy clothes that fit—
a forty waist means forty pants—rich folks
don't squeeze into thirty-eights. At spas
they are not too critical of their big asses,
and they believe in real small portions
because they can eat again pretty quick.
Rich folks resent richer folks
and they also resent poor folks
for their failures at meniality.
It's unfortunate for our theory that the same
proportion of rich folks are as pleasant
as poor folks, a pitiless seven
percent, though not necessarily the ones
who still say their prayers and finish
the morning oatmeal to help the poor.
Everyone I have ever met is deeply
puzzled.

II

Up in Michigan poor folks dream of trips
to Hawaii or "Vegas." They muttered deeply
when the banker won the big lottery—
"It just don't seem fair," they said.
Long ago when I was poor
there was something in me that craved
to get fired, to drink a shot and beer
with a lump in my throat, hitchhike
or drive to California in an old car,
tell my family "I'll write if I get work."
In California, where you can sleep outside
every night, I saw the Pacific Ocean
and ate my first food of the Orient,
a fifty-cent bowl of noodles and pork.
No more cornmeal mush with salt pork
gravy, no more shovels at dawn,
no more clothes smelling of kerosene,
no more girls wearing ankle bracelets spelling
another's name. No more three-hour waits
in unemployment lines, or cafeteria catsup
and bread for fifteen cents. I've eaten
my last White Tower burger and I'm heading
for the top. Or not. How could I dream
I'd end up moist-eyed in the Beverly Hills Hotel
when I ordered thirteen appetizers for myself
and the wheels of the laden trolley squeaked?
The television in the limousine broke down
and I missed the news on the way to look
at the ocean where there were no waves.
When I went bankrupt I began to notice cemeteries
and wore out my clothes, drank up the wine cellar.
I went to the movies and kissed my wife a lot

for the same reason—they're both in technicolor.
Everyone I met in those days was deeply puzzled.

III

Now I've rubbed rich and poor together
like two grating stones, mixed them temporarily
like oil and vinegar, male and female, until
my interest has waned to nothing. One night I saw
a constellation that chose not to reappear,
drifting in the day into another galaxy.
I tried to ignore the sound of my footsteps
in the woods until I did, and when I swam
in the river I finally forgot it was water,
but I still can't see a cow without saying *cow*.
Perhaps this was not meant to be. I dug
a deep hole out in a clearing in the forest
and sat down in it, studying the map
of the sky above me for clues, a new bible.
This is rushing things a bit, I thought.
I became a woman then became a man again.
I hiked during the night alone and gave
my dogs fresh bones until they no longer cared.
I bought drinks for the poor and for myself,
left mail unopened, didn't speak on the phone,
only listened. I shot the copy machine with my rifle.
No more copies, I thought, everything original!
Now I am trying to unlearn the universe
in the usual increments of nights and days.
Time herself often visits in swirling but gentle clouds.
Way out there on the borders of my consciousness
I've caught glimpses of that great dark bird,
the beating of whose wings is death, drawing closer.
How could it be otherwise? I thought.

Down in the hole last August during a thunderstorm
I watched her left wing-tip shudder past
between two lightning strokes. Maybe I'll see her again
during the northern lights, but then, at that moment,
I was still a child of water and mud.

DANCING

After the passing of irresistible
music you must learn to make
do with a dripping faucet,
rain or sleet on the roof,
eventually snow,
a cat's sigh,
the spherical notes that float
down from Aldebaran,
your cells as they part,
craving oxygen.

THE IDEA OF BALANCE IS TO BE FOUND
IN HERONS AND LOONS

I just heard a loon-call on a TV ad
and my body gave itself
a quite voluntary shudder,
as in the night in East Africa
I heard the immense barking cough
of a lion, so foreign and indifferent.

But the lion drifts away
and the loon stays close,
calling, as she did in my childhood,
in the cold rain a song
that tells the world of men
to keep its distance.

It isn't the signal of another life
or the reminder of anything
except her call: still,
at this quiet point past midnight
the rain is the same rain
that fell so long ago, and the loon
says I'm seven years old again.

At the far ends of the lake
where no one lives or visits—
there are no roads to get there;
you take the watercourse way,
the quiet drip and drizzle
of oars, slight squeak of oarlock,
the bare feet can feel the cold water
move beneath the old wood boat.

At one end the lordly great blue herons
nest at the top of the white pine;
at the other end the loons,
just after daylight in cream-colored mist,
drifting with wails that begin as querulous,
rising then into the spheres in volume,
with lost or doomed angels imprisoned
within their breasts.

SMALL POEM

There's something I've never known
when I get up in the morning.
Dead children fly off in the shape
of question marks, the doe's backward
glance at the stillborn fawn.
I don't know what it is
in the morning, as if incomprehension
beds down with me on waking.
What is the precise emotional temperature
when the young man hangs himself
in the jail cell with his father's belt?
What is the foot size of the Beast of Belsen?
This man in his overremembered life
needs to know the source of the ache
which is an answer without a question,
his fingers wrapped around the memory
of life, as Cleopatra's around the snake's neck,
a shepherd's crook of love.

COUNTING BIRDS

for Gerald Vizenor

As a child, fresh out of the hospital
with tape covering the left side
of my face, I began to count birds.
At age fifty the sum total is precise
and astonishing, my only secret.
Some men count women or the cars
they've owned, their shirts—
long sleeved and short sleeved—
or shoes, but I have my birds,
excluding, of course, those extraordinary
days: the twenty-one thousand
snow geese and sandhill cranes at
Bosque del Apache; the sky blinded
by great frigate birds in the Pacific
off Anconcito, Ecuador; the twenty-one
thousand pink flamingos in Ngorongoro Crater
in Tanzania; the vast flock of seabirds
on the Seri coast of the Sea of Cortez
down in Sonora that left at nightfall,
then reappeared, resuming
their exact positions at dawn;
the one thousand cliff swallows nesting
in the sand cliffs of Pyramid Point,
their small round burrows like eyes,
really the souls of the Anasazi who flew
here a thousand years ago
to wait the coming of the Manitou.
And then there were the usual, almost deadly
birds of the soul—the crow with silver
harness I rode one night as if she
were a black, feathered angel;

the birds I became to escape unfortunate
circumstances—how the skin ached
as the feathers shot out toward light;
the thousand birds the dogs helped
me shoot to become a bird (grouse, woodcock,
duck, dove, snipe, pheasant, prairie chicken, etc.).
On my deathbed I'll write this secret
number on a slip of paper and pass
it to my wife and two daughters.
It will be a hot evening in late June
and they might be glancing out the window
at the thunderstorm's approach from the west.
Looking past their eyes and a dead fly
on the window screen I'll wonder
if there's a bird waiting for me in the onrushing clouds.
O birds, I'll sing to myself, *you've carried*
me along on this bloody voyage,
carry me now into that cloud,
into the marvel of this final night.

AFTER IKKYŪ
& OTHER POEMS

1996

for Jack Turner

PREFACE

I began my Zen studies and practice well over twenty years ago in a state of rapacious and self-congratulatory spiritual greed. I immediately set about reading hundreds of books on the subject, almost all contemporary and informed by an earnest mediocrity. There was no more self-referential organism alive than myself, a potato that didn't know it was a potato.

Naturally the years have passed quickly, if not brutishly. I practiced because I value life and this seems the best way for me to get at the heart of the matter. We are more than dying flies in a shithouse, though we are that, too. There are hundreds of ways to tip off a cushion and only one way to sit there. Zen is the vehicle of reality, and I see almost as much of it in Wordsworth as I do in Ch'an texts. As I've said before, it's easy to mistake the plumbing for the river. We in the West are prone to ignore our own literary traditions, while in the East Zennists were industriously syncretic, gathering poetry, Confucius, and Taoism to their breasts. There is scarcely a better koan than Ahab before the whiteness of a whale who sees a different ocean from each side of its massive head.

The sequence "After Ikkyū" was occasioned when Jack Turner passed along to me *The Record of Tung-shan* and the new *Master Yunmen,* edited by Urs App. It was a dark period, and I spent a great deal of time with the books. They rattled me loose from the oppressive, poleaxed state of distraction we count as worldly success. But then we are not fueled by piths and gists but by practice—which is Yunmen's unshakable point, amongst a thousand other harrowing ones. I was born a baby, what are these hundred suits of clothes I'm wearing?

Of course, the reader should be mindful that I'm a poet and we tend to err on the side that life is more than it appears rather than less. I do not remotely consider myself a "Zen Buddhist," as that is too ineptly convenient, and a specific barrier for one whose lifelong obsession has been his art rather than his religion. Someone like Robert Aitken Roshi is a Zen Buddhist. I'm still a fool. Early on in my teens I suffocated myself with Protestant theology and am mindful, in Coleridge's terms, that, like spiders, we spin webs of deceit out of our big hanging asses, whether with Jesus or the Buddha.

But still practice is accretive, and who has opened doors for me like Zen creatures—Peter Matthiessen, Gary Snyder, Kobun Chino Sensei, Bob Watkins, Dan Gerber, and Jack Turner, to name a few prominent ones?

It doesn't really matter if these poems are thought of as slightly soiled dharma gates or just plain poems. They'll live or die by their own specific density, flowers for the void. The poems were written within the discreet interval described so poignantly by Tung-shan:

> Earnestly avoid seeking without,
> Lest it recede far from you.
> Today I am walking alone,
> Yet everywhere I meet him.
> He is now no other than myself,
> But I am not now him.
> It must be understood this way
> In order to merge with Suchness.

To write a poem you must first create a pen that will write what you want to say. For better or worse, this is the work of a lifetime.

J.H.

AFTER IKKYŪ

1

Our minds buzz like bees
but not the bees' minds.
It's just wings not heart
they say, moving to another flower.

2

The well pit is beneath where the pump shed burned
years ago with a living roar, a fire lion. Down
in the pit, charred timbers, green grass, one burdock,
a vernal pool where frogs live trapped in a universe.

3

I've wasted too much moonlight.
Breast-beating. I'll waste no more moonlight,
the moon bullied by clouds drifts west
in her imponderable arc, snared for a half
hour among the wet leaves in the birdbath.

4

After thirty years of work
I take three months off
and wait for the mirror's image to fade.
These chess pieces, slippery with blood.

5

Time eats us alive.
On my birthday yesterday
I was only one day older
though I began ten million eons ago
as a single cell in the old mud homestead.

6

Shoju sat all night in the graveyard
among wolves who sniffed his Adam's apple.
First light moving in the air
he arose, peed, and ate breakfast.

7

With each shot
he killed the self
until there was no one left
to bring home the bacon.

8

One part of the brain attacks another,
seven parts attack nine parts,
then the war begins to subside
from lack of ammunition,
but out there I know the mules are bringing
fresh supplies from over the mountain.

9

Poor little blind boy lost in the storm,
where should he go to be without harm?
For starters, the dickhead should get a life.
Once I had a moment of absolute balance
while dancing with my sick infant daughter
to Merle Haggard. The blind boy died in the storm
with fresh frozen laughter hot on his lips.

10

Our pup is gravely ill.
She's her own pup too,
first in her own line.

How great thou art o god,
save her, please, the same cry
in every throat. May I live forever.

    11

At Hard Luck Ranch the tea is hot,
the sky's dark blue. Behind me
the jaguar skin from the jaguar
who died so long ago from a bullet
while perched on a calf's back
tells me the same old story.

    12

Not here and now but now and here.
If you don't know the difference
is a matter of life and death, get down
naked on bare knees in the snow
and study the ticking of your watch.

    13

The hound I've known for three years
trots down the mountain road
with a nod at me, pretending he knows
what he's doing miles from home
on a sunlit morning. He's headed
for a kind of place he hasn't quite found yet
and might not recognize when he gets there.

    14

At the strip club in Lincoln, Nebraska,
she said, "I'm the Princess of Shalimar."
Doubtless, I thought, at a loss for words
but not images, the air moist but without

the promise of a rain. She's not bending
pinkly like a pretzel but a body.
At this age, my first bona fide royalty.

15

Way up a sandy draw in the foothills
of the Whetstone Mountains I found cougar
tracks so fresh, damp sand was still
trickling in from the edges. For some reason
I knelt and sniffed them, quite sure
I was being watched by a living rock
in the vast, heat-blurred landscape.

16

I went to Tucson and it gave
me a headache. I don't know how.
Everyone's a cousin in this world.
I drove down a road of enormous houses
that encompass many toilets. Down hallways,
leaping left or right, you can crap at will.
A mile away a dead Mexican child slept
out in the desert on the wrong side of a mattress.

17

Up at the Hard Luck Ranch
there's a pyracantha bush full of red berries
right outside my study window.
In December after seven hard frosts
the birds arrive to eat the fermented berries.
The birds get drunk and unwary in this saloon
and the barn cats have a bird feast.
A phainopepla landed on my head, shrieking
when my eyebrow moved, booze on its bird breath.

18

My *zabuton* doubles as a dog bed. Rose sleeps
there, full to the fur with *mu*. Glanced in
on a moonlit night; her slight white figure coiled
on the green cushion, shaking with quail dreams.
Sensing me, an eye opens, single tail-wag. Back to sleep.
When she's awake, she's so awake I'm ashamed
of my own warm water dance, my sitting too long at the fire.

19

Time gets foreshortened late at night.
Jesus died a few days ago, my father
and sister just before lunch. At dawn
I fished, then hoed corn. Married at midmorning,
wept for a second. We were poor momentarily
for a decade. Within a few minutes I made
a round trip to Paris. I drank and ate during a parade
in my room. One blink, Red Mountain's still there.

20

More lion prints in our creek bed.
Right now in the light cool rain at midnight,
coyotes. Skunk stink laden in the mist.
Hidden moon, I don't want to go home yet.
Older, the flavors of earth are more delicious.

21

Just like today eternity is accomplished
in split seconds. I read that Old Nieh
in the wilderness vastness trained a mountain
tiger to carry his firewood. A black hole the size
of 300 billion suns is gobbling up the M87
galaxy because astronomers gave it a boring name.
Time passed in sitting begs mercy from the clock.

22

Out in an oak-lined field down the road
I again saw time, trotting in circles
around the far edges. The dog didn't notice
though she's usually more attentive. She lost
the Christmas watch I gave her
in a mountain canyon at the edge of earth.

23

It certainly wasn't fish who discovered water
or birds the air. Men built houses in part
out of embarrassment by the stars
and raised their children on trivialities
because they had butchered the god within themselves.
The politician standing on the church steps thrives
within the grandeur of this stupidity,
a burnt-out lamp who never imagined the sun.

24

The monk is eighty-seven. There's no fat
left on his feet to defend against stones.
He forgot his hat, larger in recent years.
By a creek he sees a woman he saw fifty summers
before, somehow still a girl to him. Once again his hands
tremble when she gives him a tin cup of water.

25

Talked to the God of Hosts about the Native American
situation and he said everything's a matter of time,
that though it's small comfort the ghosts have already
nearly destroyed us with the ugliness we've become,
that in a few hidden glades in North America
half-human bears still dance in imperfect circles.

26

This adobe is no protection against the flossy
sweep of stars that in recent nights burn pinprick
holes in my skin, mostly in the skull despite my orange
stocking cap, hunter's orange so you won't get shot
by other hunters, a color the stars readily ignore
with beams of white fire. O stars, you forsaken suns.

27

I confess that here and there in my life
there is a vision of a great brown toad
leaking words of love and doom through his skin,
excrescences that would kill anyone, given time,
his words tinged as they are with the shapes
of death, one drumbeat, a heartbeat, the skins
of gods a rug spread beneath our feet.

28

Lin-chi says, having thrown away your head so long
ago, you go on and on looking for it in the wrong
places. The head's future can be studied in a spadeful
of dirt. The delightful girl I loved 40 years back
now weighs, according to necrologists, 30 lbs. net.
Why does she still swim in the eddy in the river's bend?

29

The four seasons, the ten oaths, the nine colors, three vowels
that stretch forth their paltry hands to the seven flavors
and the one money, the official parody of prayer.
Up on this mountain, stumbling on talus, on the north face
there is snow, and on the south, buds of pink flowers.

30

It is difficult to imagine the wordless conversations
between Jesus and Buddha going on this very moment.
These androgynous blood brothers demand our imagination.
They could ask Shakespeare and Mozart to write words
and music, and perhaps a dozen others, but they've done so.
The vast asteroid on its way toward LA goes unmentioned.

31

Come down to earth! Get your head out of your ass!
Get your head out of the clouds! Stop mooning around!
Pay attention. Get to work on time.
Time and tide that wait for no man willingly
pause for the barearmed girl brushing her hair
in a brown pickup truck on a summer evening.

32

If that bald head gets you closer to Buddha
try chemotherapy. Your hair drops casually to the floor,
eyes widen until the skull aches, the heart beats like
Thumper's foot. Heaven's near at every second.
Now you've become that lamb you refused to eat.

33

I haven't accepted the fact that I'll never understand
the universe that I saw clearly for the first time
from our roof at nineteen in miniature *kensho*.
We belonged to each other. Love at first sight,
notwithstanding the child who stared in fear
at the northern lights and noted the Milky Way's convulsive
drift. A lone star perched on the mountain's
saddle now brings tears of doubt.

34

It wasn't until the sixth century that the Christians
decided animals weren't part of the kingdom of heaven.
Hoof, wing, and paw can't put money in the collection plate.
These lunatic shit-brained fools excluded our beloved creatures.
Theologians and accountants, the same thing really, join
evangelists on television, shadowy as viruses.

35

Everywhere I go I study the scars on earth's face,
including rivers and lakes. I'm not playing God
but assessing intent. In the Patagonia Mountains
you think, "small mines, pathetic deaths." In Cabeza Prieta
men boiled in their own blood, ground temperature 170°F.
Contrails of earthen scar-tissue stink of sulfur.
Gold & copper to buy the horse that died, the woman who left.

36

Ten thousand pointless equations left just after dawn,
the city's air heavy with the fat of countless dieters.
Saw Ummon strolling down Wilshire with Yunmen,
unperturbed, disappearing into each other, emerging
with laughter. Saw thirty-three green, waking parrots
watch a single black cat raising the dew as she walked
across the golf course, the first one to the seventh tee.

37

Beware, o wanderer, the road is walking too,
said Rilke one day to no one in particular
as good poets everywhere address the six directions.
If you can't bow, you're dead meat. You'll break
like uncooked spaghetti. Listen to the gods.
They're shouting in your ear every second.

38

Who remembers Wang Chi, "the real human like
multiplied sunlight"? No one, of course,
but his words are a lamp for any fool's feet.
He can't stop you from drowning, but he can keep
you out of the boat. This water's meant for careful wading,
but imagining my ears are gills, I still dive there at night.

39

In the next installment I'll give you Crazy Horse and Anne Frank,
their conversation as recorded by Matthew of Gospel fame,
who was wont, as all scriveners, to add a bit of this and that.
God is terse. The earth's proper scripture could be carried
on a three-by-five card if we weren't drunk on our own blood.

40

Walking the lakeshore at first moonlight I can see
feathers, stones, smooth spars, seaweed,
and the doe washed up from the Manitou two days ago
has been nearly eaten by the coyotes and ravens.
I poke my stick in the moon's watery face, then apologize.

41

Home again. It looked different for a moment.
The birds, while not decrepit, flew slower.
The dogs wagged and licked their greetings,
then went back to sleep, unmindful of airplanes.
The new moon said either gather yourself for your last
decade, or slow down big pony, fat snake shed another skin.

42

Inside people fear the outside; outside, the in.
But then I'm always halfway in or out the door,
most comfortable and at home in this fear,

knowing that falling is best for my nature.
Backward works well, or gathered for the leeward
pitch, imitate the sea in perfect balance in her torment.

43

The world is wrenched on her pivot, shivering. Politicians
and preachers are standing on their heads, shitting
out of their mouths. Lucky for us Stephen Mitchell
has restored the Gospels, returning the Jesus
I imagined at fourteen, offering up my clumsy life
in a damp shroud of hormones. Most of all he said,
"Pay attention"—Buddha nodding from the wings.

44

The dawn of the day we arrived, Abel Murrietta
saw a big mountain lion sitting behind our gate.
This is not an omen but a lion, the border guard
athwart our time in the chaos of the wild, the other
that draws us to speechlessness, the lion behind the gate
turning her head, flowing up the mountainside to sit,
gazing at twilight at the casita, creek bed, our shared thickets.

45

The sound of the dog's pawsteps move away
at the precise speed of his shadow. Nothing is blurred.
The bullet tumbled toward the girl's head at 1250 feet
per second. She wasn't the president, you say,
too young for politics. Despite theological gooseshit
the gods don't keep time in light-years. We're slowed
to the brutality of clocks. Listen to the alarm. Wake up.

46

Sometimes a toothpick is the most important thing;
others, a roll of toilet paper. If you forget red wine

and garlic you'll become honky new-age incense
dressed in invisible taffeta. Eat meat or not,
try weighing your virtue on that bathroom scale
right after you crap and shower. You're just a tree
that grows shit, not fruit. Your high horse is dead meat.

47

The girl's bottom is beautiful as Peacock's dancing bear
who is 70 miles from any of our fevered instruments.
Neither girl nor bear utter a word to the world in between
in its careless sump. The Virgin said zip to the Garrison.
If you can't dance without music jump into an icy lake.
Think of the brown girl at the A&W Root Beer stand.

48

It was Monday morning for most of the world
and my heart nearly exploded according
to my digital high-blood-pressure machine,
telling me I don't want to work anymore
as the highest-paid coal miner on earth.
I want to stay up on the surface and help the heron
who's been having trouble with his creek-bed landings.
He's getting old and I wonder where he'll be when he dies.

49

Jesus wants me for a sunbeam, I sang in Sunday
school a lifetime ago, way up in cold country
where there wasn't much sun. A sunbeam in winter
made one recoil, and everyone stared mutely upward.
The bogeyman still smiles, now from a glass
of whiskey, then from a farmhouse root cellar.
A little boy bred this man with no thought of the future.

50

If I'm not mistaken, everyone seems to go back
to where they came from, ending up right
where they began. Our beloved cat died today.
She liked to sit on my head during *zazen*
back when she was a child. I bow to her magnificence
beside which all churches and temples are privy holes.

51

A lovely woman in Minnesota owned a 100-year-old horse,
actually thirty-seven, but in horse years that's at least 100.
In the third grade I read there were eleven surviving
Civil War veterans. Under the photo captions it said
they were mostly drummer boys. Now both
horse and veterans are dead, the woman married, rid
of her binding sweetheart horse. I know these peculiar
things because I'm Jim, at the right place, the right time.

52

Once and for all there's no genetic virtue.
Our cherubic baldy flounces around, fresh out of Boulder,
in black robes, Japanese words quick on his tongue.
World War II nearly destroyed my family, so I ask
him to learn Chinese. He understands I'm a fool.
Then over a gallon of wine we agree there's no language
for such matters, no happiness outside consciousness. Drink.

53

Sam got tired of the way life fudged the big issues,
drank a quart of vodka, shot himself in the parking lot
of the tavern. How could a friend do this to himself?
It was relatively easy. Anyone can do it in a blink.
We won't look for black bears again out by Barfield Lakes.
Some don't go up in smoke but are strangled off the earth.

54

This morning I felt strong and jaunty in my mail-order
Israeli commando trousers. Up at Hard Luck Ranch I spoke
to the ravens in baritone, fed the cats with manly gestures.
Acacia thorns can't penetrate these mighty pants. Then out
by the corral the infant pup began to weep, abandoned.
In an instant I became another of earth's billion sad mothers.

55

I once thought that life's what's left over after
I extricate myself from the mess. I was writing a poem
about paying attention and microwaved a hot dog
so hot it burned a beet-red hole in the roof of my mouth.
Lucrezia Borgia got shit on her fingers by not paying
attention. Chanting a sutra, the monk stepped fatally
on the viper's tail. Every gun is loaded and cocked.

56

I've emerged from the seven-going-on-eight divorces
that have surrounded me for three years. I kept on saying
look at me, I'm not wise. I've advised seven suicides.
No one's separate. Our legs grow into the horse's body.
You've ridden each other too long to get off now.
You can make a clean getaway only if you cut off your heads.
All in vain. Life won't get simple until our minds do.
Embrace the great emptiness; say again, I don't do divorces.

57

Took my own life because I was permanently crippled,
put on backward, the repairs eating up money and time.
For fifty-seven years I've had it all wrong
until I studied the other side of the mirror.
No birth before death. The other way around.
How pleasant to get off a horse in the middle of the lake.

THE DAVENPORT LUNAR ECLIPSE

Overlooking the Mississippi
I never thought I'd get this old.
It was mostly my confusion about time
and the moon, and seeing the lovely way
homely old men treat their homely old women
in Nebraska and Iowa, the lunch-time
touch over green Jell-O with pineapple
and fried "fish rectangles" for $2.95.
When I passed Des Moines the radio said
there were long lines to see the entire cow
sculpted out of butter. The earth is right smack
between the sun and the moon, the Black waitress
told me at the Salty Pelican on the waterfront,
home from wild Houston to nurse her sick dad.
My good eye is burning up from fatigue
as it squints up above the Mississippi
where the moon is losing its edge to black.
It likely doesn't know what's happening to it,
I thought, pressed down to my meal and wine
by a fresh load of incomprehension.
My grandma lived in Davenport in the 1890s
just after Wounded Knee, a signal event,
the beginning of America's *Sickness unto Death*.
I'd like to nurse my father back to health
he's been dead thirty years, I said
to the waitress who agreed. That's why she
came home, she said, you only got one.
Now I find myself at fifty-one in Davenport
and drop the issue right into the Mississippi
where it is free to swim with the moon's reflection.
At the bar there are two girls of incomprehensible beauty
for the time being, as Swedish as my Grandma,

speaking in bad grammar as they listen to a band
of middle-aged Swede saxophonists braying
"Bye-Bye Blackbird" over and over, with a clumsy
but specific charm. The girls fail to notice me—
perhaps I should give them the thousand dollars
in my wallet but I've forgotten just how.
I feel pleasantly old and stupid, deciding
not to worry about who I am but how I spend
my days, until I tear in the weak places
like a thin, worn sheet. Back in my room
I can't hear the river passing like time,
or the moon emerging from the shadow of earth,
but I can see the water that never repeats itself.
It's very difficult to look at the World
and into your heart at the same time.
In between, a life has passed.

COYOTE NO. 1

Just before dark
watched coyote take a crap
on rock outcropping,
flexing hips (no time off)
swiveled owl-like to see
in all six directions:
sky above
earth below,
points of compass
in two half-circles.
There.
And there is no distance.
He knows the dreamer
that dreams his dreams.

TIME SUITE

Just seven weeks ago in Paris
I read Chuang Tzu in my dreams
and remembered once again
we are only here for a moment,
not very wild mushrooms,
just cartoon creatures that are blown apart
and only think they are put back together,
housepets within a house fire of impermanence.
In this cold cellar we see light
without knowing it is out of reach;
not to be owned but earned
moment by moment.
But still at dawn
in the middle of Paris's heart
there was a crow I spoke to
on the cornice far above my window.
It is the crow from home
that cawed above the immense
gaunt bear eating sweet-pea vines
and wild strawberries.
Today in the garden of Luxembourg
I passed through clumps of frozen vines
and saw a man in a bulletproof
glass house guarding stone,
a girl in the pink suit
of an unknown animal,
lovers nursing at each other's mouths.
I know that at my deathbed's urging
there'll be no clocks and I'll cry out
for heat not light.

This lady is stuck
on an elevator

shuddering
between the planets.

If life has passed this quickly,
a millennium is not all that long.
At fourteen
my sex fantasies
about Lucrezia Borgia:
I loved her name, the image
of her *rinascimento* undies,
her feet in the stirrups
of a golden saddle.
She's gone now
these many years.

Dad told me that we have time
so that everything won't happen at once.
For instance, deaths are spread out.
It would be real hard on people
if all the deaths for the year
occurred the same day.

Lemuribus vertebratis,
ossibus inter tenebras—
"For the vertebrate ghosts,
for the bones among the darknesses,"
quoted the great Bringhurst,
who could have conquered Manhattan
and returned it to the natives,
who might have continued dancing
on the rocky sward.

The stillness
of dog shadows.

Here is time:
In the crotch of limbs

the cow's skull grew
into the tree
and birds nested in the mouth
year after year.

Human blood still fertilizes
the crops of Yurp.
The humus owns names:
Fred and Ted from old Missouri,
Cedric and Basil from Cornwall,
Heinz and Hans from Stuttgart,
Fyodor and Gretel in final embrace
beside raped Sylvie,
clod to clod.

The actual speed of life
is so much slower
we could have lived
exactly seven times as long
as we did.

These calendars
with pussy photos
send us a mixed message:
Marilyn Monroe stretched out
in unwingèd victory,
pink against red and reaching
not for the president or Nembutal
but because, like cats,
we like to do so.
Someday
like rockets without shells
we'll head for the stars.

On my newly devised calendar
there are only three days a month.

All the rest is space
so that night and day
don't feel uncomfortable
within my confines.
I'm not pushing them around,
making them do this and that.

Just this once
cows are shuffling over the hard rock
of the creek bed.
Two ravens in the black oak
purling whistles, coos, croaks,
raven-talk for the dead wild cow's
hindquarter in the grass,
the reddest of reds,
hips crushed when lassoed.
The cow dogs, blue heelers,
first in line for the meat,
all tugging like Africa.
Later, a stray sister
sniffs the femur bone,
bawls in boredom or lament.
In this sun's clock the bone
will become white, whiter, whitest.

The soul's decorum
dissembles
when she understands
that ashes have never
returned to wood.

Even running downstream
I couldn't step
into the same river once
let alone twice.

At first the sound
of the cat drinking water
was unendurable,
then it was broken by a fly
heading north,
a curve-billed thrasher
swallowing a red berry,
a dead sycamore leaf
suspended on its way to earth
by a breeze so slight
it went otherwise unnoticed.

The girl in the many-windowed bedroom
with full light coming in from the south
and the sun broken by trees,
has never died.

My friend's great-grandfather
lived from 1798 until 1901.

When a place is finished
you realize it went
like a truly beloved dog
whose vibrance had made
you think it would last forever;
becoming slightly sick,
then well and new again
though older, then sick
again, a long sickness.
A home burial.

They don't appear to have
firmed up their idea when time
started so we can go it alone.
"From birth to old age
it's just you," said Foyan.

So after T'ang foolery and Tancred
(the Black Pope of Umbanda)
I've lived my life in sevens,
not imagining that God could holler,
"Bring me my millennium!"
The sevens are married to each other
by what dogs I owned at the time,
where I fished and hunted,
appealing storms, solstice dinners,
loves and deaths, all the events
that are the marrow of the gods.

O lachrymae sonorense.
From the ground
paced the stars through the ribs
of ocotillo, thin and black
each o'clock till dawn,
rosy but no fingers except
these black thin stalks
directing a billion bright stars,
captured time swelling outward
for us if we are blessed
to be here on the ground,
night sky shot with measured stars,
night sky without end
amen.

NORTH

The rising sun not beet
or blood,
but sea-rose red.

I amplified my heartbeat
one thousand times;
the animals at first confused,
then decided I was another
thunder being.

While talking directly to god
my attention waxed and waned.
I have a lot on my mind.

I worked out
to make myself as strong
as water.

After all these years
of holding the world together
I let it roll down the hill
into the river.

One tree leads
to another,
walking on
this undescribed earth.

I have dreamed
myself back
to where
I already am.

On a cold day
bear, coyote, cranes.
On a rainy night
a wolf with yellow eyes.
On a windy day
eleven kestrels looking
down at me.
On a hot afternoon
the ravens floated over
where I sunk
myself in the river.

Way out there
in unknown country
I walked at night
to scare myself.

Who is this other,
the secret sharer,
who directs the hand
that twists the heart,
the voice calling out to me
between feather and stone
the hour before dawn?

Somehow
I have turned into
an old brown man
in a green coat.

Having fulfilled
my obligations
my heart moves lightly
to this downward dance.

BEAR

Bear died standing up,
paws on log,
howling. Shot
right through the heart.

The hunter only wanted the head,
the hide. I ate her
so she wouldn't go to waste,
dumped naked in a dump,
skinless, looking like ourselves
if we had been flayed,
red as death.

Now there are bear dreams
again for the bear-eater: O god,
the bears have come down the hill,
bears from everywhere on earth,
all colors, sizes, filtering
out of the woods behind the cabin.

A half-mile up
I plummeted toward the river to die,
pushed there. Then pinions creaked;
I flew downstream until I clutched
a white pine, the mind stepping back
to see half-bird, half-bear,
waking in the tree to wet
fur and feathers.

Hotei and bear
sitting side by side,
disappear into each other.
Who is to say
which of us is one?

We loaded the thousand-pound logs
by hand, the truck swaying.
Paused to caress my friend and helper,
the bear beside me, eye to eye,
breath breathing breath.

And now tonight, a big blue
November moon. Startled to find myself
wandering the edge of a foggy
tamarack marsh, scenting the cold
wet air, delicious in the moonglow.
Scratched against swart hemlock,
an itch to give it all up, shuffling
empty-bellied toward home, the yellow
square of cabin light between trees,
the human shape of yellow light,
to turn around,
to give up again this human shape.

TWILIGHT

For the first time
far in the distance
he could see his twilight
wrapping around the green hill
where three rivers start,
and sliding down toward him
through the trees until it reached
the blueberry marsh and stopped,
telling him to go away, not now,
not for the time being.

RETURN TO YESENIN

25 years later

For only in praising is my heart still mine, so violently
do I know the world.
Rainer Maria Rilke, *Fragment of an Elegy*

I forgot to say that at the moment of death Yesenin
stood there like a misty-eyed pioneer woman trying
to figure out what happened. Were the children
still in the burning barn with the bawling cows?
He was too sensitive for words, and the idea of a rope
was a wound he couldn't stop picking at. To step
back from this swinging man twisting clockwise
is to see how we mine ourselves too deeply,
that way down there we can break through the soul's
rock into a black underground river that sweeps us away.
To be frank, I'd rather live to feed my dogs,
knowing the world says *no* in ten thousand ways
and *yes* in only a few. The dogs don't need another
weeping Jesus on the cross of Art, strumming the scars
to keep them alive, tending them in a private
garden as if our night-blooming tumors were fruit.
I let you go for twenty years and am now only
checking to see that you are really dead. There was an urge
to put a few bullets through Nixon's coffin or a big,
sharp wooden stake, and a girl told me she just saw
Jimi Hendrix at an AIDS benefit in Santa Monica.
How could I disbelieve her when her nipples
were rosebuds, though you had to avoid the snakes
in her hair. If you had hanged yourself in Argentina
you would have twisted counterclockwise. We can't
ask if it was worth it, can we? Any more than we can
ask a whale its mother's name. Too bad we couldn't

go to Mexico together and croak a few small gods
back to life. I've entered my third act and am
still following my songs on that thin line between
woods and field, well short of the mouth of your hell.

SONORAN RADIO

Looking at a big moon too long
rusts the eyes.

The raped girl stood all day naked
in the cold rain holding a plastic Virgin.
Their colors ran into the ground.

Tonight the Big Dipper poured down
its dark blood into the Sea of Cortez,
El Oso Grande, the hemorrhaged bear.

In the supermarket beef feet, chicken feet,
one lone octopus losing its charm.
An old woman named Octavia
who stared at my blind eye
carried out the 100 lb. gunnysack of pintos,
a bag of groceries in the other hand.

Just over the mountains
this other country, despised
and forsaken, makes more sense.
It admits people are complicated,
it tries to ignore its sufferings,
it cheats and loves itself,
it admits God might be made
of stone.

The red bird sits
on the dead brown snake.

The lobo admits its mistake
right after eating
the poisoned calf.

In the forms of death
we are all the same;
destinies are traded
at the very highest levels
in very high buildings
in clear view of the dump-pickers.

My heart and your heart!

The horses are running from flies.
Twenty-three horses run
around and around from the flies
in the big mesquite *retaque* corral
while five boys watch,
each one smaller
than the next biggest.

In the valley of the Toltecs
the American hunter from Palm Beach
shot one thousand white-winged doves
in a single day, all by himself.

The shark was nearly on shore
when it ate the child in three bites
and the mother kicked the shark in the eye.

The dopers killed the old doctor
in the mountain village,
but then the doctor's patients
stoned the dopers to death,
towing their bodies through town
behind Harley Davidsons.

It is the unpardonable music
stretching the soul
thinner than the skin.
Everyone knows they are not alone

as they suffer the music together
that gives them greater range
for greater suffering.

In the vision
the Virgin who sat in the sycamore
speaks in the voice
of the elegant trogon,
a bird so rare it goes
mateless for centuries.

The lagoon near the oil refinery
outside Tampico caught fire one night.
Everywhere tarpon were jumping
higher than a basketball hoop,
covered with oily flames,
the gill-plates rattling,
throwing off burning oil.

The black dove and white dove
intermarried, producing not brown doves,
but some white doves and black doves.
Down the line, however,
born in our garden a deep-yellow dove
more brilliant than gold
and blind as a bat.
She sits on my shoulder
cooing night songs in the day,
sleeping a few minutes at noon
and always at midnight, wakes
as if from a nightmare
screaming "Guadalupe!"

She said that outside Magdalena
on a mountainside
she counted thirteen guitarists

perched just below a cave
from which they tried to evoke
the usual flow
of blood and flowers.

Up in the borderland mountains
the moon fell slowly on Animas Peak
until it hit it directly
and broke like an egg,
spilling milk on the talus
and scree, sliding in a flood
through a dozen canyons.
The wind rose to fifty knots,
burning the moon
deep into the skin.

In a seaside restaurant
in Puerto Vallarta
a Bosnian woman killed a Serbian man
with a dinner fork,
her big arm pumping the tines
like a jackhammer
before the frightened diners
who decided not to believe it.
She escaped the police net,
fleeing into the green mountains,
fork in hand.

The praying mantis crawled
up the left nostril of our burro
and killed it.

Nightjars and goat suckers,
birds from the far edge of twilight
carrying ghosts from place to place—
Just hitching a ride, the ghosts

say to the birds, slapping
on the harness of black thread.
Even in *el norte* the whippoorwill's
nest is lined with the gossamer thread
of this ghost harness.

The cow dogs
tore apart
and ate
the pregnant housecat.

The gray hawk
(only twenty pair left in the U.S.)
flew close over
the vermilion flycatcher
perched on the tip
of the green juniper tree.

The waitress in the diner
where I ate my *menudo*
told me that Christ actually
bled to death. Back in those days
nails were the same as railroad spikes,
and the sun was hot as hell.
She sees the Resurrection
without irony or backspin.
"We are so lucky," she said.
"I couldn't live with all the things
I've done wrong in my life.
I feel better when I'm forgiven."

His dog sneezed
and crawled under a pickup
to get away from the sun.
The guitar and concertina music
swept down the mountainside

from the old cowboy's funeral,
hat and bridle
hanging from a white cross
in a cluster of admirable
plastic flowers.

The ravens are waiting
in the oak at twilight
for the coyotes to come
and open up the dead steer.
The ravens can't break through
cowhide with their beaks
and have been there since dawn
eager for the coyotes to get things started.
There's plenty for everyone.

These black beetles,
big as a thumb,
are locked in dead embrace
either in love or rage.

The bull does not want
to be caught. For five
hours and as many miles
on a hot morning
three cowboys and a half-dozen
cow dogs have worked
the bull toward the pen.
The truck is ready to take
him to the sale. He's known
as a baloney bull, inferring
his destiny: old, used up,
too lazy and tired to mount cows.
Meanwhile he's bawling, blowing
snot, charging, hooking a horn

at the horses, dogs, a stray tree.
Finally loaded, I said good-bye
to his blood-red eyes.
He rumbles, raises his huge neck
and bawls at the sun.

The cow dog licks her cancerous
and bloated teats.
Otherwise, she's the happiest
dog I know, always smiling,
always trying to help out.

I gave the woman seven roses
and she smiled, holding
the bouquet a couple of hours
at dusk before saying good-bye.
The next day I gave her
a brown calf and three chickens
and she took me to bed.
Over her shoulder a rose
petal fell for an hour.

From a thicket full
of red cardinals
burst seven black javelinas,
including three infants
the size of housecats.

There were so many birds
at the mountain spring
they drove one insane
at dawn and twilight;
bushes clotted with birds
like vulgar Christmas trees.
I counted thirteen hundred

of a hundred different kinds,
all frozen in place
when the gray hawk flew by,
its keening voice
the precise weight of death.

Magdalena kept taking off her clothes
for hours until there was nothing left,
not even a trace of moisture on the leather chair.
Perhaps it was because
she was a government employee
and had lost a child.
It was the sleight of her hand.
I never saw her again.

Another bowl of *menudo*
and she's on a rampage in a black
Guadalupe T-shirt: "We can't keep
working through the used part every day.
Everyone is tired of dope. Day in, day out,
the newspapers are full of dope news,
people are shot dead and not-so-dead,
sent to prison, and both police and criminals
are so bored with dope they weep
day and night, going about their jobs,
living and dying from this stupid dope.
There has to be more than dope. Understand?"

I dreamed here
before I arrived.
Chuck and whir
of elf owls above firelight,
dozens in the black oak
staring down into the fire
beyond which a thousand white sycamore

limbs move their legs into the night.
Sonoran moon gets red
again as she sets in the dust
we've colored with blood.

from THE SHAPE
OF THE JOURNEY:
NEW AND
COLLECTED POEMS

1998

to Lawrence Sullivan

Uncollected Poems

1968–1991

DREAMS

to D.G.

In the West the cities of the North
New York cool as a fresh apple,
girls who shower and change their underpants
marriage to Lee Remick
my distant love of the moment, dreams
of great power over nothing in particular,
poet dreams of "not since Dante . . ."
terror dreams that I dream awake
stream flowing through pigfarms
glutted with muck and shit
the largest watersnake on earth
upon its bank.

I dream not to dream
my other who stunned with waking
sees a scythe awake
moving through the dark
make me still, give me an eye
that moves toward earth, some giant
anti-observatory, glistening, huge thick
glass toward ground.

Stony Brook Holographs, 1968

HELLO WALLS

to Willie Nelson

How heavy I am. My feet sink into the ground and my knees
are rubbery, my head and brain propped with aluminum braces.
Life is short! I'm sinking through it at the speed of sound.
A feather is dropping with me in the vacuum. At bottom we'll
prove nothing except the fall is over for both of us. No matter
that I am richer than Satanta the Kiowa chief if you subtract
those millions of verdant acres which we did. In the prison
hospital he hurls himself headfirst from the third-story window.
Who wants to die like a white Christian? Even his animal skins
forgave him. But this has nothing to do with me—out the window
I can't see the army approach with cocked howitzers. There's
nothing but snow. How to lift myself out of this Egypt, wriggle
free, fly out of the page, out of the human condition like
a miraculous crow, like Satanta from the window, like birds
beneath the buffalo feet, griffins to a nest at the cathedral's
top. *Fly, fly away* the old song goes, climb a single note
and follow it, crazed mariachi, a shot tomcat, or Huxley
near death from cancer drops ten thousand hits of acid to go out
on a truly stupendous note, far above King David's zither,
the shriek of our space probe hitting Venus plum in the middle.

Aisling, Summer 1976

CLEAR WATER 4

for Irby

"Turn the world around the other way"
the song says. The continent tips us off,
the tide's unreplenished. And all this
in my yellow Chevy pickup. Outside
Topeka eighteen years ago, stopped while hitchhiking,
I say, "What's wrong?" and the deputy says "Nothin', thought
we'd have a chat." 104 in the shade with only
donuts in my guts and Kansas imitating Texas
to no particular purpose as if continents needed
purposes other than the way we skate around.
We'll find the rest of the bodies when the ice
melts in twelve years, she said. Tell Eileen
we pee outdoors with our legs spread because
we are still dogs, however Jungian. The Jungian Dog.
Dorn's wrong and right. In the saddlebag along
the road near Fallon you're best off with a Derringer
plus a .44 and a Bisley to shoot the old ones, a Sharps
for ghost buffalo, a .305 for cars. Who controls words
controls, only if you don't leave the bathroom.
Say that Max is heartbreaking music of Delius,
that we slip off earth without knowing we're on,
that it has to be waited out as a moving target
or sitting hidden on the mountain near Livingston Montana
with a buddha face.

Aisling, Summer 1976

SCRUBBING THE FLOOR THE NIGHT
A GREAT LADY DIED

Ruffian, 1972–1975

Sunday, with two weeks of heat lifting from us in a light rain. A good
day for work with the break in weather; then the race, the great horse
faltering, my wife and daughter leaving the room in tears, the dinner
strangely silent, with a dull, metallic yellow cast to the evening sun. We
turn from the *repeats,* once is so much more than enough. So the event
fades and late in the night writing in the kitchen I look at the floor soiled
by the Airedales in the heat wave, tracking in the brackish dirt from the
algae-covered pond. I want the grace of this physical gesture, filling the
pail, scrubbing the floor after midnight, sweet country music from the
radio and a drink or two; then the grotesque news bringing me up from
the amnesia of the floor. How could a creature of such beauty merely
disappear? I saw her as surely as at twilight I watched our own horses
graze in the pasture. How could she wake so frantic, as if from a terrible
dream? Then to continue with my scrubbing, saying it's only a horse but
knowing that if I cannot care about a horse, I cannot care about earth
herself. For she was so surely of earth, in earth; once so animate, sprung
in some final, perfect form, running, running, saying, *Look at me, look at
me, what could be more wonderful than the way I move, tell me if there's something
more wonderful, I'm the same as a great whale sounding.* But then who am I
sunk on the floor scrubbing at this bitterness? It doesn't matter. A great
creature died who took her body as far as bodies go toward perfection
and I wonder how like Crazy Horse she seems to leave us so far behind.

Natural World, 1982

A CEDAR POEM

for Rose Nimkiins Petoskey

If you've been frying fish, burn cedar.
If your old dog farts, burn cedar.
When the enemy leaves your home, burn cedar.
When a friend arrives, burn cedar.
When a child is born, burn cedar.
When the mind's light goes out, burn cedar.
In honor of your beloved dead, burn cedar.
Green boughs or dry wood, burn cedar.
It is the godsmoke, crackling, curling upward,
earth's breath that lets your heart breathe free.

April 25, 1991

Geo-Bestiary

1998

I can hear the cow dogs sleeping
in the dust, the windmill's
creak above thirty-three
sets of shrill mating birds.
The vultures fly above the corrals
so softly the air ignores them.
In all of the eons, past and future,
not one day clones itself.

I walked the same circular path today
in the creek bottom three times.
The first: a blur, roar of snowmelt
in creek, brain jumbling like the rolling
of river stones I watched carefully
with swim goggles long ago, hearing
the stones clack, click, and slow shuffle
along the gravel.
The second time: the creek is muddy,
a Mexican jay follows me at a polite
distance, the mind slows to the color
of wet, beige grass, a large raindrop
hits the bridge of my nose, the remote
mountain canyon has a fresh dusting
of snow. My head hurts pleasantly.
The third time: my life depends
on the three million two hundred seventy-seven
thousand three hundred and thirty-three
pebbles locked into the ground so I
don't fall through the thin skin of earth
on which there is a large coyote-turd full
of Manzanita berries I stepped over twice
without noticing it, a piece of ancient chert,

a fragment of snakeskin, an owl eye
staring from a hole in an Emory oak,
the filaments of eternity hanging in the earthly
air like the frailest of beacons seen
from a ship mortally far out in the sea.

    3

That dew-wet glistening wild iris
doesn't know where it comes from,
what drove the green fuse, the poet said,
up and out into the flowering I see
in the dank flat of the creek, my eye
drawn there by a Virginia rail who keeps
disappearing as they do, unlike the flower
which stays exactly in the place the heron stands
every day, the flower no doubt fertilized
by heron shit, or deeper—those rocky bones
my daughter found of the Jurassic lizard.
I said to the flower one brain-bleeding morning
that I don't know where I came from either
or where I'm going, such a banal statement
however true. O wild iris here today and soon gone,
the earth accepts us both without comment.

    4

Some eco-ninny released
at least a hundred tame white doves
at our creek crossing. What a feast
he innocently offered, coyotes in the yard
for the first time, a pair of great horned
owls, male and then the female
ululating, two ferruginous hawks,
and then at dawn today all song-
birds vamoosed at a startling shadow,

a merlin perched in the willow,
ur-falcon, bird-god, sweetly vengeful,
the white feathers of its meal,
a clump, among others, of red-spotted snow.

    5

The little bull calf gets his soft pink
nuts clipped off, then is released
in a state of bafflement, wandering
this way and that, perhaps feeling
a tad lighter, an actual lacuna.
But like the rest of the culture these creatures
are quick healers, have been dumbed down
so far from their wild state they think we're harmless.
In the old days sometimes longhorns,
like the Lakota had, had the sense to attack
Cavalry contingents, goring what could be gored.
Even now a few, not quite bred or beaten
into senescence, struggle wildly with these invisible
telemetric collars wrapped tightly around our necks
though it's fatally illegal to take them off.

    6

O BLM, BLM, and NFS,
what has your mother, the earth,
done to you that you rape and scalp
her so savagely, this beautiful woman
now mostly scar tissue?

    7

O that girl, only young men
dare to look at her directly
while I manage the most sidelong of glances:
olive-skinned with a Modigliani throat,

lustrous obsidian hair, the narrowest
of waists and high French bottom, ample
breasts she tries to hide in a loose blouse.
Though Latina her profile is from a Babylonian
frieze and when she walks her small white dog
with brown spots she fairly floats along,
looking neither left nor right, meeting no one's
glance as if beauty was a curse. In the grocery
store when I drew close her scent was jacaranda,
the tropical flower that makes no excuses.
This geezer's heart swells stupidly to the dampish
promise. I walk too often in the cold shadow
of the mountain wall up the arroyo behind the house.
Empty pages are dry ice, numbing the hands and heart.
If I weep I do so in the shower so that no one,
not even I, can tell. To see her is to feel
time's cold machete against my grizzled neck,
puzzled that again beauty has found her home in threat.

8

Many a sharp-eyed pilot has noticed
while flying in late October
that remnant hummingbirds rob piggyback
rides on the backs of southward-flying geese.

9

I hedge when I say "my farm."
We don't ever own, we barely rent this earth.
I've even watched a boulder age,
changing the texture of its mosses
and cracking from cold back in 1983.
Squinting, it becomes a mountain fissure.
I've sat on this rock so long we celebrate
together our age, our mute geologic destiny.

I know a private mountain range with a big bowl in its center that you find by following the narrowest creek bed, sometimes crawling until you struggle through a thicket until you reach two large cupped hands of stone in the middle of which is a hill, a promontory, which would be called a mountain back home. There is iron in this hill and it sucks down summer lightning, thousands and thousands of strokes through time, shattering the gigantic top into a field of undramatic crystals that would bring a buck a piece at a rock show. I was here in a dark time and stood there and said, "I have put my poem in order on the threshold of my tongue," quoting someone from long, long ago, then got the hell off the mountain due to tremors of undetermined source. Later that night sleeping under an oak a swarm of elf owls (*Micrathene whitneyi*) descended to a half-dozen feet above my head and a thousand white sycamores undulated in the full moon, obviously the living souls of lightning strokes upside down along the arroyo bed. A modern man, I do not make undue connections though my heart wrenches daily against the unknowable, almighty throb and heave of the universe against my skin that sings a song for which we haven't quite found the words.

11

Today the warblers undulate
fishlike, floating down,
lifting up with wing beats
while below me in the creek
minnows undulate birdlike,
floating down, lifting up with fin beats.
For a minute I lose the sense
of up and down.

12

I was hoping to travel the world
backward in my red wagon,
one knee in, the other foot pushing.

I was going to see the sights I'd imagined:
Spanish buildings, trellised with flowers,
a thousand Rapunzels brushing their long
black hair with street vendors singing
the lyrics of Lorca. I'd be towed
by a stray Miura over the green Pyrenees,
turning the bull loose before French customs.
At the edge of the forest René Char was roasting
a leg of lamb over a wood fire. We shared
a gallon of wine while mignonettes frolicked for us.
This all occurred to me forty-two
years ago while hoeing corn and it's time
for it all to come to pass along with my canoe
trip through Paris, with Jean Moreau trailing
a hand in the crystalline Seine, reading me Robert Desnos.
Why shouldn't this happen? I have to rid
myself of this last land mine, the unlived life.

13

Try as you might there's nothing
you can do about bird shadows
except try to head them off
and abruptly stop, letting them pass
by in peace. Looking up and down
at the very same moment is difficult
for a single-eyed man.
The ones coming behind you,
often cautious crows or ravens,
strike hard against the back and nape nerve.
Like most of life your wariness
is useless. You wobble
slightly dumbstruck, queasy,
then watch the shadow flit across
the brown wind-tormented grass.

14

As a geezer one grows tired of the story
of Sisyphus. Let that boulder stay
where it is and, by its presence,
exactly where it wished to be,
but then I'm old enough to have
forgotten what the boulder stood for?
I think of all of the tons of junk
the climbers have left up on Everest,
including a few bodies. Even the pyramids,
those imitation mountains, say to the gods,
"We can do it too." Despite planes
you can't get off the earth for long.
Even the dead meat strays behind, changing
shape, the words drift into the twilight
across the lake. I'm not bold enough
to give a poetry reading while alone
far out in the desert to a gathering
of saguaro and organ-pipe cactus
or listen to my strophes reverberate off a mountain
wall. At dawn I sat on a huge boulder
near Cave Creek deep in the Chiricahuas
and listened to it infer that it didn't want
to go way back up the mountain but liked
it near the creek where gravity bought
its passage so long ago. Everest told me
to get this crap off my head or stay at home
and make your own little pyramids.

15

Concha is perhaps seven. No one knows this cow dog's age for sure but
of course she could care less. Let us weep for the grandeur of rebellious
women. After a lifetime of service as a faithful tender of cattle her mind
has changed itself. She's become daffy and won't do her job. She's the

alpha bitch and leads the other cow dogs off on nightly runs after javelina and deer, maybe herding steers when she shouldn't, driving horses mad. They return worthlessly exhausted. Now the death sentence hangs above her mottled gray head like a halo of flies. She's chained to a mesquite, barking for hours without pause. I bring her biscuits on frosty mornings and she shivers without in her solitary confinement but inside it's obvious that she's hot and singing. Her head with its streaks of barbed-wire scars awaits the trigger finger. But then on a dark, wet morning, the grace of El Niño in this parched land, her reprieve arrives. She's being exiled to a ranch in Mexico just south of here where they need a crazed bitch who's kick-ass with range bulls. She'll drive one into an outhouse if that's what you want. This is a triumph beyond good-byes and I watch through the window as she leaves the barnyard in the back of a pickup, the wind and rain in her face, baring her teeth in anger or a smile, her uncertain future, which by nature she ignores, so much better to me than none.

16

My favorite stump straddles a gully a dozen
miles from any human habitation.
My eschatology includes scats, animal poop,
scatology so that when I nestle under this stump
out of the rain I see the scats of bear, bobcat,
coyote. I won't say that I feel at home
under this vast white pine stump, the roots
spread around me, so large in places no arms
can encircle them, as if you were under the body
of a mythic spider, the thunder ratcheting
the sky so that the earth hums beneath you.
Here is a place to think about nothing,
which is what I do. If the rain beats down
hard enough tiny creeks form beside my shit-strewn
pile of sand. The coyote has been eating mice,
the bear berries, the bobcat a rabbit. It's dry
enough so it doesn't smell except for ancient

wet wood and gravel, pine pitch, needles. Luckily
a sandhill crane nests nearby so that in June
if I doze I'm awakened by her cracked
and prehistoric cry, waking startled, feeling
the two million years I actually am.

17

I was sent far from my land of bears.
It wasn't an asylum but a resting place
to get well buttoned-up against my fugal state
wherein whirl is both the king and queen,
the brain-gods who stir a thousand revolutions
a second the contents of this graying cocotte.
Stop it please. Please stop it please.
There was one other poet from Yankeeland
who rubbed himself, including private parts,
with sandpaper. His doctor searched his room,
even his anus where he had secreted a tightly
bound roll. Across the wide yard and women's
quarters a lovely soprano sang TV jingles.
One day it was, "Fly the friendly skies of United,"
over and over. Her friend fed her peanut butter
and marshmallows to quell her voice, plus
a daily goblet of Thorazine. If you dive down deep
enough there are no words to bring you up. Not my
problem. If you fly too high there are no words
to help you land. I went back to my land of bears
and learned to bob like an apple on the river's surface.

18

I was commanded, in a dream naturally,
to begin the epitaphs of thirty-three friends
without using grand words like love pity pride
sacrifice doom honor heaven hell earth:

1. O you deliquescent flower
2. O you always loved long naps
3. O you road-kill Georgia possum
4. O you broken red lightbulb
5. O you mosquito smudge fire
6. O you pitiless girl missing a toe
7. O you big fellow in pale-blue shoes
8. O you poet without a book
9. O you lichen without tree or stone
10. O you lion without a throat
11. O you homeless scholar with dirty feet
12. O you jungle bird without a jungle
13. O you city with a single street
14. O you tiny sun without an earth
15. Forgive me for saying good-night quietly
16. Forgive me for never answering the phone
17. Forgive me for sending too much money
18. Pardon me for fishing during your funeral
19. Forgive me for thinking of your lovely ass
20. Pardon me for burning your last book
21. Forgive me for making love to your widow
22. Pardon me for never mentioning you
23. Forgive me for not knowing where you're buried
24. O you forgotten famous person
25. O you great singer of banal songs
26. O you shrike in the darkest thicket
27. O you river with too many dams
28. O you orphaned vulture with no meat
29. O you who sucked a shotgun to orgasm
30. Forgive me for raising your ghost so often
31. Forgive me for naming a bird after you
32. Forgive me for keeping a nude photo of you
33. We'll all see God but not with our eyes

19

I sat on a log fallen over a river and heard
that like people each stretch had a different voice
varying with the current, the nature
of its bed and banks, logjams, boulders,
alder or cedar branches, low-slung
and sweeping the current, the hush of eddies.
In a deep pool I saw the traces of last night's moon.

20

Who is it up to if it isn't up to you?
In motels I discover how ugly I am,
the mirrors at home too habitual to be noted.
I chose methodically to be anti-beautiful,
Christian fat keeps you safe from adultery!
With delight I drown my lungs in smoke
and drink that extra bottle of wine
that brings me so much closer to the gods.
Up the road a dozen wetbacks were caught
because one stopped at a ranch house, desperate
for a cigarette. Olive oil and pork sausage
are pratfalls, an open secret to the stove.
In the newspaper I read that thirty-two
dairy cows ate themselves to death on grain
by shaking loose an automatic feeder
("They just don't know any better," the vet said).
Of course false modesty is a family habit.
The zone-tailed hawk looks like and mimics
the harmless turkey vultures with which it often
flies for concealment, stoops in flight and devours
the creatures who thought, "It's just a vulture."

21

In the Cabeza Prieta from a hillock I saw no human sign for a thousand square miles except for a stray intestinal vapor trail with which we mar the sky. I naturally said, "I'm alone." The immense ocotillo before me is a thousand-foot-high rope to heaven but then you can't climb its spiny branches. In Daniel's Wash I heard and saw the great mother of crotalids, a rattler, and at a distance her rattles sounded exactly like Carmen Miranda's castanets, but closer, a string of firecrackers. In 1957 in New York I was with Anne Frank who was trying to be a writer but they wouldn't buy her dark stories. We lived on MacDougal south of Houston and I worked as a sandhog digging tunnels until I was crushed to death. She cooked fairly well (flanken, chicken livers, herring salad). Now Ed Abbey rides down from the Growler Mountains on a huge mountain ram, bareback and speechless. This place is a fearsome goddess I've met seven times in a decade. She deranges my mind with the strangest of beauties, her Venusian flora mad to puncture the skin. It's ninety degrees and I wonder if I'm walking so far within her because I wish to die, so parched I blow dust from my throat. Finally I reach the hot water in my car and weep at the puny sight. Is this what I've offered this wild beauty? Literally a goddamned car, a glittering metallic tumor.

22

"Life's too short to be a whore anymore,"
I sang out to the Atlantic Ocean
from my seaside room in St. Malo,
the brain quite frugal until I took
a long walk seaward at low tide
and watched closely old French ladies
gathering crustaceans. When they left
they shook their fingers saying, "*marée, marée,*"
and I watched them walk away toward shore
where I had no desire to go. A few
stopped and waved their arms wildly.
The tide! The tide goes out, then comes in

in this place huge, twenty feet or so,
the tidal bore sweeping slowly in
but faster than me. I still didn't want to leave
because I was feeling like a very old whore
who wanted to drown, but then this wispy
ego's pulse drifted away with a shitting gull.
Before I die I must eat the three-leveled
"plateau" of these crustaceans with two bottles
of Sancerre. It's dinner that drives the beaten
dog homeward, tail half-up, half-down,
no dog whore but trotting legs, an empty stomach.

23

My soul grew weak and polluted during captivity, a zoo creature, frantic
but most often senescent. One day in the Upper Peninsula I bought a
painting at a yard sale of the supposed interior of a clock. The tag said,
"Real Oil Painting Nineteen Bucks." People around me grinned, knowing
I wasn't a yard-sale pro. Never go to a supermarket when you're hungry,
my mother said, or a yard sale after a Côtes du Rhône. The painting was
quite dark as there's little sunlight within clocks but the owners had wiped
it with oil and there was a burnished glow to its burnt sienna. I couldn't
see into the cavern in the center but I didn't have my glasses with me. Back
at the cabin I was lucky enough to have the magnifying glass that comes
with the *Compact Oxford English Dictionary,* the true source of agony. There
were grinning mice sailing along on Eilshemius-type clouds in a corner of
the clock's metallic shell, and miniature assemblage print that said, "fly-
ways, byways, highways" in a lighter cavern, also "Je souffre but so what,"
also "I am a buggered cherubim," an alarming statement. On the central
cavern walls there were the usual cogs and wheels, straightforward, not
melting Dalí-esques. In the lower left-hand corner it was signed "Felicia"
with a feminine bottom from which emerged a candle, lighting the art-
ist's name. Here was a wedding present for a couple you didn't really like.
Children, even future artists, should never take the backs off of discarded
Big Bens. They'll never make sense of these glum, interior stars with
their ceaseless ticking, saying that first you're here and then you're not.

24

A whiff of that dead bird along the trail
is a whiff of what I'd smell like
if I was lucky enough to die
well back in the woods or out in the desert.
The heavy Marine compass doesn't remind
me that I'm somewhere in America,
likely in northern Michigan by the maple and alder,
the wildly blooming sugarplum and dogwood,
wandering aimlessly in great circles
as your gait tends to pull you slowly aside,
my one leg slightly distorted at birth
though I was fifty before my mother told me,
but then from birth we're all mortally wounded.
When I was a stray dog in New York City
in 1957, trying to eat on a buck a day
while walking thousands of blocks
in that human forest I thought was enchanted,
not wanting to miss anything but missing
everything because at nineteen dreams
daily burst the brain, dismay the senses,
the interior weeping drowning your steps,
your mind an underground river
running counter to your tentative life.
"Our body is a molded river," said wise Novalis.
Bloody brain and heart, also mind and soul finally
becoming a single river, flowing in a great circle,
flowing from darkness to blessed darkness,
still wondering above all else what kind of beast am I?

25

The resplendent female "elegant trogon,"
her actual name, appeared at my study
window the very moment my heroine died

(in a novel of course) so that my hair
bristled like the time a lion coughed right
outside our thin screen-walled shack.
What does this mean? Nothing whatsoever,
except itself, I am too quick to answer.
This bird is so rare she never saw it.
I had expected her soul to explode
into a billion raindrops, falling on the farm
where she was born, or far out in the ocean
where she drowned, precisely where I once saw
two giant sea turtles making love.
Full fathom five thy lovely sister lies,
tumbling north in the Gulfstream current,
but then the soul rose up as vapor, blown west-
ward to the Sea of Cortez, up a canyon, inhabiting
this quetzal bird who chose to appear at my window.
This all took three seconds by my geologic watch.

        26
In Montana the badger looks at me in fear
and buries himself where he stood
in the soft sandy gravel
only moments ago. I have to think
it's almost like our own deaths
assuming we had the wit to save money
by digging our own graves or gathering
the wood for the funeral pyre.
But then the badger does it to stay alive, carrying
his thicket, his secret room in his powerful claws.

        27
She said in LA of course that she'd be reincarnated as an Indian princess,
and I tried to recall any Lakota or Anishinabe princesses. I said how about
wheat berries, flakes of granite on a mountainside, a green leaf beginning

to dry out on the ground, a microbe within a dog turd, the windfall apple
no one finds, an ordinary hawk fledgling hitting a high-tension wire, apri-
cot blossoms from that old fallow tree? Less can be more she agreed. It
might be nice to try something else, say a tree that only gets to dance if
the wind comes up but I refuse to believe this lettuce might be Grandma
—more likely the steak that they don't serve here. We go from flesh to
flesh, she thought, with her nose ring and tongue tack, inscrutable to me
but doubtless genetic. There is no lesser flesh whether it grows feathers
or fur, scales or hairy skin. The coyote wishes to climb the moonbeam
she cannot be, the wounded raven to stay in the cloud forever. Whatever
we are we don't quite know it, waiting for a single thought as lovely as
April's sycamore.

28

The wallet is as big as earth
and we snuffle, snorkel, lip lap
at money's rankest genitals,
buried there as money gophers, money worms,
hibernate our lives away with heads
well up money's asshole, eating, drinking,
sleeping there in money's shitty dark.
That's money, folks, the perverse love
thereof, as if we swam carrying an anchor
or the blinders my grandpa's horses wore
so that while ploughing they wouldn't notice
anything but the furrow ahead, not certainly
the infinitely circular horizon of earth.
Not the money for food and bed but the endless
brown beyond that. I'm even saving
up for my past, by god, healing the twelve-hour
days in the fields or laying actual concrete blocks.
The present passes too quickly to notice
and I've never had a grip on the future,
even as an idea. As a Pleistocene dunce

I want my wife and children to be safe
in the past, and then I'll look up from my money-
fucking grubbing work to watch the evening
shadows fleeing across the green field next door,
tethered to these shadows dragging toward night.

29

How can I be alone when these brain cells
chat to me their million messages
a minute. But sitting there in the ordinary
trance that is any mammal's birthright, say on a desert
boulder or northern stump, a riverbank,
we can imitate a barrel cactus, a hemlock tree,
the water that flows through time as surely
as ourselves. The mind loses its distant
machine-gun patter, becomes a frog's
occasional croak. A trout's last jump in the dark,
a horned owl's occasional hoot,
or in the desert alone at night
the voiceless stars light my primate
fingers that I lift up to curl
round their bright cosmic bodies.

30

How much better these actual dreams
than the vulgar "hoped for," the future's
golden steps which are really old
cement blocks stacked at a door that can
never open because we
are already inside.
Is all prayer just barely short of the lip
of whining as if, however things are,
they can't possibly be quite right
(what I don't have I probably should),

the sole conviction praying for sick children?
But true dreams arrived without being
summoned, incomprehensibly old and without
your consent: the animal that is running
is you under the wide gray sky, the sound
of those banal drumbeats is the heart's true reflection,
all water over your head is bottomless,
the sky above we've learned quite without limits.
Running, he wears the skins of animals
to protect his ass in the misery of running,
stopping at the edge of the green earth
without the fulsome courage to jump off.
He builds a hut there and makes the music
he's never heard except in the pulse of dreams.

31

A few long miles up Hog Canyon
this rare late-March heat is drawing forth
the crotalids from their homes of earth and rock
where they had sensed me scrambling over them
while hunting quail. It is the dread
greenish brown Mojave I fear the most,
known locally as "dog killer," lifting
its wary head higher than you think possible,
coiling its length beneath itself
as if a boxer could carry a single, fatal punch.
This is the farthest reach from the petting zoo
like my Africa's dream black mamba.
I tell her I'm sorry I shot a cousin rattler
in our bedroom. How idiotic. She's a cocked
.357 snake, rattling "Get the hell out of here.
This land is my land when I awake.
Walk here in the cool of morning or not at all."
She's my childhood myth of the kiss of death

and I'm amazed how deftly I fling myself backward
down a long steep hill, my setter Rose frightened
by my unconscious, verbless bellows. Perhaps
if I'm dying from some painful disease
I'll catch and hold you like Cleopatra's asp
to my breast, a truly inventive suicide.

    32

How the love of Tarzan in Africa haunted my childhood, strapped with
this vivid love of an imaginary wild, the white orphan as king of nature
with all creatures at his beck and call, monkey talk, Simba! Kreegah!
Gomanganini! The mysterious Jane was in his tree house in leather loin-
cloth and bra before one had quite figured out why she should be there.
Perhaps this was all only a frantic myth to allay our fear of the darkest
continent and help us defeat a world that will never be ours after we had
tried so hard to dispose of our own Indians. The Blacks were generally
grand if not influenced too much by an evil witch doctor, or deceived
by venal white men, often German or French, while a current Tarzan,
far from the great Johnny Weissmuller, has the body builder's more than
ample tits, tiny waist and blow-dried hair, Navajo booties somehow, while
the newest Jane has a Dutch accent and runs through a Mexican forest (if
you know flora) in shorts and cowboy boots screaming in absolute alarm
at nearly everything though she simply passed out when a Black tied her
rather attractively way up in a tree. What can we make of this Aryan myth
gone truly bad, much worse than Sambo's tigers turning to butter for his
pancakes, much more decrepit than noble Robin Hood; or how we made
our landscape safe for mega-agriculture and outdoor cow factories by
shooting all the buffalo, and red kids fast asleep in tents at Sand Creek
and elsewhere, the Church climbing to heaven on the backs of Jews; or
that we could destroy the Yellow Plague in Vietnam? The girl or boy
with their brown dog in the woods on Sunday afternoon must learn first
to hold their noses at requests to march. But Tarzan swinging over the
whole world on his convenient vines, knows that bugs, snakes, beasts
and birds, are of the angelic orders, safe forever from men and their

thundersticks and rancid clothes, and Jane's lambent butt and English
accent singing him to sleep in their treetop home, she waving down at
the profuse eyelashes of a sleeping elephant.

33

Coyote's bloody face makes me
wonder what he ate, also reminds
me of when I sliced my hand
sharpening the scythe to cut weeds.
What the hell is this blood we mostly see
on TV, movies, the doctor's office, hospitals?
The first two remote and dishonest,
the second two less so but readily expunged,
but not the massive dark-red pool beneath
the shrimper's neck in 1970, his trachea
a still-pulsing calamari ring.
I don't care how many quarts of this red
juice I'm carrying around as it flows
through its pitch-dark creeks and rivers.
We must learn to rock our own cradles.
I don't want to get ahead or behind myself
fueled by this red gasoline, legs stretching
as if eager to pass over the edge of earth
or trotting backward into the inglorious past.
Tonight its pump is thumping as when an airplane's
engine stutters, thinking too much of those I loved
who died long ago, the girl sitting in the apple
tree, the red sun sinking beneath her feet,
how god plucked her off earth with his careless
tweezers because she plucked a flower with her toes.

34

Not how many different birds I've seen
but how many have seen me,
letting the event go unremarked
except for the quietest sense of malevolence,
dead quiet, then restarting their lives
after fear, not with song, which is reserved
for lovers, but the harsh and quizzical
chatter with which we all get by:
but if she or he passes by and the need
is felt we hear the music that transcends all fear,
and sometimes the simpler songs that greet sunrise,
rain or twilight. Here I am.
They sing what and where they are.

BRAIDED CREEK

A CONVERSATION IN POETRY,
WITH TED KOOSER

2003

to Dan Gerber

INTRODUCTION

It plays to our western point of view to assign a literary work some part of its value on the virtue of its author's name. If Olive Oyl is touched by the poem she finds in the spinach can, should she care whether it was written by Popeye or Bluto? This little book is an assertion in favor of poetry and against credentials.

Jim Harrison
Ted Kooser

How one old tire leans up against
another, the breath gone out of both.

Old friend,
perhaps we work too hard
at being remembered.

Which way will the creek
run when time ends?
Don't ask me until
this wine bottle is empty.

While my bowl is still half full,
you can eat out of it too,
and when it is empty,
just bury it out in the flowers.

All those years
I had in my pocket.
I spent them,
nickel-and-dime.

Each clock tick falls
like a raindrop,
right through the floor
as if it were nothing.

In the morning light,
the doorknob, cold with dew.

The Pilot razor-point pen is my
compass, watch, and soul chaser.
Thousands of miles of black squiggles.

Under the storyteller's hat
are many heads, all troubled.

At dawn, a rabbit stretches tall
to eat the red asparagus berries.

The big fat garter snake
emerged from the gas-stove burner
where she had coiled around the pilot light
for warmth on a cold night.

Straining on the toilet
we learn how
the lightning bug feels.

For sixty-three years I've ground myself
within this karmic mortar. Yesterday I washed
it out and put it high on the pantry shelf.

All I want to be
is a thousand blackbirds
bursting from a tree,
seeding the sky.

Republicans think that all over the world
darker-skinned people are having more fun
than they are. It's largely true.

Faucet dripping into a pan,
dog lapping water,
the same sweet music.

The nuthatch is in business
on the tree trunk,
fortunes up and down.

Oh what dew
these mortals be.
Dawn to dark.
One long breath.

The wit of the corpse
is lost on the lid of the coffin.

A book on the arm of my chair
and the morning before me.

Everyone thought I'd die
in my twenties, thirties, forties, fifties.
This can't go on forever.

There are mornings
when everything brims with promise,
even my empty cup.

Two squirrels fight
to near death,
red blood flecking green grass,
while chipmunks continue feeding.

What pleasure: a new straw hat
with a green brim to look through!

Rowing across the lake
all the dragonflies are screwing.
Stop it. It's Sunday.

Throw out the anchor
unattached to a rope.
Heart lifts as it sinks.
Out of my mind at last.

On every topographic map,
the fingerprints of God.

When we were very poor one spring
I fished a snowy river and caught
a big trout. It changed our lives
that day: eating, drinking, singing, dancing.

Lost: Ambition.
Found: A good book,
an old sweater,
loose shoes.

Years ago
when I became tough as a nail
I became a nail.

An old song from my youth:
"I'm going to live, live, live
until I die." Well, perhaps not.

Still at times I'm a dumb little boy
fishing from a rowboat in the rain
wanting to give the family a fish dinner.

Only today
I heard
the river
within the river.

Clear summer dawn,
first sun steams moisture
redly off the cabin roof,
a cold fire. Passing raven
eyeballs it with a *quawk*.

The rabbit is born
prepared for listening,
the poet just for talk.

As a boy when desperate I'd pray with bare knees
on the cold floor. I still do,
but from the window I look like an old man.

Two buzzards
perched on a hay bale
and a third just gliding in.

I want to describe my life in hushed tones
like a TV nature program. *Dawn in the north.*
His nose stalks the air for newborn coffee.

Turtle has just one plan
at a time, and every cell
buys into it.

The biomass of ants,
their total weight on earth,
exceeds our own.
They welcome us to their world
of small homes, hard work, big women.

But the seventeen-year cicada
has only one syllable.

What prizes and awards will I get for revealing
the location of the human soul? As Nixon said,
I know how to win the war but I'm not telling.

Some days
one needs to hide
from possibility.

She climbed the green-leafed apple tree
in her green Sunday dress. Her white panties
were white as the moon above brown legs.

Is this poem a pebble,
or a raindrop coated with dust?

Each time I go outside the world
is different. This has happened
all my life.

When I found my tracks in the snow
I followed, thinking that they might
lead me back to where I was. But
they turned the wrong way and went on.

I schlump around the farm
in dirty, insulated coveralls
checking the private lives of mice.

I heard the lake cheeping
under the ice, too weak
to break through the shell.

Nothing to do.
Nowhere to go.
The moth just drowned
in the whiskey glass.
This is heaven.

Wind in the chimney
turns on its heel
without crushing the ashes.

Way out in the local wilderness
the only human tracks are mine, left foot
pigeon-toed, aimless.

Trust snow to keep a secret.

Old white soup bowl
chipped like a tooth,
one of us is always empty.

I used to have time by the ass
but now I share it in common
and it's going away.

These legs
are wearing out.
Uphill, downhill.
They'll love
their flat earth rest.

Old centipede
can't keep himself
from leaving.

My dog girlfriend Rose was lost
for three endless days and nights
during which I uncontrollably sobbed.

Fear is a swallow
in a boarded-up warehouse,
seeking a window out.

The brown stumps
of my old teeth
don't send up shoots
in spring.

In New York
on a wet
and bitter street
I heard a crow from home.

Mouse nest in the toe of my boot,
have I been gone that long?

I haven't forgotten
to look in the mirror,
I just don't
do it anymore.

When Time picks apples,
it eats them with the yellow teeth
of bees.

We flap our gums, our wattles, our
featherless wings in non-native air
to avoid being planted in earth,
watching the bellies of passing birds.

On its stand on the empty stage
the tuba with its big brass ear
enjoys the silence.

So what if women
no longer smile to see me?
I smile to see them!

Why do I behave so badly?
Just because. That's still
a good answer.

Now an outlander, once a poet in NY
crisscrossing Gotham for food and drink,
the souls of Lorca and Crane a daily solstice.

Open the shoe-store door
and a bell rings:
two shoehorns on a shoelace.

Let go of the mind, the thousand blue
story fragments we tell ourselves
each day to keep the world underfoot.

How foolish the houseplant looks
as it offers its droopy leaves
like hands to be kissed.

I trace my noble ancestry back
to the first seed, the first cell
that emerged reluctantly from the void.

The crow comes from
a broken home.
She is so loud because
no one will listen.

Dog days
for me and the dogs,
afloat clockwise
in the river's eddy.

The deer hung flapping
high on the buffalo fence,
pushed by an inner wind.

The pigeon
has swallowed a fountain!
Listen!

The goofy young bald eagle
is ignored by the seagulls and ravens
as these enemies share
a barrel of fish heads and guts.

On Everest there are pink concealed
gnats that when falling
learn decisively that they can't fly.

Surely someone will help
the mourning mourning dove,
but who, but who?

Trees stay in place.
Fish spend a lifetime underwater.
Our last track is a skull.

A coffin handle
leaves a lasting impression
on a hand.

Oh the dark, rank, brackish rut
of money. The news from the inside
is fine. Outside, a sucking cold vacuum.

A nephew rubs the sore feet
of his aunt,
and the rope that lifts us all toward grace
creaks in the pulley.

The cups of the tulips
tip forward, spilling their snow.

Sometimes my big front teeth bite
my lower lip and my food gets bloody.
What is this argument all about?

"Do you feel your age?" she asked,
so I squeezed my age till it hurt,
then set it free.

Rising from a cramped position
before the fireplace I discover
that there's blood in my legs.

So much to live for.
Each rope rings
a different bell.

Fifty-two degrees at noon, July 2.
At the senior citizens' carwash
all the oldsters try to look vigorous.

The mirror, backed in black,
and grief behind each face.

When you drink from dawn's light
you see the bottom of the cup.

I am wherever I find myself to be,
of all places. At 6 a.m. the Paris lights
shine through the cool November rain.
Only a few hours ago there was a moon.

My new trifocals hurt my nose.
All that lifting them up and down
just to find my way.

The fat snake's gone this year.
She's been transplanted to a place
she won't hear my startled yelp
when she emerges from the stove top.

Winter knows
when a man's pockets
are empty.

Old willow
taps the river
with his cane.

I was paralyzed from the waist up
for three months. My feet walked me.
The birds all turned brown. I fell
out of a tree I hadn't climbed.

An empty boat
will volunteer for anything.

When the dollhouse was built in a month's work
a red ghost was trapped in a tiny closet.
You can hear its breathing a thousand miles.

Gentle readers, tomorrow I undergo
radical brain surgery, but don't worry.
Win some. Lose some. Mostly ties.

Wanted: Looking for owl roosts
for pellets for Science project.
Call Marli.

In each of my cells Dad and Mom
are still doing their jobs. As always,
Dad says *yes,* Mom *no.* I split the difference
and feel deep sympathy for my children.

At the tip of memory's
great funnel-cloud
is the nib of a pen.

At my cabin
to write a poem
is to throw an egg across
the narrow river into the trees.

A dozen dead houseflies,
bits of green glass from the bottle
of summer, smashed on the sill.

Getting older I'm much better at watching
rain. I skip counting individual drops
in favor of the general feeling of rain.

Like a fist, the toad
knocks on the dirt road
wanting in.

Strange world indeed:
a poet keeping himself awake
to write about insomnia.

The sparrow is not busy,
but hungry.

I remember being a cellular oyster
in a tiny geode before being prodded
into a world of lilacs and blood.

Next to a gravestone,
a green tin cup
brimful of shadows.
Must we drink?

There is just one of us.
Already you are what you are.
Old rooster crowing with a stretched neck.

I might have been a welder,
kneeling at a fountain of sparks
in my mask of stars.

The moon put her white hands
on my shoulders, looked into my face,
and without a word
sent me on into the night.

Coming home late from the tavern.
A mouse has drowned in the toilet.
A metaphor of the poet, I think.
But no, the death of a glorious mouse.

The drunken man
spills most of his importance
on his shoes.

After carefully listing my 10,000 illusions
I noticed that nearly all that I found
in the depths was lost in the shallows.

Raindrops on your glasses;
there you go again,
reading the clouds.

Dewdrops are the dreams
of the grass. They linger, shining,
into the morning.

If you can awaken
inside the familiar
and discover it strange
you need never leave home.

The birds,
confused by rain clouds,
think it's evening.

Another spring,
and a long trail of grease ants
over the breadboard.

The girl with blue shorts and brown legs
the color of the dog beside her
ran through the green orchard
kicking her butt with her own heels.

Lost for a while,
I found her name
when I scratched through
my hair.

To prevent leakage,
immerse yourself in clouds and birds,
a jubilant drift downward.

With her brush, the artist
touches one part of her life
with another.

You told me you couldn't see
a better day coming,
so I gave you my eyes.

How can Lorca say he's only the pulse
of a wound that probes to the opposite side?
I'm wondering if he ever rowed a boat backwards.

The black sleeve falls back
from the scalded fist:
a turkey vulture.

At 62 I've outlived 95 percent
of the world. I'll be home
just before dark.

All my life
I've been in the caboose
with blind glands
running the locomotive.

Letters from beautiful women.
What do they tell me?

Woodpecker,
why so much effort
for such little gain?

In Mexico the big, lovely
woman took off her blue outfit
becoming a normal woman
only more so.

The way a springer spaniel
hops through deep grass,
I was once a lover like that.

When she left me
I stood out in the thunderstorm,
hoping to be destroyed by lightning.
It missed, first left, then right.

When a hammer sings
its head is loose.

Actresses I've known grow younger
while I don't, but after my Vietnam head
wounds, I won three Olympic gold medals.

The one-eyed man must be fearful
of being taken for a birdhouse.

As a child I loved to square-dance,
a junior beast sniffing my fingers
after it touched a new girl's hand.

Reading poetry late at night
to try to come back to life.
Almost but not quite.

Now it's the body's dog, pain,
barking and barking.
A stranger has come to the gate
with an empty sack.

The hay in the loft
misses the night sky,
so the old roof
leaks a few stars.

Rain clouds gone,
and muddy paw prints
on the moon.

I've never learned from experience.
What else is there? you ask.
How about ninety billion galaxies.

What is it the wind has lost
that she keeps looking for
under each leaf?

I grow older.
I still like women, but mostly
I like Mexican food.

Sleeping on my right side I think
of God. On my left side, sex.
On my back I snore with my dog.

Some nights are three nights long,
some days a mere noon hour, then whistled
back to work, the heart dredging sludge.

The nightmare we waken from,
grateful, is somebody else's life.

Mirrors have always given the wrong
impression of me. So do other people.
So do I. Let's stop this right now.

The face you look out of
is never the face
your lover looks into.

The crumpled candy wrapper
is just another flower
to the rain.

How can I disappoint myself?
How many are within this brown
and wrinkled skin? Just one in pieces.

The stones turn their backs to us.
Our lives are light as flyspecks.

What has become
of the great hunter?
Today he won't kill flies.

Out in a field, an immense empty
pasture, clouds of leaves fell
from no visible trees. I was scared.

God's hand is cupped
over the crickety heart
of the turtle.

At the cabin I left the canola bottle open
and eleven mice drowned in this oil bath.
I had invented the mouse atom bomb.

The firefly's one word:
darkness!

A bumblebee,
a straggly rosebush
staining the air with her scent.
A blue and black butterfly—
too many *B*s but life is like that.

How tall would I be
without my enemies
to measure me?

One grows tired of the hoax of up
and down. Jesus descended into a universe
of neither perfect lines, squares, nor circles.

Bought a broken pocket watch
at the church rummage sale.
"Need it for parts," I lied.

You step in the same river once only
for an instant. Panhandle time with
the bruised fingers of what might have been.

"Charred beyond recognition" is bad news.
Yet it happens to us all. Ashes
have never returned to wood.

In an egg yolk,
an artery fine as the touch
of a feather.

The cow dogs caught their first jackrabbit.
Ace, the big male, is curled in the dirt
growling to protect his trophy, the bloody ears.

First deerfly emerged solstice morning
bent on hell, creature torture. But like Bush
among his fly friends he's a nice guy.

How lucky in one life to see
the sun lift a cloud from a pool!

This slender blue thread,
if anything,
connects everything.

The ninth time I screwed Ophelia
in a row I was still a garden hose
but then I woke up in Nebraska.

The Great Gourmand rows his boat
all day on a peanut butter sandwich
and warm water.

At my age,
even in airports,
why would you wish
time to move faster?

The clock stopped at 5:30 for three months.
Now it's always time to quit work,
have a drink, cook dinner.

The butterfly
jots a note on the wind
to remind itself of something.

How can it be
that everyone my age
is older than I?

Twisted my ankle
until it's blue.
Now I can feel my heart
beating in my foot.

How attentive the big bear resting his chin
on the bird feeder, an eye rolling toward my window
to see if he has permission for sunflower seeds.

On my desk two
indisputably great creations:
duct tape and saltine crackers.

The red-naped sapsucker
doesn't know its name is silly.
Oh you white guys, again.

In a pasture, wild turkeys
flip cow pies, looking for bugs.

Suddenly my clocks agree.
One has been stopped for several
months, but twice a day
they have this tender moment.

In deer season,
walking in the woods,
I sing like Pavarotti.

"What I would do for wisdom,"
I cried out as a young man.
Evidently not much. Or so it seems.
Even on walks I follow the dog.

The owl is a bronze urn of ashes
till one of the round seals blinks.

Crow with a red beak
looks over his shoulder.

After rowing my blue and brown boat
for three hours I liked the world again,
the two loons close by, the theory of red wine.

Waited all day for the moon to rise.
It just happened.
I can't believe my luck.

I saw a black butterfly
as big as a raven
flapping through the night.
Maybe it was an owl.

Ten mousetraps in the cellar
and one dead mouse.
Pretty good odds for living.

In 1947 a single gold nugget was found
hereabouts. Old men still look for a second one.
In between life has passed.

In my garden
the late sun glows
through a rabbit's ears.

Midday silence is different
from nighttime silence.
I can't tell you how.

Between the four pads
of a dog's foot,
the fragrance of grass.

July, and fat black flies
so slow you can bat them
right out of the air.

Dead raccoon, legs in the air,
washes his paws in the sky.

Flecks of foam
on the fountain's lips
as it reads aloud from
the scripture of water.

This morning,
fish bleed into nacreous clouds
and an iron bird walks to town
on the bottom of the river.

I'm so pleased that Yeats
never got off his stilts
though I have only one.

I have used up more than
20,000 days waiting to see
what the next would bring.

It's hard to believe there's a skeleton
inside us, not certainly in the beautiful
girl getting out of her red car.

Elaborate is the courtliness
of the imagination, on one sore knee
before beauty.

When I touched her long feet
I stopped walking.
When I tasted her mouth
I quit eating.

When I watched her hands
as she peeled a potato,
I gave up everything I owned.

I have grown old, and know
how an owl feels,
seeing a man with a lantern.

November cold. Hey, grasshopper!
What goes? Once all that armor
weighed nothing!

In winter, don't ever
touch your tongue
to someone cold.

Fresh snow standing deep
on the phone wire. If you call me,
speak softly.

Well before dawn I woke
up crying because my teeth hurt.
Lucky for me there was soothing rain
on the cabin roof.

I woke up as nothing. Now start piling
it on. No. Yes. No. Maybe. Indoors.
Outdoors. Me. You. Her corpse said stop.

Birds and bugs
flying left and right.
Always the question,
What to do next?

The wasp
has built his palace
in a bell.

Life has always yelled at me,
"Get your work done." At least
that's what I think she says.

The patience of the spider's web
is not disturbed by dew.

Time makes us supplicant whores.
Ray Carver told me he was missing years.
The bottle's iron mouth suckles the brain dry.

The old Finn (85) walks
twenty-five miles to see his brother.
Why? "I don't have no car."

Look again: that's not
a yellow oak leaf on the path,
but the breastplate from a turtle.

The robins are back,
so weary from flying that they walk
wherever they go.

When we were young we talked
about bottomless lakes, which meant to us
the same lakes were bottomless in China.

You had to milk the cows at 5 a.m.
and 5 p.m. or they'd start bawling.
Even udders can become brutal clocks.

That winter the night fell seven
times a day and horses learned
to run under the ground.

Time flew in and out of the window
until she dropped dead in the kitchen.

At the end, just a pinch of the world
is all we have left to hold on to,
the hem of a sheet.

What if everyone you've loved
were still alive? That's the province
of the young, who don't know it.

A new spring and it's still 5:30
on the cabin's clock. It's always dawn
or time for dinner. My favorites.

If a camel can stretch its muzzle
out of its own stink
so can I.

Lazed on the floor like an old baby
for three hours, then rowed my blue
and brown boat.

Oh, to be in love,
with all five buckets
of the senses
overflowing!

On the shoulder, the turtle
warily holds out his head
on the end of a stick.

The moon, all lordly white,
an anti-rose embedded
at dawn in a thin veil
of red clouds.

Their balls were so swollen they collided
their motorcycles at 70 mph
with only momentary regret.

It's nice to think that when
we're fossils we'll all be in the same
thin layer of rock.

Oh, to write just one poem
that would last as long as that rose
tattooed on her butt!

The imagination's kisses
are a cloud of butterflies.

We should
sit like a cat
and wait for the door
to open.

In our farthest field,
between one walk
and the next,
the arrival of ten billion
grasshoppers.

How sharp must be the fletcher's knife
to split a feather
and leave in both halves flight.

The old hen scratches
then looks, scratches then looks.
My life.

Every time I've had a sea change
I thought I was dying.
I probably was.

My stopped clock is always
jumping ahead,
a sure winner in the race with time,
with every day as long as I wish it to be.

A vermilion flycatcher flew too far north
and died in Montana. The same for a Michigan wolf
in Missouri. I get butchered in New York
but don't mind it. I rise again the third day.

Bucket in the rain,
rejoice!

Deerflies die by the billions, the cool air
so clear you drink it in gulps
and the moon drifts closer to the cabin door.

Sometimes fate will steal a baby
and leave an old man
soft as a bundle of rags.

So happy with my fat old body,
still quick enough to slap a fly.

Black dog on white snow
beside the flooding, brown river.
This is where I live!

I feel
the bear's heart
in her footprints.

To have reverence for life
you must have reverence for death.
The dogs we love are not taken from us
but leave when summoned by the gods.

You asked, *What makes you sure?*
I have the faith of the blind,
I answered.

Wish-wash. Ten thousand tons of peanuts
free to us monkeys for 10,000 years.
Oh taste and see, but not in a hurry.

One barred owl harried by
eight loud crows.
A thief besieged by thieves.

A light snow shows
that even the old wagon track
is new.

I hope there's time
for this and that,
and not just this.

Pout and drift. The poet self-sunk
for three months looks up at the dark
heavens, puzzled by moon and stars.

The butterfly's brain,
the size of a grain of salt,
guides her to Mexico.

Buddhists say everything is led by mind.
My doubts are healed by drinking
a bottle of red wine in thirty-three minutes.

DNA shows that I'm the Unknown Soldier.
I can't hear the birds down here,
only politicians shitting out of their mouths.

The water spider
bounces on his legs
but cannot shake the lake.

The low ceiling grazes
the tops of the tall pines
encircling the yard.
Even the air feels crushed.

Peach sky
at sunset,
then (for god's sake)
one leaf across
the big October moon.

Dust too
is drawn on wings
to light.

Last year the snake
left her skin on the floor,
diaphanous like the name
of a lovely girl you've forgotten—
but not her flesh.

I'm sixty-two and can drop dead
at any moment. Thinking this in August
I kissed the river's cold moving lips.

The colder the raindrops
the harder they knock
on the door.

Come to think of it,
there's no reason to decide
who you are.

Stars from horizon to horizon.
A whole half universe
just to light the path.

Rilke says the new year brings things that have
never been, forgetting "won't be again."
Even a dog is never lost in the same place.

Awake in Paris all night listening to rain.
It's lucky there's nothing to eat, a fat dog
waiting for the luck of a roadkill possum.

I prefer the skyline
of a shelf of books.

Imagine a gallery
where all the paintings
opened and closed their wings!

In Brazil I leapt
out of my skin, then back
into it, a onetime-only trick.

Sometimes all it takes
to be happy
is a dime on the sidewalk.

When women pleasure themselves, I heard
at age twelve, they tweak their left ear
then move on to greatness.

Her voice had a deep resonance
that must have made her pubic hair
buzz.

The moon put her hand
over my mouth and told me
to shut up and watch.

I surely understand paper and how poets
disappear despite it. These days I write
so lightly I don't quite touch it.

A man pays court with his poems.
A woman dismisses him with hers.

Monkeys search each other
and so do we. Another sign
of our advancement.

All those spin butchers drooling
public pus. Save your first
bullet for television.

Rate the hours. One and 5 a.m.
are fine while 3 is the harshest.
The fool always feels safe at noon.

I thought my friend was drinking
too much, but it was the vodka
that was drinking him.

An uncommon number of us die
on our birthdays. You turn a bend
and abruptly you're back home.

Now that I'm older I perfectly
recall the elephant's eye
and the whale's eye that blinked.

That little red eye behind the toilet?
And we think poets
have a baleful look.

This is the county fair
and everything has a bull's ring
through its nose.
Who is leading?

After fifty years of tracking clouds
I've become cold rain upon my life.
How odd to see the mist so clearly.

Autumn dusk, and in the grass
the spiders' gray funnels
drain off the light.

In the electric chair's harness,
one man hauls all the darkness.

Our lives as highlights on TV:
our best lays and meals,
our backward flights of drunken
fancy down the stairs.

These house-trailer fires kill thousands
who will no longer suffer
the opinions and scorn of the rich.

Coming home from the tavern—
I see the pile of dirty clothes
on the cabin floor move.
Doglike, the snake is getting comfortable.

The path disappeared. There was a field
with no edges over which I walked
through the sky which blanketed the ground.

In this lowbrow wilderness
in the area of the black-phase wolf,
I give up my opinions.

A house will turn itself
to catch a little moonlight
on a bedpost.

It's the Devil's
blessing
that flies sleep
at night.

In the house the lizard's enemy
is porcelain. They struggle in the sink.
Warren, the cat, finds them there.

The tree also died the exact
moment the old raven fell off
a lower branch.

A frosty morning,
and one mosquito
at rest on the lip
of the tub.

Sometimes the teakettle rattles
over the flame with the And! And! And!
of a child telling a story too big
to pour out all at once.

So the Greeks had amphorae
with friezes of nymphs.
We have coffee mugs with ads
for farm equipment!

How evil all priesthoods.
All over the earth Holy Places
soaked with extra blood.

The handle of its neck
clucks back and forth
and ratchets the turkey
forward.

How is it the rich always know
what is best for the poor?

Trelawny burned Shelley's heart
while thousands of poets
were waiting for transplants.

Lush petals
and glistening thorns—
this college
full of experts.

The poet holds the podium
in both hands
like a garbage bag of words.

See how the rich and famous
sniff the tips of their fingers.
What have they been touching?

Ikkyū was awakened by a crow's caw,
which is not the same as an alarm clock.
He adored the whore dressed in gold brocade.
O master, why count flowers that are gone?

On the nightstand,
a copy of *Prevention* magazine
and the night coming on.

Like an old dog
I slowly lower and arrange myself
in a heap of sighs.

Scientists say the moon grows 1½ inches
farther away every year. I'll fight
this cosmic terrorism hand to hand.

What I learned: Dogs walk upstairs
for nothing. Don't eat with your nose.
Tonight the moon owns this river.

Often I travel at night and am surprised
where I end up at dawn. All road signs and maps
are hoaxes. Don't forget the earth is round.

Earth touched Moon
with his shadow, and Moon
blushed. Everyone saw it.

"When the roll is called up yonder
I'll be there," they sang. Hopefully.
Maybe. But maybe not.

Foolish me,
to think my wine
would never turn.

Come close to death
and you begin to see
what's under your nose.

On the cabin floor a trapped mouse
covers maggots that writhe.
With this in sight,
allow me to squeak.

I've been married since birth.
All other women sense the bottomless
depth of my insincerity.

She owns a perfect butt
but her loutish husband calls
it his "reserved seat."

Without her scarves
the weeping willow
has a twisted body.

They're putting a new green tin roof
on my moss-covered cabin.
Bang, what violence.

It rained so hard the sky became water
and under a mantle of trees I gulped for air.
Here on the bottom the water rose to my chin,
and my face ached to grow gills.

A welcome mat of moonlight
on the floor. Wipe your feet
before getting into bed.

Bullfrog groans.
He is the wooden floor
under the cold feet of the night.

The full moon often rises
in the wrong place. Tonight I sense
activity up there, a general unrest.

My wife's lovely dog, Mary, kills
butterflies. They're easier than birds.
I wonder if Buddha had dog nature.

Three teeth pulled including
a prime buck. Tongue probes
the jaw's lonesome holes.

Alone in the car
we try to tell ourselves
some good news.

These headlights
swim right through
the seine of falling snow.

In our October windfall time red
apples on frostbitten green grass.
You learn to eat around the wormholes.

As long as the woodpecker
taps on my roof I'll be fine,
a little life left in the shell.

The blind man navigates
by stars behind the daylight.

Just before I fly out of myself
I'll say a puzzled goodbye.
Our bodies are women who were never
meant to be faithful to us.

I was born a baby.
What has been
added?

Treasure what you find
already in your pocket, friend.

Today a pink rose in a vase
on the table.
Tomorrow, petals.

The pastures grow up
with red cedars
once the horses are gone.

SAVING DAYLIGHT

2006

for Linda (again)

WATER

Before I was born I was water.
I thought of this sitting on a blue
chair surrounded by pink, red, white
hollyhocks in the yard in front
of my green studio. There are conclusions
to be drawn but I can't do it anymore.
Born man, child man, singing man,
dancing man, loving man, old man,
dying man. This is a round river
and we are her fish who become water.

CABBAGE

If only I had the genius of a cabbage
or even an onion to grow myself
in their laminae from the holy core
that bespeaks the final shape. Nothing
is outside of us in this overinterpreted world.
Bruises are the mouths of our perceptions.
The gods who have died are able to come
to life again. It's their secret that they wish
to share if anyone knows that they exist.
Belief is a mood that weighs nothing on anyone's
scale but nevertheless exists. The moose
down the road wears the black cloak of a god
and the dead bird lifts from a bed of moss
in a shape totally unknown to us.
It's after midnight in Montana.
I test the thickness of the universe, its resilience
to carry us further than any of us wish to go.
We shed our shapes slowly like moving water,
which ends up as it will so utterly far from home.

MOM AND DAD

Gentle readers, feel your naked belly button where
you were tied to your mother. Kneel and thank
her for your jubilant but woebegone life. Don't
for a moment think of the mood of your parents
when you were conceived which so vitally affects
your destiny. You have no control over that and
it's unprofitable to wonder if they were pissed
off or drunk, bored, watching television news,
listening to country music, or hopefully out in
the orchard grass feeling the crunch of wind-
fall apples under their frantic bodies.

NIGHT DHARMA

How restlessly the Buddha sleeps
between my ears, dreaming his dreams
of emptiness, writing his verbless poems.
(I almost rejected "green tree
white goat red sun blue sea.")
Verbs are time's illusion, he says.

In the stillness that surrounds us
we think we have to probe our wounds,
but with what? Mind caresses mind
not by saying *no* or *yes* but *neither*.

Turn your watch back to your birth
for a moment, then way ahead beyond
any expectation. There never was a coffin
worth a dime. These words emerge
from the skin as the sweat of gods
who drink only from the Great Mother's breasts.

Buddha sleeps on, disturbed when I disturb
him from his liquid dreams of blood and bone.
Without comment he sees the raven carrying
off the infant snake, the lovers' foggy
gasps, the lion's tongue that skins us.

One day we dozed against a white pine stump
in a world of dogwood and sugar plum blossoms.
An eye for an eye, he said, trading
a left for my right, the air green tea
in the sky's blue cup.

MODERN TIMES

I

Each man should own three
belts just as he once had three
legs the better to turn corners.
Women had three arms
the better to hold things.
Now without these extra limbs
men and women can't remember
the life they don't know they've forgotten
packed away with dried plum buds
and evening primroses. They've traded
their limbs for clocks and ideas,
their hearts packed in salt. They thought
it was noon but it's nearly midnight.

II

Every poem is the poem
before the last. We know this absurd
feeling of wishing to live on the lip
of a future that can't quite
manage to happen, the ache
of the girl who decided not to exist
before she was born, the quizzical
trashcan behind the abortion clinic,
the unacknowledged caskets that always
arrive on night flights. We assumed
God loved most the piety of beggars,
that we should properly cower before
our elected murderers, that we could
sit tight behind our locked doors
and try to pretend we were rich
and happy children until time wore out.

III

We worked for food and shelter
and then bought the arts and better cars,
bigger houses, smarter children
who couldn't really learn to read and write.
It was too hard. The arts escaped
to a different heaven to get rid of us.
We misunderstood food and shelter,
flies crawling on a window,
fluttering up and down,
seeing the outside beyond reach
because of the invention of glass
that couldn't be undone. We lived
within the outside for two million years
and now it's mostly photos.
We chose wallpaper and paint over leaves
and rivers. In our dream of safety
we decided not to know the world.

IV

The question is, does the dog
remember her childhood?
If so, our universe changes,
tilts a bit. We do not willingly
offer much to the creature world,
a little food to amuse our loneliness.
We made funeral pyres of the houses
of bears and birds because they neglected
to console our paths to fortune.
They commit love with an intensity
unknown to us and without advice.
They read the world rather than books
and don't bother with names to identify
themselves. To them we're a Chinese film

without subtitles. Meanwhile my dog
dreams back to her seven-week childhood
in Wisconsin, over so soon before she took
a flight west to Montana, emerging
from a crate with a quizzical smile.

V

Do more people die asleep or awake?
We can easily avoid both conditions
but I'm not telling you how.
Why interrupt the ancient flow?
There's nothing more solid in life
than the will toward greed and self-destruction
but also beauty, who doesn't mind
sitting on her own tired knees.
How can I find my mother and father,
a sister and a brother if they're dead?
I've had to learn other languages
to make contact, the creature world
and flora, the mute landscape
offering a quiet music without verbs
and nouns. This is the language
of the departed ones. Those who have become
birds seem happy to be no longer us.
Salvation isn't coming. It's always been here.

VI

I've been on a full-time moon
watch this winter for reasons
I can't determine. Maybe I'm helping out?
My government is so loathsome I've turned
to other, much more important things.
The beetle takes a half hour on a leisurely
stroll across the patio, heading

northwest as if it truly mattered.
I think of Wallace Stevens in his office
doing insurance work as if it truly mattered.
He stays late on a spring afternoon
watching swallows swoop for insects
that haven't yet hatched in Hartford,
an old poet greedy for the life
he was never remotely to have;
a white marriage, love as a cold
cinderblock never to arise from the rubble,
his life a long slow Dresden
burning its own jealous ashes.

      VII

I can freely tie myself up without rope.
This talent is in the realm of antimagic
and many people have it. On a dawn
walk despite the creek, birds and forest
I have to get through the used part,
the murky fluid of rehearsals
and resentments, but then they drain away
and I'm finally where I already am,
smack-dab in the middle of each step,
the air you can taste, the evening
primrose that startled by my visit
doesn't turn away. When I read
the ancient manuscripts of earth
many of the lines are missing
that I'm expected to complete.
I'm the earth, too, sharing this song
of blood and bone with the whale,
monkey and housecat. At eye level
with toad our eyes share the passage
of this ghost ship we boarded at birth.

VIII

There are a lot of muted grays in life,
dull bronzes, mornings the color
of a lead sinker that will never help
you catch a fish, and then a trace
of sun allows you to see down into the water
where three minnows pass diagonally above
a sunken log, two tadpoles, the pebble-
circular swirl of a spawning bed, a glutinous
clot of frog eggs, and farther out
a turtle peering above a lily pad's edge.
Salvation from mood can be slow
in coming. Two song sparrows pick
this moment to fight over a lady,
a private woodland Iraq shrieking
"She's mine," as she pretends to be otherwise
occupied. The sky doesn't study
our immobility. When the mood has fled
I listen to the air, and a cloud is only
a cloud again though I'd like to see a dragon
emerging upward to the water's surface,
a gesture to lift us above our human weight.

IX

I salute the tiny insect crawling
back and forth across my journal,
perhaps eating the infinitesimal particles
of dried sweat from the effort to make music
and reason out of the ocean of life
most often opaque as dirty cream.
I tell this insect how unlucky for him.
He should be outside eating the tender cores
of spring flowers or alighting on a bird's
back the better to fly away on another's wings.

Our lives are novels we don't want to read
and we so gracelessly translate their world
for our own purposes. We live morosely
in this graveyard long before we're buried.
Still we love our green and blue world
and leap out of our lives from sea to shining
sea. We know that our despised world
is our Great Mother's breast warm to our desert lips.

X

What I'm doing is what I'm already
doing. The mind can't accept the ordinary.
The pope fed through his nose would prefer
pasta marinara as he grabs at heaven
as a gentle old monkey might at a vine
while hanging from a tree because of the waiting
jaguar far below. Finding myself where I already
am is a daily chore. Chaos herself is fragile.
A step takes seconds. Clocks leak our invisible
blood in invisible increments. I'd rather say,
"sun is up, high brutal noon, sun is down,
night comes," in rhythm with the bird's superior
clock. I can no longer reshape the unbearable
world and have given up to count birds.
Up the mountain in a mesquite thicket
two pale-blue female lazuli buntings yield
to the tally clicker in my vest pocket,
their souls intact, ignoring my glorious smile.
I've abandoned the culture's ghost not my life,
Jim on the south slope at dawn counting birds.

ADDING IT UP

I forgot long division but does one
go into sixty-six more than sixty-six times?
There's the mother, two daughters, eight dogs,
I can't name all the cats and horses, a farm
for thirty-five years, then Montana, a cabin,
a border casita, two grandsons, two sons-in-law,
and graced by the sun and the moon, red wine
and garlic, lakes and rivers, the millions of trees.
I can't help but count out of habit, the secret
door underneath the vast stump where I founded
the usual Cro-Magnon religion, a door
enveloped by immense roots through which one day
I watched the passing legs of sandhill cranes,
napping where countless bears have napped,
an aperture above where the sky and the gods
may enter, yet I'm without the courage to watch
the full moon through this space. I can't figure
out a life. We're groundlings who wish to fly.
I live strongly in the memories of my dead dogs.
It's just a feeling that memories float around
waiting to be caught. I miss the cat that perched
on my head during *zazen*. Since my brother died
I've claimed the privilege of speaking to local rocks,
trees, birds, the creek. Last night a broad moonbeam
fell across my not-so-sunken chest. The smallest
gods ask me what there is beyond consciousness,
the moment by moment enclosure the mind
builds to capture the rudiments of time.
Two nights ago I heard a woman from across
the creek, a voice I hadn't heard since childhood.
I didn't answer. Red was red this dawn
after a night of the swirling milk of stars

that came too close. I felt lucky not to die.
My brother died at high noon one day in Arkansas.
Divide your death by your life and you get
a circle, though I'm not so good at math.
This morning I sat in the dirt playing
with five cow dogs, giving out a full pail of biscuits.

YOUNG LOVE

In my "Memoir of an Unsuccessful Prostitute"
I questioned what was it like to be nineteen
in New York City in 1957, fresh from northern
Michigan farmland, looking for sex and food.
First of all the edges of buildings were sharp
and if you walked around a corner too close
to them you could cut yourself. Even though it
was summer the daylight was short and when it
was hot you sweated inward. You walked the streets
as a shy elephant who within the cruelty
of his neurons had conceived a love of women.
A Black woman said you were too white
and a white woman said you were too brown.
Another said you were a red Indian ("How
exciting"). You became very thin and fell asleep
beside fountains, on park benches, in the library
where they roused you with a shake. Pigeons
avoided you as a breadless monster. The circus women
paid in used popcorn, their secret currency.
The beatnik girl paid with crabs who tugged
at the roots of your eyebrows, your tiny friends.
Late one night the moon split in pieces
and you could see two yellow shards at the ends
of Forty-Second Street where a herring sandwich
was a quarter, Italian sausage fifty cents.
The drug of choice was a Benzedrine inhaler
plus three beers, after which you jumped over the hood
of an approaching taxi with your invisible pogo stick.
You hitchhiked the trail of a letter from a girl back home
and New York City became more beautiful
with each mile west.

THE MOVIE

I'm making a movie about my life
which never ends. The plot thickens
and thickens like an overcooked soup.
The movie features tens of thousands
of characters including those who passed
me on the street without knowing
that I was a star. The film includes
my long horizontal dives above fields
of corpses. I've become proud that I'm part
dog favoring perceptions over conclusions.
I'm not sexy enough at my age
to carry a movie so I'm filming my mind
at play, with the rudiments of Eros
backing into the camera with the force
of a drop forge. Ultimately the poet, filmmaker,
is the girl who didn't have a date for the prom.
She takes a walk and hears the music
from the gymnasium, imagining the crepe
paper and wilting corsages vibrating
with the wretched music. She walks past
the graveyard with its heavy weight
of dirt nappers and climbs a hill steep
as a cow's face. From the top of the hill
she sees the world she never made
but has changed with words into the arena
of the sacred. The sky becomes
dumbfounded with her presence. If she decides
to shoot herself it's only to come to life again.
The thin slip of the moon speaks French
but the voice is compressed by trees and translated
by fireflies. This girl is far more interesting
than I am and that's why I'm filming

her rather than my trip to the mailbox
avoiding the usual rattlesnakes in the tallgrass.
It's not truth that keeps us alive
but invention, no actual past but the stories
we've devised to cover our disappearing
asses. Near a pond she hears the millions of
tree frogs, peepers, and thinks this noise is sex.
For a split second she wonders what it would
be like to make love to that older poet she heard
read in Grand Rapids, the way he grasped
her hand when he gave her a free book. My god,
now we're nearly together in my movie though
the camera is the unwilling POV and when it
comes CLOSE she pushes down her jeans
near the thicket where I've been waiting.
In the faintest moonlight I see her pelvic curls.
Now it is time to back away from heaven's mouth.
I don't film dreams that lack narrative drive,
and besides I have no legs to leave the thicket,
only an imagination whose camera has chosen
to BACK AWAY far above the crucified dogs
and the soldiers writhing in alien courtyards,
above the swirling cumuli where those who we
thought were dead watch us while sitting on plastic
lounge chairs, up where the finest music still rises,
up there out of harm's way where I store my life film
in microversion around the neck of a hawk who has
never landed since birth.

LIVINGSTON SUITE

in memory of T.J. Huth

Shorn of nature,
here but in small supply,
townspeople adore their dogs.

     ⌐

Our dogs have never lived
in a town. Neither have I
since 1967. I adore
the puzzlement of our dogs.

     ⌐

Each morning I walk four blocks
to this immense river,
surprised that it's still there,
that it won't simply disappear
into the ground like the rest of us.

     ⌐

In the burnt July air
the strange cool odor
of sprinkler water
creating its own little breeze
in the Livingston Park
where there are twelve rings for playing
horseshoes built before the fathers of lies
built the clouds above our heads.

     ⌐

A lovely girl passes on her bicycle
with a fat cat
on her shoulder who watches me

disappear through heavy lids,
then a lovely soiled girl on her knees
in a garden looks up at me
to say hello. A Christian urge tries
to make me ignore her pretty butt
cocked upward like a she-cat's.

—

Four churches within a block,
Methodist, Lutheran, Episcopal, Congregational,
surrounding me with maudlin holiness,
Sunday's hymns a droning hum
against the ceilings. Crows and magpies think,
Oh it's that day again.
Christ in the New World like Milne's Eeyore,
a lumpen donkey sweating with our greed,
trying to make us shepherd his billions of birds.

—

Under the streets are the remnants
of an older town with caches
of Indian skulls, also wizened
white scalps from those who jumped
the gun on the westward movement
that is still ending in Santa Monica
where a girl who I knew, after taking three
California speedballs, had her brain hurled into eternity
like a jellied softball. Oh Cynthia.

—

I walk my dog Rose in the alleys
throughout town. Maybe it's where poets belong,
these substreets where the contents of human life
can be seen more clearly, our shabby backsides

disappearing into the future at the precise rate
of the moon's phases. Rose turns, hearing
an upstairs toilet flush, the dead cows,
pigs and chickens turning semiliquid
in the guts of strangers, the pretty tomato
changing shape, the potatoes that once held leaves
and blossoms in their spindly green arms. Holy days
of early summer with lilacs drooping laden
under the weight of their moist art. From a kitchen
a woman laughs a barking laugh over
something I'll never know. A ninety-year-old
couple emerges from the Methodist church smiling,
masters of a superior secret. Back in the alley
a dirty yellow cat emerges from a garbage can
with trout remains, a sure sign of feline victory.
She holds the carcass tightly as if I might take it.

      —

Our newspaper, *The Enterprise,* said,
"Grizzlies feasting on storm-killed cattle."
An early June blizzard dropped four feet
of snow, killing a thousand cows and calves,
a few foals, and the grizzlies hungry and fresh
from hibernation are feasting. "The bears
are just thick. It's really kind of dangerous
up here right now," said Gus V., a rancher.
Interesting news on the summer solstice.
The cow protrudes from the snowbank with ravens
perched around the eyes & udders watching for a coyote
or bear to open the hidebound meat, nearly
a million pounds of meat spread around the
countryside. What pleasure in this natural terrorism.

      —

On a twilight walk a violent storm moved swiftly
toward the east and south of me with the starkest
lightning striking against the slate-colored
Absaroka mountains. Closer, on a green mountainside
white trucks passed on Interstate 90,
then closer yet Watson's Black Angus cattle
sprinkled like peppercorns against shiny
wet pale green grass. Closer, a tormented
cottonwood thicket in the rising wind, maybe
60 knots, branches flailing, closer the broad
and turbulent brown river. And finally
only me on which all things depend, standing
on the riverbank, bent to the wind, the solitary
twilight watcher wondering who is
keeping the gods alive this evening or whether
they have given up on us and our tiny forked tongues,
our bleating fears and greed, our pastel anxieties.

In 1968 when I was first here
there was a cool scent of pines
and melting snow from the mountains
carried by a southwind through the river's
canyon. The scent is still here,
the sure fresh odor of the West.

At the oars of the drift boat
in the thrash and churn of a rapid
I have no more control over the boat,
or my life, than I had in 1968.
Swept away. And not quite understanding
that this water is heading toward
the Caribbean. A grizzly bear pisses

in a creek in the Absarokas and traces end up
nonchalantly passing New Orleans
into the Gulf of Mexico. This fuzzy air
above is from dust storms in China.
The underground river far below me
started in the Arctic and heads toward
the equator. During the Bush colonoscopy
narwhals were jousting over lady narwhals
and an immense Venezuelan anaconda gave birth
to a hundred miniatures of her kind, all quickly
eaten by waiting caimans and large wading birds.
Trapped in the compartment of a sunken ship
a man writes a letter in the dark to his wife
and children in Missouri which will never be read.
I watch a blind sheep who loves to roll in the grass.

—

At the rodeo the bucking horse
leaps then buckles to its knees,
recovers, then bucks up. And up.
The rider thrown, eating a face-
ful of dirt while behind the announcer's
shack and across the river,
up a cliff and a broad green slope,
trucks pass east and west on I-90
unmindful of the cowboy spitting dirt.

—

Around here they're still voting
for Eisenhower as a write-in candidate.
Around here people still have memories
and honor their war dead. In the park
to each road guardrail a flag and white cross
are attached, and a name that is gone

but not forgotten. An old man carrying
a portable oxygen unit breathes deeply
with moist eyes looking at his brother's name,
lost in Iwo Jima. We bow slightly
to each other, and my memory repeats the prayer
I offered at age five for my uncles Art and Walter
off in the South Pacific on warships fighting
the Japanese and the satanic Tojo. At church
we sang "Fairest Lord Jesus" and the minister
announced that a deacon's son was lost
in what I heard as "yurp."
Some of the men and women sobbed loudly.
I remembered him playing baseball and driving
around town in his old Ford coupe with an actual
squirrel tail attached to the aerial, and just out
of kindergarten I had it all wrong thinking who will
drive Fred's car now? Our mothers and fathers embraced.

—

From different upstairs windows I see four different
mountain ranges not there to accompany the four churches:
the Absarokas, the Gallatins, the Bridgers, the Crazies.
You naturally love a mountain range called Crazies.
Of course naked women, Native and white,
run through the Crazies on moonlit nights
howling for husbands and lovers
lost to our wars. I've followed their red footprints
while hunting in these mountains, the small toes.

—

A community can drown in itself,
then come to life again. Every yard seems
to have flowers, every street its resident magpies.
In the outfield of the baseball diamond

there are lovely small white flowers that a gardener
told me are the "insidious bindweed." All my life
I've liked weeds. Weeds are botanical
poets, largely unwanted. You can't make a dollar
off them. People destroy the obnoxious dandelion
that I've considered a beautiful flower since early
childhood, blowing off the fuzzy seeds when they died,
sending the babies off into the grim universe,
but then I'm also fond of cowbirds and crows,
cowbirds and poets laying their eggs for others
to raise then drifting away for no reason.

—

Search & Rescue is "combing" the river
this morning for a drowned boy. If it were me
I'd rather float east through the night toward the rising
sun. But it's not me. The boy probably
wasn't literary and the parents want the body
to bury, the fourth body in the river this summer.
Currents can hold a body tight to the bottom.
A vet friend found residual gills in the head
of a dog but at our best we're ungainly in water
compared to the clumsiest of fishes. Against the song,
we won't fly away. Or float. We sink into earth.

—

In this prolonged heat wave the snow
is shrinking upward to the mountain tip-tops
to a few crevasses and ravines. On Mount Wallace
ancient peoples, likely the Crow, the Absarokas,
carved out of flat stone the imprint of a man
so you could lie there in a grizzly-claw necklace
and see only sky for three days and nights,
a very long session in your own private church.

—

It's ninety-five degrees at four p.m.
and two girls in their early teens step
from the cooler cement sidewalk onto the street's hot
asphalt in their bare feet, beginning to dance,
jump, prance, one in shorts and the other
in a short summer dress. It is good enough
so that only Mozart would contribute to this pure
dance that is simply what it is, beyond passing
lust, sheer physical beauty, the grace of *being*
on a nearly insufferable hot day in Montana.
The girls skidded their feet on sprinkler-wet grass
under a maple tree, then went indoors out of my life.

—

Everyone seems to have loved the drowned boy.
Destiny is unacceptable. This grand river
he'd seen thousands of times didn't wait for him.
Nobody seems to have a clue. He died two days ago
and they're still searching the river. Some men
carry ominous long poles with a hook in the end.
This morning walking Rose I looked at the wide
eddy with a slow but inexorable whirlpool coiling
in upon itself that no human could swim against.
You might survive by giving up the struggle
and hope that the water would cast you aside
into the steady current, and that it wouldn't force you
downward beyond the limit of your breath.
In high school I flunked chemistry, unable to bear
up under the foreign odors or comprehend the structure
of water. It's one thing to say out loud "H-two-O"
and another to have spent thousands of days in the company
of lakes, creeks and rivers seeing fish breathe
this liquid air. An old man feels the slow struggle

of dying, say for ten years, which drowning shortens
to a minute or so. People say it's the best way to die.
Once in the Humboldt current off the coast of Ecuador
I looked into the eye of a whale and later wondered
if she communed with the soul of water. At nineteen
or twenty the cup is overflowing but not understood.
The dread is there won't be time to drink it.

      —

Kooser called from Nebraska to say he'd found
a large cinder on a long walk along abandoned
country railroad tracks, a remnant of steam
trains, the cinder similar to those our fathers
shoveled from coal furnaces in the early winter mornings
before stoking the fire. In your dark bedroom
you'd hear the scrape of the shovel and the thump
when cinders were dropped in metal washtubs.
Now the trains are all diesel and in Livingston at night
I hear them pass, Burlington & Northern, the horn
an immense bassoon warning the drunks at crossings.
Some complain but I love this night music,
imagining that a few of the railroad cars are from
my youth when I stood in a pasture and thrilled
to my favorite, "Route of Phoebe Snow."
To be excited by a cinder is to be excited about life.

      —

There's a dullish ache, a restlessness in those
who walk their dogs along the river's levee.
None of us wants to find the body
but then it's our duty to look in this early morning
light with a cool breeze coming off the crumpled water.
A tree plucked from the bank sails by and beauty
is visited by the terror of power. When my sister

was killed at nineteen I began to disbelieve
in destiny, in clocks and calendars, that the downward
thrust of time that hammers us into the ground
is planned, that the girl in France who wrote
me a letter before suicide was drawn to that place
by an ignored, thus insignificant, universe where God
wakes up cross, yawns and the dead are tossed
like confetti into the void. If there's a divinity
that shapes our ends it's beyond our ken. A tree
by its nature seeks its future moment by moment.
The child in grade-school science looks out the window
bemused that his singularity was chosen from millions
of his parents' eggs and sperms. There's much less time
than he thinks no matter how long he lives. The heart
can never grasp these unbearable early departures.

⎯

A concert in the park on the 4th of July sponsored
by the networks in New York. Someone named Sheryl Crow,
Hank Williams Junior not Senior, and my old favorite,
Los Lobos. As a claustrophobe I can't walk the four blocks
into the crowds but from my studio
I can hear the Latino music wafting through maple
trees, imagining I'm at our winter casita near Patagonia,
Arizona, on the Mexican border, the music so much
closer to love and death than our own, the heart
worn on the sleeve, the natural lament of flowers, the moon
visible. Smiling skeletons are allowed to dance
and the gods draw closer to earth, the cash registers
drowned out in the flight of birds, the sound of water.

⎯

You can't row or swim upstream on the river.
This moving water is your continuing past

that you can't retrace by the same path
that you reached the present, the moment by moment
implacable indifference of time. At one point
in my life nearly every tree on earth was shorter
than me, and none of the birds presently here
were here at my birth except an aged macaw
in Bahia. Not a single bear or bug, dog or cat,
but a few turtles and elephants who greeted
my arrival. We can't return for a second
to those golden days of the Great Depression, World War II,
the slaughter of the Jews, the Stalinist purges,
the yellow horde of China feeding on its afterbirth,
the Japanese gearing up scientific experiments
that would kill a quarter of a million. How auspicious
it is when people talk of the marvelous sixties
with the extermination of JFK, Bobby Kennedy,
Martin Luther King, Vietnam, and enough music
to divert us from the blood-splattered screen
of immediate history. Within time and the river
no one catches their breath, a vast prayer wheel
without a pivot spinning off into the void.
We're wingless birds perpetually falling north.

⸺

Maybe I'm wrong. After years of practice
I learned to see as a bird but I refuse
to do it now, not wanting to find the body.
I traveled east to our cabin in Michigan
where I learned that my Zen master, Kobun
Chino Sensei, drowned in a cold pond trying to save
his three-year-old daughter, who also drowned.
I make nothing of this but my mind suddenly
rises far upward and I see Kobun in his black
robes struggling in the water and he becomes

a drowning raven who then frees himself for flight,
his daughter on the pond's bottom rising to join him.
What could the vision mean but a gift? I said
maybe I'm wrong. The Resurrection is fatally correct.

—

As an early and relentless swimmer I couldn't imagine
death by water until I saw a spring runoff
in the Manistee River, a shed floating by
as if powered by a motor, a deafening wave curling
upward at a logjam. I don't want to die
in a car, at war, in an airliner where I searched
for the pulse of an old lady who collapsed
in the aisle, found nothing, and everyone said
she seemed to be smiling. She left the plane behind.
But water at least is an earthly embrace.
It was my wife who found the body while walking
her dog Mary beside the river at Mayor's landing.
I was in Michigan in a cabin beside the river
made turbulent by an hour-long cloudburst.
I wish it wasn't you, I said. "But it was," she said.
"It had to be someone. Why not me?"

—

In Livingston I'm back home in Reed City
over fifty years ago when trains were steam but the cows
and alleys were the same, the friendly town mongrels
I said hello to, one who walked with me an hour
before turning home when we crossed his street.
From the park bridge I watch a heron feed and at the edge
of town there were yellow legs, Wilson's phalaropes
wandering a sand and rock bar, at home in the river
because they could fly over it. I'm going to swim
across it on a moonlit night. Near the porch steps

of the house next door are two stone Chinese lions
looking at the street with the eyes of small gods,
the eyes that were given us that we don't wish to use
for fear of madness. Beside the river's bend
where he drowned colored stones are arranged
to say "We love you, T.J." Not loved in past
tense but love in the way that the young have the grace
of their improbable affections, their hearts
rising to the unkempt breath and beat of the earth.

HILL

For the first time
far in the distance
he could see his twilight,
wrapping around the green hill
where three rivers start,
and sliding down toward him
through the trees until it reached
the blueberry marsh and stopped,
telling him to go away, not now,
not for the time being.

BURIED TIME

Our bodies leap ahead
and behind our years.

Our bodies tracked the sun
with numbers at play and curiosity
not for slavery.

Time often moves sideways,
its mouth full and choking
on rubbery clocks.

In the elephant's heart
the uncounted sunrises, the muscle
pumping blood to its
red music.

The world's air is full
of orphaned ghosts and on the ground
so many mammals that feed
at night for safety.

Our bodies move sideways
and backwards of their own accord
in scorn of time.

I didn't divorce the sun and moon
but we had an amicable separation
for a while.

I established myself in the night.
I organized seven nights in a row
without any days.
I liked best the slender cracks
between nights and days where I bloomed
like an apple tree.

I collected dawns and twilights.
They are stored in my room between
two volumes of poetry, their titles secret.

In geologic time we barely exist.
I collected memories of my temporary host
leaving a trace of words, my simian tracks.

The universe is the Great Mother.
I haven't met the father. My doubt
is the patina of shit the culture
paints on my psyche.

There is no "I" with the sun and moon.
Time means only the irretrievable.
If I mourn myself, the beloved dead,
I must mourn the deaths of galaxies.

Despite gravity we're fragile as shadows.
They crushed us with time-as-money,
the linear hoax.

At the cabin standing in the river
on a warm night the female coyote
near the logjam can see the moon's glint
off my single front tooth.

When she barks her voice wraps
itself with me in the moving water,
the holy form of time.

ANGRY WOMEN

Women in peignoirs are floating around
the landscape well out of eyesight
let alone reach. They are as palpable
as the ghost of my dog Rose whom I see
on long walks, especially when exhausted
and my half-blind eyes are blurred by cold wind
or sleet or snow. The women we've mistreated
never forgive us nor should they, thus their ghostly
energies thrive at dawn and twilight in this vast
country where any of the mind's movies can be played
against this rumpled wide-screened landscape.
Our souls are travelers. You can tell when your own
is gone, and then these bleak, improbable
visits from others, their dry tears because you were
never what you weren't, so that the world
becomes only what it is, the unforgiving flow
of an unfathomable river. Still they wanted you otherwise,
closer to their dreamchild, just as you imagined
fair maidens tight to you as decals to guide
you toward certainties. The new pup, uncrippled by ideals,
leaps against the fence, leaps at the mountains beyond.

BEFORE THE TRIP

When old people travel, it's for relief
from a life that they know too well,
not routine but the very long slope
of disbelief in routine, the unbearable
lightness of brushing teeth that aren't all
there, the weakened voice calling out
for the waiter who doesn't turn;
the drink that once was neither here
nor there is now a singular act of worship.
The sun that rises every day says
I don't care to the torments of love
and hate that once pushed one back
and forth on the blood's red wagon.
All dogs have become beautiful
in the way they look at cats and wonder
what to do. Breakfast is an event
and bird flu only a joke of fear the world
keeps playing. On the morning walk
the horizon is ours when we wish.
We know that death is a miracle for everyone
or so the gods say in a whisper of rain
in the immense garden we couldn't quite trace.

PARIS TELEVISION

Thinking of those Russian schoolchildren. How can what we call depression be approached directly? It can't. I have this triumverate of ghosts— John, Rose, Suzanne Wilson—who visit me. Mortality is gravity, the weight we bear up under daily. I can only create lightness out of doors— walking, fishing, standing in the yard looking at Linda's flowers or the Absaroka mountains, or in the Upper Peninsula looking at the peculiar vastness of Lake Superior, the night sky, watching my grandsons. How can I lift my weight each day when my own words began to fail me this year, or my perceptions began to fail my words? When both my inside and outside worlds became incomprehensible? But then the source of all religion is incomprehension. The first day of school for the Russian children. Their dogs walk halfway, figure it out, return home to wait in the just-beginning-to-wane summer heat, with all flowers shedding themselves and neglected wheat stalks in the corners of fields dropping their grains, some dogs howling at the fireworks, and then the parents of the children joining them. My voice becomes small as a molting bird's, barely a whisper until I can fly again, if ever.

OPAL

O Opal, your ear
in my heart
both hear
the glorious void,
preferring the birds.

THE MAN WHO LOOKED FOR SUNLIGHT

Nine days of dark, cold rain
in October, some snow, three gales
off Lake Superior with the cabin's tin roof
humming Beethoven, the woodcock weather vane
whirling and thumping like a kettledrum,
tree limbs crashing in the woods;
at dawn a gust made small whitecaps on the river.
Marquette NPR promised sunlight
on Thursday. I sit here reflecting
I've burned a whole cord of wood this week.
I'm ten years old again sitting here waiting
for the sunlight, petting my dog Rose,
sitting by the window straining for sunlight.
I'm not going to drown myself in the cold
dark river but I really would like sunlight.
Finally clouds rush by well beyond the speed
limit, and there's a glimpse of sunlight,
a few seconds of sunlight, enough for today,
the sunlight glistening on the wet forest
and my dog sleeping by the window.

ALCOHOL

In the far back room of the school
for young writers are two big illegal
formaldehyde glass jars holding the kidneys
and livers of Faulkner and Hemingway
among the tens of thousands of empty bottles
of everything they drank to fuel themselves
through their bloody voyages. Alive, their arms
were crooked out as question marks trying
to encircle the world. Dead, they are crazy
old men who convinced us of the reasonableness
of their tales, their books deducted from their caskets
at the last possible moment. And now we hold
them tightly as if they ever truly cared.
No one should wish to enter this room
but still some of us hurl ourselves against
the invisible door as if our stories and alcohol
were Siamese twins ineluctably joined at the head,
our hearts enlarged until they can barely beat.

EN VERACRUZ EN 1941

Giselle me dio una estatuilla primitiva
de la Virgen de Sonora, estrellas radiando de su cabeza,
labios y cejas astillados, nariz descascarada
y debajo de su manto el niño
Jesús mira saludando con dos manos
elevadas, anunciando su llegada entre nosotros.
Giselle, ningún hombre puede acostarse con las tres:
madre, amante, Virgen.
Confieso que tus pezones son rojo rubí
pero en la muerte se tornarán turquesas.
Con tu pie desnudo sobre mi falda confieso también
que me despojaré de tu insoportable estatuilla,
o camino a La Habana la dejaré caer en el océano,
para que descanse en la falda del poeta de América, Hart Crane,
quien no pudo aprender el lenguaje de los chiles y las flores,
que la mar es madre no padre. No podemos estar solos.
¿Dónde estaba el perro para acariciar la mano con la que escribía?
Perro, te doy mi segunda empanada,
la sonrisa roja de mi corazón, el crepúsculo que lleva la mar
a mi cuarto donde Giselle duerme bien desnuda
sobre su vientre para que yo aúlle sin voz
al Caribe, porque no soy un perro de buena fe,
soy un perro poético a quien la luna devuelve con un aullido
su mensaje espantoso de llegada y despedida.
Madre, Virgen, amante sobre su vientre. Las tres son una,
pero estamos en partes, pies y cabeza de alguna manera
arrastrándose hacia nuestros cuerpos, moviéndose como yo ahora
bajo el ventilador, meciéndonos perpetuamente. Madre, Virgen,
perdónennos nuestras amantes. Una vez ustedes fueron mujeres.

~ probablemente escrito por Pablo Neruda

IN VERACRUZ IN 1941

Giselle gave me a primitive statuette
of the Virgin from Sonora, stars spoked from her head,
chipped lips and eyebrows, flaked nose,
and from underneath her skirt the infant
Jesus peeks out saluting with two raised
hands, announcing his arrival among us.
Giselle, no man can sleep with all three:
mother, lover, Virgin.
I confess that your nipples are ruby
but at death they will become turquoise.
With your bare foot in my lap I also confess
I'll leave your unbearable statuette behind,
or en route to Havana drop it in the ocean,
to rest in the lap of America's poet, Hart Crane,
who could not learn the language of chilies and flowers,
that the sea is mother not father. We can't be alone.
Where was the dog to caress his writing hand?
Dog, I give you my second empanada,
my heart's red smile, the twilight that carries the sea
into my room where Giselle sleeps quite naked
on her belly so that I give a voiceless howl
to the Caribbean, not being a bona fide dog
but a poetic dog at whom the moon howls back
her terrifying message of arriving and leave-taking.
Mother, Virgin, lover on her belly. The three are one,
but we are in parts, feet and head somehow
crawling toward our bodies, moving as I do now
under the fan endlessly rocking, Mother, Virgin,
forgive us our lovers. You were women once.

~ very likely by Pablo Neruda (translated by Jim Harrison)

DREAM LOVE

How exhausted we can become
from the contents of dreams:
long, too long nights of love
with whirling corrupted faces,
unwilling visits from the dead
whom we never quite summoned;
the animals who chased our souls
at noon when we were children
so that we wished to be magical dogs
running backwards off the world's
edge into a far better place
than a hot noon with earth herself
a lump in our weary young throats.
In dream love we're playing
music to an empty room.
On leaving the room the music
continues and surrounds those we loved
and lost who are at roost
in their forested cemeteries,
visible but forever beyond our reach.
They won't fly away until we join them.

FLOWER, 2001

Near a flowershop off boulevard Raspail
a woman in a sundress bending over,
I'd guess about 49 years of age
in a particular bloom, just entering
the early autumn of her life,
a thousand-year-old smile on her face
so wide open that I actually shuddered
the same shudder I did in 1989
coming over the lip of a sand dune
and seeing a big bear below me.

PATAGONIA POEM

Here in the first morning sunlight I'm trying
to locate myself not by latitude 31.535646° N,
or longitude 110.747511° W, but by the skin
of my left hand at the edge of the breakfast plate.
This hand has the skin and fingers of an animal.
The right hand forks the egg of a bird, a chicken.
The bright yellow yolk was formerly alive
in the guts of the bird waiting for the absent rooster.
Since childhood it has been a struggle
not to run away and hide in a thicket and sometimes
I did so. Now I write "Jim" with egg yolk
on the white plate in order to remember my name,
and suddenly both hands look like
an animal's who also hides in a remote thicket.
I feel my head and the skull ever so slightly
beneath the skin, a primate's skull that tells
me a thicket is a good idea for my limited
intelligence, and this hand holding a pen, a truly
foreign object I love, could with its brother hand
build a shelter in which to rest awhile and take
delight in life again, to wander in the moonlight
when earth achieves its proper shape, to rest looking
out through a tangle of branches at a daylight
world that can't see back in at this animal shape.

READING CALASSO

I'm the pet dog of a family of gods
who never gave me any training.
Usually they are remote.
I curl up in an empty house
and they peek in the window when I'm sleeping.
Their children feed me table scraps
from ink-stained fingers.
Sometimes they lock me in a shed
and keep calling my name outside the door.
They expect me to bark day and night
because nearly everyone is their enemy.

THE BEAR

When my propane ran out
when I was gone and the food
thawed in the freezer I grieved
over the five pounds of melted squid,
but then a big gaunt bear arrived
and feasted on the garbage, a few tentacles
left in the grass, purplish white worms.
O bear, now that you've tasted the ocean
I hope your dreamlife contains the whales
I've seen, that one in the Humboldt current
basking on the surface who seemed to watch
the seabirds wheeling around her head.

BARS

Too much money-talk sucks the juice
out of my heart. Despite a fat wallet
I always become a welfare mother trying to raise
the price of a chicken for my seven children,
the future characters of my novels
who are inside me wanting to go to a bar.
They're choking on unwritten book dust and need
a few drinks as much as I do. (We're all
waiting to see what we become when we're grown up.)
Everyone smart knows that alcohol is life's
consolation prize for the permanently inconsolable.
Even my unborn characters who right now
are simpleminded demons sense the drinks
waiting for them when their bodies reach solid ground.
At four p.m. I resist for moments, head for the Bluebird
where in the parking lot I become a prescient animal,
probably a stray dog, hearing the ass-cheek squeak
of a woman passing on the sidewalk. A small male
fly follows her swinging left ankle and smiles
looking upward in the season of summer dresses.
One drink and I'm petulant. Men in golf clothes
are talking about the stock market where once
men talked of farming, hunting, fishing, the weather.
If Holly weren't sitting jauntily on a bar stool
I'd gulp and bolt. Something about a bar stool
that loves a woman's bottom. Vodka makes me young
but not young enough and the men keep saying Lucent
Lucent Lucent. Secret powers only allow
me two drinks before dinner so I head for Dick's Tavern
where actual working men talk of fishing,
crops, bankrupt orchards, the fact that the moon
is a bit smaller than it used to be. No one says Lucent,

only that the walleyes are biting short, but Lucent,
this preposterous French word afflicting so many
with melancholy, carries me back to Paris
where dozens of times I've entered the Select
on Montparnasse with hungry heart and mind.
When I'm there next month I'll order my bottle
of Brouilly, perhaps a herring salad, say "Lucent"
loudly to a woman to see what happens. Wine
makes me younger than vodka and while I drink
I'll pet the cat who after a dozen years will finally
sit on my lap, and think we're better at nearly
everything than the French except how to live life,
a small item indeed. Once I left the Select
for the airport, de Gaulle, and twenty-four hours
later I was sitting in my cabin in the Upper Peninsula
waiting for a sow bear and two cubs to leave
the clearing so I could go to the bar, The Dunes Saloon,
and think over France in tranquility. The idea
of going to this bar draws in creature life. Once in the driveway
a female wolf stood in my headlights and nodded,
obviously the reincarnation of a girl I knew
who drowned in Key West where I first discovered
that one drink can break the gray egg that sometimes
encloses you, two drinks help you see this world.
Three drinks and you're back inside the gray egg.

DIABETES

I'm drawing blood the night of the full moon,
also a full eclipse of the full moon.
When will this happen again in my life,
if ever? Maybe in yours, of course.
I'm drawing blood not in Vampirism
but in diabetes. Few can find the Carpathians
on the map. It would be unhealthy for a vampire
to drink my sugary blood, which is a river
miles in length, a rare round river,
billions of round rivers walking the earth
and flowing with blood. A needle pops
the finger and out it comes, always a surprise,
red as a rose rose red my heart pumps flower red.
You wonder who created this juice of life?
And what power in the blood, as the hymn goes.
The grizzly flips the huge dead buffalo like a pancake.
The bloody brain concocts its mysteries, Kennedy's
fragments flying forever through the air in our neurons.
Walking outside with a bloody smear on my tingling
finger I stare at the half-shadowed bloodless
moon. Fifty yards away in September wolves killed
three of Bob Weber's sheep. My wife Linda called
me in Paris to say that from our bedroom window
before dawn you could hear them eating the sheep.
Red blood on the beige grass of late September.

SEARCHERS

At dawn Warren is on my bed,
a ragged lump of fur listening
to the birds as if deciding whether or not
to catch one. He has an old man's
mimsy delusion. A rabbit runs across
the yard and he walks after it
thinking he might close the widening distance
just as when I followed a lovely woman
on boulevard Montparnasse but couldn't equal
her rapid pace, the click-click of her shoes
moving into the distance, turning the final
corner, but when I turned the corner
she had disappeared and I looked up
into the trees thinking she might have climbed one.
When I was young a country girl would climb
a tree and throw apples down at my upturned face.
Warren and I are both searchers. He's looking
for his dead sister Shirley, and I'm wondering
about my brother John who left the earth
on this voyage all living creatures take.
Both cat and man are bathed in pleasant
insignificance, their eyes fixed on birds and stars.

MOTHER NIGHT

When you wake at three a.m. you don't think
of your age or sex and rarely your name
or the plot of your life which has never
broken itself down into logical pieces.
At three a.m. you have the gift of incomprehension
wherein the galaxies make more sense
than your job or the government. Jesus at the well
with Mary Magdalene is much more vivid
than your car. You can clearly see the bear
climb to heaven on a golden rope in the children's
story no one ever wrote. Your childhood horse
named June still stomps the ground for an apple.
What is morning and what if it doesn't arrive?
One morning Mother dropped an egg and asked
me if God was the same species as we are?
Smear of light at five a.m. Sound of Weber's
sheep flock and sandhill cranes across the road,
burble of irrigation ditch beneath my window.
She said, "Only lunatics save newspapers
and magazines," fried me two eggs, then said,
"If you want to understand mortality look at birds."
Blue moon, two full moons this month,
which I conclude are two full moons. In what
direction do the dead fly off the earth?
Rising sun. A thousand blackbirds pronounce day.

THE CREEK

One. Two. Three.
Before six a.m. waking
to the improbable ache of confused
dreams so that the open world
of consciousness was to jump into hell.
Fled the house with my dog Rose,
crossed the creek and into a thicket
after counting three different beer cans
by the road, two varieties of water bottles.
Who hears?
asked the man with ears.
Eleven different birdcalls
and a vermilion flycatcher just beyond
my nose fluttering along a willow
branch unsure of my company
during his bug breakfast.
Who hears? Far above a soundless gray hawk
attacks and chases away two turkey vultures.
Looked up again and sensed the dead
lounging upon those billowing cumulus clouds.
I'll check on this the next time I fly.

BIRDS AGAIN

A secret came a week ago though I already
knew it just beyond the bruised lips of consciousness.
The very alive souls of thirty-five hundred dead birds
are harbored in my body. It's not uncomfortable.
I'm only temporary habitat for these not-quite-
weightless creatures. I offered a wordless invitation
and now they're roosting within me, recalling
how I had watched them at night
in fall and spring passing across earth moons,
little clouds of black confetti, chattering and singing
on their way north or south. Now in my dreams
I see from the air the rumpled green and beige,
the watery face of earth as if they're carrying
me rather than me carrying them. Next winter
I'll release them near the estuary west of Alvarado
and south of Veracruz. I can see them perching
on undiscovered Olmec heads. We'll say goodbye
and I'll return my dreams to earth.

BECOMING

Nowhere is it the same place as yesterday.
None of us is the same person as yesterday.
We finally die from the exhaustion of becoming.
This downward cellular jubilance is shared
by the wind, bugs, birds, bears and rivers,
and perhaps the black holes in galactic space
where our souls will all be gathered in an invisible
thimble of antimatter. But we're getting ahead of ourselves.
Yes, trees wear out as the wattles under my chin
grow, the wrinkled hands that tried to strangle
a wife beater in New York City in 1957.
We whirl with the earth, catching our breath
as someone else, our soft brains ill-trained
except to watch ourselves disappear into the distance.
Still, we love to make music of this puzzle.

PORTAL, ARIZONA

I've been apart too long
from this life we have.
They deep-fry pork chops locally.
I've never had them that way.
In the canyon at dawn the Cooper's hawk
rose from her nest. Lion's pug marks
a few miles up where the canyon narrowed
and one rock had an eye with sky beyond.
A geezer told me Nabokov wrote here
while his beloved Vera tortured the piano.
He chased butterflies to their pinheaded doom
but Lolita survived. What beauty
can I imagine beyond these vast rock walls
with caves sculpted by wind where perhaps
Geronimo slept quite innocent of television
and when his three-year-old son died
made a war these ravens still talk about.

EASTER MORNING

On Easter morning all over America
the peasants are frying potatoes
in bacon grease.

We're not supposed to have "peasants"
but there are tens of millions of them
frying potatoes on Easter morning,
cheap and delicious with catsup.

If Jesus were here this morning he might
be eating fried potatoes with my friend
who has a '51 Dodge and a '72 Pontiac.

When his kids ask why they don't have
a new car he says, "These cars were new once
and now they are experienced."

He can fix anything and when rich folks
call to get a toilet repaired he pauses
extra hours so that they can further
learn what we're made of.

I told him that in Mexico the poor say
that when there's lightning the rich
think that God is taking their picture.
He laughed.

Like peasants everywhere in the history
of the world ours can't figure out why
they're getting poorer. Their sons join
the army to get work being shot at.

Your ideals are invisible clouds
so try not to suffocate the poor,
the peasants, with your sympathies.
They know that you're staring at them.

CORRIDO SONORENSE

para la banda Los Humildes

Cuando ella cantó su canción
aun los conejos y los perros rabiosos escucharon.
Vivía en una choza de estaño
a mitad de camino de una montaña cerca de Caborca.
Sólo tenía doce años, criada por un hermano
que algún viernes se fue a Hermosillo
para engañar a los ricos y poderosos
que le habían robado su cosecha.
Tres días y tres noches
esperaba con el corazón en la boca
al final de su sendero al borde
del camino polvoriento que conducía a Caborca.
Hacía calor y estaba tomando el aire
en sollozos cuando un camión se acercó
y le tiró un saco con la risa
de un diablo frío. En el saco
estaban la lengua de su hermano y su dedo
con el anillo hecho de crin.
Ahora se convertiría en puta o moriría de hambre,
pero se cortó las venas para reunirse con su hermano.
Si deseas engañar a los ricos y poderosos
tienes que hacerlo con un arma.

SONORAN CORRIDA

for the band Los Humildes

When she sang her song
even rabbits and mad dogs listened.
She lived in a tin shack
halfway up a mountain near Caborca.
She was only twelve, raised by a brother
who one Friday went to Hermosillo
to cheat the rich and powerful
who had stolen his crop.
Three days and three nights
she waited with her heart in her throat
at the end of their path down
to the dusty road that led to Caborca.
It was hot and she was drinking the air
in sobs when a truck drew up
and threw her a bag with a cold
devil's laughter. In the bag
were her brother's tongue and finger
with its ring made of a horsehair nail.
Now she would become a whore or starve,
but she cut her wrists to join her brother.
If you wish to cheat the rich and powerful
you must do it with a gun.

OLDER LOVE

His wife has asthma
so he only smokes outdoors
or late at night with head
and shoulders well into
the fireplace, the mesquite and oak
heat bright against his face.
Does it replace the heat
that has wandered from love
back into the natural world?
But then the shadow passion casts
is much longer than passion,
stretching with effort from year to year.
Outside tonight hard wind and sleet
from three bald mountains,
and on the hearth before his face
the ashes we'll all become,
soft as the back of a woman's knee.

LOS VIEJOS TIEMPOS

En los viejos tiempos no oscurecía hasta medianoche
y la lluvia y la nieve emergían de la tierra
en vez de caer del cielo. Las mujeres eran fáciles.
Cada vez que veías una, dos más aparecían,
caminando hacia ti marcha atrás al tiempo que su ropa caía.
El dinero no crecía en las hojas de los árboles sino abrazado
a los troncos en billeteras de ternero,
pero sólo podías sacar veinte dólares al día.
Ciertos hombres volaban tan bien como los cuervos mientras otros
    trepaban
los árboles cual ardillas. A siete mujeres de Nebraska
se les tomó el tiempo nadando río arriba en el Misuri;
fueron más veloces que los delfines moteados del lugar. Los perros basenji
podían hablar español, mas decidieron no hacerlo.
Unos políticos fueron ejecutados por traicionar
la confianza pública y a los poetas se les dio la ración de un galón
de vino tinto al día. La gente sólo moría un día
al año y bellos coros surgían como por un embudo
a través de las chimeneas de los hospitales donde cada habitación tenía
un hogar de piedra. Algunos pescadores aprendieron a caminar
sobre el agua y de niño yo trotaba por los ríos,
mi caña de pescar siempre lista. Las mujeres que anhelaban el amor
sólo necesitaban usar pantuflas de oreja de cerdo o aretes
de ajo. Todos los perros y la gente en libre concurso
se tornaban de tamaño mediano y color marrón, y en Navidad
todos ganaban la lotería de cien dólares. Ni Dios ni Jesús
tenían que descender a la tierra porque ya estaban
aquí montando caballos salvajes cada noche
y a los niños se les permitía ir a la cama tarde para oírlos
pasar al galope. Los mejores restaurantes eran iglesias
donde los anglicanos servían cocina provenzal, los metodistas toscana
y así. En ese tiempo el país era dos mil millas

THE OLD DAYS

In the old days it stayed light until midnight
and rain and snow came up from the ground
rather than down from the sky. Women were easy.
Every time you'd see one, two more would appear,
walking toward you backwards as their clothes dropped.
Money didn't grow in the leaves of trees but around
the trunks in calf's leather money belts,
though you could only take twenty bucks a day.
Certain men flew as well as crows while others ran
up trees like chipmunks. Seven Nebraska women
were clocked swimming upstream in the Missouri
faster than the local spotted dolphins. Basenjis
could talk Spanish but all of them chose not to.
A few political leaders were executed for betraying
the public trust and poets were rationed a gallon
of Burgundy a day. People only died on one day
a year and lovely choruses funneled out
of hospital chimneys where every room had a field-
stone fireplace. Some fishermen learned to walk
on water and as a boy I trotted down rivers,
my flyrod at the ready. Women who wanted love
needed only to wear pig's ear slippers or garlic
earrings. All dogs and people in free concourse
became medium sized and brown, and on Christmas
everyone won the hundred-dollar lottery. God and Jesus
didn't need to come down to earth because they were
already here riding wild horses every night
and children were allowed to stay up late to hear
them galloping by. The best restaurants were churches,
with Episcopalians serving Provençal, the Methodists Tuscan,
and so on. In those days the country was an extra

más ancho, y mil millas más
profundo. Había muchos valles para caminar aún no descubiertos
donde tribus indígenas vivían en paz
aunque algunas tribus eligieron fundar naciones nuevas
en las áreas desconocidas hasta entonces en las negras
grietas de los límites entre los estados. Me casé
con una joven pawnee en una ceremonia detrás de la catarata acostumbrada.
Las cortes estaban administradas por osos durmientes y pájaros cantaban
fábulas lúcidas de sus pájaros ancestros que vuelan ahora
en otros mundos. Algunos ríos fluían demasiado rápido
para ser útiles pero se les permitió hacerlo cuando acordaron
no inundar la Conferencia de Des Moines.
Los aviones de pasajeros se parecían a barcos aéreos con múltiples
alas aleteantes que tocaban un tipo de música de salón
en el cielo. Las consólidas crecían en los cañones de pistola
y cada quien podía seleccionar siete días al año
con libertad de repetir pero este no era un programa
popular. En esos días el vacío giraba
con flores y animales salvajes desconocidos asistían
a funerales campestres. Todos los tejados en las ciudades
eran huertas de flores y verduras. El río Hudson era potable
y una ballena jorobada fue vista cerca del muelle
de la calle 42, su cabeza llena de la sangre azul del mar,
su voz alzando las pisadas de la gente
en su tradicional antimarcha, su inocuo desarreglo.
Podría seguir pero no lo haré. Toda mi evidencia
se perdió en un incendio pero no antes que fuera masticada
por todos los perros que habitan la memoria.
Uno tras otro ladran al sol, a la luna y las estrellas
tratando de acercarlas otra vez.

two thousand miles wider, and an additional thousand
miles deep. There were many undiscovered valleys
to walk in where Indian tribes lived undisturbed
though some tribes chose to found new nations
in the heretofore unknown areas between the black
boundary cracks between states. I was married
to a Pawnee girl in a ceremony behind the usual waterfall.
Courts were manned by sleeping bears and birds sang
lucid tales of ancient bird ancestors who now fly
in other worlds. Certain rivers ran too fast
to be usable but were allowed to do so when they consented
not to flood at the Des Moines Conference.
Airliners were similar to airborne ships with multiple
fluttering wings that played a kind of chamber music
in the sky. Pistol barrels grew delphiniums
and everyone was able to select seven days a year
they were free to repeat but this wasn't a popular
program. In those days the void whirled
with flowers and unknown wild animals attended
country funerals. All the rooftops in cities were flower
and vegetable gardens. The Hudson River was drinkable
and a humpback whale was seen near the Forty-Second Street
pier, its head full of the blue blood of the sea,
its voice lifting the steps of people
in their traditional anti-march, their harmless disarray.
I could go on but won't. All my evidence
was lost in a fire but not before it was chewed
on by all the dogs who inhabit memory.
One by one they bark at the sun, moon and stars
trying to draw them closer again.

TWO GIRLS

Late November (full moon last night),
a cold Patagonia moon, the misty air
tinkled slightly, a rank-smelling bull
in the creek bottom seemed to be crying.
Coyotes yelped up the canyon
where they took a trip-wire photo of a jaguar
last spring. I hope he's sleeping or eating
a delicious deer. Our two little girl dogs
are peeing in the midnight yard, nervous
about the bull. They can't imagine a jaguar.

THE LITTLE APPEARANCES OF GOD

I

When god visits us he sleeps
without a clock in empty bird nests.
He likes the view. Not too high.
Not too low. He winks a friendly wink
at a nearby possum who sniffs the air
unable to detect the scent
of this not-quite-visible stranger.
A canyon wren lands on the bridge
of god's nose deciding the new experience
is worth the fear. He's an old bird
due to flee the earth
not on his own wings. This is a good
place to feel his waning flutter
of breath, hear his last delicate musical
call, his death song, and then he hopes
to become part of god's body. Feeling
the subdued dread of his illness
he won't know for sure until it's over.

II

He's now within the form of a whippoorwill
sitting on a faded gravestone in the twilight
while children pass by the cemetery
almost enjoying the purity of their fright.
Since he's god he can read the gravestone
upside down. Little Mary disappeared
in the influenza epidemic back in 1919.
He ponders that it took a couple of million
years to invent these children but perhaps microbes
must also have freedom from predestination.
He's so tired of hearing about this ditzy Irishman,

Bishop Ussher, who spread the rumor that creation
only took six thousand years when it required twelve billion.
Man shrank himself with the biological hysteria
of clocks, the machinery of dread. You spend twelve billion
years inventing ninety billion galaxies and who appreciates
your work except children, birds and dogs, and a few
other genius strokes like otters and porpoises, those humans
who kiss joy as it flies, who see though not with the eye.

III

Years ago he kept an eye on Deprise Brescia,
a creature of beauty. He doesn't lose track of people
as some need no help, bent to their own particulars.
No dancing or music allowed.
The world in front of their noses has disappeared.
Dickinson wrote, "The Brain is just the weight of God."
We said goodbye to our farm and a stately heron walked up the steps
and looked in our window. I had suffocated myself
but then south of Zihuatanejo just outside the Pacific's
crashing and lethal surf in a panga I heard the billions
of cicadas in the wild bougainvillea on the mountainsides,
a new kind of thunder. He gave Thoreau, Modigliani
and Neruda the same birthday to tease with his abilities.

WAVES

A wave lasts only moments
but underneath another one is always
waiting to be born. This isn't the Tao
of people but of waves.
As a student of people, waves, the Tao,
I'm free to let you know that waves
and people tell the same story
of how blood and water were born,
that our bodies are full of creeks
and rivers flowing in circles,
that we are kin of the waves
and the nearly undetectable ocean currents,
that the moon pleads innocence
of its tidal power, its wayward control
of our dreams, the way the moon tugs
at our skulls and loins, the way
the tides make their tortuous love to the land.
We're surely creatures with unknown gods.

TIME

Nothing quite so wrenches
the universe like time.
It clings obnoxiously
to every atom, not to speak
of the moon, which it weighs
down with invisible wet dust.
I used to think the problem
was space, the million miles
between me and the pretty waitress
across the diner counter stretching
to fill the coffee machine with water,
but now I know it's time
which withers me moment by moment
with her own galactic smile.

AN OLD MAN

Truly old men, he thought, don't look too far past the applesauce and cottage cheese, filling the tank of the kerosene heater over there in the corner of the cabin near the stack of *National Geographic*s from the forties containing nipples from Borneo and the Amazon, tattooed and pierced. He carries extra cash because he woke up on a recent morning thinking that the ATM at the IGA had acted suspiciously. The newspaper said pork steak was ninety-nine cents a pound but it turned out to be a newspaper from last week and pork steak had shot up to one thirty-nine. He can't eat all the fish he catches and sometimes the extras get pushed toward the back of the refrigerator so that the rare visitor says, "Jesus Christ Frank something stinks." A feral tomcat that sometimes sleeps in the pump shed will eat it anyway. He read that his thin hair will continue growing in the grave, a nice idea but then cremation is cheaper. His great-granddaughter from way downstate wears an African-type nose ring and brought him a bird book but he'd rather know what birds call themselves. He often dreams of the nine dogs of his life and idly wonders if he'll see them again. He's not counting on it but it's another nice idea. One summer night in a big moon he walked three miles to his favorite bend of the river and sat on a stump until first light when a small bear swam past. In the night his ghost wife appeared and asked, "Frank, I miss you, aren't you holding on too long?" and he said, "It's not for me to decide." Last November he made a big batch of chili from a hindquarter of a bear a neighbor shot. There are seven containers left and they shouldn't go to waste. Waste not, want not.

TO A MEADOWLARK

for M.L. Smoker

Up on the Fort Peck Reservation
(Assiniboine and Sioux)
just as I passed two white crosses
in the ditch I hit a fledgling meadowlark,
the slightest thunk against the car's grille.
A mean-minded God
in a mean-minded machine, offering
another ghost to the void to join the two
white crosses stabbing upward in the insufferable
air. Wherever we go we do harm, forgiving
ourselves as wheels do cement for wearing
each other out. We set this house
on fire forgetting that we live within.

Driving south of Wolf Point down by the Missouri:
M.L. Smoker is camped with her Indians,
tepees in a circle, eating buffalo meat for breakfast,
reminding themselves what life may have been.
She says that in the evenings the wild horses
from the *terra incognita* to the south come
to the river to drink and just stand there
watching the Indians dance. I leave quickly,
still feeling like a bullsnake whipping through
the grass looking for something to kill.

NOVEMBER

The souls of dogs,
big toes of ladies,
original clouds,
the winter life
of farm machinery,
the hammer lost
in the weeds,
the filaments of sunlight
hugging the bare tree,
then slipping off the bark
down into night.

COLD POEM

A cold has put me on the fritz, said Eugene O'Neill,
how can I forget certain things?
Now I have thirteen bottles of red wine
where once I had over a thousand.
I know where they went but why should I tell?
Every day I feed the dogs and birds.
The yard is littered with bones and seed husks.
Hearts spend their entire lives in the dark,
but the dogs and birds are fond of me.
I take a shower frequently but still
women are not drawn to me in large numbers.
Perhaps they know I'm happily married
and why exhaust themselves vainly to seduce me?
I loaned hundreds of thousands of dollars
and was paid back only by two Indians.
If I had known history it was never otherwise.
This is the song of the cold when people
are themselves but less so, people
who haven't listened to my unworded advice.
I was once described as "immortal"
but this didn't include my mother who recently died.
And why go to New York after the asteroid
and the floods of polar waters, the crumbling
buildings, when you're the only one there
in 2050? Come back to earth.
Blow your nose and dwell on the shortness of life.
Lift up your dark heart and sing a song about
how time drifts past you like the gentlest, almost
imperceptible breeze.

INVASIVE

Coming out of anesthesia I believed
I had awakened in the wrong body,
and when I returned to my snazzy hotel room
and looked at *Architectural Digest*
I no longer recognized large parts of the world.
There was a cabin for sale
for seven million dollars, while mine had cost
only forty grand with forty acres. An android
from drugs I understood finally that life
works to no one's advantage. From dawn
until midnight I put together a jigsaw puzzle
made of ten million pieces of white confetti.
On television I watch the overburdened world
of books and movies, all flickering trash, while outside
cars pass through deep puddles on the street,
the swish and swash of life, patterns of rain
drizzle on the windows, finch yodel and Mexican raven squawk
until I enter the murder of sleep and fresh demons,
one of whom sings in basso profundo Mickey and Sylvia's
"Love Is Strange." In the bathroom mirror it's someone else.

ON THE WAY TO THE DOCTOR'S

On Thursday morning at seven a.m. seven surgeons will spend seven hours taking me apart and putting me back together the same way. Three of the surgeons don't have medical degrees but are part-time amateurs trying to learn the ropes. One is a butcher who wants to move up. A butcher's salary is twenty-seven thousand and the average surgeon makes two hundred twenty-seven, the difference being the proximity of the nearest huge asteroid to the moon, which could be destroyed any minute now. In anticipation of the unmentionable I've put my life in order. Anyone with blood-slippery hands can drop a heart on the floor. I've sent a single-page letter of resignation to the Literary World but they haven't had time to read it. They're exhausted from reading Sontag's obituaries, a nasty reminder that everyone dies. Assuming I survive, Jean Peters and Jean Simmons will reemerge as twenty-seven-year-olds and trade shifts nursing me around the clock. They're goddesses and never get tired. Since the surgeons are cutting me open like a baked potato, sex will be put aside for the time being. It's unpleasant to burst your stitches on a Sunday morning dalliance when you're due on your gurney in the hospital Chapel of Black Roses. I'm not afraid of death. I've been told I'll immediately return as a common house finch, but it's all the stuff between here and death falsely called life. Right now we're actually in the car with my wife driving to the doctor's. I say, "Turn left on Ruthrauff onto La Cholla." I always drive when we go to Tucson but I'm in too much pain half-reclining in the seat peeking out like the little old man I might not get to be. At the entrance to the office the doctor meets us with an immense bouquet of Brazilian tropical flowers. The doctor resembles a photo of my mother in 1933, so much so that I'm uncomfortable. The office is full of dozens of identical framed photos of a desperate sunset in the desert trying to look original. The office temperature is kept at 32 degrees to reduce odors. I've been recently sleeping under seven blankets and am quite cold. The pages of the magazines on the coffee table are blank so that you can make up your own *National Geographic*s. I haven't eaten for days except rice and yogurt, but my wife is out in the car having a baguette stuffed with prosciutto, imported provolone, mortadella and roasted peppers. They turn out the lights so my eyes don't tire reading blank pages. Now I see that the mirror on the wall is two-way and in another room the seven surgeons are rolling up their sleeves, hot to get started. "We don't have time to wash our hands," they say in unison.

ESPAÑOL

Por años he creído que el mundo debe hablar español.
He soñado que hablaba y leía español,
pero cuando desperté no fue verdad. Tal vez las Naciones Unidas
puedan poner freno al inglés pero lo dudo.
El inglés es el lenguaje de la conquista, el dinero, el asesinato.

Dios me envió un e-mail diciendo que el sexo sería mejor
en español. Dios estaba fumando un "Lucky Strike"
mientras Bush mordisqueaba chicle "Dentyne" y estudiaba "Baywatch"
     en la tele.

Mi viejo amigo Jesús se convirtió en una película de terror
que ganó millones en inglés, el cual pensaba no había sido inventado.
Jesús habla español pero no entiende bien el inglés,
por eso nuestras oraciones erran y las chicas son deshimenizadas.

Niños y niñas yacen en sus camas pataleando
en desesperación a los dioses que juegan al boliche
con sus cabezas. No pasaría si hablaran español.
La televisión mexicana dijo que la Virgen llevaba calzones los domingos.

El dibujo animado es nuestra forma de arte mientras que los españoles
     escriben
poesía, miles de Lorcas de quinta elogiando a la luna
pero sin el contragiro de los dibujos en sus corazones. El sexo no nos
     conducirá
al cielo en español pero nos acercará más que los dibujos.

María Magdalena dijo que si no hubiera sido por la historia
se habría ahogado en el pozo o inventado
la pistola para que se la dispararan. Es tan compleja
que no puede ser entendida excepto en español.

Me arrojé de un avión pero aterricé en una nube de español.
El inglés me había perseguido a muerte. Los santos caen
sobre plumas ensangrentadas justo antes que la historia termine.

SPANISH

For years I've believed the world should speak Spanish.
I've dreamt that I spoke and read Spanish,
but when I awoke it wasn't true. Perhaps the U.N.
can put a halt to English but I doubt it.
English is the language of conquest, money, murder.

God e-mailed me that sex would be better
in Spanish. God was smoking a Lucky Strike
while Bush snapped Dentyne and studied *Baywatch* on TV.

My old pal Jesus became a horror film that made
millions in English that he thought hadn't been invented.
Jesus speaks Spanish but understands English poorly,
thus our prayers go awry and girls are dehymenized.

Boys and girls lie on their beds kicking their feet
in desperation at the gods who are bowling
with their heads. It wouldn't happen if they spoke Spanish.
Mexican TV said the Virgin wore underpants on Sunday.

The cartoon is our art form while the Spanish write
poetry, thousands of fifth-rate Lorcas praising the moon
but without cartoon backspin in their hearts. Sex won't take
us to heaven in Spanish but closer than cartoons.

Mary Magdalene said that if it hadn't been for history
she would have drowned herself at the well or invented
the gun for them to shoot her. She's so complex
that she can't be understood except in Spanish.

I jumped out of a plane but landed on a Spanish cloud.
English had chased me to death. The saints fall
on bloody feathers just before history ends.

PICO

I don't know what. I don't know what.
I'm modern man at the crossroads,
an interstice where ten thousand roads meet
and exfoliate. Meanwhile today a hundred
dense blue never-seen-before pinyon jays
land in the yard for a scant ten minutes.
The pinyon jays are not at any crossroads
but are finding their way south by celestial navigation.
You're not on a road, you fool. This life
is pathless with ninety billion galaxies
hovering around us, our home truly away from home.

THE SHORT COURSE

For my new part I'm in makeup
        each day for twenty-four hours.
We can die from this exhaustion
        of shooting without a script;
the lines that didn't come right disappeared
        into the thickest air
        without the vacuum of intentions.
New lines appeared in miraculous succession.
We found love by writing it down
        only moments before she appeared.
The door opened itself.
Steps were taken.
A new day dawned crimson.
We went outside among the inhuman trees.
A creek appeared from nowhere.
Everyone is raised by the gods
but we never learned our lines.

SCIENCE

It was one of those mornings utterly distorted by the night's dreams. Why go to court to change my name to Gaspar de la Nuit in order to avoid thinking of myself as a silly, fat old man? At midmorning I looked at the dogs as possibilities for something different in my life. I was dogsitting both daughters' dogs plus our own: Lily, Grace, Pearl, Harry, Rose and Mary. I shook the biscuit box and they assembled in the living room on a very cold windy morning when no one wanted to go outside except for a quick pee and a bark at the mailman. I sang, "He's got the whole world in his hands," as they waited for their snack. Harry was embarrassed and furtive and tried to leave the room but I called him back. I tried, "Yes, we have no bananas, we have no bananas today," and Lily, the largest of the dogs, became angry at the others who looked away intimidated. I tried something religious, "The Old Rugged Cross," to no particular response except that Mary leapt up at the biscuit box in irritation. I realized decisively that dogs don't care about music and religion and thus have written up this report. This scarcely makes me the Father of the A-bomb, I thought as I flung the contents of the full box of biscuits around the room with the dogs scrambling wildly on the hard maple floor. Let there be happy chaos.

THE FISH IN MY LIFE

When I was younger I walked the floor
of the Baltic looking for a perfect herring.

Off Ecuador when I swam underneath the boat
the hooked marlin was wreathed in curious sea snakes.

I stepped on a scorpion in Key West. It bit me.
It's not a fish but it looks like a shrimp.

The nude girl ate the brook trout I fried. A morsel
plummeted from her lips to the left aureole.

Fish spend their lives underwater except for skyward jumps
for food, or to shake off gill lice, look around in dismay.

In the house of water the bottom and the top
do not go away. Our drowned bodies are kissed.

With my grandson's Play-Doh I shaped
a modest fish, also the brown girl of my dreams.

O fish, my brothers and sisters, some scientists
think that our sinuses are merely vestigial gills.

Fish, we both survive among countless thousands
of dead eggs. We're well chosen by the gods of chaos.

A LETTER TO TED & DAN

France to Michigan

Just another plane trip
with the mind wandering
at large in the bowels
of life. How am I to land this?
At Godthåb, above Greenland,
we're disappointing compared to the immensity
of our scientific reality, the trillions
of unresolved particles, though there were
those improbable unrecorded celebrations,
over a million at the samba festival,
a thousand bands, a million doves
eaten raw because there was no wood for fire,
an immense dance with no words with nonstop
loving in the fashion of lions and porpoises.
Off in the jungle anacondas perked up their heads
and slowly moved toward the music,
the largest snake of all wrapped around
the world's waist, holding us together
against our various defilements, our naive
theocracies at war with one another.

　　　　　—

Almost forgot that, over Iceland,
seven miles below I saw children
sledding in the first snow of the year,
small as motes of dust on silver-edged
sleighs, the glistening of the frosted sweat
of the shaggy pony that pulled them
back up the hill. I've long wondered
at the way certain children, even babies,
decide to become songbirds because they could see

the endless suffering in their future.
They've been using this method for centuries.

—

I've asked the French government,
Richelieu in fact, for the use of a one-room
cabin in the Dordogne where I can recreate
the local origin of man in this birthplace
of the Occident, riding the spear
of the Occident into the future, the iron horse
that makes us glue the life of mankind
together with blood.

—

In France I went to a place
of grandeur though it was only
a thicket as large as the average hotel room.
I learned that we'll float into eternity
like the dehydrated maggots I saw
in Mexico around the body of a desert tortoise
missing an interior that had fled
seven days before. How grand.

—

For after death I've been given
the false biblical promise of smoking privileges
and the possession of hundreds of small
photos of all the dogs and women I've known.

—

The beasts (the plane and I) land on earth.
Time for a hot dog and a small pizza.
I glance at the mellifluous rubbing
of a melancholy woman's buttocks.
I tell her to celebrate her tears.

EFFLUVIA

Tonight the newish moon is orange
from the smoke of a forest fire, a wedge of fresh orange.

The mystery of ink pumped up from three
thousand feet in northern Michigan from the bed
of a Pleistocene sea. A meteor hit
a massive group of giant squid, some say
millions, from whose ink I write this poem.

A bold girl I once knew made love
on lysergic acid to a dolphin and a chimp,
though not the same day. She said the chimp
was too hairy, too fast, and improbably insensitive.

An artist friend made me a cocktail shaker
from a rubbery translucent material and in the pinkish
form of a human stomach. Shake it and the vodka
drops like rain into a sea of happiness.

I am a relic in a reliquary.
All of these damp skulls of ghosts,
many of them feathered, telling
me that the past isn't very past.

On an airliner going to both dream coasts
I'm a Romantic Poet so alone and lonely.
Lucky for me there are pilots up front.

We must give our fantasy women homely names
to keep our feet barely on the ground of this dismembered
earth: Wilma, Edna, Ethel, Blanche, Frida.
Otherwise we'll fly away on the backs
of their somnambulistic lust, fleas in their plumage.
The birds above the river yesterday: Swainson's

hawk, prairie and peregrine falcons, bald and golden
eagles, osprey, wild geese, fifty-two sandhill cranes.
Their soaring bodies nearly lifting us from the river.

JOSEPH'S POEM

It's the date that gets me
down. It keeps changing.
Others have noticed this.
Not long ago up at Hard Luck Ranch,
Diana, the cow dog, was young.
Now her face looks like my own.
Surprise, she doesn't say, with each
halting step, the world is going away.
How could I have thought otherwise,
these dogging steps pit-patting
to and fro, though when the soul
rises to the moment, moment by moment
it is otherwise. Dog's foot is holy
and the geezer, childish again,
is deep up a canyon with his dog
close to the edge of the world,
the heart beating a thousand times
a minute, probably more,
as if it were an interior propeller
to whir us upward, but it's not.
Once I held the heart of a bear
that was about my size. Stewed it back
at the cabin and thought that the sky
opened up and changed her colors,
smelled the fumes of a falling contrail,
sensed the world behind my back
and beneath my feet, ravens above,
each tree its individual odor,
the night no longer night,
the burst of water around my body,
the world unfolding in glory with each step.

UNBUILDING

It's harder
to dismantle your life
than build it.
One Sunday morning at Hard Luck Ranch
the roadrunner flits around the backyard
like an American poet,
ignored by nine cow dogs lying in patches
of sun, also by three ravens,
and finally by seven Gambel's quail
who do not know that they're delicious roasted
when they come to the bowl of water.
It is always possible to see the traceries of birds,
but on the scrambled porn channel the woman's
mouth that prays is used otherwise and the ground
delivers up insects I've never noticed before.
I found myself in the slightest prayer
for Diana who I fear will die like her
namesake did far across the ocean blue.
She's fourteen with cancer of the mouth
and throat though around Christmastime
I found her making love with her son Ace.
When they finished I gave her extra biscuits
for being so human, for staying as young
as her mind and body called out for her to be.
No rain now for one hundred twenty-three days
so I read Su Tung-p'o where it's always raining,
Rain drenches down as from a tilted basin,
and recall I owe forty thousand on my credit cards.
Carried along by red wine and birds, dogs,
the roadrunner's charm, I take apart my life
stone by mortared stone while I'm still strong
enough to do so, or think that I am,

wishing that I could smile like a lazy
dog curled in the dust on Sunday morning,
far from the shroud I sewed for my life.

SUZANNE WILSON

Is it better to rake all the leaves
in one's life into a pile
or leave them scattered? That's a good question
as questions go, but then they're easier to burn
in one place. The years take their toll,
our lives, to be exact. We burn without fire
and without effort so slowly the wick of this lamp
seems endless. And then the fire is out,
a hallowed time. And those who took the light
with them pull us slowly toward their breasts.

CURRENT EVENTS

I'm a brownish American who wonders
if civilization can be glued together with blood.
The written word is no longer understood.
We've had dogs longer than governments.
Millions of us must travel to Washington
and not talk but bark like dogs.
We must practice our barking and in unison
raise a mighty bark. The sun turns amber
and they're opening the well-oiled gates of hell.

POEM OF WAR (I)

The old rancher of seventy-nine years
said while branding and nutting young bulls
with the rank odor of burned hairs and flesh
in the air, the oil-slippery red nuts
plopping into a galvanized bucket,
"This smells just like Guadalcanal."

POEM OF WAR (II)

The theocratic cowboy forgetting Vietnam rides
into town on a red horse. He's praying to himself
not God. War prayers. The red horse
he rides is the horse of blasphemy. Jesus
leads a flower-laden donkey across the Red Sea
in the other direction, his nose full of the stink
of corpses. Buddha and Muhammad offer
cool water from a palm's shade while young
men die in the rockets' red glare.
And in the old men's dreams
René Char asked, "Who stands on the gangplank
directing operations, the captain or the rats?"
Whitman said, "So many young throats
choked on their own blood." God says nothing.

RACHEL'S BULLDOZER

The man sitting on the cold stone hearth
    of the fireplace
considers tomorrow, the virulent
    skirmishes with reality
he takes part in, always surprised,
    in order to earn a living.
On most days it's this villain
    reality making the heart ache,
creeping under the long shirtsleeves
    to suffocate the armpits,
each day's terror pouring vinegar
    into the heart valve.
Today it's Rachel Corrie making me
    ashamed to be human,
beating her girlish fists against
    the oncoming bulldozer blade.
Strangled mute before the television screen
    we do not deserve to witness this courage.

AFTER THE WAR

God wears orange and black
on Halloween. The bumblebee hummingbird
in Cuba weighs less than a penny.

I was joined by the head to this world.
No surgery was possible.
We keep doing things together.

There's almost never a stoplight
where rivers cross each other.

Congress is as fake as television sex.
The parts are off a few inches and don't actually
meet. It's in bad taste to send the heads
of children to Washington.

Just today I noticed that all truly valuable
knowledge is lost between generations. Of course
life is upsetting. What else could be upsetting?

From not very far in space I see the tiny pink
splotches of literature here and there upon
the earth about the size of dog pounds.

Reporters mostly reported themselves.
This was a new touch. They received
producer credits and director's perks.

Tonight I smell a different kind
of darkness. The burning celluloid of news.
The Virgin strolls through Washington, D.C.,
with an ice pick shoved in her ear.
Who is taking this time machine
from the present into the present?

One of the oldest stories: dead dicks playing
with death toys. Plato said war is always greed.
Red blood turns brown in the heat. It's only
the liquid shit of slaves.

Un mundo raro. The angel is decidedly female.
She weighs her weight in flowers.
She has no talent for our discourse,
which she said was a septic tank burble.

Of the 90 billion galaxies a few are bad
apples, especially a fusion of male stars
not unlike galactic gay sex. Washington
is concerned, and the pope is stressed.

All over America people appear to be drinking
small bottles of water. Fill them with French
red wine and shoot out the streetlights.

As a long-lived interior astronaut
it was mostly just space. The void
was my home in which I invented
the undescribed earth.

This is Rome. There are no Christians
so we throw Muslims to the lions of war.
We have the world in the dentist's chair.

I pray daily for seven mortally ill women,
not to say that life is a mortal illness.
It's always been a matter of timing.
Lives are as hard to track as flying birds.
To understand the news is to drag a dead dog
behind you with a paper leash.
Once you loved the dog.

Try to remember all of the birds
you've heard but didn't see.
This is called grace.

I was living far too high in my mind
and started fishing like the autistic child
they found the next morning still fishing.
The war became X-rated. No American bodies.

During these times many of us
would have been far happier as fish, making
occasional little jumps up above the water's
surface for a view of the new century.

It seems that everything is a matter
of time, from cooking to dropping dead.
Just moments earlier the dead soldier
drank warm orange juice, scratched his ass
and thought about the Chicago Cubs.

Mrs. America is smothering the world
in her new pair of enormous fake tits.
She's the purgatorial mother
who can't stop eating children.

Rose was struck twice by a rattler
in the yard, a fang broken off in her eyeball.
Now old dog and old master each
have an eye full of bloody milk.

The end of the war was announced
by the Leader in a uniform from the deck
of an aircraft carrier, one of those deluxe
cruise ships that never actually touches
the lands they visit.

A girl of a different color kissed me once.
I think it was in Brazil. Celestial buttocks.
Honeysuckle dawn. Imanja rose from the sea,
her head buried in a red sun.

Hot August night, a forty-day heat wave.
Thousands of the tiniest bugs possible
are dying in this old ranch house. Like humans
they are easily attracted to the wrong light.

Tonight the moon is an orange ceiling globe
from a forest fire across the river. In the dark
animals run, stumble, run, stumble.

I stopped three feet from the top
of Everest. Fuck it, I'm not going
a single inch farther.

We need a poetry of fishscales, coxcombs,
soot, dried moss, the heated aortas of whales,
to respond to the vulpine sniggers of the gods.

Throughout history soldiers want to go to war
and when they get there straightaway wish
to go home.

Change the lens on this vast picture show.
See the mosquito's slender beak penetrate
the baby's ass. A touch of evil.

I read the unshakable dreams of the hundred-
year-old lesbian, life shorn of the perfection
of the pork chop. Everyone lacks inevitability.

Michael and Joseph never truly returned
home because they weren't the same people
they were when they left home.

My dog Rose can't stop chasing curlews
who lead her a mile this way and that.
I have to catch her before she dies of exhaustion.
This is a metaphor of nothing but itself.

The motives were somewhat imaginary but people
died in earnest. Some were
shoveled up like flattened roadkill.

During World War II my brother John
and I would holler "bombs over Tokyo"
when we pooped. A different kind of war.

She kicked her red sandal at the sun
but it landed in a parking-lot mud puddle.
"We're de-haired chimps," she said
finishing her pistachio ice-cream cone.

Osama won really big I heard on a game
show. We changed our institutions,
the surge toward a fascist Disneyland.

I wish I had danced more, said the old man
drawing nearer his death bedstead in a foot
of grass in the back forty. Where's my teddy bear?

Of late, on television we are threatened
by crocodiles, snakes and bears
in full frontal nudity. Politicians are clothed.

My childhood Jesus has become an oil guy
but then he's from the area. Seek and ye shall
find an oil well. The daughter of murder is murder.

Nothing can be understood clearly. A second into
death we'll ask, "What's happening?" Viola said
that there's an invisible world out there and we're
living within it. Rose dreams of ghost snakes.

Of late, politicians remind me of teen prostitutes
the way they sell their asses cheap, the swagger
and confusion, the girlish resolutions. They can't go
home because everyone there is embarrassed.

I nearly collapsed yesterday but couldn't find
an appropriate place. Our pieces are anchored
a thousand miles deep in molten rock. A spider-
web draws us an equal distance toward the heavens.

The Leader is confident that Jesus and the Apostles
are his invisible SWAT team. His God
is a chatterbox full of martial instructions.

I worry about the soul life of these thousand
tiny bugs that die on the midnight coffee
table. Here today, gone tomorrow, but then
in cosmic time we live a single second.

Once a year all world leaders should be put
in an Olympic swimming pool full of rotten
human blood to let them dog-paddle in their creation.
The lifeguard is a blind child playing a video war game.

Men look at women's tits and flip out.
This is the mystery of life, but then they have a line
of coke, some meth, a few beers, and beat up or rape
or shoot someone. They make movies about this.

We must adore our fatal savagery. The child
thrown naked into the snowbank for peeing the bed
then kills the neighbor's cat, etc., etc. The midget
dreamt he grew two feet. Between the Virgin
and the garrison the flower becomes a knife.

My, how our government strains us
through its filthy sheets. We're drawn

from birth through the sucking vortex
of greed. It all looked good on paper.

To change Rhys, God is a doormat in a world
full of hobnailed boots. Proud of his feet
the Leader is common change. He's everywhere.

I've been looking closely at my smaller
mythologies the better to love them, those colorful
fibs and false conclusions, the mire
of private galaxies that kept
ancient man on earth and me alive.

BROTHERS AND SISTERS

I'm trying to open a window in this very old house of indeterminate age
buried toward the back of a large ranch here in the Southwest, abandoned
for so long that there's no road leading into it but a slight indentation in
the pastureland, last lived in by the owner's great-uncle who moved to
New York City to listen to music, or so he said, but his grandnephew
said that the man was "light in his loafers," which was hard to be back in
New Mexico in those days. In the pantry under a stained vinegar cruet is
a sepia photo of him and his sister in their early teens on the front porch
of the house, dressed unconvincingly as vaqueros, as handsome as young
people get. The photo is dated 1927 and lights up the pantry. I find out
that the girl died in childbirth in the middle thirties in Pasadena, the boy
committed suicide in Havana in 1952, both dying in the hands of love.
Out in the yard I shine my flashlight down a hole under a massive juniper
stump. A rattlesnake forms itself into anxious coils surrounding its pretty
babies stunned by the light.

FENCE LINE TREE

There's a single tree at the fence line
here in Montana, a little like a tree
in the Sandhills of Nebraska, which may be miles
away. When I cross the unfertile pasture strewn
with rocks and the holes of gophers, badgers, coyotes,
and the rattlesnake den (a thousand killed
in a decade because they don't mix well with dogs
and children) in an hour's walking and reach
the tree, I find it oppressive. Likely it's
as old as I am, withstanding its isolation,
all gnarled and twisted from its battle
with weather. I sit against it until we merge,
and when I return home in the cold, windy
twilight I feel I've been gone for years.

SAVING DAYLIGHT

I finally got back the hour
stolen from me last spring.
What did they do with it
but put it in some nasty cold storage?
Up north a farm neighbor wouldn't change
his clocks, saying, "I'm sticking with God's time."
All of these people of late seem to know
God rather personally. God even tells
girls to limit themselves to heavy petting
and avoid the act they call "full penetration."
I don't seem to receive these instructions
that tell me to go to war, and not to look
at a married woman's butt when she leans
over to fetch a package from her car's
backseat. I'm enrolled in a school without
visible teachers, the divine mumbling
just out of earshot, the whispering from the four-million-
mile-an-hour winds on the sun. The dead rabbit
in the road spoke to me yesterday, also the owl's wing
in the garage likely torn off by a goshawk.
In this bin of ice you must carefully
try to pick the right cube.

INCOMPREHENSION

We have running water in our
home though none of us know
why dogs exist.

Nevertheless, we love both water
and dogs and believe God might
fix our lives with his golden wrench.

This is the day the moon is closest
to us, the new moon slender
as a gray hair I pulled from my head.

The man said that there is no actual
life, only what we remember. In the
tropics the lizard is the God of the rock
he lives upon and under.

We didn't know the pages were
stuck together and we'd never
understand anything.

The church says God is a spy
who keeps track of how we misuse
our genitals. He always yawns
at the beginning of work.

I can only offer you the ten numbers
I wrote down when I read the
thermometer today, this incredible
machine I worship but don't understand.

I was the only one to see the boat sunken
on land. There were no survivors except
the few human rats that leapt like
flying squirrels.

The Queen of Earth is thought to be
up for grabs. She makes us shiver
in fear to keep us warm.

MEMORIAL DAY

Things I didn't know about until today:
Clip your toenails when wet and they won't crack.
The white in birdfeathers comes from the moon,
the yellow from the sun,
the black from night herself.
And that at three p.m. today
when we have our full minute of silence
for our millions of war dead,
their ghosts beyond the invisible carapace
above the green and blue turning earth
(from which birds get other colors),
the ghosts will vomit up the remnants
of their bone dust on hearing the strident
martial music rising up to them,
the hard-peckered music of the living,
the music of the machineries of war
in the wallets of the rich. And the ghosts ask us
to send up the music of earth:
three tree frogs, two loons, splash of fish
jumping, the wind's verbless carols.

LETTER POEM TO SAM HAMILL
AND DAN GERBER

I've been translating the language with which creatures
address God, including the nonharmonic bleats
of dying sheep, the burpish fish, the tenor groan
of the toad in the snake's mouth, the croak
of the seagull flopping on the yellow line,
misnamed mockingbird and catbird singing hundreds
of borrowed songs, coyotes' joyous yipe when they
bring down a fawn that honks like a bicycle
horn for his helpless mother. The ladybug on the table
was finally still. I strained my ear close to her
during the final moments but only heard Mozart
from the other room. She was beyond reach.
One night under a big moon I heard the massive-
lunged scream of a horse pounding in the pasture
across the creek, then his breathing above the creek
gurgle. This language is closer to what we spoke
in Africa seventy thousand years ago before
we started writing things down and now we can't
seem to stop. I can't imagine how we thought that
we're better than any other creatures except that
we wrote ourselves into it. Someone looked down
from Babel's tower and got the wrong idea, ignoring
the birds above him. I learned all this one day
listening to a raven funeral in a fir tree behind
my cabin, and learned it again listening to a wolf
howling from the river delta nearby. It's an old
secret past anyone's caring, or so it seems.

HAKUIN AND WELCH

Driving with implacable Hakuin, the cruelest
teacher who ever lived, across the reaches
of Snoqualmie Pass, snow and ice after moving
upward through dense rain. The sky cleared
for a moment and did I see ornate space vehicles
against the mountain wall? I'm frankly scared
but Hakuin steadies me, not Mom who said
shame on you, or Dad so long dead his spirit
only returns to me when I'm fishing. At Jim Welch's
memorial in Seattle I could again see all human
beings and creatures flowering and dying in the void,
which is all that we are given along with the suffering
so ignored by angels. In Butte I picked up a bum
on crutches, a leg jellied in Vietnam, who took seven
prescriptions drawn from his pocket with a bottle
of pop. "Time isn't on our side," he said with the air
of a comic. I either drove through the mountains
or the mountains moved past me, the valley
rivers often flowing the wrong way. This is God's
nude world. Home, I watched the unclothed moon
rise while holding our new unruly pup
who speaks the language of Hakuin.
Protect your family. You don't know much.
Don't offer yourself up to this world.
A sense of destiny is a terrible thing.

L'ENVOI

All of my life I've held myself
at an undisclosed location.
Sometimes I have a roof over my head
but no floor, and sometimes a floor but no roof.
This is the song of a man who wrote songs
without music, dog songs, river songs,
bear songs, bird songs though they didn't
need my help, and many people songs.
The just-waking universe returned the favor
with spherical carols as if creation
hadn't stopped a minute, which it hadn't,
as if our songs helped it become itself.
We gave no voice to the bear but watched
our minds allow the bear to become a bear.
At a brief still point on the whirling earth
we saw both the stars and the ground we walked
upon, struggling to recognize each other at noon,
talked ourselves deaf and blind on the sharp
edge of disappearing for reasons we never
figured out. I was conceived near a dance hall
on a bend of a river, now sixty-seven years
downstream I'm singing a water song
not struggling against the ungentle current.

MARCHING

At dawn I heard among birdcalls
the billions of marching feet in the churn
and squeak of gravel, even tiny feet
still wet from the mother's amniotic fluid,
and very old halting feet, the feet
of the very light and very heavy, all marching
but not together, crisscrossing at every angle
with sincere attempts not to touch, not to bump
into each other, walking in the doors of houses
and out the back door forty years later, finally
knowing that time collapses on a single
plateau where they were all their lives,
knowing that time stops when the heart stops
as they walk off the earth into the night air.

IN SEARCH OF SMALL GODS

2009

to Ted and Dan

Walker, your footsteps
are the road, and nothing more.
Walker, there is no road,
the road is made by walking.
Walking you make the road,
and turning to look behind
you see the path you never
again will step upon.
Walker, there is no road,
only foam trails on the sea.

—

Caminante, son tus huellas
el camino, y nada más;
caminante, no hay camino,
se hace camino al andar.
Al andar se hace camino,
y al volver la vista atrás
se ve la senda que nunca
se ha de volver a pisar.
Caminante, no hay camino,
sino estelas en la mar.

Antonio Machado, "Proverbs and Songs #29,"
translated by Willis Barnstone

I BELIEVE

I believe in steep drop-offs, the thunderstorm across the lake
in 1949, cold winds, empty swimming pools,
the overgrown path to the creek, raw garlic,
used tires, taverns, saloons, bars, gallons of red wine,
abandoned farmhouses, stunted lilac groves,
gravel roads that end, brush piles, thickets, girls
who haven't quite gone totally wild, river eddies,
leaky wooden boats, the smell of used engine oil,
turbulent rivers, lakes without cottages lost in the woods,
the primrose growing out of a cow skull, the thousands
of birds I've talked to all of my life, the dogs
that talked back, the Chihuahuan ravens that follow
me on long walks. The rattler escaping the cold hose,
the fluttering unknown gods that I nearly see
from the left corner of my blind eye, struggling
to stay alive in a world that grinds them underfoot.

CALENDARS

Back in the blue chair in front of the green studio
another year has passed, or so they say, but calendars lie.
They're a kind of cosmic business machine like
their cousin clocks but break down at inopportune times.
Fifty years ago I learned to jump off the calendar
but I kept getting drawn back on for reasons
of greed and my imperishable stupidity.
Of late I've escaped those fatal squares
with their razor-sharp numbers for longer and longer.
I had to become the moving water I already am,
falling back into the human shape in order
not to frighten my children, grandchildren, dogs and friends.
Our old cat doesn't care. He laps the water where my face used to be.

LARSON'S HOLSTEIN BULL

Death waits inside us for a door to open.
Death is patient as a dead cat.
Death is a doorknob made of flesh.
Death is that angelic farm girl
gored by the bull on her way home
from school, crossing the pasture
for a shortcut. In the seventh grade
she couldn't read or write. She wasn't a virgin.
She was "simpleminded," we all said.
It was May, a time of lilacs and shooting stars.
She's lived in my memory for sixty years.
Death steals everything except our stories.

NEW MOON

Why does the new moon give anyone hope?
Nevertheless it does and always has for me
and likely does for that Mexican poet with no pesos,
maybe a couple of tortillas, chewing them while sitting
on a smooth rock beside a creek in the Sierra Madres
seeing the new moon tilted delicately away from Venus,
the faint silver light, the ever-so-small sliver
of white enamel rippling in the creek, the same moon,
he thinks, that soothed the Virgin in her great doubt
over the swollen belly beneath her breasts.
The fatherless son had two new moons in his forty days
in the wilderness, the second one telling him it was time
to become God and enter the beast of history.
This poet, though, ignores the sacraments of destiny
and only wants a poem to sing the liquid gift of night.

TOMORROW

I'm hoping to be astonished tomorrow
by I don't know what:
not the usual undiscovered bird in the cold
snowy willows, garishly green and yellow,
and not my usual death, which I've done
before with Borodin's music
used in *Kismet,* and angels singing
"Stranger in Paradise," that sort of thing,
and not the thousand naked women
running a marathon in circles around me
while I swivel on a writerly chair
keeping an eye on my favorites.
What could it be, this astonishment,
but falling into a liquid mirror
to finally understand that the purpose
of earth is earth? It's plain as night.
She's willing to sleep with us a little while.

HARD TIMES

The other boot doesn't drop from heaven.
I've made this path and nobody else
leading crookedly up through the pasture
where I'll never reach the top of Antelope Butte.
It is here where my mind begins to learn
my heart's language on this endless
wobbly path, veering south and north
informed by my all-too-vivid dreams
which are a compass without a needle.
Today the gods speak in drunk talk
pulling at a heart too old for this walk,
a cold windy day kneeling at the mouth
of the snake den where they killed 800 rattlers.
Moving higher my thumping chest recites the names
of a dozen friends who have died in recent years,
names now incomprehensible as the mountains
across the river far behind me.
I'll always be walking up toward Antelope Butte.
Perhaps when we die our names are taken
from us by a divine magnet and are free
to flutter here and there within the bodies
of birds. I'll be a simple crow
who can reach the top of Antelope Butte.

AGE SIXTY-NINE

I keep waiting without knowing
what I'm waiting for.
I saw the setting moon at dawn
roll over the mountain
and perhaps into the dragon's mouth
until tomorrow evening.

There is this circle I walk
that I have learned to love.
I hope one day to be a spiral
but to the birds I'm a circle.

A thousand Spaniards died looking
for gold in a swamp when it was
in the mountains in clear sight beyond.

Here, though, on local earth my heart
is at rest as a groundling, letting
my mind take flight as it will,
no longer waiting for good or bad news.

Often, lately, the night is a cold maw
and stars the scattered white teeth of the gods,
which spare none of us. At dawn I have birds,
clearly divine messengers that I don't understand
yet day by day feel the grace of their intentions.

SUNDAY DISCORDANCIES

This morning I seem to hear the nearly inaudible
whining grind of creation similar to the harmonics
of pine trees in the wind. My outrageously lovely
hollyhocks are now collapsing of their own weight,
clearly too big for their britches. I'm making notes
for a novel called *The End of Man, and Not Incidentally,
Women and Children,* a fable for our low-living time.
Quite early after walking the dogs, who are frightened
of the sandhill cranes in the pasture, I fried some ham
with a fresh peach, a touch of brown sugar and clove.
Pretty good but I was wondering at how the dogs
often pretend the sandhill cranes don't exist despite
their mighty squawks, the way we can't hear
the crying of coal miners and our wounded in Iraq.
A friend on his deathbed cried and said it felt good.
He was crying because he couldn't eat, a lifelong habit.
My little grandson Silas cried painfully until he was fed
macaroni and cheese and then he was merry indeed.
I'm not up to crying this morning over that pretty girl
in the rowboat fifty-five years ago. I heard on the radio
that we creatures have about a billion and a half
heartbeats to use. Voles and birds use theirs fast
as do meth heads and stockbrokers, while whales
and elephants are slower. This morning I'm thinking
of recounting mine to see exactly where I am.
I warn the hummingbirds out front, "Just slow down,"
as they chase me away from the falling hollyhocks.

HOSPITAL

No poems about copious blood in the urine,
tumors as big as a chicken beneath the waistline.
We've long since found these truths quite evident.
Life has never been in remission or rehabilitation.
Life doesn't sing those homely words we invented
to blind our eyes to this idyll of metamorphoses
which can include unbearable pain and unbearable joy.
Death by starvation or gluttony are but a block away
in some cities known to us for their artifacts.
Today I regretted closing this lowly stinkbug in the gate,
feeling the crunch of it beneath my foot to push it on.
My heart must open to the cosmos with no language
unless we invent it moment by moment in order to breathe.
A girl in a green bathing suit swam across the green river
above which swallows flocked in dark whirls.
She swam toward a green bank lined with green willows.
The guiding light of our sun averages half a day.

CHILD FEAR

Sour milk. Rotten eggs. Bumblebees.
Giant women. Falling through the privy hole.
The snake under the dock that bit my foot.
Snapping turtles. Electric fences. Howling bears.
The neighbor's big dog that tore apart
the black lamb. Oil wells. Train wheels.
Dentists and doctors. Hitler and Tōjō. Eye pain.
School superintendent with three gold teeth.
Cow's infected udder, angry draft horse.
School fire. Snake under hay bale. Life's end.

That your dead dogs won't meet you in heaven.

ANOTHER OLD MARIACHI

His voice cracks on tremolo notes.
He recalls the labia of women
as the undersides of dove wings,
the birds he retrieved as a boy for rich hunters.
Now in a cantina outside of Hermosillo
he thinks, I don't have much life left
but I have my songs. I'm still the child
with sand sticking to my dew-wet feet
going to the fountain for morning water.

SPRING

This small liquid mouth in the forest
is called a spring, but it is really
a liquid mouth that keeps all of the secrets
of what has happened here, speaking in the unparsed
language of water, how the sky was once closer
and a fragment of a burned-out star boiled its water.
This liquid mouth has been here since the glaciers
and has seen a few creatures die with its billions
of moving eyes—an ancient bear going bald who went to sleep
and never knew that it died, and an Indian woman
who plunged in her fevered face, deciding to breathe
the water. Since it is a god there is a delight
in becoming unfrozen in spring, to see the coyote
jump five feet into the air to catch a lowly mouse,
or to reflect a hundred thousand bright moons,
to sleep under a deep mantle of snow or feel
the noses of so many creatures who came to drink,
even the man who sits on the forest floor, enjoying
the purity of this language he hopes to learn someday.

MANUELA

When I left Seville I wanted to write
a poem as large as the soul of Manuela,
but no book could contain her. You need a country,
Spain, the sun-gristled murderer of poets.

On the train to Granada I read a newspaper
that said children in Somalia were eating
their own lips in desperation, gulping the air
as if the sky herself was something to eat.
The train slowed in the middle of a ranch
of fighting bulls, bulls as mean as the world.

Several gods walking south through Somalia
saw the Black tinkertoy children and decided
to leave the earth after being here before
Helen's face sank so many ships.

Manuela dances the eyes of the children,
a moon without golf clubs, the muddy Guadalquivir,
her fear and love of the bull of the earth.

Back when I was young and still alive
there were almost too many gods. You could see
them ripple in the water before the lake's ice
melted in April, the loons and curlews giving them voice.

COW MEDITATION

Whenever I'm on the verge of a book tour I begin to think
of Guadalajara. This has been going on for decades.
On tote boards in airports in Chicago and Dallas
and Los Angeles you see Guadalajara listed, so far away
from signing books in Salt Lake and Denver, and from here
at Hard Luck Ranch near the Mexican border
where they're loading cattle for market on a cold,
rainy day with distant Guadalajara a new kind of moon.
Sleet is melting on the back of a baloney bull. He broke
his dick somehow and is destined to be lunch meat.
Twelve cattle are near the end of their lives without knowing it,
ten quite old and two young and scrawny with illness.
In this rough country no one survives with bad teeth.
A rare Aztec thrush visits the pyracantha tree
two feet from my window, looking for a mate.
Last year it was a male waiting for a female to show up.
Life is an honor, albeit anonymously delivered.
Before Rancher Bob leaves for market he tells me
that a cow as old as a sixty-five-year-old woman escaped
by jumping three six-foot-high corral fences and running
up a canyon back into the mountains. "She's too smart
to be caught again," he says. When my plate is too full
I think, Clean the plate by flying to Guadalajara.

PRAYER

Are all of these wrongful prayers gumming
up the skies like smog over Los Angeles?
We never stop making a special case for ourselves.
May the Coyotes kill the Lobos in the Regional Finals.
The lottery would be nice. Bring my dead child back to life.
May the weather clear for the church picnic on Saturday.
Let Christina be my true love not Bob's or Ralph's.
May we destroy all terrorist countries except the children.
In France the sun through stained-glass windows
quilted the sanctuary with the faint rose light of Jesus' blood.
10,000 different asses, clutched in fear, sat on these pews.
Perhaps planes fly holes in all our stalled prayers,
and birds migrate through them as they rise up
or down toward the ninety billion galaxies we know of,
those seeds of the gods in this endlessly flowering universe.
As a child I prayed in my hiding place beneath the roots
of an overturned tree that the sight would return to my blind eye.
The sight is only enough to see the moon,
the rising sun, the blur of stars.

LUNAR

Out in the nighttime in the caliche-gravel driveway
doing a shuffle dance to the music of the lunar eclipse,
a dark gray and reddish smear blocking the moon.
I'm embarrassed by my dance steps learned
from the Ojibwe over fifty years ago,
but then who's watching but a few startled birds,
especially a canyon wren nesting in a crack of the huge
rock face? Without the moon's white light the sky
is suddenly overpopulated with stars like China and India
with people. The stars cast the longest of shadows.
I dance until I'm a breathless old fool thinking
that the spirit of this blinded moon is as real
as that enormous toad that used to bury itself
between the house and the barn of our farm
in Lake Leelanau. One evening I watched him slowly
erupt from the ground. Now the moon's white light
begins to show itself, shining off looming Red Mountain
where years ago I'm told a Mexican boy climbed
to the top to play a song more closely to his dead sister.
Luna, luna, luna, we must sing to praise living and dead.

SINGER

My dream of becoming a Mexican singer
is drifting away.
It reminds me of the etching on my journal
of a naked girl
grasping the cusp of the moon with
both hands.
She's surrounded by stars. No one is strong enough
to hold the moon for long.
I simply wanted my musical sobs to drift
on the airways
to a larger audience with songs about
hearts and pistols,
the curious nonresistance of our human
flesh to bullets,
the love my eye developed in the doctor's office
for a girl
fifty years younger than me. And sadder
songs about the dogs
that ate the child in Tucson, or the twelve-year-
old virgin girl
falling before the red hammer of the lout who
loved to lick tears,
the boy who stabbed his own heart on flunking
the rigors of geometry,
the relentless yips of the coyotes chasing
a deer last night.
What can I make of this world of details
that doesn't yield
to literature, that doesn't feel quite right
enclosed in a slender book?
The Indian boy born without a tongue
is a soup eater,

and the fourteen-year-old girl in Iraq has her teeth frozen
together in rape.
In the night of our age how can I translate
their unworded words?

POOR GIRLS

They're amputating the head of the poor girl
to put it on a rich girl who needs it to survive.
This is always happening to poor girls
who are without defense. They've sold the contents
of their hope chests on eBay. The never-worn
size 18 wedding dress is cheap because it's black.
I've watched poor girls in diners eat piles of cheap potatoes.
Of course they sometimes marry poor guys
who leave them to work in oil fields or join the army.
I know one who has four children and takes care
of her vegetable husband home from sunny Iraq
with the mental age of a baby in big diapers.
Unmarried poor girls often have bowling clubs
and drink lots of beer Tuesday nights at Starlight Lanes.
They know they're largely invisible cleaning motels:
receptionists, waitresses, fast-food cooks, nannies.
Still they're jolly with friends and nephews and nieces.
I see a great big one wearing a bright blue bathing suit
when I go trout fishing. She parks her old Plymouth
and floats on a truck inner tube on a mile of fast water,
gets out, wheels the tube back through a pasture, does it again.

LIMB DANCERS

Of course we're born in the long shadow
of our coffins or urns. So what can we do except
open ourselves wide to life herself
rather than the numbers game of time and money?
You'd best avoid the voyage to the bottom of the sea
from which most don't arise, or come up
only halfway, struggling for the light of childhood
before they named themselves Self, a temporary measure.
Back then you did not separate yourself very far
from birds or cows, though you failed all attempts
to fly, or moo with deep basso strength. Fishing
and dogs carried you through months of pain,
and also hard rain playing the tin-roof instrument.
The heart opened wider and wider and the skin grew
thinner and thinner until a few insignificant gods
who had lost their jobs in the city parks took up residence
in the forest behind our old house, then moved farther
on down here on the Mexican border where they joined
the Chihuahuan ravens along the creek, those noisy
limb dancers. When they wish they move inside each other.
We can find them by looking when we give up our skin.

NIGHT RIDE

The full moon dark orange from another forest
fire, and at four a.m. the massive sound of elephants
trumpeting in the yard and in Weber's sheep
pasture next door. Out the bedroom window I saw
the elephants big as shadowy dump trucks drifting
to and fro. Sat there at the window watching
until the elephants disappeared at first light
when nature became livid with its essence,
oceans of grass as blade-thin green snakes writhing,
birds flying in ten dimensions of Dürer perfection.
I then circled earth in a warm clear bubble,
remembering the Black girl from another life
who became the Virgin Mary and gave me the gift
of seeing the white moon behind a thunderstorm
where she was washed as if by a waterfall,
gave me the gift of seeing these cows and sheep,
the bear near the garden, on all sides at once.
Here I was Jim the poet drifting the edges of night,
not sure he wished to be kidnapped by the gods.

THE GOLDEN WINDOW

By accident my heart lifted with a rush.
Gone for weeks, finally home on a darkish day
of blustery wind, napped, waking in a few minutes
and the sun had come clean and crept around the house,
this light from one of trillions of stars
falling through the window skeined
by the willow's greenish bright yellow leaves
so that my half-asleep head opened wide
for the first time in many months, a cold sunstroke,
so yellow-gold, so gold-yellow, yellow-gold,
this eye beyond age bathed in yellow light.

—

Seventy days on the river with a confusion between
river turbulence and human tribulation. We are here
to be curious not consoled. The gift of the gods
is consciousness not my forlorn bleating prayers
for equilibrium, the self dog-paddling in circles
on its own algae-lidded pond. Emily Walter wrote:
> "We are given rivers so we know our hearts
> can break, but still keep us breathing."

—

When you run through the woods blindfolded
you're liable to collide with trees, I thought
one hot afternoon on the river. You can't drown yourself
if you swim well. We saw some plovers
and then a few yellowlegs with their peculiar cries,
and I remembered a very cold, windy September day
with Matthiessen and Danny when the birds lifted
me far out of myself. It was so cold and blustery the avian

world descended into the river valley and while fishing
we saw a golden eagle, two immature and two adult
bald eagles, two prairie falcons, two peregrines, Cooper's
hawks, two Swainson's, a sharp-shinned,
a rough-legged, a harrier, five turkey vultures,
three ospreys, and also saw buffleheads, wigeon,
teal, mallards, mourning doves, kingfishers,
ring-billed gulls, killdeer, spotted plovers,
sandpipers and sandhill cranes.
They also saw us. If a peregrine sees fifty times better
than we, what do we look like to them?
Unanswerable.

⸺

Nearing seventy there is a tinge of the usually
unseen miraculous when you wake up alive
from a night's sleep or a nap. We always rise in the terrifying
posture of the living. Some days the river is incomprehensible.
No, not the posture, but that a terrifying beauty
is born within us. I think of the twenty-acre thicket
my mother planted after the deaths forty years ago,
the thicket now nearly impenetrable as its own beauty.
Across the small pond the green heron looked at me quizzically—
who is this? I said I wasn't sure at that moment
wondering if the green heron could be Mother.

⸺

Now back in the Absarokas I'm awake
to these diffuse corridors of light. The grizzlies
have buried themselves below that light cast down
across the mountain meadow, following a canyon
to the valley floor where the rattlesnakes will also sleep
until mid-April. Meanwhile we'll travel toward the border

with the birds. The moon is swollen tonight
and the mountain this summer I saw bathed
in a thunderstorm now bathes itself in a mist of snow.

—

Rushing, turbulent water and light, convinced by animals
and rivers that nature only leads us to herself,
so openly female through the window of my single eye.
For half a year my alphabet blinded me to beauty,
forgetting my nature which came from the boy lost
comfortably in the woods, how and why he suspected home,
this overmade world where old paths are submerged
in metal and cement.

—

This morning in the first clear sunlight making its way
over the mountains, the earth covered with crunchy frost,
I walked the dogs past Weber's sheep pasture
where a ram was covering a ewe who continued eating,
a wise and experienced woman. I headed due west
up the slope toward Antelope Butte in the delicious
cold still air, turning at the irrigation ditch hearing
the staccato howl of sandhill cranes behind me,
a couple of hundred rising a mile away from Cargill's
alfalfa, floating up into the white mist rising
from the frost, and moving north in what I judge
is the wrong direction for this weather. Birds make mistakes,
so many dying against windows and phone wires.
I continued west toward the snake den to try to catch
the spirit of the place when it's asleep, the sheer otherness
of hundreds of rattlesnakes sleeping in a big ball
deep in the rocky earth beneath my feet. The dogs,
having been snake trained, are frightened of this place.
So am I. So much protective malevolence. I fled.

Back home in the studio, a man-made wonder. We planted
a chokecherry tree near the window and now through cream-
colored blinds the precise silhouette of the bare branches,
gently but firmly lifting my head, a Chinese screen
that no one made which I accept from the nature of light.

—

I think of Mother's thicket as her bird garden.
How obsessed she was with these creatures. When I told
her a schizophrenic in Kentucky wrote, "Birds are holes
in heaven through which a man may pass," her eyes teared.
She lost husband and daughter to the violence of the road
and I see their spirits in the bird garden. On our last night
a few years ago she asked me, "Are we the same species as God?"
At eighty-five she was angry that the New Testament wasn't fair
to women and then she said, "During the Great Depression
we had plenty to eat," meaning at the farmhouse,
barn and chicken coop a hundred yards to the north
that are no longer there, disappeared with the inhabitants.
The child is also the mother of the man.

—

In the U.P. in the vast place southeast of the river
I found my way home by following the path
where my shadow was the tallest
which led to the trail which led
to another trail which led to the road home
to the cabin where I wrote to her:
"Found two dead redtail hawks, missing
their breasts, doubtless a goshawk took them
as one nests just north of here a half mile
in a tall hemlock on the bend of the river."

—

With only one eye I've learned
to celebrate vision, the eye a painter,
the eye a monstrous fleshy camera
which can't stop itself in the dark
where it sees its private imagination.
The tiny eye that sees the cosmos overhead.

—

Last winter I lost heart between each of seven cities.
Planes never land with the same people who boarded.

—

Walking Mary and Zilpha every morning I wonder
how many dogs are bound by regret
because they are captured by our imaginations
and affixed there by our need to have them do
as we wish when their hearts are quite otherwise.

—

I hope to define my life, whatever is left,
by migrations, south and north with the birds
and far from the metallic fever of clocks,
the self staring at the clock saying, "I must do this."
I can't tell the time on the tongue of the river
in the cool morning air, the smell of the ferment
of greenery, the dust off the canyon's rock walls,
the swallows swooping above the scent of raw water.

—

Maybe we're not meant to wake up completely.
I'm trying to think of what I can't remember.
Last week in France I read that the Ainu in Japan
receive messages from the gods through willow trees,
so I'm not the only one. I looked down into the garden

of Matignon and wondered at the car trip the week before
where at twilight in Narbonne 27,000 blackbirds swirled,
and that night from the window
it was eerie with a slip of the waning moon
off the right shoulder of the Romanesque cathedral
with Venus sparkling shamelessly above the moon,
Venus over whom the church never had any power.
Who sees? Whose eye is this? A day later in Collioure
from the Hermitage among vineyards in the mountains
I could look down steep canyons still slightly green
from the oaks in November to the startling blue of the Mediterranean,
storm-wracked from the mistral's seventy-knot winds,
huge lumpy whitecaps, their crests looking toward Africa.

—

I always feared losing my remaining eye,
my singular window to the world. When closed it sees
the thousands of conscious photos I've taken with it,
impressionist rather than crystalline, from a lion's mouth
in the Serengeti in 1972 to a whale's eye in the Humboldt current,
to the mountain sun gorged with the color of forest
fires followed by a moon orange as a simple orange,
a thousand girls and women I've seen but never met,
the countless birds I adopted since losing the eye in 1945
including an albino grouse creamy as that goshawk's breast
that came within feet of Mother in our back pasture,
the female trogon that appeared when Dalva
decided to die, and the thousands of books out of whose print
vision is created in the mind's eye, as real as any garden at dawn.

—

No rhapsodies today. Home from France
and the cold wind and a foot of snow have destroyed
my golden window, but then the memory

has always been more vivid than the life. The memory
is the not-quite-living museum of our lives.
Sometimes its doors are insufferably wide open
with black stars in a gray sky, and horses
clattering in and out, our dead animals resting here
and there but often willing to come to life again
to greet us, parents and brothers and sisters sitting
at the August table laughing while they eat twelve
fresh vegetables from the garden. Rivers, creeks, lakes
over which birds funnel like massive schools of minnows.
In memory the clocks have drowned themselves, leaving
time to the life spans of trees. The world of our lives
comes unbidden as night.

ADVICE

A ratty old man, an Ojibwe alcoholic who lived to be eighty-eight and chewed Red Man tobacco as a joke, told me a few years back that time lasted seven times longer than we "white folks" think. This irritated me. We were sitting on the porch of his shack drinking a bottle of Sapphire gin that I brought over. He liked expensive gin. An old shabby-furred bear walked within ten feet of us on the way to the bird feeder for a mouthful of sunflower seed. "That bear was a pissant as a boy. He'd howl in my window until I made him popcorn with bacon grease. You should buy a green Dodge from the fifties, a fine car but whitewash it in the late fall, and scrub it off May 1. Never drive the highways, take back roads. The Great Spirit made dirt not cement and blacktop. On your walks in the backcountry get to where you're going, then walk like a heron or sandhill crane. They don't miss a thing. Study turtles and chickadees. These bears and wolves around here have too much power for us to handle right. I used to take naps near a female bear who farted a lot during blueberry season. Always curtsey to the police and they'll leave you alone. They don't like to deal with what they can't figure out. Only screw fatter women because they feed you better. This skinny woman over near Munising gave me some crunchy cereal that cut my gums. A bigger woman will cook you ham and eggs. I've had my .22 Remington seventy years and now it looks like it's made out of duct tape. Kerosene is your best fuel. If you row a boat you can't help but go in a circle. Once I was so cold and hungry I ate a hot deer heart raw. I felt its last beat in my mouth. Sleep outside as much as you can but don't close your eyes. I had this pet garter snake that lived in my coat pocket for three years. She would come out at night and eat the flies in my shack. Think of your mind as a lake. Give away half the money you make or you'll become a bad person. During nights of big moons try walking as slow as a skunk. You'll like it. Don't ever go in a basement. Now I see Teddy's fish tug coming in. If you buy a six-pack I'll get us a big lake trout from Teddy. I got three bucks burning a hole in my pocket. Women like their feet rubbed. Bring them wildflowers. My mom died when I was nine years old. I got this idea she became a bird and that's why I talk to birds. Way back then I thought the Germans and Japs would kill the world but here we are about ready to cook a fish. What more could you want on an August afternoon?"

FIBBER

My bird-watching friends tell me, "You're always seeing birds that don't exist." And I answer that my eye seems to change nearly everything it sees and is also drawn to making something out of nothing, a habit since childhood. I'm so unreliable no one asks me, "What's that?" knowing that a sandhill crane in a remote field can become a yellow Volkswagen. In moments, the girl's blue dress becomes the green I prefer. Words themselves can adopt confusing colors, which can become a burden while reading. You don't have to become what you already are, which is a relief. Today in Sierra Vista while carrying six plastic bags of groceries I fell down. Can that be a curb? What else? The ground rushed up and I looked at gravel inches away, a knee and hands leaking blood. Time and pain are abstractions you can't see but you know when they're with you like a cold hard wind. It's time to peel my heart off my sleeve. It sits there red and glistening like a pig's heart on Grandpa's farm in 1947 and I have to somehow get it back into my body.

EARLY FISHING

There was a terrible mistake when I checked my driver's license today and saw that I'd be seventy next week. At 3:30 a.m. I was only ten and heard Dad with that coal shovel on a cool May morning in the basement, his steps on the stairs, then he woke me for trout fishing with scrambled eggs, a little coffee in my milk, and then we were off in the car, a '47 Chevy two-tone, blue and beige, for the Pine River about an hour's distance up through Luther, the two-track off the county road muddy so he gunned it. He settled me near a deep hole in the bend of the river and then headed upstream to his favorite series of riffle corners. The water was a little muddy and streamer flies didn't work so I tied on a bright Colorado spinner and a gob of worms. In the next four hours I caught three good-sized suckers and three small brown trout. I kept the trout for our second breakfast and let the suckers go. It was slow enough that I felt lucky that I'd brought along a couple dozen Audubon cards to check out birds. Back then I wanted to see a yellow-bellied sapsucker and I still do. While I dozed I hooked my biggest brown trout, about two pounds, and wished I had been awake. When Dad came back downstream and started a small fire I fibbed about my heroism catching the trout, a lifelong habit. He fried the fish with bacon grease stored in a baby food jar. He cut up a quarter-loaf of Mother's Swedish rye bread and we ate the fish with the bread, salt and pepper. Dad napped and I walked back into the dense swampy woods getting a little lost until he called out after waking. Midafternoon we packed up to leave with a creel full of trout for the family and I left my fly rod in the grass behind the car and Dad backed over it. I had paid ten bucks for it earned at fifteen cents an hour at lawn and garden work. Dad said, "Get your head out of your ass, Jimmy." They're still saying that.

MAPMAN

I like to think that I was a member of the French Resistance though I
was only three years old and lived on a farm in northern Michigan when
Germany invaded France, an unforgivable act but then the seams of
history burst with the unforgivable. The mind itself is a hoax that feeds
on its own fanciful stories. In Marseille the Germans cut off my feet at
the ankle and left me for dead, as they say. I cauterized my stumps on
the coals of a bonfire near the Vieux-Port and took several weeks to
crawl over the hills past Cassis to Bandol. The German soldiers ignored
me crawling along with my knees wrapped in burlap. In Bandol I was
recognized as the Mapman by a vintner and was smuggled back to Mar-
seille under the straw in a cartload of pigs. Pig shit repels prying noses.
I was hidden behind a false wall in the basement and from my candlelit
table spread with the maps of war I helped direct the routes of passage
through the countryside for the Resistance. Intensely detailed maps of
southern France were my wallpaper and improbably intimate to me. We
lost thousands of brave men but saved thousands or so they said. San-
drine who worked at the bakery sent down nude photos of herself and I
considered them maps of the mysteries of women. I grew fat on all the
bread sent down to me with summer vegetables. I began to grow thin in
November when a Nazi colonel set up a desk in the bakery to avoid the
bitterness of the mistral and the employees had to be careful about the
use of the dumbwaiter. Once in the middle of the night someone coura-
geous sent down a case of simple red wine which I drank in two days to
experience the glories and ample delusions of drunkenness. I even tried
to dance to silence on my healed stumps, an unsuccessful venture. The
logical question anyone might ask is how an American could be of any
use to the Resistance? My father was an archaeologist from the University
of Chicago and my mother was a French anthropologist. They spent the
entirety of the 1920s and '30s in the south of France investigating the
remnants of ancient cultures. This period of time included my childhood
and youth and I was happy indeed to accompany them on their research
wanderings. Both parents were executed in Aix-en-Provence in 1942 for
hiding Jews in their rural home. My own obsessions from an early age

were botany and cartography. I was a child "crazed with maps," as the poet Rimbaud would have it. My specialty in cartography was topography, the peculiarities of varying elevations. Many of us understand that along with geological upheavals the world has been shaped by the movement of water. Water is the primal signatory of earth shape. I certainly don't wish to overstate my importance to the underground. It finally wasn't that much because of human frailty and the lunar, impassive cruelty of the Gestapo. I was only the Mapman giving the latitudinal and longitudinal coordinates for relatively safe foot passage from place to place. Consider the deer. There are tens of thousands of them and they are rarely seen because they don't wish to be seen. Learn the traits of peasants and deer, was my advice. They do their best not to be shot. I was a Mercator genius of sorts having hiked the countryside for nearly twenty years and studied the terrain with the attention a farmer offers to his own land. Animal tracks are the safest route of passage on this earth. When liberation came I remained in the bakery basement. Why try to see the world when history had stolen my feet? I was helped upstairs on my stumps once a week and could see down a narrow street to a blue slice of the Mediterranean but had never acquired a particular interest in the sea so it was merely one of those banal Sunday paintings and other people were only marionettes who smelled oddly after my four years of solitary confinement. Finally an old shipwright and an army doctor carved me feet out of wood and leather. The shipwright spoke a peculiar Marseille patois that I didn't understand and that made him a good companion after war made one properly speechless. Unfortunately as I began to be up and around I found I could go nowhere in my former beloved landscapes that I had known since childhood. As with history the landscape became only the story of the dead, the invisible crosses of my compatriots obscenely obvious in my mapmaker's brain. I moved north to the Morvan about thirty kilometers from Autun to a small woodcutter's cottage where I was quite ignorant of the invisible graves in the landscape. Soon enough there will be no one left capable of reimagining my past, my story, and we will become the victims of books. I do have the fond memory of a goodbye picnic I had with a poet friend near L'Isle-sur-la-Sorgue. We stared down into a tiny rock pool in a creek, confident that it held no ghosts.

THE *PENITENTES*

It is hard not to see poets as *penitentes* flaying their brains for a line. They have imaginary tattoos that can't be removed. They think of themselves as mental Zorros riding the high country while far below moist and virginal señoritas wait impatiently in the valley. Poets run on rocks barefoot when shoes are available for a dime. They stand on cliffs but not too close to the fatal edge. They have examined their unfamiliar motives but still harvest the wildflowers they never planted. The horizon has long since disappeared behind them. They have this idea that they have been cremated but aren't quite dead. Their ashes are eyes. At night the stars sprinkle down upon them like salt. At noon they are under porches with the rest of the world's stray and mixed-breed dogs, only momentarily noticed, and are never petted except by children and fools.

VERY SMALL WARS

There's no flash here among the troops. We just want to protect our freedom, well-being and safety. It occurred to me that if I were a vehicle I wouldn't be a Maserati but a John Deere or Farmall tractor, nothing special. Way out here in the country Linda runs a trapline and I patrol daily for rattlers though I can't find the one she saw in the garage behind her gardening tools. She kills a half-dozen mice a day but is now thinking of a device called "Mice Cube" which traps them alive so I could release them on a Republican's lawn when I drive to town for a drink. I'm squeamish about killing mice, once having tried to save one with a broken neck in the trap who looked up at me imploringly. I was drunk and actually sobbed, putting the little critter on a cotton bed in a matchbox. In the morning she was gone and probably eaten by our retarded cat Elie who sits under the bird feeder all day waiting for lunch to fall from the heavens. Also there's a sentimentality about murder as I intend to shoot Hungarian partridge, grouse, woodcock, maybe an antelope for the table this fall. Linda is rather matter-of-fact about killing mice but women are natural hunters. Rattlesnakes aren't innocent. One killed my dog Rose. Our little grandson Silas walks in the flower beds, which we pre-check for vipers. The mind tires of this war but my peace plan is faulty: let rattlers in the house to kill and eat the mice. The last rattler I shot was within a foot of the front door and struck at our old, deaf cat Warren. I blew the snake's head into oatmeal with my *pistola* in a surge of anger. I am a man of peace. Send suggestions. It's not known in Washington, D.C., but death is death.

LAND DIVERS

On the TV screen it said, "Warning: Indigenous Nudity," which sets you up for what you saw in *National Geographic* as a kid in the forties. These natives have the smiles we haven't seen since we were children. They own a lot of pigs on this island, and raise taro, and have the ocean for fish. Their religion is real complicated like some of our own. It's a tough job to explain the meaning of life when you have no idea. They build towers of logs and poles and jump off them headfirst with a long vine tied to an ankle, just long enough to stop them short of the ground or else they'd dash out their brains. Is this to threaten inevitable death? It is to say, Yes I know I'll die, but right now I'm flying if only for a moment. I'm wondering when I watch this film, which nearly everyone has seen like the Budweiser Clydesdales, whether native peoples didn't take this ritual a step further. There was a primitive oceanic culture that believed that after death we're capable of swimming around under the ground and wherever we finally come up is the afterlife we deserve. Some bad people had to swim for years but if you were good it was a mere dunking and you would come up where you already were as a new grandchild. Should we believe this? Why not? Unfortunately the only mammal I know vaguely capable of this is the badger, always a lonely and irascible creature, who can bury himself in a minute and chew off a dog's leg in less time than that. A friend shot a badger in the head to make him turn loose a dog but in death the badger continued chewing. Meanwhile, up on a tower we poise for the jump hoping we're not so fat our vine-bound leg will pull off, unmindful that the gods favor ordinary blackbirds in this art.

EASTER 2008

Death is liquid the scientists are saying. We'll enter the habitat of water after giving up the control we've never had. There will be music as when we used to hear a far-off motorboat while swimming underwater. Some of the information is confusing though water makes music simply being itself. Since we won't have ears and mouths it will be a relief to give up language, to sense a bird flying overhead without saying *bird* and not to have to hear our strenuous blood pumping this way and that. You don't need ears to hear the planets in transit, or the dead who have long since decided there is nothing more to say but *glory* in their being simply part of the universe held in the area of a thrall called home. When Christ rose from the water he wondered at seeing the gods he had left far behind when he finished his forty days in the wilderness.

SHORTCOMINGS

Only thirteen birds at first light. Some are near the French doors to tell me that they need more food. I did poorly at French and Italian but know how to ask for food in their countries. So did birds up north where chickadees would peck at the window saying the feeder is empty. Down here the different types of orioles say, "More grapes please." I know dog language fairly well but then dogs hold a little back from us because we don't know their secret names given them by the dog gods. Nature withholds and hides from us until we try to learn her languages. Yesterday a Chihahuan raven replied to me in a voice I had never heard before saying, "You don't speak very well." In 20,000 walks you're bound to learn a little. Doors finally open where you didn't know there were doors and windows lose their dirty glass. After a night of extreme pain I had glimpses of a new world. A rock brought me to red tears. Of course death will interrupt us soon enough, or so they say, but right now walking through a canyon I can't imagine not walking through a canyon. On a new side of night I asked the gods to not let me learn too much.

THE WORLD'S FASTEST WHITE WOMAN

I saw this documentary about the fastest white woman in the world, ever so little behind a Black woman by tenths of seconds in the 100 and 200 meters. Or at least I think I saw a documentary or perhaps my mind created this true-to-life story. She was running along the wonderful paths in the ravines in Toronto and you could see skyscrapers through the green leafy trees. In a ditzy TV interview she said that she easily outran a group of rapists in LA. They wanted to shoot at her when they couldn't catch her but a wise rapist said that he had stopped the shooting under the accurate presumption that she would eventually run in a circle back to them due to the fact that one leg is always slightly shorter than the other and no one can run very far in a straight line. That's why tracks are always circular. I run in very tight circles due to a deformed left leg my parents couldn't afford to get fixed, another mark of Cain. I may as well put on track shoes and twirl. Anyway this fastest white woman in the world is both sad and angry that she can't run around the world because of the water problem. The oceans, whether in their placidity or torment, are not friendly to feet. Even Jesus while walking on the Sea of Galilee knew that sinking was a possibility. After I met her a single time briefly (she was running in place) in Toronto I introduced myself by letter as a famed physiologist curious about her speed. I bought a white smock and latex gloves and examined the juncture of her hips and thighs and buttocks that propelled her at such an alarming rate. Of course she was more muscular but I found nothing unlike the other eleven women in my life. We were in Austin at the University of Texas and after the minute examination we went down to the track and I tried to film her running but I couldn't figure out the cheap video camera I had bought at Costco. We then went to a BBQ shack where she ate a huge triple-portion brisket platter with the hottest of sauces and an ample bowl of pickled jalapeños. She was bereft by her inability to run around the world but somehow managed to eat saying that she needed 7,000 calories a day to maintain her weight of 119 pounds. It was then that I wiped away her tears with a blue paper napkin and suggested that we go to the North

Pole where she could run around the world in seconds, but like many of the young she apparently didn't understand geography. We then went to my not-so-lavish hotel suite where she quickly ate the entire contents of the complimentary fruit bowl. During a long night of love in which we discovered that we didn't like each other I explained to her that her obsession was to beat a dead horse over and over until it became an actual dead horse in the brain, stinking and immovable. I had to be cautious in our lovemaking because her feet had callused spurs that reminded me of the female duckbill platypus that has poisonous spurs on her back feet that can kill a small dog. She wept and at dawn confessed that everyone in her family was morbidly obese and that her speed was never more than a second ahead of her prodigious appetite. I called room service for the dozen scrambled eggs, one-pound sausage patty, quart of OJ and seven pieces of toast she needed. I drank a pot of coffee and read a newspaper to see if the world deserved to exist. We drove into the country until we found a remote road where she ran in front of my Hertz. I admired the way she was staying a single step in front of her madness in the way that so many of us do by merely watching the clock where each tick brings us safely over the lip of the future, our madness a split second behind us.

MY LEADER

Now in the dog days of summer Sirius is making a dawn peek over the mountains, or so I think being fairly ignorant of stars. It's been over 90 degrees for thirty days and here in Montana the earth has begun to burn. I recall a hot late morning down in Veracruz in a poor-folks cemetery waiting for a restaurant to open so I could eat my lunch, a roasted robalo with lime and garlic, a beer, a nap and then to start life over again watching ships in the harbor that needed to be watched. The old cemetery keeper points out a goat in the far corner and shrugs, making hand and finger gestures to explain how the goat crawls over the stone fence or wriggles though the loose gates. I follow the goat here and there and he maintains what he thinks is a safe distance. He eats fresh flowers and chews plastic flowers letting them dribble in bits from his lips. A stray dog trots down a path and the goat charges, his big balls swinging freely. The dog runs howling, squeezing through a gate. The goat looks at me as if to say, "See what I have done." Now he saunters and finds fresh browse in the shade of the catafalque of the Dominguez family. I sit down in the shade and he sits down facing me about ten feet away, his coat mangy and his eyes quite red. I say, "I'm waiting for my roasted fish." He stares, only understanding Spanish. I say, "In this graveyard together we share the fatal illness, time." He stretches for a mouthful of yellow flowers quickly spitting them out. Baptists say the world is only 6,000 years old, but goats are fast learners. They know what's poisonous as they eat the world.

COLD WIND

I like those old movies where tires and wheels run backwards on horse-drawn carriages pursued by Indians, or Model A's driven by thugs leaning out windows with tommy guns ablaze. Of late I feel a cold blue wind through my life and need to go backwards myself to the outback I once knew so well where there were too many mosquitoes, blackflies, curious bears, flowering berry trees of sugar plum and chokeberry, and where sodden and hot with salty sweat I'd slide into a cold river and drift along until I floated against a warm sandbar, thinking of driving again the gravel backroads of America at thirty-five miles per hour in order to see the ditches and gulleys, the birds in the fields, the mountains and rivers, the skies that hold our 10,000 generations of mothers in the clouds waiting for us to fall back into their arms again.

BURNING THE DITCHES

Over between Dillon and Butte in the valley near Melrose they're burning out the ditches on a moist, sad morning when my simpleminded heart aches for another life. Why can't I make a living trout fishing? The same question I posed sixty years ago to my father. I got drunk last night, an act now limited to about twice a year. It was the olive-skinned barmaid Nicole who set me off as if the dead filaments of my hormones had begun to twitch and wiggle again. In the morning I walk a canyon two-track and hear a canyon wren for the first time outside Arizona. Up the mountainside I see the long slender lines of the billowing smoke from the ditch fires, confused because the wren song is drawing me south to my winter life on the Mexican border. The ditches get choked with veg-etation and they burn them out in the spring so the irrigation water can flow freely. I suddenly determine that the smell of spring is the smell of the rushing river plus the billions of buds on trees and bushes. Back in the home ground, the Upper Peninsula of Michigan, when loggers went to town one day a month, they called getting drunk "burning out the grease." In 1958 a friend in San Francisco burned out his veins shooting up hot paregoric, a cheap high. It's safer for me to continue smoldering just below the temperature of actual flame wondering if there's a distant land where life freely flows like a river. Years ago in a high green pasture near timberline I watched a small black bear on its back rolling back and forth and shimmying to scratch its back, pawing the air with pleasure, not likely wanting to be anywhere or anyone else.

ALIEN

It was one of those mornings when my feet seemed unaware of each
other and I walked slowly up a canyon wash to avoid tripping. It was
warmish at dawn but the sun wouldn't quite come out, having missed
a number of good chances, or so I thought studying the antic clouds
that were behaving as sloppily as the government. I was looking for a
wildflower, the penstemon, but stopped at a rock pool in a miniature
marsh seeing a Mojave rattlesnake curled up in the cup of a low-slung
boulder. Since this snake can kill a cow or horse I detoured through a
dense thicket then glimpsed the small opening of a side canyon I had
not noticed in my seventeen years of living down the road. How could I
have missed it except that it's my habit to miss a great deal? And then the
sun came out and frightened me as if I had stumbled onto a well-hidden
house of the gods, roofless and only a hundred feet long, backed by a
sheer wall of stone. I smelled the telltale urine of a mountain lion but no
cave was visible until I looked up at a passing Mexican jay who shrieked
the usual warning. We move from fear to fear. I knew the lion would be
hiding there in the daytime more surely than I had seen the snake. They
weren't guardians. This is where they lived. These small rock cathedrals
are spread around the landscape in hundreds of variations but this one
had the rawness of the unseen, giving me an edge of discomfort rarely
felt in nature except in Ecuador and the Yucatán where I had appeared as
a permanent stranger. I sat down with my back tight against a sheer wall
thinking that the small cave entrance I faced by craning my neck must be
the home of the old female lion seen around here not infrequently and
that she could only enter from a crevasse at the top, downward into her
cave. This is nature without us. This is someone's home where I don't
belong.

SNAKE WOMAN

She moved like a snake if a snake had feet. I was sitting in a café when she passed on a narrow side street in Modena, Italy. Her head twitched on a thin neck, the tip of her pink tongue testing the air. Her feet were too far behind a body almost too slender to walk, and under her long skirt it was unlikely that there were actual legs. From a few blocks away near the military school the cadet band was playing our own Marine hymn for the Zampone Festival, which is stuffed pig's leg, but the rhythm of her walking was against the music. She must be a local fixture because no one else noticed her. I recall as a boy I found a tiny bird the size of a thumb-nail but Mother said it was just a bumblebee so I fed it to a blacksnake that lived under our dock. Now fifty yards down the street the woman is definitely a snake, undulating upright, defying gravity on the way home to eat bugs and mice. I think of following her but I'm a little frightened. I once stepped on our blacksnake in my bare feet. I bet she crawls up her stairs. I wish I had never seen her.

LATE

What pleasure there is in sitting up on the sofa late at night smoking cigarettes, having a small last drink and petting the dogs, reading Virgil's sublime *Georgics,* seeing a girl's bare bottom on TV that you will likely never see again in what they call real life, remembering all the details of when you were captured by the Indians at age seven. They gave you time off for good behavior but never truly let you go back to your real world where cars go two ways on the same streets. The doctors will say it's bad for an old man to stay up late petting his lovely dogs. Meanwhile I look up from Virgil's farms of ancient Rome and see two women making love in a field of wildflowers. I'm not jealous of their real passion trapped as they are within a television set just as my doctors are trapped within their exhausting days and big incomes that have to be spent. Lighting a last cigarette and sipping my vodka I examine the faces of the sleeping dogs beside me, the improbable mystery of their existence, the short lives they live with an intensity unbearable to us. I have turned to them for their ancient language not my own, being quite willing to give up my language that so easily forgets the world outside itself.

NINETY-SIX-YEAR-OLD ESTONIAN

Just before World War II I was smuggled into America on a tramp freighter. There were a hundred of us and only one toilet on the stormy seas. We were never allowed up on deck during our entire passage. The dark was good practice for twenty-five days because a job had been arranged for me in a basement in Brooklyn, twelve hours a day seven days a week so that I didn't see America in the daylight for five months since I arrived in November. In fact I only saw daylight in the late spring, summer, and early fall for ten years. I was held there by fear, working for a Chinaman who had paid my passage. My job was stamping out rubber guns and knives for novelty stores. After a decade of this I strangled the Chinaman and stole his money and consequently had a happier life working on freighters between New York City and ports in Central and South America as a deckhand, taking extra shifts to get daylight hours. For a while I was a thief and gambler but quit this profitable life because it was night work. It was far better to work on vegetable farms in New Jersey, all in the wonderful daylight. Now that I can barely move I have this small room in my nephew's junky house in Nyack. I spend every day from dawn to dusk sitting in this chair watching the light off the Hudson River, which changes every second.

VALLEJO

I keep thinking of César Vallejo's wine bottles, the moldy ones he picked up on the streets to return for *sous*. His girlfriend helped though on certain days it was slim pickings and they only shared a baguette sitting on a bench in the Montparnasse Cemetery, the location of his destiny, also one of the best places to watch birds in Paris what with all of those trees and upright stones to perch upon. A baguette is to eat with something else but if you have nothing else it will work for half an hour until it seems your stomach has begun to eat itself because it has. So many years after he died I still wanted him to go back to Peru before it was too late and settle for their 350 varieties of potatoes rather than die on a cold, rainy Thursday in Paris as he predicted he would. I started reading him fifty years ago and still do, seeing him write his poems in incomprehensible Paris, selling empty bottles, eating his bread, dying. He sailed off on a dream ship of food and full wine bottles. I don't want to keep thinking about César Vallejo as I sit on the sofa at midnight having just heard on television that everything in nature is disappearing. Someone is always trying to scare us. Everyone wants to be a hit man for God these days. Meanwhile it's the first week of May and I'm waiting for the curlews to arrive in the soon-to-be-flooded pasture across the road, also the tiniest of wildflowers only recently noticed in the spavined field to the south. I keep seeing the orioles, grosbeaks, warblers, lazuli buntings I left behind last week on the border wearing their clearly unimaginable colors as if they'll never disappear. Vallejo stands more revealed today. The gods loved him, dead or alive. They don't care if we're pissing blood or that our hearts strangle themselves to do their bidding.

LATE SPRING

Because of the late, cold wet spring the fruit of greenness is suddenly upon us so that in Montana you can throw yourself down just about anywhere on a green grassy bed, snooze on the riverbank and wake to a yellow-rumped warbler flittering close to your head then sipping a little standing water from a moose track. Of course pitching yourself downward you first look for hidden rocks. Nothing in nature is exactly suited to us. Meanwhile everywhere cows are napping from overeating, and their frolicsome calves don't remember anything except this bounty. And tonight the calves will stare at the full moon glistening off the mountain snow, both snow and moon white as their mother's milk. This year the moisture has made the peonies outside my studio so heavy with their beauty that they droop to the ground and I think of my early love, Emily Brontë. The cruelty of our different ages kept us apart. I tie and prop up the peonies to prolong their lives, just as I would have nursed Emily so she could see another spring.

OLD BIRD BOY

Birds know us as "the people of the feet." I am watched as I walk around and around my green studio, a man of many beaten paths. Near me a willow flycatcher arcs in its air dance to catch a grasshopper, a swift move that I compare to nothing whatsoever that I do. They own the air we breathe. I've studied the feet of the bridled titmouse for years, how they seem to be made of spiderwebs so precariously attached to perch or ground, also the feet of the golden eagle which are death angels, and then the wings of all birds which on close inspection don't seem possible. Most birds own the ancient clock of north and south, a clock that never had hands, the god-time with which the universe began. As the end draws nearer I've taken to praying to be reincarnated as a bird, and if not worthy of that, a tree in which they live so I could cradle them as I did our daughters and grandsons. Three times last April down on the border a dozen Chihuahuan ravens accompanied me on walks when I sang the right croaking song. I was finally within them. For the first time in my life I dared to say aloud, "I am blessed."

ON HORSEBACK IN CHINA

I followed this man across China for three months. I had a string of five horses though two were daffy and didn't ride well in the western mountains except with my interpreter in the saddle. She was less than four feet and weighed but fifty pounds at most. She said that her name meant Jane in Chinese and she had studied at Oxford for three free years because the Englishmen decided not to notice her. She had a tiny dog that lived in the sleeve of her robe. The horses were fond of this little dog as they often are of barn cats. My interpreter's dog ate a mere three thimblefuls of pork broth every day and unlike other dogs was without curiosity for our eclectic meals of yellow snake, monkey udders, a stew of duck rectums. Our journey began on the mainland near Hong Kong appropriately enough on April Fool's Day and ended on July 4, and when I dropped a string of firecrackers from a fiftieth-floor window I prayed they didn't land in a baby carriage. Hotel windows don't open anymore but I keep a glass cutter in my checked luggage with which I carve a tiny opening to relieve my claustrophobia. The trip itself was exhausting and to a degree hastened my aging, plus I depleted a goodly portion of my life's savings in my attempt to trace a man who didn't want to be traced except in the 2,400 messages he left here and there, encoded in poems. My route was circular and at no time could I give up or I would lose the exorbitant deposit on the horses. A low point was at the former hunting lodge of the famed Prince of Nine Gongs (T'ang dynasty) where I became ill from a soup made of the rumen of yak bellies smuggled in from the Arctic Circle of Alaska by a diplomat. After three days of purging I resolved to eat only rice, an impossible program except for those who wish to die, as Jane pointed out. The landscape and my thoughts dissolved into each other, becoming liquid, and I recalled a line from a poet I disliked, "You are only where you are minus you." In honor of our liquidity we become the landscape down to the horse beneath us. One evening in the mountains camped by a waterfall I heard the screaming of monkeys and then the roar of a tiger at which point the monkeys fell silent. My motive for the trip? To discover if we are only the varying sums of our everyday lives. Up until this trip to China I had no clear understanding of my past and certainly no interest in seeing into the future. A decisive moment of satori came when a giant black mastiff that had been guarding a nearby herd of sheep entered the circle of light cast by our campfire and swallowed Jane's teeny dog in a single impulsive gulp that resembled a reverse burp. Jane wept piteously, flopping around like a freshly caught fish on the bottom of a wooden boat. I tried to console her but she explained that the dog was actually her soul. Later that day one of our horses got loose, swam through the rapids of a vast river and on the other side looked back for a moment in farewell before escaping into the green foothills of distant mountains. One day camped by a small lake it occurred to me that the fish we were eating were essentially the same fish eaten by Jesus and the Buddha. I was alarmed by the idea that the contents of life are indeed limited. That evening Jane told me that she was seventy years old after we collected an encrypted message in a despondent village that had lost its mayor when his wife stabbed him on learning of his affair with a retarded girl. This could have happened anywhere in the world. As time passed, as it will, I was becoming generally less mournful and after spending the night at a farm I apologized to a mother pig for eating a piglet of hers the night before but she pardoned me saying that she had eaten a human child when she escaped into the forest as a wild young girl-pig. I began to enjoy my lack of direction after I lost our compass at the beginning of the third month. Confusion ensued because Jane was useless over her lost soul and spent much of her time wrapped in her child's red sleeping bag. My gestures at a Chinese version of a department store were misunderstood and we were directed to the mountain dwelling of the hermit rather than a place to purchase a compass. At the store they seemed amused at the business card my interpreter had devised for me giving my name as Lord Zero. My travels had been eased by my semidiplomatic passport arranged by a friend, a U.S. congressman famed in China for removing trade barriers. Of course world trade is more important than marriage or religion. In any event we arrived after three days' ride into the mountains and the hermit immediately restored Jane's soul by serving her a boiled potato. He said that everything is to be found in the ordinary. It was then that it occurred to me that without travel we can't understand the madness of travel. This separates us slightly from the brief journey of the potato. I certainly lack courage and am no man's hero except to my children when they were young. My only peculiarity is swimming rivers alone at night. However, all my life I've seemed to love what our British cousins call the "edgelands," those grand pieces of land without economic value of any consequence. This is even more so in China where the press of more than a billion souls covers land of value as a swarm of honeybees collected around their queen. After riding two thousand miles I was no less a fool when I returned home. Since I was absolutely witless with the language Jane was my mind and I was merely antennae for my future memories which arrived in moments. I ate my meals, rode a horse, studied the landscape, all too often forgetting why I had made the journey. For better or much worse the hands on the reins were my own. One night I slept with a peasant woman who tasted like a tart green apple sprinkled with salt. In the morning she made me a soup of rice, chicken's feet, garlic, green onions and hot peppers. My feet were bare and the resemblance between my feet and chicken's feet was apparent. A dog I called Black Muzzle in honor of a dog who lived a thousand years ago shared the soup. It is possible in life to feel fairly good about nothing in particular. The only conclusions I can offer are the obvious biological ones. I've always had the modest embarrassment of a nearly size 10 head and when I arrived at our home my little grandson Johnny was kneading pasta dough on our kitchen table. He asked, "Grandpa, your head is big, what's in it?" I said, "On this day nothing in particular."

A STRANGE POEM

The birds and beard turn gray.
You twist from the hips
and the black door is closer.
The neighbor's baby goes to college
and two pet dogs have their graves
hallowed by a bed of varied flowers.
You play with their toys in the yard
and eat from their sparkling bowls.
The woman you loved killed you
with her ass as a scorpion does.
At sea you die from drinking the water.
It took so many years to build this blood
that leaks out on the straw in Grandpa's barn.
The simpleminded mirror can't find me.
Like everyone else I took myself for granted.
Still I praised god who spawned me
from one of a billion hopeless eggs
in this river of air. I tried to run away
with the girl who stayed behind
like everyone else. Here on the lip of earth
the air is as fresh as the cyclamen the color of blood.
Back at my beloved dog bowl I bow
to the gods who gave me this life,
my fins, the water.

NEW WORLD

This moment says no to the next.
Now is quite enough for the gathering birds
in the tall willows above the irrigation ditch.
It's autumn and their intentions are in their blood.
Looking up at these chattering birds I become dizzy,
but statistics say old men fall down a lot.
The earth is fairly soft here, so far from the world
of cement where people must live to make a living.
Despite the New Covenant you can't eat the field's lilies.
Today I think I see a new cold wind rushing through the air.
Of course I stare up too long because I love cedar waxwings,
their nasalate click and hiss, their cantankerous joy.
I fall and the dogs come running. Mary licks my face.
I tell them that this is a world where falling is best.

BARKING

The moon comes up.
The moon goes down.
This is to inform you
that I didn't die young.
Age swept past me
but I caught up.
Spring has begun here and each day
brings new birds up from Mexico.
Yesterday I got a call from the outside
world but I said no in thunder.
I was a dog on a short chain
and now there's no chain.

RENÉ CHAR

In the morning when the tilt of the world
is just so
the sunlight races down the small mountain
facing our porch
so fast you couldn't possibly
beat it in track shoes
nor would you want to try. It's too steep
and the rock is crumbly.
Once in Three R Canyon I saw a mountain
lion a half mile
distant flow up such a rock face and suddenly
was struck by my fleshy
limitations. I read that some women run with wolves
but I walk with opossums
and someday will slow to the desert tortoise's
stately pace.
Char says that a poet has only to be there when the bread
comes fresh from the oven.

PEONIES

The peonies, too heavy with their beauty,
slump to the ground. I had hoped
they would live forever but ever so slowly
day by day they're becoming the soil of their birth
with a faint tang of deliquescence around them.
Next June they'll somehow remember to come alive again,
a little trick we have or have not learned.

GOOD FRIDAY

Release yourself. Life is a shock to the system.
It was to the small javelina ever flattening
on the yellow line on a hot afternoon.
Release yourself. You've always doubted cars,
remembering when trains and horses were enough
and boats kept our ocean skies unmarred.
Release yourself. Your doubt is only the patina
of shit the culture paints on those in the margins.
Tomorrow the full moon is on Good Friday,
the blind face of the gods who can't see us anymore.

INSIGHT

After we die we hover for a while
at treetop level with the mourners
beneath us, but we are not separate
from them nor they from us.
They are singing but the words
don't mean anything in our new language.

THE HOME

If my body is my home
what is this house full of blood
within my skin? I can't leave it
for a moment but finally will. It knows
up and down, sideways, the texture
of the future and remnants of the past.
It accepts moods as law no matter
how furtively they slip in and out
of consciousness. It accepts dreams as law
of a different sort as if they came from
a body well hidden within his own.
He says, "Pull yourself together," but he
already is. An old voice says, "Stay close to home."

OLD TIMES

When I revived at dawn I didn't know
where I had been in the manner that occasionally life
imitates the childishness of science fiction.
The local mountains had become immense stupas
and there was a long band of fire in the east.
I bounded along in silly fifty-foot strides
unable to identify the huge orange birds that became
that color from flying low through the fire.
What am I to make of this? Where did it come
from to the weary human who'd rather parse
the mysteries of oatmeal topped with strawberries,
but then any kid knows that during a long night
the imagination thumbs its nose at civilization
as the lid of a jar screwed on too tight
that has no idea what its true contents are.
The billions of neurons fed by a couple of trillion
cells aren't confused. Perhaps a simpleminded
neuron remembers when the mountains were stupas
where small gods lived and 500-pound
birds fled from grass fires on the vast savannas
and man's ancestors wore seven-league boots
getting places either quickly or slowly without clocks.

MIDNIGHT BLUES PLANET

We're marine organisms at the bottom of the ocean
of air. Everywhere esteemed nullities rule our days.
How ineluctably we travel from our preembryonic
state to so much dead meat on the ocean's hard floor.
There is this song of ice in our hearts. Here we struggle
mightily to keep our breathing holes opened
from the lid of suffocation. We have misunderstood the stars.
Clocks make our lives a slow-motion frenzy. We can't get
off the screen back into the world where we could live.
Every so often we hear the current of night music
from the gods who swim and fly as we once did.

COMPLAINT & PLEA

Of late I've been afflicted by too many hummingbirds,
a red moon rising again in the smoke of forest fires,
a record long heat tsunami, the unpardonable vigor
of the hollyhocks pressing against the green studio,
their gorgeous trashiness as flowers (some call
them weeds), the fledgling redtail hawks crying
all day because they don't want to fly, the big rattler
I shot near our front door twisting itself into
the usual question mark, the river I want to fish
turbulent and brown from a distant thunderstorm,
the studio steps I fell off with the ground I used
to love floating up to meet me, the deepest sense
that life which is a prolonged funeral service
won't behave, that I'm living within a glass orb
that a monster brat won't stop shaking. A friend
wrote, "I have moments when I think life
may have gotten to be too much for me or that
I haven't gotten to be enough for it." Yes, life
is a holographic merry-go-round that whirls
at the speed of light in all directions at once.
To whom may I address my plea that the river
clear so that I might go fishing? The fish
must learn that pretty flies can have hooks in them.

FRIENDS

Dogs, departed companions,
I told you that the sky would fall in
and it did. How will we see each other again
when we're without eyes? We'll figure it out
as we used to when you led me back
to the cabin in the forest in the dark.

SMALL GODS

My hope is that this minuscule prayer
will reach out to the god unknown I just sensed
passing in the rivulet of breeze above the mere rivulet
of water in this small arroyo. To the skittering insect
this place is as large as the Sea of Galilee.
In prayer I'm a complicated insect, moving
this way and that. The insect before me puzzles
over its current god, my dog Zilpha, who watches
with furrowed brow and thinks, "Should I paw
at this bug in this shallow pool, bite it, roll
on it in this tiny creek in the late afternoon heat,
or perhaps take another nap?" She looks at her god,
which is me, understanding as her eyes close
that the gods make up their minds as they go.
They are as patient as the water in which they live,
and won't be surprised when they reach the sea
with their vast collection of reflections, the man, the dog,
the stars and moon and clouds, the javelina and countless
birds, bugs and minnows, the delicate sips of rattlers,
the boughs of mesquite, the carapace of the desert tortoise,
the heron footprints, the water's memories of earth.

GOAT BOY

I no longer lead my life. I'm led.
The sexuality of insects tells us that intentional
life is a hoax but the gods tell us
that we are also gods. The sun kindly rises
on the snoring goat out by the barn.
He'll only do what he wants to do.
He eats potato peels and stares at the rising moon.
I believe in my calling like he believes in the moon.
How else could I see clearly at night?
We are nature, too, and some of us do less well
in this invented world, or if we do well for a while
there is that backward stare from these overplowed fields
to the wild woodlot and creek in the distance.
At seven I went out to play and was lost in the woods
for a day and never understood the way back home.

NIGHT WEATHER

I was thinking that weather might be the reason
the phases of night can be laminated with melancholy
so that we sit tightly against our Formica desks
with tears arising as we plan our own funerals.
Verdi's *Requiem* won't play well in Montana
just as "A Mighty Fortress Is Our God" doesn't work in Paris.
If it's Arizona you can't sing "Shall We Gather at the River."
Funerals fade abruptly in this desert night when rain begins to fall
and I see the future blooming of April's penstemon and primrose,
and bird hatchlings much smaller than a marble,
hearts beating as they break the shells that still contain us
or if the shell's not there we still can't quite leave.

UP

Here I am at the gateless gate again hoping
to see father, mother, sister, brother.
Where did they come from? Where did they go?
I keep climbing this tree as old as the world
and have lost my voice up here in the thin air.

TIME

Time our subtle poison runs toward us,
and through us, and out the other side.
We've never been in the future except for a moment.
Time's poison is in the air we breathe
and the faint taste in the water we drink.
We are dogs who love their morning walks
but not their names. They don't know they're dogs,
but no one had the right to give them the wrong names.
Time never told us to have faith in the sepulchre
that awaits us. The night carves us into separate acts,
but I do have faith in that turbulent creek
of blood within me.

FATHER

The old man's angleworm stares
at the ground where it was born.

He remembers his red wagon speeding
down the steep sidewalk and tipping over.

He followed the girl up the ladder
to the haymow, his face hot as the sun.

Sailing from the north into his alien homeland
he put his bony shoulder against the human glacier.

He failed to find a new bird species or the nymph
with golden snakes in her raven hair.

He aimed so high that his cousin clouds were ice.
Below, the green carapace of earth, the backs of birds.

He dug a hole in the woods for a perfect hiding place,
and when he finally emerged he was a book.

He reminded himself daily that he lived
in a world of elephants, dandelions, butterflies.

Now walking the thin, sharp edge of the grave
he thinks of oceans and birds, a missing brother.

The girl across the subway tracks in 1957 is still there
amid brackish ozone, boarding the train.

ELEVEN DAWNS WITH SU TUNG-P'O

1

On my seventieth birthday reading Su Tung-p'o
in the predawn dark waiting for the first birdcall.
"I'm a tired horse unharnessed at last," he said.
Our leaders say "connect the dots" but the dots
are the 10,000 visible stars above me.

2

Morning. Twenty-five degrees. Heavy frost descending
at 6:30 a.m. The only sound the whisper
of green hackberry leaves falling,
a deep green carpet under each tree.
First bird, a canyon wren.
Sky azure, sun-gold mountain.
My ears not frozen shut,
my one eye open
to this morning in a cold world.

3

At dawn my mind chattered like
seven schoolgirls,
seven pissed-off finches at the feeder,
seven ravens chasing the gray hawk.
How to calm it down? Let the creek
run through it from ear to ear.

4

You can't expect anything.
Even dawn is a presumption.
More raptors this year after two
good monsoons. I found a lush
and hidden valley I couldn't bear

to enter today. It frightened me
as if it might be home to new species
of creatures God had forgotten to invent.
The old man is also a timid boy.

            5
On solstice dawn I'm an old brat
lifting a hundred mental bandages.
Mt. Everest is covered with climbers' junk
and a golf club was left behind on the moon,
the East suffocates in malice and the West
in pink cotton candy. Sixty years ago
my brother told me that the rain was angel piss
and that turtles might kill me when I swam.
The solstice says "everything on earth is True."

            6
Waiting for the light. I stand by her door
listening for breath. We've had 18,000 nights
but one of us will go first. The big moon
speaks to me with the silence
of a sleeping dog. First bird, the canyon wren.
I hear her say to her dog Mary, "Move over."

            7
Press the coffee button, December 24, with the moon
the bright eyeball of a god. For a couple of
million years people were outside
and now they're mostly inside. Had Su Tung-p'o
heard of Jesus from the trade routes exchanging
gunpowder and pasta? He knew the true wilderness
is the soul which doesn't wear
the old shoes of time and space.

8

I felt ignored waking up in the cold dark
and planned a parade for myself leading
the dogs, Mary and Zilpha, down the creek bed.
I wield my walking stick like a drum major
pointing out the earth and sky to the earth and sky.
The dogs like javelina tracks but cringe at the paw prints
of the mountain lion. Five ravens sound the alarm.
I never was the lord of all I survey.

9

Late in life I've lost my country.
Everywhere there is the malice of unearned
power, top to bottom, bottom to top,
nearly solid scum. Very few can read or write.
Lucky for me we winter in this bamboo thicket
near a creek with three barrels of bird food.
With first light things seem a little better.

10

Don't probe your brain's sore tooth in the dark.
Let your mind drift to the mountains
where migrants are doubtless freezing
on the coldest night of the year. The dogs
found a nest beneath the roots of a big sycamore
tipped over in July's flood. The ashes of a tiny fire,
an empty water bottle, a pop-top can of beans
scorched by the coals. These dangerous people
whom we're being taught to hate like the Arabs.

11

I can't find the beginning, middle and end in the dark.
Will a kindly lightbulb help? Su Tung-p'o is dead
but I keep talking to him as I do my father

gone now these fifty years. I have no moves
left except to feed the birds at first light.
I have nearly lived out my exile, the statistics
say. Who knows what glorious wine comes next
in my sunny kingdoms of dogs, birds and fish?

THE QUARTER

Maybe the problem is that I got involved with the wrong crowd of gods when I was seven. At first they weren't harmful and only showed themselves as fish, birds, especially herons and loons, turtles, a bobcat and a small bear, but not deer and rabbits who only offered themselves as food. And maybe I spent too much time inside the water of lakes and rivers. Underwater seemed like the safest church I could go to. And sleeping outside that young might have seeped too much dark into my brain and bones. It was not for me to ever recover. The other day I found a quarter in the driveway I lost at the Mecosta County Fair in 1947 and missed out on five rides including the Ferris wheel and the Tilt-A-Whirl. I sat in anger for hours in the bull barn mourning my lost quarter on which the entire tragic history of earth is written. I looked up into the holes of the bulls' massive noses and at the brass rings puncturing their noses which allowed them to be led. It would have been an easier life if I had allowed a ring in my nose, but so many years later I still find the spore of the gods here and there but never in the vicinity of quarters.

SONGS OF UNREASON

2011

for Will Hearst

Life never answers.
It has no ears and doesn't hear us;
it doesn't speak, it has no tongue.
It neither goes nor stays:
we are the ones who speak,
the ones who go,
while we hear from echo to echo, year to year,
our words rolling through a tunnel with no end.

That which we call life
hears itself within us, speaks with our tongues,
and through us, knows itself.

Octavio Paz, from "Response and Reconciliation,"
translated by Eliot Weinberger

BROOM

To remember you're alive
visit the cemetery of your father
at noon after you've made love
and are still wrapped in a mammalian
odor that you are forced to cherish.
Under each stone is someone's inevitable
surprise, the unexpected death
of their biology that struggled hard, as it must.
Now to home without looking back,
enough is enough.
En route buy the best wine
you can afford and a dozen stiff brooms.
Have a few swallows then throw the furniture
out the window and begin sweeping.
Sweep until the walls are
bare of paint and at your feet sweep
until the floor disappears. Finish the wine
in this field of air, return to the cemetery
in evening and wind through the stones
a slow dance of your name visible only to birds.

SUITE OF UNREASON

> Nearly all my life I've noted that some of my thinking was atavistic,
> primitive, totemistic. This can be disturbing to one fairly learned.
> In this suite I wanted to examine this phenomenon.

The moon is under suspicion.
Of what use is it?
It exudes its white smoke of light.

—

Her name was imponderable.
Sitting in the grass seven feet
from the lilacs she knew
she'd never have a lover.
She tends to her knitting
which is the night.

—

That morning the sun forgot to rise
and for a while no one noticed
except a few farmers, who shot themselves.

—

The girl near the Théâtre de l'Odéon
walked so swiftly
we were astonished.

—

The fish with the huge tumor
jumped higher than my head
from my hand when released.

—

The girl in the green dress
sang a wordless carol
on the yellow school bus.

—

The truest night of the hunter
is when like his prey
he never wakes up.

—

Only one cloud
is moving the wrong way
across the sky
on Sunday morning.

—

The girl kissed a girl,
the boy kissed a boy.
What would become of them?

—

The violent wind.
The violent wind.
The violent wind.

—

On watch on the ship's stern.
The past disappears
with the ship's wake
and the furling dark waters.

—

A local girl walked over the top
of the Absaroka Mountain Range
and was never seen again. Some say
a grizzly bear got her, some say aliens,
I think that fueled by loneliness
she is still walking.

—

One day a heron walked
up our front steps and looked
into the front-door window.
Was it a heron and also
something else?

—

Years ago at the cabin when returning
from the saloon at night
I'd scratch the ears of a bear
who'd rest his chin on the car windowsill.

—

Azure. All told a year of water.
Some places with no bottom.
I had hoped to understand it
but it wasn't possible. Fish.

—

She told me in white tennis shorts
that when you think you can't
take it anymore you're just getting started.
No pieces can be put back together.

—

Last week in this pasture it was 75.
Today it's 29 and snowing. The world is too small
with a limited amount of weather
with no cosmic 15,000-mph winds.
A piece of luck!

—

These birds. Cutting up often dreary
life and letting joy seep through.
What are they? It's not for me to know
but to sense, to feel flight and song,
even in today's gray snowy sky.

—

Why does the mind compose this music
well before the words occur? The gods
created the sun and we the lightbulb
and the medicine that kept the happy child alive.

—

Some of my friends sought their deathbeds,
Celtic dogs with their death tails
in their teeth. I thought I knew
them but I didn't. They ignored birds.

—

Late October and now I wear a wool
cap around the clock, take three naps a day.
I've no clear memory why this happens,
something about the earth tilting on an axis.
Yesterday twenty-three sandhill cranes flew north. Why?

—

I pray for seven women I know
who have cancer. I can't tell you why
they have cancer and neither can doctors.
They are beaten by a stranger with no face.

—

Recently ghosts are more solid than we are,
they have color and meat on their bones,
even odor and voices. You can only tell them
by what's missing. A nose, ear, feet on backward,
their hair that floats though the air is still.

—

We fear the small hole in our brain
that made its tubular descent to the center of the earth
when we were born. In the loveliest landscape,
the tinge of death. The photo of the mammoth grizzly
gaining on the young buffalo? No, the tinge is in the air.

—

Fifty years ago in our cold, snowbound
house in the north, Carlos Montoya brought sunlight.
When I finally went to Seville and Granada,
the cold house sometimes entered my hotel rooms,
a flash of snowdrifts among the orange trees.

—

Off Ecuador the whale was so close I could smell
her oily smell, look into a soccer-ball eye.
I was frightened when the motor quit
and I couldn't see land. Now I can't see
the ocean in the mountains, only watch the rivers run.

—

After a long siege of work
I wake up to a different world.
I'm older of course, but colors and shapes
have changed. The mountains have moved a bit,
our children are older. How could this happen?

—

When young I read that during the Philippine War
we shot six hundred Indians in a wide pit. It didn't seem fair.
During my entire life I've been helpless
in this matter. I even dream about it.

—

I read so much that my single eye became hot
as if it had been staring into nebulae.
Of course it had. On some clear nights in the country
the stars can exhaust us. They only mean what they are.

—

In summer I walk the dogs at dawn
before the rattlesnakes awake. In cold weather
I walk the dogs at dawn out of habit.
In the pastures we find many oval deer beds
of crushed grass. Their bodies are their homes.

—

The tree only intends what it is with its dictator
genome. Like us they don't see what's coming.
They often rot from inside out though it can take
decades. When sawed down you smell the sharp
edged ripeness of their lives, their blood.

—

The clouds are only a foot above my head
and there's a brisk cold wind from the north.
Still, when I pass the yard headed for the hills
the garden is lavish with dying and dead
flowers, so many wild immutable colors
that my cold head soars up through the clouds.

—

Out in the pasture I found the second concealed
hole descending to a room sculpted from hard dirt.
The previous owner was frightened of atomic attack.
Now it's the home of the beast god forgot to invent.
This is where our bodies will sit down to eat us.

—

On television I saw a tall willowy girl jump
seven feet in the air. How grand to have a dozen
of these girls weaving in and out of the pines
and willows in the yard and jumping so high,
perhaps to Stravinsky, the landscape visible
under their bodies. They don't have to be nice.
Art often isn't though it scrubs the soul fresh.
The beauty of the rattlesnake is in its threat.

—

As the Bulgarians say, the moon is to blame.
Come to think of it that's right. The moon
works in waves of power like the ocean
and I was swept away into wrongdoing
when the moon was large. I am innocent.

—

Of late I can wake up and the world
isn't quite recognizable or I'm finally

with age losing my touch, my control.
Three days seemed identical but then they were
and perhaps in losing my self all became lucid.
This isn't a brave new world but one finally revealed.

—

The brush I scrub my soul with each morning
is made of the ear-hairs of a number of animals:
dogs, pigs, deer, goat, raccoon, a wolverine,
and pinfeathers of particular birds, a secret.
Brush too hard, your ambitions will be punished.

—

I took the girl to the dance but she returned
with another. I forgave her. I took her to another
dance and she went home with two men. I forgave
her again. This became a pattern, I forgave
her so the maggots of hatred wouldn't eat my brain.

—

The night is long for a hungry dog.
We're not with them in spirit. They're alone.
The small teddy bear Lulu gave me in France
suddenly tipped over on my desk. Does this mean
my beloved is dead? She's ninety-three. Her
food and wine were the essence of earth.

—

In the Upper Peninsula of Michigan
and mountains of the Mexican border
I've followed the calls of birds
that don't exist into thickets
and up canyons. I'm unsure
if all of me returned.

—

I left this mangy little
three-legged bear two big fish
on a stump. He ate them at night
and at dawn slept like a god
leaning against the stump
in a chorus of birds.

—

The day was so dulcet and beautiful
I could think about nothing.
I lost my head.

—

A big warm wind in November,
yellow willow leaves
swirl around one hundred
white sheep.
This world is going to sleep.

—

Woke up from a nap and in an instant
knew I was alive. It was startling
to the point of fear. Emotions and sensations
were drowning me. This had never happened before.
On a blue chair in a pasture I relearned the world.

—

I've heard it three times from the woods,
le cri de Merlin. Fear is the price
you pay for remoteness, pure fear, somber
and penetrating. Maybe it's just that female wolf
I saw. The world is not what we thought it was.

—

In the Yucatán the jungle was from the movies
until the second day, then became itself.
I go away then come home but the jungle's
birds and snakes are with me in the snow.
You carry with you all the places you've ever been.

—

In a foreign city, even New York, I'm never
convinced I'll get back home where I wish to be.
It seems unlikely. The routes disappear.
You can follow the birds home but they're too fast
and often change their minds. Especially crows.

—

Reading Gilfillan's *Warbler Road* I learn
what I don't care about anymore by its absence.
These tiny birds are the living jewelry of the gods.
They clothe my life in proper mystery telling me
that all is not lost, harboring as they do stillborn children.

—

I'm quite tired of beating myself up
to write. I think I'll start letting
the words slip out like a tired child.
"Can I have a piece of pie" he asks,
and then he's asleep back on the cusp of the moon.

—

Again I wonder if I'll return.
France twice this fall, then New York. Will I know
if I don't return? The basic question of life.
Does Robert Frost know he's dead? His Yankee wit
a dust mote. God's stories last until no one hears.

—

The fly on the window is not a distant crow
in the sky. We're forced into these decisions.
People are forever marrying the wrong people
and the children of the world suffer.
Their dreams hang in the skies out of reach.

—

There's no question about circles, curves,
and loops, life's true structures, but the edges,
straight lines, squares come from us.
We must flee these shapes, even linear sentences
that limit us to doors, up and down ladders,
straight trajectories which will curve in eternity.

—

In Africa back in 1972 one day I studied
a female lion with blood on her fluttering whiskers,
traces of dark blood on her muzzle. A creature died
as we all must. In my seventies I see the invisible
lion not stalking but simply waiting, the solution
of the mystery I don't want to solve. She's waiting.

—

One day near here there was an earthquake
that started a new river in the mountains. During
the ponderous snowmelt in spring the river
is hundreds of feet deep and massive boulders roll
crashing along the bottom though you can't see them.

—

I've traveled back to the invention of trees
but never water. Water is too far in the blind past

whereas trees have eyes that help us see
their penetration of earth. Much that you see
isn't with your eyes. Throughout the body are eyes.

—

Of course we are condemned to life without parole
until the gods usher us in to our executioners
who live in a hot windowless room, always dark.
But then our fragility imagines everything
and the final moment is a kiss from the lipless gods.

—

Years before Hubble I thrust myself
far up into the night and saw that the constellations
were wildly colored. This frightened me
so I swam a river at night waiting for the stars
to resume their whiteness to adapt to my limits.

—

Where's my medicine bag? It's either hidden
or doesn't exist. Inside are memories of earth:
corn pollen, a bear claw, an umbilical cord.
If they exist they help me ride the dark
heavens of this life. Such fragile wings.

—

In Fillmore, Utah, night of the full moon,
Nov. 20, a day of blizzard, driving rain,
at 4:44 a.m. I'm arranging my tiny petrified
truffles from the Dordogne on the motel table.
They look like the decayed teeth of a small predator.
I'll leave one behind to start a new civilization.

—

The birds of winter. How I brooded
about them in my childhood. Why not fly south?
In the kingdom of birds everyone lives until they don't.

—

It's sudden. The chickadee hanging on a barb
of wire half eaten by the northern shrike. Birds kill
each other like we do but to eat. We're both five billion.
Whoever destroys their home rapes the gods.

—

The body wins another little argument
with doom. You wake to a crisp, clear morning
and you're definitely not dead. The golden light
flows down the mountain across the creek. A little vodka
and twelve hours of sleep. Nature detonates your mind
with the incalculable freshness of the new day.

—

The creek bed in front of our casita
has many tracks: javelina, deer, mountain
lion, and sometimes in the sand the serpentine
trace of a fat rattler. Foremost I love
the tracks left by hundreds of species of birds
that remain in the air like we do.

—

What vices we can hold in our Big Heads
and Big Minds, our Humor and Humility.
We don't march toward death, it marches toward us
as a summer thunderstorm came slowly across
the lake long ago. See the lightning of mortality dance,
the black clouds whirling as if a million crows.

—

Doom should be ashamed of itself.
It's so ordinary happening to billions
of creatures. It's common as a toilet seat,
the discarded shoes of a lifetime. It's proper
that it often hides itself until the last moment
and then the eternal silent music begins.

—

I'm unaware of what kind of singer I've become.
Each night there's a glass of vodka that quickly
becomes the color of my blood, the color of the guts
of archangels, the color pumped in dirt by the hearts
of soldiers. Any more than one glass of vodka
smears the constellations, the true source of light.

—

In my final moment I'll sing a nonsense ditty
of reconciliation knowing that music came
before words. I'm only a painter in Lascaux.
I've sold my destiny for a simple quarter that bought
me the world that I've visited at twilight.

—

I will sing even with my tongue sliced
into a fork. At the hospital this morning
I learned I'll be a nursemaid forever
or exactly as long as forever lasts. I study birds
that give me the tentative spaciousness of flight.

NOTATION

They say the years are layers, laminae.
They lie. Our minds aren't stuck together
like trees. We're much nearer to a ball of snakes
in winter, a flock of blackbirds, a school of fish.
Your brain guides you away from sentences.
It is consoled by the odor of the chokecherry tree
that drifts its sweetness through the studio window.
Chokecherry trees have always been there
along with crab apples. The brain doesn't care
about layers. It is both vertical and horizontal
in a split second, in all directions at once.
Nearly everything we are taught is false
except how to read. All these poems that drift
upward in our free-floating minds hang there
like stationary birds with a few astonishing
girls and women. Einstein lights a cigarette
and travels beyond the galaxies that have
no layers. Our neurons are designed after 90 billion galaxies.
As a shattered teenager I struggled to paint
a copy of El Greco's *View of Toledo* to Berlioz's *Requiem*.
The canvas was too short but very deep. I walked
on my knees to see what the world looked like
to Toulouse-Lautrec. It didn't work. I became seven
again. It was World War II. I was about
to lose an eye. The future was still in the sky
above me, which I had to learn to capture
in the years that never learned as clouds
to be layered. First warm day. Chokecherry burst. Its song.

AMERICAN SERMON

I am uniquely privileged to be alive
or so they say. I have asked others
who are unsure, especially the man with three
kids who's being foreclosed next month.
One daughter says she isn't leaving the farm,
they can pry her out with tractor
and chain. Mother needs heart surgery
but there is no insurance. A lifetime of cooking
with pork fat. My friend Sam has made
five hundred bucks in 40 years
of writing poetry. He has applied for 120
grants but so have 50,000 others. Sam keeps
strict track. The fact is he's not very good.
Back to the girl on the farm. She's been
keeping records of all the wildflowers
on the never-tilled land down the road,
a 40-acre clearing where they've bloomed
since the glaciers. She picks wild strawberries
with a young female bear who eats them. She's being
taken from the eastern Upper Peninsula down
to Lansing where Dad has a job in a
bottling plant. She won't survive the move.

ARTS

It's better to start walking before you're born.
As with dancing you have to learn the steps
and after that free-form can be the best.
Stevens said technique is the proof of seriousness,
though the grace of a Maserati is limited to itself.
There is a human wildness held beneath the skin
that finds all barriers brutishly unbearable.
I can't walk in the shoes cobbled for me.
They weren't devised by poets but by shoemakers.

BIRD'S-EYE VIEW

In the Sandhills of Nebraska
the towns are mere islands, sandspits,
in the ocean of land while in the Upper Peninsula
of Michigan, the towns seem not very successful
attempts to hold back the forest. In Montana
the mountains are so dominant that some days
the people refuse to look at them as children
turn away from the fathers who beat them.
But of course in most places the people
have won, the cities and highways have won.
As in nearly all wars both sides have lost
and the damage follows until the end of our time.
It seems strange that it could have been done well.
Greed has always fouled our vast nest.
Tiring of language, the mind takes flight
swimming off into the ocean of air thinking
who am I that the gods and men have disappointed me?
You walk through doorways in the mind you can't walk out
then one day you discover that you've learned to fly.
From up here the water is still blue, the grass green
and the wind that buoys me is 12 billion years old.

POET WARNING

He went to sea
in a thimble of poetry
without sail or oars
or anchor. What chance
do I have, he thought?
Hundreds of thousands
of moons have drowned out here
and there are no gravestones.

A PART OF MY HISTORY

I took the train from Seville to Granada with a vintner friend. I had been reading Federico García Lorca for over fifty years and needed to see where he was murdered on the mountainside near Granada. Beware old man! We visited the site of the murder, drank a little wine, and I began to drown in melancholy. We went to our hotel where I planned to stay in Lorca's room but it frightened me and I moved to another. We toured the city in the morning and I stared at the Sierra Nevada glistening with snow that was somehow somber as the jewelry of the dead. I took a nap and wept for no reason. We went to a magnificent flamenco concert on a hill across from the Alhambra and ate very late in the evening. I became quite ill. My friend had to leave for her home in Collioure. I spent the day reading my empty journal, the white pages swarming with nothing. At 5 a.m. I went to an airport hours away in the darkness, flew to Madrid, then from Madrid to Chicago sitting next to a girl of surpassing beauty who said that she was an Erasmus scholar, an honor of sorts. I slept for eight hours and dreamt that Erasmus was a girl. At a Chicago airport hotel I thought I was slipping away and was taken to a hospital in an ambulance and my journal was crushed in my pocket. I stayed in ER for seven hours and a Chinese magician restored me. At dawn I flew to Montana and barely recognized our dog. My advice is, do not try to inhabit another's soul. You have your own.

THE MUSE IN OUR TIME

We were born short boys in tall grass.
We became the magicians who actually
sawed the girl in half. We were prosecuted
unfairly by the gods for this simple mistake
and exiled to the tropics where we wore
the masques of howler monkeys
until we became howler monkeys
in the fabulous zoo of our culture.
Now as an amateur surgeon I'm putting
the girl back together stitch by painful stitch
beside the creek in the winter twilight.
She begs me to stop. She wants to become
a night-blooming cereus only seen
every decade or so in the random dark.

MUSE II

Pretty girls most often have pretty
parents but then for unknown genetic
reasons a beautiful woman is born
of homely parents. She is not happy
about being set aside by the gods.
At family gatherings truly ugly relatives
want to murder her but this is rarely
done in poetry since William Shakespeare.
Out in the orchard she is buggered
nearly to death by her cousins who all
become scientists who devise products
we never imagined we would need.
She is sent into the world. She crawls
into the low door of the city but yearns
to stand straight. She floats up a river
into the country and lives with wild dogs
who are soon hunted to death for sport.
She wants to step off the world but can't find
the edge. A man flies her to Mexico
and makes her a prostitute. She escapes
but a pimp slashes her face, a happy
moment because now she's not beautiful.
She walks twenty miles down an empty beach
and lives with an old, deaf fisherman.
Now her soul swells with the grandeur of the ocean,
the beauty of fish, the silence of man,
the moon and stars she finally understands.

POET AT NINETEEN IN NYC

The poet looking for an immortal poem
from his usual pathetic position as a graduate
student in a university that doesn't exist.
He knows three constellations, this expert
of the stars, and sometimes notices the moon
by the time it reaches its first quarter.
He's admirable and keeps his chin high
in the city's arctic winds. He drinks
a hundred drinks a month, three a day
and a bit more for courage. He has a room
and a half, the half a tiny kitchenette,
and his table for writing and eating
is a piece of plywood he places on the bed.
Tacked above the bed are pictures of his heroes,
Dostoyevsky, Whitman, Lorca and Faulkner,
and of course Rimbaud. He doesn't fear rejection
because he keeps his work to himself. He thinks
he's as inevitable as a river but doesn't have time
to keep time. The hardest part is when the river
is too swift and goes underground for days on end.

SISTER

I wanted to play a song for you
on our old $28 phonograph
from 1954 but the needle is missing
and they no longer make the needles.
It is the work of man to make a voice
a needle. You were buried at nineteen
in wood with Daddy. I've spent a lifetime
trying to learn the language of the dead.
The musical chatter of the tiny yellow finches
in the front yard comes closest. It's midnight
and I'm giving my nightly rub to the dog's
tummy, something she truly depends on.
Maybe you drifted upward as an ancient
bird hoping to nest on the moon.

SKULL

You can't write the clear biography
of the aches and pains inside your skull.
Will I outlive my passport expiration?
Will the knots of the past beat me to death
like limber clubs, the Gordian knots
that never will be untied, big as bowling balls?
Maybe not. Each time I row the river
for six hours or so the innards of my skull
slightly change shape. Left alone knots
can unravel in the turbulence of water.
It isn't for me to understand why loved ones
died. My skull can't withstand
the Tao of the mighty river carrying me along
as if I were still and the mountains
capped by clouds were rushing past.
After we submerge do we rise again in another form?
Meanwhile I speculate on the seven pills
I must take each day to stay alive.
I ask each one, "Are we doing your job?"
The only answer I've found is the moving
water whose music is without a single lyric.

HORSES

In truth I am puzzled most in life
by nine horses.

I've been watching them for eleven weeks
in a pasture near Melrose.

Two are on one side of the fence and seven
on the other side.

They stare at one another from the same places
hours and hours each day.

This is another unanswerable question
to haunt us with the ordinary.

They have to be talking to one another
in a language without a voice.

Maybe they are speaking the wordless talk of lovers,
sullen, melancholy, jubilant.

Linguists say that language comes after music
and we sang nonsense syllables

before we invented a rational speech
to order our days.

We live far out in the country where I hear
creature voices night and day.

Like us they are talking about their lives
on this brief visit to earth.

In truth each day is a universe in which
we are tangled in the light of stars.

Stop a moment. Think about these horses
in their sweet-smelling silence.

RENÉ CHAR II

What are these legitimate fruits
of daring?
The natural brain, bruised by mental
somersaults.
On a bet to sleep naked
out in the snow.
To push your forefingers into your ears
until they meet the brain.
To climb backwards into the heavens because
we poets live in reverse.
It is too late to seduce the heroine
in my stories.
How can enough be enough
when it isn't?
The Great Mother has no ears and *hallelujah*
is the most impossible word in the language.
I can only say it to birds, fish, and dogs.

XMAS CHEESEBURGERS

I was without Christmas spirit
so I made three cow dogs,
Lola and Blacky and Pinto,
cheeseburgers with ground chuck
and French St. André cheese
so that we'd all feel better.
I delivered them to Hard Luck Ranch
and said, "Chew each bite 32 times."
They ignored me and gobbled.
The world that used to nurse us
now keeps shouting inane instructions.
That's why I ran to the woods.

MARY THE DRUG ADDICT

Mary, spayed early so a virgin like her ancient namesake, is a drug addict. She was stomped on as a puppy by an angry little girl and thus a lifetime of spinal problems. Now an old woman she waits for her pain pills every day and then she's a merry animal. Up until a few years back she'd run much farther than her Lab sister until she was a tiny black peppercorn in the alfalfa field. She walks much closer now turning to check if I'm following along. She's an English cocker and sniffs the ground then pauses to meditate on the scent. To understand Mary we have to descend into the cellar, the foundation of our being, the animal bodies we largely ignore. She sleeps a lot, eats kibble without interest and craves meat tidbits with the pleasure making her wiggle. Outdoors, her eyes wide to the open she acts with exuberance, our lost birthright. Like all beautiful women she has become beautifully homely. In the evening I lift her onto the couch despite her brush with a skunk, and we speak a bone-deep language without nouns and verbs, a creature-language skin to skin.

NIGHT CREATURES

"The horses run around, their feet
are on the ground." In my headlights
there are nine running down the highway,
clack-clacking in the night, swerving
and drifting, some floating down the ditch,
two grays, the rest colorless in the dark.
What can I do for them? Nothing, night
is swallowing all of us, the fences
on each side have us trapped,
the fences tight to the ditches. Suddenly they turn.
I stop. They come back toward me,
my window open to the glorious smell of horses.
I'm asking the gods to see them home.

DEAF DOG'S BARK

A bit flinty. Trace of a squeak.
Does she hear herself?
"I hear only my own music," said Beethoven.
Is it an announcement or warning
from one so small and crippled
in youth by a child
who stomped her spine?
She listens to the glory of her past.
She knows where she is
in our home. She's Mary,
the deer chaser, a woman
of power, a lion in her mind,
roaring so weakly into the dark,
trying to make hips follow chest.

JUNE THE HORSE

Sleep is water. I'm an old man surging
upriver on the back of my dream horse
that I haven't seen since I was ten.
We're night riders through cities, forests, fields.

I saw Stephanie standing on the steps of Pandora's Box
on Sheridan Square in 1957. She'd never spoken
to me but this time, as a horse lover, she waved.

I saw the sow bear and two cubs. She growled
at me in 1987 when I tried to leave the cabin while her cubs
were playing with my garbage cans. I needed a drink
but I didn't need this big girl on my ass.

We swam up the Neva in St. Petersburg in 1972
where a girl sat on the bank hugging a red icon
and Raskolnikov, pissed off and whining, spat on her feet.

On the Rhône in the Camargue fighting bulls
bellowed at us from a marsh and 10,000 flamingos
took flight for Africa.

This night-riding is the finest thing I do at age seventy-two.
On my birthday evening we'll return to the original
pasture where we met and where she emerged from the pond
draped in lily pads and a coat of green algae.
We were children together and I never expected her return.

One day as a brown boy I shot a wasp nest with bow and arrow,
releasing hell. I mounted her from a stump and without
reins or saddle we rode to a clear lake where the bottom
was covered with my dreams waiting to be born.
One day I'll ride her as a bone-clacking skeleton.
We'll ride to Veracruz and Barcelona, then up to Venus.

POET NO. 7

We must be bareback riders. The gods
abhor halters and stirrups, even a horse
blanket to protect our asses is forbidden.
Finally, our legs must grow into the horse
because we were never meant to get off.

A PUZZLE

I see today that everyone on earth
wants the answer to the same question
but none has the language to ask it.
The inconceivable is clearly the inconceivable.
Bum mutter, teethchatter, brain flotsam,
we float up from our own depths
to the sky not the heavens, an invention
of the murderers. Dogs know the answer
by never asking the question but can't advise us.
Here is the brain that outran the finish line:
on a dark day when the world was slate
the yellow sun blasted the mountain across
the river so that it flung its granitic light
in the four directions to which we must bow.
Life doesn't strangle on ironies, we made
that part up. Close after dawn the sheep next door
leave their compound, returning at twilight.
With the rains this was a prodigious green year,
and now the decay of autumn sleeps in dead comfort.
Words are moving water—muddy, clear, or both.

RUMINATION

I sit up late dumb as a cow,
which is to say
somewhat conscious with thirst
and hunger, an eye for the new moon
and the morning's long walk
to the water tank. Everywhere
around me the birds are waiting
for the light. In this world of dreams
don't let the clock cut up
your life in pieces.

DAN'S BUGS

I felt a little bad about the nasty earwig
that drowned in my nighttime glass of water,
lying prone at the bottom like a shipwrecked mariner.
There was guilt about the moth who died
when she showered with me, possibly a female.
They communicate through wing vibrations.
I was careful when sticking a letter
in our rural mailbox, waiting for a fly to escape,
not wanting her to be trapped there in the darkness.
Out here in the country many insects invade our lives
and many die in my nightcap, floating and deranged.
On the way to town to buy wine and a chicken
I stopped from 70 mph to pick up
a wounded dragonfly fluttering on the yellow line.
I've read that some insects live only for minutes,
as we do in our implacable geologic time.

INVISIBLE

Within the wilder shores of sky
billions of insects are migrating
for reasons of sex and food,
or so I'm told by science,
in itself as invisible as the specters
of love and death. What can I see
from here but paper and the mind's
random images? A living termite
was found on sticky paper at 19,000 feet.
Perhaps she thought she had lost
the world as I think I must, barring
flora, fauna, family, dogs, the earth,
the mind ground of being as it is.
A few years back I began to lose
the world of people. I couldn't hold on.
Rüppell's vulture was seen at 36,000 feet
for reasons the gods keep from us.

MARY

How can this dog on the cushion
at my feet have passed me
in the continuum of age, a knot
in our hearts that never unwinds? This dog
is helplessly herself and cannot think otherwise.
When called she often conceals herself
behind a bush, a tree, or tall grass
pondering if she should obey. Now crippled
at twelve, bearing up under pain
on the morning run, perhaps wondering
remotely what this is all about, the slowness
that has invaded her bones. Splayed out
now in a prone running pose
she moves in sleep slowly into the future
that does not welcome us but is merely
our destiny in which we disappear
making room for others on the long march.
The question still is how did she pass me
happily ahead in this slow goodbye?

REMOTE FRIENDS

Yes, in the predawn black
the slim slip of the waning moon,
the cuticle of an unknown god,
perhaps Mother Night, the outline
of her back between points of stars,
she's heading south toward Mexico
preferring mountains, rivers, oceans, jungles
that return her affection for earth.
It's been hard work to guide migrating
birds for 150 million years. To her
we're newcomers, but then she married
me, a stranger whom she's worn thin as water.

POET SCIENCE

In my recent studies I have discovered cancer.
Last year it was the language of birds
and the year before, time by drowning a clock in the toilet.
It is life's work to recognize the mystery
of the obvious. Cancer is a way the gods
have learned to kill us. In numbers it's tied
with war and famine. Time is the way
our deaths are numbered precisely. The birds
and their omnipresent language, their music,
have resisted conclusions as surely as the stars
above them which they use for navigation.
I have prayed willingly to their disinterest,
the way they look past me into the present,
their songs greeting both daylight and dark.
They've been on earth fifty times longer than us
right down to the minute, and they've told me
that cancer and time are only death's music,
that we learned this music before birth without hearing it.
Like cancer cells we've lost our way and will do anything to live.
My mind can't stop its only child so frightened of the dark.

ACHE

All this impermanence and suffering
we share with dogs, bees, crows,
the aquatic insect that lives but a single
minute on a summer evening
then descends to its river burial,
perhaps into the mouth of a trout
already full of its brothers and sisters
while in a nearby meadow the she
wolf approaches an infant elk
she'll share with her litter.
Many of us live full term never seeing
the bullet, the empty plate of hunger,
the invisible noose of disease.
We can't imagine the rings of the bristlecone
that lived for millennia. We cut it down
to number the years like our own insolent birthdays.

ORIOLE

Emerging after three months to the edge
of the hole of pain I arrange
ten orange halves on a stiff wire
off the patio between a small tree
and the feeder. Early next morning
five orioles of three species appear:
Scott's, hooded, Bullock's. Thinking
of those long nights: this is what agony wanted,
these wildly colored birds to inhabit
my mind far from pain.
Now they live inside me.

BLUE SHAWL

The other day at the green dumpsters,
an old woman in a blue shawl
told me that she loved my work.

RIVER I

I was there in a room in a village
by the river when the moon fell into the window
frame and was trapped there too long.
I was fearful but I was upside down
and my prayers fell off the ceiling.
Our small dog Jacques jumped on the sofa
near the window, perched on the sofa's back
and released the moon to head south.
Just after dawn standing in the green yard
I watched a girl ride down the far side
of the railroad tracks on a beauteous white horse
whose lower legs were wrapped in red tape.
Above her head were mountains covered with snow.
I decided we were born to be moving water not ice.

RIVER II

Another dawn in the village by the river
and I'm jealous of the 63 moons of Jupiter.
Out in the yard inspecting a lush lilac bush
followed by five dogs who have chosen
me as their temporary leader, I look up
through the vodka jangle of the night before,
straight up at least 30,000 feet where the mountains
are tipping over on me. Dizzy I grab the lilacs
for support. Of course it's the deceitful clouds
playing the game of becoming mountains.
Once on our nighttime farm on a moonlit walk
the clouds pushed by a big western wind
became a school of whales swimming hard
across the cold heavens and I finally knew
that we walk the bottom of an ocean we call sky.

RIVER III

Saw a poem float by just beneath
the surface, another corpse of the spirit
we weren't available to retrieve.
It isn't comforting to admit that our days
are fatal, that the corpse of the spirit
gradually becomes the water and waits
for another, or perhaps you, to return
to where you belong, not
a shaker sprinkling its salt
everywhere. You have to hold your old
heart lightly as the female river holds
the clouds and trees, its fish
and the moon, so lightly but firmly
enough so that nothing gets away.

RIVER IV

The river seems confused today because it
swallowed the thunderstorm above us. At my age
death stalks me but I don't mind. This is to be
expected but how can I deal with the unpardonable
crime of loneliness? The girl I taught to swim
so long ago has gone to heaven, the kind of thing
that happens while we're on the river fishing and
seeing the gorgeously colored western tanagers and the
profusion of nighthawks that some call bullbats,
nightjars, and down on the border they call them
goatsuckers for stealing precious milk. I love
this misfiring of neurons in which I properly
understand nothing, not the wild high current
or the thunderstorm on which it chokes. Did the
girl swim to heaven through the ocean of sky?
Maybe. I can deny nothing. Two friends are mortally
ill. Were it not for the new moon my sky
would collapse tonight so fed by the waters of memory.

RIVER V

Resting in an eddy against dense greenery
so thick you can't see into it but can fathom
its depth by waning birdcalls, hum of insects.
This morning I learned that we live and die
as children to the core only carrying
as a protective shell a fleshy costume
made up mostly of old scar tissue
from before we learned how to protect ourselves.
It's hard to imagine that this powerful
river had to begin with a single drop
far into the mountains, a seep or trickle
from rocks and then the runoff from snowmelt.
Of course watershed means the shedding
of water, rain, a hundred creeks, a thousand
small springs. My mind can't quite
contain this any more than my own inception
in a single sperm joining a single egg
utterly invisible, hidden in Mother's moist
dark. Out of almost nothing, for practical
purposes nothing, then back as ancient
children to the great nothing again,
the song of man and water moving to the ocean.

RIVER VI

I thought years ago that old Heraclitus was wrong.
You can't step into the same river even once.
The water slips around your foot like liquid time
and you can't dry it off after its passage.
Don't bother taking your watch to the river,
the moving water is a glorious second hand.
Properly understood the memory loses nothing
and we humans are never allowed to let our minds
sit on the still bank and have a simple picnic.
I had an unimaginable dream when young
of being a river horse that could easily plunge upstream.
Perhaps it came from our huge black mare June
whom I rode bareback as she swam the lake
in big circles, always getting out where she got in.
Meanwhile this river is surrounded by mountains
covered with lodgepole pines that are mortally diseased,
browning in the summer sun. Everyone knows
that lightning will strike and Montana burn.
We all stay quiet about it, this blessed oxygen
that makes the world a crematory. Only the water is safe.

RIVER VII

The last trip to the river this year. Tonight I think
of the trout swimming in a perfect, moonless
dark, navigating in the current by the tiny pinpoint
of stars, night wind rippling the eddies,
and always if you stick your head under
the surface, the slight sound of the pebbles
rubbing against pebbles. Today I saw two dead
pelicans. I heard they are shot because they eat
trout, crows shot because they eat duck eggs,
wolves shot for eating elk or for chasing
a bicyclist in Yellowstone. Should we be shot
for eating the world and giving back our puke?
Way down in Notch Bottom, ancient winter camp
for long-gone Indians, I am sweetly consoled
by our absolute absence except for a stretch
of fence on the bank, half washed away
by the current, a sequence of No Trespassing signs
to warn us away from a pricey though miasmic swamp.
The river can't heal everything. You have to do your part.
We've even bruised the moon. Still the birds are a chorus
with the moving flow, clearly relatives of Mozart,
the brown trout so lovely the heart flutters. Back home
something has eaten the unfledged swallows. It wasn't us.
I'm on another river now, it's swollen and turbulent.
"The spirit is here. Are you?" I ask myself.

SPRING

Something new in the air today, perhaps the struggle of the bud to become a leaf. Nearly two weeks late it invaded the air but then what is two weeks to life herself? On a cool night there is a break from the struggle of becoming. I suppose that's why we sleep. In a childhood story they spoke of "the land of enchantment." We crawl to it, we short-lived mammals, not realizing that we are already there. To the gods the moon is the entire moon but to us it changes second by second because we are always fish in the belly of the whale of earth. We are encased and can't stray from the house of our bodies. I could say that we are released, but I don't know, in our private night when our souls explode into a billion fragments then calmly regather in a black pool in the forest, far from the cage of flesh, the unremitting "I." This was a dream and in dreams we are forever alone walking the ghost road beyond our lives. Of late I see waking as another chance at spring.

SKY

Here along the Mexican border
working on the patio between
two bamboo thickets and facing
the creek, all that I hear while
staring down at the unforgiving paper
is chatter and song,
the crisp fluff of birds flying
back and forth to the feeders,
the creek that actually burbles,
and the nearly imperceptible sound
of the sky straining to keep
us on earth despite our disappointments,
our fatal cries that disappear
into her blueness, her blackness.

MARCH IN PATAGONIA, AZ

Some days in March are dark
and some altogether too glittery
and loud with birds. There is recent news
of ancient cosmic events that have lost
significance. I recognize the current
moon from Granada several years
ago, a big Spanish moon though here
it hangs over Mexico, shining on blood
and the music wandering lost in the air.
At the ranch starving cattle
bawl loudly in the drought.

BRAZIL

"It rains most in the ocean off Trinidad
so that the invisible sea flowers
never stop blooming on the lid of water."

Or so she said on a balcony in Bahia
in 1982, brushing her long black hair
upward into the wet moonlit night.

I'm staring east at the island of Itaparica
spangled with light a dozen miles at sea.
I think that it's not for me to determine the truth.

A half hour ago it was a snake far to the west
in the jungle which only ate flowers the color
of blood and laid seven red eggs every year.

In Brazil I'm adding to my knowledge
of the impossible. In her remote hometown
a condor stole and raised a child as its own.

At dinner of a roasted fish she said the child
had learned to fly and I broke, saying no,
that our arms have the wrong kind of feathers.

She was pissed and said, "I went to Miami
with an aunt when I was seven to fix my heart.
You only make guns, bombs, cars, and count money.

"Your ocean stank of gasoline, your food was white.
I saw an alligator eat a dog. A river
didn't run into the sea but went backwards.

"A century ago in my hometown the Virgin Mary
appeared and sang about her lost child in the river
of men. If you don't believe me you're wicked."

Back home in the cold our dogs run across
clear ice, their feet and shadows watched by fish.
I drop three lighted candles into moving water to survive Brazil.

GRAND MARAIS

The wind came up so strongly at midnight
the cabin creaked in its joints and between
the logs, the tin roof hummed and shuddered
and in the woods you could hear the dead
trees called widow-makers falling
with staccato crashes, and by 3 a.m.
the thunderous roar of Lake Superior miles away.
My dog Rose comes from the sofa
where she invariably sleeps. Her face is close
to mine in the dark, a question on her breath.
Will the sun rise again? She gets on the bed trembling.
I wonder what the creature life is doing
without shelter? Rose is terribly frightened
of this lordly old bear I know who visits
the yard for the sunflower seeds I put out
for the birds. I placed my hand on his head one night
through the car window when I was drunk.
He doesn't give a shit about violent storms
knowing the light comes from his mind, not the sun.

DESERT SNOW

I don't know what happens after death
but I'll have to chance it. I've been waking
at 5 a.m. and making a full study of darkness.
I was upset not hearing the predicted rain
that I very much need for my wildflowers.
At first light I see that it was the silent rain
of snow. I didn't hear this softest sigh
of windless snow softly falling
here on the Mexican border in the mountains,
snow in a white landscape of high desert.
The birds are confounded by this rare snow
so I go out with a spatula to clean the feeders,
turn on the radio not to the world's wretched news
but to the hot, primary colors of cantina music,
the warbles and shrieks of love, laughter, and bullets.

REALITY

Nothing to console the morning but the dried grasshopper
on my desk who fell apart at my powerful touch.
Two days ago at dawn I awoke with a large black tear
stuck to my cheek that felt like a globule of tar.
The MRI machine at the Nogales hospital revealed
that the black tear is connected to heart, brain, penis
with three pieces of nearly invisible spiderweb.
My friend the urologist said that if even one breaks
Eros is dead in my body, a corpse of the memory of love.
Luckily I was diverted for a day by helping my wife
make Thanksgiving dinner for ten friends and neighbors,
brooding about the souls of 35 million turkeys
hovering visibly in the blue sky above our naked earth.
They can't fly away like the game birds I hunt, doves and quail.
As with people we've bred them so that they're unable to escape.
At certain remote locations they see through the fence
their mysterious cousins flying to tree limbs
and weep dry turkey tears of bitter envy.
I made the gravy, the most important substance on earth,
but now on Friday morning I'm back to my black tear
on my old brown cheek of barely alive Eros.
In slightly more than a week I'll be seventy-two.
How can I concoct this intricate fantasy of making love
to three French girls on a single Paris afternoon?
It begins with a not very good pot of coffee
in my room at the Hôtel de Suède on rue Vaneau
where at night I heard an owl, a chouette in the garden.
I meet two of the girls in the Luxembourg on a morning walk
where one, astoundingly, is reading a novel I wrote.
I demand ID to make sure they're of legal age.
One must be safe from the police in fantasies.

We go shopping and I buy them 100-euro
tricornered hats. We go to an apartment
and meet the older sister of one. She's twenty-three.
I sign my books they own and when I turn
they sit on the sofa with soft cotton skirts raised.
I forgot to add that it's a warm day in April.
Should I choose by saying, "Eeny, meeny, miney, mo,"
or would this Michigan idiom frighten them?
I make a dream swan dive into a day of love and laughter
then suddenly I'm back at Hard Luck Ranch
giving the cow dogs biscuits. Old nitwit Petey
pisses in his food and water as Man in Our Time.
I am liberated back into the fragility of childhood.

SHE

Nothing is as it appears to be.
What is this aging? What am I to make
of these pale, brutal numbers? For a moment I'm fourteen.
The sky didn't fall in, it fell out.
Men suck on their sugary black pistols
but the world isn't ruled for a second.
The pen is mightier than the sword
only in the fretwork of a poet's language.
At fourteen green was green and women
were the unreachable birds of night,
their fronts and backs telling us
we might not be alone in the universe,
their voices singing that the earth is female.
The humid summer night was as warm as birth,
and she swam out into the night beyond the dock light.

LOVE

Love is raw as freshly cut meat,
mean as a beetle on the track of dung.
It is the Celtic dog that ate its tail in a dream.
It chooses us as a blizzard chooses a mountain.
It's seven knocks on the door you pray not to answer.
The boy followed the girl to school eating his heart
with each step. He wished to dance with her
beside a lake, the wind showing the leaves'
silvery undersides. She held the moist bouquet
of wild violets he had picked against her neck.
She wore the sun like her skin
but beneath, her blood was black as soil.
At the grave of her dog in the woods
she told him to please go away forever.

BACK INTO MEMORY

The tears roll up my cheek
and the car backs itself south.
I pull away from the girl and reverse
through the door without looking.
In defiance of the body the mind
does as it wishes, the crushed bones
of life reknit themselves in sunlight.
In the night the body melts itself
down to the void before birth
before you swam the river into being.
Death takes care of itself like a lightning
stroke and the following thunder
is the veil being rent in twain.
The will to live can pass away
like that raven colliding with the sun.
In age we tilt toward home.
We want to sleep a long time, not forever,
but then to sleep a long time becomes forever.

DEBTORS

They used to say we're living on borrowed
time but even when young I wondered
who loaned it to us? In 1948 one grandpa
died stretched tight in a misty oxygen tent,
his four sons gathered, his papery hand
grasping mine. Only a week before, we were fishing.
Now the four sons have all run out of borrowed time
while I'm alive wondering whom I owe
for this indisputable gift of existence.
Of course time is running out. It always
has been a creek heading east, the freight
of water with its surprising heaviness
following the slant of the land, its destiny.
What is lovelier than a creek or riverine thicket?
Say it is an unknown benefactor who gave us
birds and Mozart, the mystery of trees and water
and all living things borrowing time.
Would I still love the creek if I lasted forever?

PRISONERS

In truth I have lost my beauty
but this isn't as important as the violation
of the myth of the last meal due those
about to be executed. I believe in the sacred
obligation to give a man about to be dead
what he wants to eat. Not true. In Texas
it's limited to what's on hand, the hundreds
of tons of frozen garbage prisoners feed on.
Not to worry. I'm ineligible to be executed,
not being convicted of killing anyone, but after
a lifetime of chewing I'd choose a saltine cracker.
After all, we chew and chew and chew. Pigs, fish,
melancholy cows and gamboling lambs pass
through us, not to speak of fields of wheat
and lettuce, tomatoes and beans. Our jaws are strong
as a woman's thighs pumping up the stairs
of a tall building to throw herself from the roof
because she's tired of chewing, being penetrated
by swallowing, and of a man who chews
as if his life depended on it, which it does.

CORRUPTION

Like Afghanistan I'm full of corruption.
My friend McGuane once said, "I'd gladly
commit a hundred acts of literary capitulation
to keep my dog in Alpo." The little ones needed
dental braces and flutes, cars and houses.
Off and on I've had this dangerous golden touch
like a key to a slot machine streaming 20-dollar
gold pieces. It was so easy to buy expensive
French wine that purges the grim melancholy
of livelihood, the drudgery of concocting fibs.
I know a man, happily married, who bought
a girl a hundred-dollar pair of panties. I was stunned.
For this price I buy a whole lamb each fall.
Now lamb and panties are gone though the panties
might be on a card table at a yard sale.
Right now a wind has come up and there's a strange
blizzard of willow buds outside my studio.
I'm on death row but won't give up corruption.
I've waterboarded myself. I'm guilty of everything.

OUR ANNIVERSARY

I want to go back to that wretched old farm
on a cold November morning eating herring
on the oil tablecloth at daylight, the hard butter
in slivers and chunks on rye bread, gold-colored
homemade butter. Fill the woodbox, Jimmy.
Clots of cream in the coffee, hiss and crackle
of woodstove. Outside it's been the hardest freeze
yet but the heels still break through into the earth.
A winter farm is dead and you want to head for the woods.
In the barn the smell of manure and still-green hay
hit the nose with the milk in the metal pails.
Grandpa is on the last of seven cows,
tugging their dicklike udders, a squirt in the mouth
for the barn cat. My girlfriend loves another
and at twelve it's as if all the trees have died.
Sixty years later seven hummingbirds at the feeder,
miniature cows in their stanchions sipping liquid sugar.
We are fifty years together. There are still trees.

DOORS

I'm trying to create an option for all
these doors in life. You're inside
or out, outside or in. Of late, doors
have failed us more than the two-party system
or marriages comprising only one person.
We've been fooled into thousands of dualisms
which the Buddha says is a bad idea.
Nature has portals rather than doors.
There are two vast cottonwoods near a creek
and when I walk between them I shiver.
Winding through my field of seventy-seven
large white pine stumps from about 1903
I take various paths depending on spirit.
The sky is a door never closed to us.
The sun and moon aren't doorknobs.
Dersu Uzala slept outside for forty-five years.
When he finally moved inside he died.

GREED

I'm greedy for the pack rat to make
it across the swift creek. It's my first swimming
pack rat and I wonder why he wants the other side.
The scent of a pack-rat woman perhaps.
I'm greedy for those I prayed for to survive
cancer, greedy for money we don't need,
for the freshest fish to eat every day
without moving to the ocean's shore,
to have many lovers who don't ruin my marriage
and that my dog will live longer than me
to avoid the usual sharp boyhood heartbreak,
to regain the inch and a half I lost with age, to see
my youngest aunt pull up her nylons again in 1948.
Oh how I wanted a real sponge, a once-living
creature, and a wide chamois cloth to wash
cars for a quarter, a huge twenty-cent burger
and a five-cent Coca-Cola for lunch, greedy
that my beloved wife will last longer than me,
that the wind will blow harder up the girl's
summer dress, for three dozen oysters
and a bottle of 1985 Pétrus at twilight,
to smoke a cigarette again in a bar, that my
daughters live to be a hundred if they so wish,
that I march to heaven barefoot on a spring morning.

CEREAL

Late-night herring binge causes sour
gut. My dog ate the Hungarian partridge
eggs in the tall grass, her jaws dripping
yolk, therefore I ate a cereal for breakfast
guaranteed to restore my problematic health.
Soon enough I'll be diving for my own
herring in the North Atlantic, or running so fast
I nearly take off like the partridge mother
abandoning her eggs to the canine monster.
It will be strange to be physically magnificent
at my age, the crowds of girls cooing
around me as I bounce up and down
as if my legs cannot contain their pogo strength,
but I leave the girls behind, bouncing across
a river toward the end of the only map we have,
the not very wide map of the known world.

D.B.

A winter dawn in New York City
with people rushing to work
eating rolls, drinking paper cups
of coffee. This isn't the march of the dead
but people moving toward their livelihoods
in this grim, cold first sign of daylight.
I watched the same thing in Paris
and felt like the eternal meddler sitting
at the window, trying to avoid
conclusions about humans, their need
to earn their daily bread, as we used to say.
In Paris I know a lovely woman
who wears a twenty-foot-long wool skirt
to hide her legs from men. Who can blame
her though I fear the grave dangers
of this trailing garment clipped and woven
from lowly sheep. What a burden
it is to drag this heavy skirt
throughout the workday to hide from desire
as if her sexuality had become a car bomb
rather than a secret housepet hidden
from the landlords of the world who are always there.

SUNLIGHT

After days of darkness I didn't understand
a second of yellow sunlight
here and gone through a hole in clouds
as quickly as a flashbulb, an immense
memory of a moment of grace withdrawn.
It is said that we are here but seconds in cosmic
time, twelve and a half billion years,
but who is saying this and why?
In the Salt Lake City airport eight out of ten
were fiddling relentlessly with cell phones.
The world is too grand to reshape with babble.
Outside the hot sun beat down on clumsy metal
birds and an actual ten-million-year-old
crow flew by squawking in bemusement.
We're doubtless as old as our mothers, thousands
of generations waiting for the sunlight.

BRUTISH

The man eating lamb's tongue salad
rarely thinks of the lamb.
The oral surgeon jerking twenty teeth out
in a day still makes marinara sauce.
The German sorting baby shoes at Treblinka
writes his wife and children frequently.
The woman loves her husband, drops two kids
at day care, makes passionate love
to an old boyfriend at the Best Western.
We are parts. What part are you now?
The shit of the world has to be taken
care of every day. You have to choose
your part after you take care of the shit.
I've chosen birds and fish, the creatures
whose logic I wish to learn and live.

NIGHTFEARS

What is it that you're afraid of at night?
Is it the gunman at the window, the rattler
slipping into your boot on the patio, the painful
quirk in your tummy or the semitruck
drifting across the centerline because the driver
is text-messaging a she-male girlfriend in El Paso?
Is it because so many birds these days are born
with one wing like poets in campus infirmaries,
that the ghouls of finance, or the post office,
have taken your paycheck to pay for Kool-Aid
parties around their empty pools? The night
has decided to stick around for a week
and people are confused, we creatures of habit
who took the sun for granted. She had decided
on whim to keep herself from us, calling down
the descent of a galactic cloud, to let flowers
wilt and die. Whole countries expire in hysteria
and troops must march in the glare of headlights.
When the red sun decides to rise again we humans
of earth swim through the acrid milk of our brains
toward the rising light, a new song on our lips,
but all creatures retreat from us, their murderers.
In real dawn's early light my poached egg is only an egg.

BLUE

During last night's blue moon
the Great Matter and Original Mind
were as close as your skin.
In the predawn dark you ate muskmelon
and the color of the taste lit up the mind.
The first finch awoke and the moon
descended into its mountain burial.

THE CURRENT POOR

The rich are giving the poor bright-colored
balloons, a dollar a gross, also bandages,
and leftover Mercurochrome from the fifties.
It is an autumn equinox and full moon present,
an event when night and day are precisely
equal, but then the poor know that night
always wins, grows wider and longer
until Christmas when they win a few minutes.
Under the tree there's an orange big as a basketball.
It is the exiled sun resting in its winter coolness.

MOPING

Please help me, gentle reader. I need advice.
I need to carbonate my brain
before nightfall. One more night
with this heaviness will suffocate me.
It's probably only the terror
of particulars. Memories follow us
like earaches in childhood. I'm surrounded
by sad-eyed burros, those motel paintings
I thought were book reviewers and politicians
but no, they're all my dead friends
who keep increasing in numbers until
it occurs to me that I might join them one day
floating out there in the anemic ether
of nothingness, but that's not my current business.
Just for the time being my brain needs oxygen
though I'm not sure what it is, life's puzzle
where you wake in a foreign land and the people
haven't shown themselves but the new birds
are haunting. The mind visits these alien Egypts,
these incalculable sunrises in a new place,
these birds of appetite with nowhere to land.

CHURCH

After last night's storm the tulip
petals are strewn across the patio
where they mortally fluttered. Only the gods
could reconnect them to their green stems
but they choose not to perform such banal
magic. Life bores deep holes in us
in hopes the nature of what we are
might sink into us without the blasphemy
of the prayer for parlor tricks. Ask the gods
to know them before you beg for favors.
The pack rat removes the petals one by one.
Now they are in a secret place, not swept away.
The death of flowers is unintentional. Who knows
if either of us will have a memory of ourselves?
If you stay up in the mountains it's always cold
but if you come down to the world of men you suffocate
in the folds of the overripe ass of piety, the smell
of alms not flowers, the smiling beast of greed.

CHATTER

Back on the blue chair before the green studio
I'm keeping track of the outside world
rather than the inside where my brain seethes
in its usual mischief. Like many poets
I'm part blackbird and part red squirrel
and my brain chatters, shrieks, and whistles
but outside it tends to get real quiet
as if the greenery, garden, and mountains
can be put into half sleep though a female
blackbird is irritated with me. She's protecting
her fledgling child that died last Friday.
I placed a small white peony on its body.
Meanwhile the outside is full of the stuff of life.
Inside it's sitting there slumped with the burden
of memory and anecdotal knowledge, the birds of appetite
flitting here and there singing about sex and food,
the girl bending over with her impossible target,
or will it be foie gras or bologna and mayo?
The fish back then were larger and swam past
along with a few horses and dogs. Japanese
archers once used dogs for target practice
and that's why we won the war. A dead friend
still chatters his squirrel chatter like the squirrel
in the TV hunting program shot in the gut,
scurrying in a circle carrying the arrow
on a narrowing route. Funerals, parties,
and voyages greet the mind without gentleness.
Outside the mother blackbird shrieks. I can't help.

RETURN

Leaving on an exciting journey
is one thing, though most of all
I am engaged in homecoming—
the dogs, the glass of wine, a favorite
pillow that missed your head, the local
night with its familiar darkness.
The birds that ignored your absence
are singing at dawn assuring you
that all is inconceivable.

PRADO

After the ghostly Prado and in the Botanic
Gardens I tried to get in touch with Goya's
dogs. I called and called near the tiny blue roses
but likely my language was wrong
for these ancient creatures. Maybe they
know we destroyed the good hunting
in Spain and won't leave their paintings.
I can't give up. My waning vision
is fairly good at seeing dog souls. I wait
listening to unknown birds, noting the best voice
comes from one small and brown.
I feel a muzzle on my hand and knee
while thinking of the Caravaggio with David
looking down at the slain Goliath. This never
happens, this slaying of the brutal monster.
We know the ones that have cursed our lives.
Franco can't hear me talking to the ghost dog.
I was lucky that early on the birds and fish
disarmed me and the monster in my soul fled.
But where am I? Where can an animal hide?

DEATH AGAIN

Let's not get romantic or dismal about death.
Indeed it's our most unique act along with birth.
We must think of it as cooking breakfast,
it's that ordinary. Break two eggs into a bowl
or break a bowl into two eggs. Slip into a coffin
after the fluids have been drained, or better yet,
slide into the fire. Of course it's a little hard
to accept your last kiss, your last drink,
your last meal about which the condemned
can be quite particular as if there could be
a cheeseburger sent by God. A few lovers
sweep by the inner eye, but it's mostly a placid
lake at dawn, mist rising, a solitary loon
call, and staring into the still, opaque water.
We'll know as children again all that we are
destined to know, that the water is cold
and deep, and the sun penetrates only so far.

DEAD MAN'S FLOAT

2016

in memory of Valerie de la Valdene

WHERE IS JIM HARRISON?

He fell off the cliff of a seven-inch *zafu*.
He couldn't get up because of his surgery.
He believes in the Resurrection mostly
because he was never taught how not to.

HOSPITAL

I was chest-high in the wheat field with wind blowing in shimmering circles. A girl on horseback came by on a trail and the horse smelled sweet with the wheat. How blessed horses smell in this bitter world.

I could see the hospital in the distance and imagined the surgeons in the basement sharpening their knives. Tomorrow they will cut me from neck bone to tailbone to correct mysterious imperfections that keep me from walking. I want to walk like other kids in the fields with my noble dog.

After surgery I didn't get well and they sent me to Mayo in Minnesota, an immense Pentagon of health machinery. In an ambulance-plane I ate a bad sandwich in keeping with the tradition of bad food that would last until my secretary brought takeout from a nearby restaurant.

Each night I sang along with a bedsore cantata from the endless halls, the thousand electronic gizmos beeping, and also people entering my room for "tests." I was endlessly sacrificed at the medical gizmo altar. There was no red wine and no cigarettes—only the sick who tore at the heart.

A beautiful girl Payton couldn't walk. I'd shudder whenever I passed her room.

On very long sleepless nights I'd gaze at the well-lit statue of Saint Francis across the courtyard. I'm not Catholic but he bore me up with birds on his shoulders. One night the planet Venus dropped unwelcome on his neck. Francis with Venus is not right. I don't think he knew a woman. I saw the same thing in Narbonne, France, one night with a million blackbirds flocking above the canal for the trip south across the Mediterranean. Venus was blurred on the peak of the cathedral.

My spine aches from top to bottom. Also my shingles burn, a special punishment. Francis heard my crying over Payton. He doesn't care about her beauty I suppose. There were no beauty contests among his birds.

I heard Mozart's last trio late last night, a spine-tickler, like the night I heard Thelonious Monk in Grand Central. There are so many emotions on earth, especially trapped here where moment by moment I surge with emotions. I'm told this place is admired throughout the world, though my brain waves tell me different. The nurses are kind and friendly while the doctors tend toward smug and arrogant. Hundreds of doctors looking for something wrong are suspicious.

The old bugaboo of depression slid in. I wanted to sleep on the floor but was frozen in an electric bed. I began to have delusions and at one point I was in Paris at my favorite food store buying cheeses with my grandson. Another night I was wailing and the attendant shook me awake. "I'm dying," I said. "No you're not, you're just wailing." I ate an apple and went back to staring at Saint Francis and his birds. Without birds I'm dead. They are my drug that lifts me up to flight. Thousands of kinds of birds I've studied, even in the rain when they seem more blessed on the branches.

What *is* wailing? A death-drawn crooning. It hurts to hear noises from the pediatric ward—the innocent crying out. I am thoroughly guilty in a long life.

I wanted to be a cello. I hear cellos when I'm trout fishing. The green banks with wild roses capture the cellos and thousands of birds, many sweet-sounding warblers and colorful western tanagers. Will I fish again with this badly ruptured spine? The scar looks like the bite of an ancient creature.

There is a place in us to weep for others. I found it at night with daytime eyes, whirling the memories so fresh you could smell the pain within is dark and raw. This great sprawl of sick people craving the outside, to walk in a forest beside a lake, the air full of birds in the greenery. Saint Francis dozing against a tree, a yellow warbler perched on his shoulder. There is no way out of this prison we have built so clumsily, hellish in its ugliness. Most of us want to stay. I can't die when I want to go back to Narbonne and my secret room where I write so much. They cut me open in a long strip and luckily sewed me back up. In hospitals we are mostly artful sewage systems.

I need my secret place in the Upper Peninsula near Lake Superior, my dark thicket covered by winter. It is night in there but I can watch passing animals, a deer, bear, even possums, which I love for their humility. The thicket is flooded with birds, a few inches from my good eye. Francis would love this thicket. Maybe I'll take him there someday. And best of all a stump in a gully that I can crawl into and sit up. My place of grace on earth, my only church. The gods live there.

How to get out of this hospital? I planned three departures but a doctor won't sign my release. I am desperate for home and my lovely wife. They want to keep me here though departure is supposedly voluntary. Finally a friend in California sent a jet and saved me. We loaded up my daughter, my secretary, and her daughter and were soaring back to Montana.

A green glade of soft marsh grass near a pool in a creek. There are a dozen white birches and I curl in the grass. The last day I saw a drop of blood on a tile. Be careful, our blood falls easily.

BIRDS

The birds are flying around frantically
in the thunderstorm that just began, the
first in weeks and weeks. They are enjoying
themselves. I think I'll join them.

SOLSTICE LITANY

I

The Saturday morning meadowlark
came in from high up
with her song gliding into tall grass
still singing. How I'd like
to glide around singing in the summer
then to go south to where I already was
and find fields full of meadowlarks
in winter. But when walking my dog
I want four legs to keep up with her
as she thunders down the hill at top speed
then belly flops into the deep pond.
Lark or dog I crave the impossible.
I'm just human. All too human.

2

I was nineteen and mentally
infirm when I saw the prophet Isaiah.
The hem of his robe was as wide
as the horizon and his trunk and face
were thousands of feet up in the air.
Maybe he appeared because I had read him
so much and opened too many ancient doors.
I was cooking my life in a cracked clay
pot that was leaking. I had found
secrets I didn't deserve to know.
When the battle for the mind is finally
over it's late June, green and raining.

3

A violent windstorm the night before
the solstice. The house creaked and yawned.

I thought the morning might bring a bald earth,
bald as a man's bald head but not shiny.
But dawn was fine with a few downed trees,
the yellow rosebush splendidly intact.
The grass was all there dotted with Black
Angus cattle. The grass is indestructible
except to fire but now it's too green to burn.
What did the cattle do in this storm?
They stood with their butts toward the wind,
erect Buddhists waiting for nothing in particular.
I was in bed cringing at gusts,
imagining the contents of earth all blowing
north and piled up where the wind stopped,
the pile sky-high. No one can climb it.
A gopher comes out of a hole as if nothing happened.

4

The sun should be a couple of million miles
closer today. It wouldn't hurt anything
and anyway this cold rainy June is hard
on me and the nesting birds. My own nest
is stupidly uncomfortable, the chair
of many years. The old windows don't keep
the weather out, the wet wind whipping
my hair. A very old robin drops dead
on the lawn, a first for me. Millions
of birds die but we never see it—they like
privacy in this holy, fatal moment or so
I think. We can't tell each other when we die.
Others must carry the message to and fro.
"He's gone," they'll say. While writing an average poem
destined to disappear among the millions of poems
written now by mortally average poets.

5

Solstice at the cabin deep in the forest.
The full moon shines in the river, there are pale
green northern lights. A huge thunderstorm
comes slowly from the west. Lightning strikes
a nearby tamarack bursting into flame.
I go into the cabin feeling unworthy.
At dawn the tree is still smoldering
in this place the gods touched earth.

ANOTHER COUNTRY

I love these raw moist dawns with
a thousand birds you hear but can't
quite see in the mist.
My old alien body is a foreigner
struggling to get into another country.
The loon call makes me shiver.
Back at the cabin I see a book
and am not quite sure what that is.

ZONA

My work piles up,
I falter with disease.
Time rushes toward me—
it has no brakes. Still,
the radishes are good this year.
Run them through butter,
add a little salt.

SEVEN IN THE WOODS

Am I as old as I am?
Maybe not. Time is a mystery
that can tip us upside down.
Yesterday I was seven in the woods,
a bandage covering my blind eye,
in a bedroll Mother made me
so I could sleep out in the woods
far from people. A garter snake glided by
without noticing me. A chickadee
landed on my bare toe, so light
she wasn't believable. The night
had been long and the treetops
thick with a trillion stars. Who
was I, half-blind on the forest floor
who was I at age seven? Sixty-eight
years later I can still inhabit that boy's
body without thinking of the time between.
It is the burden of life to be many ages
without seeing the end of time.

EASTER AGAIN

Christ rose so long ago but the air
he rose through hasn't forgotten
the slight red contrail from the wounds.
I think he was headed
to that galaxy with six trillion stars
to cool off from the Crucifixion.
I have often heard the spikes
being driven through hands
and feet—in my mind, that is.
The sky was truly dark blue
that day and earth a tiny
green-and-blue ball.

THE PRESENT

I'm sitting on the lip of this black hole, a well
that descends to the center of the earth.
With a big telescope aimed straight down
I see a red dot of fire and hear the beast howling.
My back is suppurating with disease,
the heart lurches left and right,
the brain sings its ditties.
Everywhere blank white movies wait to be seen.
The skylark flew within inches of the rocks
before it stopped and rose again.
The cost of flight is landing.

SOUL

My spirit is starving.
How can it be fed?
Not by pain in the predictable future
nor the pain in the past
but understanding the invisible flower
within the flower that tells it what is,
the soul of the tree that does the same.
I don't seem to have a *true character*
to discover, a man slumped on his desk
dozing at midmorning. I'm an old poet.
That's it. Period. A three-legged goat
in mountain country. It's easier in the woods
where you have trees to lean on. There at times
I smelled bears right behind the cabin
coming to eat sunflower seeds put out for birds.
This dawn it's primroses, penstemon,
the trellis of white roses. On Easter
Jesus is Jesus. When did God enter him or us?

THUNDER

Thunder before dawn,
thunder through dawn,
thunder beings they were called.
It had to be a person or animal up there.
Outside, walking to my work shed
the clouds were low, almost black, and turbulent.
You could nearly jump up and touch them.
I love thunder. I could listen to it all day long.
Like birdsong it's the music of the gods.
How in childhood I adored these cloud voices
that could lift me up above my troubles,
far above the birds. I'd look down
at their flying backs, always in circles
because earth is round. What a gift
to have my work shed shudder with thunder.

REVERSE PRAYER

I pray for Mandelstam hiding covered
with snow in a ditch. The Stalinists want to kill
him and finally succeed. I want him to escape
to Nebraska, please God. I pray for Lorca
that the assassin's guns won't work and he'll
escape like a heron flying west to the Mediterranean
then across the ocean to Michigan where he might
dislike the snow but at least he's alive.
He loved Cuba and Brazil for their music which
we don't have much of here. Please God, save him.
I even pray for Keats that he won't die
so young but get another thirty years or so
to write poems in Rome. He likes
sitting with my girlfriend on the Spanish
Steps. Can I trust him? Probably not
but I want more of his poems so I'll overlook
his behavior. And of course Caravaggio
the king of painters must live longer,
God. Why create a great painter
then let him die early?

A BALLAD OF LOVE AND DEATH ABOUT ELSA

The ambulance driver told me in a bar
about the car accident—Elsa's head torn off
and her eyes stayed open.
I went to the site with a bouquet of flowers.
The road's shoulder was short green grass and along
the fence there were primroses and California
poppies. In the field a brown-and-white cow
watched me wander around. I wondered
how long Elsa could see, and what.
I found a patch of blood-crisp grass
where her head must have rested
surrounded by shards of windshield.
She was a fine gardener with a sweet,
warm voice.

MOLLY THE BRAVE

Molly was the bravest.
In April she would swing out
over the river on a rope
tied to an elm branch. There was still
ice along the bank and one day
her body was found down by the weir
with a bruised head, which meant she hit ice.
One summer evening she hugged me in her wet
black bathing suit after I brought her a milk shake.
My blood became hot and moved in all directions.
When we caught frogs to eat their legs
she said, "We are animals." And on the hill
by the river we illegally picked trillium.
All the boys wanted to marry her.
We kept putting the wildflowers she loved
on her grave. More than sixty years
later I see clearly that no one gets over anything
least of all Molly by the river,
swinging up through the air—
                                                a bird.

REPORT FROM VALENCIA

The girl ran across the cemetery
with the wind at her back looking
for the empty grave she commissioned. She ran
the same speed as the wind so that the air
around her was still. She threw
herself weeping into the empty hole
screaming to be covered with soil.
Four boys who had been smoking dope
threw handfuls of dirt on her
and one small rock hit her on the head
and subdued her. She curled up
on the damp earth. This happened on the
outskirts of Valencia in Spain. Her lover
had left her. He wanted to go to America
and become rich and have a new car.
Compared to old Spain America is a new car.
She wanted to stay in Valencia and have
a baby. Eventually, the gravedigger came
along and said he couldn't bury her
without a government-stamped death certificate.
He helped her out of the grave with his rope ladder,
peeking up her legs.

WOOD AND WAR

Way back in the forest a dozen miles south of my log cabin there's a cabin on a high finger into a swamp with no path. Long ago a trapper lived there with a wife and three sons who went to World War II. Only one came home and lived the rest of his life in seclusion. The father was an ex-professor who died by freezing after breaking both hips running his snowmobile into a tree. The mother, batty and mute, lived in Duluth with her sister. Little Walter, the last son, was all that was left and starved himself to death in twenty years. Hunters and wanderers knew enough to stop by and help him cut and haul in wood. Winter got as low as 40 below. All the locals knew he was dying slow. Women sent out casseroles but the casseroles ended up with the bears. Walter had a bag of beans and a bag of rice. "O my brothers lost in war," he'd think, his heart broken in half by their absence. In February he was found naked, frozen, draped over his dwindled woodpile.

He looked like wood.

STICKING TO IT

The old Finn hadn't washed his cup
in fifty years. "It ain't dirty,"
he said, "there just been coffee in it."
His wife and baby both died in childbirth
fifty-seven years ago. Inside his cabin
there's a dust woman near
an unused cradle he made by hand.

WARMTH

The lettuce pushed up through the cold, cold ground.
There is this relentless struggle for warmth on earth.
Mandelstam lay in the snowy ditch
in an outsized ratty black overcoat
hearing a troika go past with harness bells,
the thud of horse hooves. His face
was cold so he pulled his head down
into darkness like a turtle.
A piece of bread would have helped.
Recently in Nebraska a pretty girl
got lost in a blizzard and froze to death.
They fail to revive so many of us
in these halls of ice. So many drunks
freeze to death in Russia it's a public
scandal. They're tripling the price
of vodka to keep the poor from dying drunk.
So many American Indians freeze
walking home from bars on the reservation edge.
A friend died leaning and dozing against
his mailbox, so near home.

COW

A cow is screaming across the arroyo.
It's a blasting Warsaw Ghetto scream.
It speaks of the end of time on earth.
I know her calf didn't die,
a little bull standing off to the side
staring at her with a "What's wrong with Mom?"
look. Next morning she's dead,
already smelling badly in the heat.
I think of the Bishop of Lyon in the ninth century
who said animals don't go to heaven because
they don't contribute to the church.
I see that the cow dogs are getting ready to eat her.
I see her spirit struggling to ascend to heaven.
That's no lie. I help her push off,
lifting her big head above a mass of bugs.

SEVENTY-FOUR

I can't be seventy-four.
It's plainly impossible.
Is this a near-death experience?
At dawn there were layers and layers
of birdsong from multiple willow thickets,
and an irritable kingfisher on the phone line
over the creek. They are always irritable
in my memory's storehouse of creeks, rivers,
lakes. "Get out of here! This is my place!"
they shriek. The Mexican green kingfisher
says the same thing. Such anger at dawn.
Meanwhile seventy-four years of birds
have passed. Most have died of course
so I shouldn't complain about the nearing
end of it all. I once saw a bird fall out
of a tree stone dead. I nudged it surprised
at its feather lightness that allowed it to fly.
I buried it in earth where they don't belong
any more than we do. Dead birds should be
monuments suspended forever in the air.

OLD MAN

An old man is a spindly junk pile.
He is so brittle he can fall
through himself top to bottom.
No mirror is needed to see the layers
of detritus, some years clogged with it.
The red bloody layer of auto deaths
of dad and sister. Deaths piled like cordwood
at the cabin, the body 190 pounds of ravaged
nerve ends from disease. The junk pile is without
sympathy for itself. A life is a life,
lived among birds and forests and fields.
It knew many dogs, a few bears and wolves.
Some women said they wanted to murder him
but what is there worth murdering?
The body, of course, the criminal body
doing this and that. Some will look
for miraculous gold nuggets in the junk
and find a piece of fool's gold in the empty
cans of *menudo,* a Mexican tripe stew.

RISEN

We were so happy when the pretty girl
rose from the dead.
It was just past lilac time and the scent still hung
in the air like the death of the gods.
She didn't stay around for long. Once you've
been dead you're not happy to return.
She had been to the ends of the universe
and back and was a bit unearthly,
a bit too luminous to have a hamburger
or go running in the dark.

NYC

Hot, hungry, eighteen and reading
Lorca's *Poet in New York*.
Scholars say he lost his duende in NYC.
I don't think so. He got it back in Harlem,
then Havana. I walked three months
until my soles became paper and
I finally understood *Poet in New York*.
Homesick, I went home and worked on a farm.
Homesick, he went home and got murdered.

A VARIATION ON MACHADO

I worry much about the suffering
of Machado. I was only one when he carried
his mother across the border from Spain to France
in a rainstorm. She died and so did he
a few days later in a rooming house along a dry canal.
To carry Mother he abandoned a satchel
holding his last few years of poetry.
I've traveled to Collioure several times
to search for Machado's lost satchel.
The French fed him but couldn't save him.
There's no true path to a death—
we discover the path by walking.
We turn a corner on no road
and there's a house on a green hill
with a thousand colorful birds sweeping in a circle.
Are the poems in the basement of the house on the hill?
We'll find out if we remember earth at all.

VOWS

I feel my failure intensely
as if it were a vital organ
the gods grew from the side of my head.
You can't cover it with a hat and I no longer
can sleep on that side it's so tender.
I wasn't quite faithful enough
to carry this sort of weight up the mountain.
When I took my vows at nineteen
I had no idea that gods were so merciless.
Fear makes for good servants
and bravery is fraudulent. When I awoke
I wasn't awake enough.

PURPLE

It's criminal to claim you've earned
a Purple Heart if you didn't.
Politicians do this. I say, "Off with their heads."
Last spring in our bushy front yard
two mountain lions, mother and son
killed a deer—the leftovers of the meal were strikingly
red. I claim the Red Heart medal for inspecting
the carcass on this dangerous field of battle.
One took a mouthful then ripped
out the heart, stripping veins and arteries.
Lions with bloody faces, then ravens with bloody
beaks, about twenty yelling out victory
when the lions left. Once in Tanzania
I saw a big male lion with bloodred mane and face
after he had his whole head in the innards
of a zebra. He ignored us and the flies,
dozing with a full tummy in the midday heat.
I'm sharing the Red Heart medal with this lion.

SPIRIT

Rumi advised me to keep my spirit
up in the branches of a tree and not peek
out too far, so I keep mine in the very tall
willows along the irrigation ditch out back,
a safe place to remain unspoiled by the filthy
culture of greed and murder of the spirit.
People forget their spirits easily suffocate
so they must keep them far up in tree
branches where they can be summoned any moment.
It's better if you're outside as it's hard for spirits
to get into houses or buildings or airplanes.
In New York City I used to reach my spirit in front
of the gorilla cage in the children's zoo in Central Park.
It wouldn't come in the Carlyle Hotel, which
was too expensive for its taste. In Chicago
it won't come in the Drake though I can see it
out the window hovering over the surface
of Lake Michigan. The spirit above anything
else is attracted to humility. If I slept
in the streets it would be under the cardboard with me.

WOLVES OF HEAVEN

It had been very hot for three weeks
so I worked well into a cool night
when at three a.m. a big thunderstorm hit.
I went out in the yard naked and sat
at the picnic table for a rain bath
careful about the rattlesnake on the sidewalk.
The sky drowned the mosquitoes
feeding on me. The lightning was relentless
and lit up the valley so I could see
the ghosts who had me ill this past year.
Then I was part of a battle from two
hundred years ago when the Cheyenne
from the east attacked the Absaroka,
the Crow, in this valley. A group of the Cheyenne
were *massaum,* the wolves of heaven,
warriors who painted themselves solid yellow.
One on a black horse stopped at our gate
but decided not to kill me.
I want to be a yellow wolf of heaven.
They disappeared into the lightning.

LOST MEDICINE

I lost my medicine bag
from back when I believed
in magic. It's made from a doe's stomach
and holds a universe:
grizzly teeth and claw, stones from Tibet,
the moon, the garden, the beach
where the baby's ashes are buried.
Now I expect this bag to cure my illnesses—
I can't walk and the skin on my back
pulses and moans without a mouth.
The gods exiled me into this loneliness
of pain for their own good reasons.

PRIVATE DIAMONDS

Pain guides our lives very well.
Take the stone from your shoe
and by a miracle it replaces itself,
a private diamond. The peony buds
know exactly who they are and say so.

LAZULI TRANCE

I had to skin a 12 lb. pork shank
which is a tough job if you're not a butcher.
Even when dead, animals want to keep their skin.
Antelope, deer, and bear are far easier than pigs.
So is a cow. I must have wanted to keep
the molar I had jerked the other day. It took
an hour to wrestle the sucker out by which time
I had entered the body of a lazuli bunting
back home twenty miles away. In bad times trances
help. The bird was marvelous as my bones had
never been so light though the new vision
was a little frightening but far from the dentist's office.
During my recent ninety days of shingles
I was in many creatures and many places.
You still inhabit the pain but are not miserably
trapped in its location. So my precious tooth
is gone forever, and I praise the lazuli bunting,
its miraculous colors of blue, a little white,
a chest patch of beige and orange, for taking
me to a far better place to suffer.

> (Author's advice: Choose small creatures,
> birds, salamanders, otter. Megafauna are
> dangerous and are far beyond the
> capabilities of almost anyone.)

MOUNTAIN TRAVEL

The clouds are unmoving near Cambria
but the mountain I am on
drifts south with the wind,
a new way to travel, riding
a mountain as a horse made
of stone and earth. Only a few
miles but enough to flush a condor
from the ridge, the shadow passing
near my feet, the bird glancing at me
asking, "What are you doing here?"
I was a little frightened nestled
beneath a Santa Lucia fir, cushioning
my head on a giant cone,
wary of rattlesnakes among wildflowers
but had read of this experience in Buddhism
before Christ, hermits riding mountains.
Did people stop walking on water
or riding mountains after Christ?
What is a man to do if he can't ride mountains?
Tomorrow a walk upriver on the water.
Meanwhile, the earth flowed beneath my feet.
A round river floating in the sky.

GOD'S MOUTH

The girl thought that the sky was God's
wide-open mouth. After discussion, arguing,
I decided to agree. She was so sure
of herself, adamant in fact, as if stomping
a foot made anything true. I suppose
that at the back of the mouth is the brain
that created insects and galaxies, the girl
herself who is now singing a banal popular song
in a thin reedy voice. Then she told me
about a huge African catfish who keeps
her unruly children in her mouth. They come
and go, retreating when in danger. God is like
that, the girl said. We can go in and out.

JUNK PILE

God throws us out the back door
onto a huge junk pile in another
galaxy. There are billions of bodies.
It's 1,000 degrees below
zero but compacted souls don't need heat.
It's logical because we
came in the front door. All of us die
in the caboose not of our choosing
but then we've always seen life
disappearing behind us, most always
into what we clumsily call the past.
Most of the girls I loved are now crones
with me a geezer, shuffling toward the moon.
So many years ago the girl with brown legs
in the green dress got off the yellow school bus.
Sometimes the past flips over and determines
what we are today. The girl's sandy
feet were on the dashboard. Beneath, thighs
were speaking the language of thighs.
Godspeed is the speed of light.

CARPE DIEM

Night and day
seize the day, also the night—
a handful of water to grasp.
The moon shines off the mountain
snow where grizzlies look for a place
for the winter's sleep and birth.
I just ate the year's last tomato
in the year's fatal whirl.
This is mid-October, apple time.
I picked them for years.
One McIntosh yielded sixty bushels.
It was the birth of love that year.
Sometimes we live without noticing it.
Overtrying makes it harder.
I fell down through the tree grabbing
branches to slow the fall, got the afternoon off.
We drove her aqua Ford convertible into the country
with a sack of red apples. It was a perfect
day with her sun-brown legs and we threw ourselves
into the future together seizing the day.
Fifty years later we hold each other looking
out the windows at birds, making dinner,
a life to live day after day, a life of
dogs and children and the far wide country
out by rivers, rumpled by mountains.
So far the days keep coming.
Seize the day gently as if you loved her.

MARRIAGE

I just remembered a serious argument.
On my seventy-fifth birthday I had the firm sense
that I was a hundred seventy-five. She disagreed.
"Look at your driver's license," she said. I said you know
the state of Montana took my license from me. She
went to my briefcase and got out my passport.
"You're a mere seventy-five," she said.
I said, "How can you trust the government
in this important matter?" I went to bed
after a couple of drinks believing I was a hundred
seventy-five. In the morning I felt
only seventy-five and apologized at breakfast.
I'd lost a hundred years and felt light,
younger, more energetic. As a boy I saw in *Life*
magazine photos of the Civil War veterans. I don't
think there are any left, are there?
They would have to be a hundred seventy-five.
Sometimes I remember aspects of that damnable war.

ROUND

My head is round, not perfectly so as that would be against nature. At any given time I don't know what's in it unless I pick up pen and paper and even this can be evasive. Sometimes our minds don't want to know what's in them. The girl or boy you were looking at in the coffee shop was distinctly illegal. Rebuff thoughts or go to prison, chums. Prisons no longer allow Tabasco, which could be used as a weapon or so they say. From a distance the head is a bowling ball on the shoulders, but not so: a carapace and inside, the contents are what children call "gushy." The soft brain has its own improbable life containing galaxies, tens of thousands of people met, the microcosm of life in one place and on the diaphanous and often filthy cloth of memory, hanging there and battered on the clothesline in so many years of bad weather, wet and stiff with ice or blasted by sun and heat, part of it in shreds. The bad is frankly more memorable than the good. The big truck knocking off my side-view mirror, a close call indeed. I saw his alarmed eyes, on my side of the road. I shuddered at death's door. The bowling ball is neutral but weighs the same as the head. Dropped from 35,000 feet they both can cause small earthquakes.

DEAD MAN'S FLOAT

Dr. Guevara said that I'm hollow-eyed
and exhausted from writing too much.
I should take a break but I don't know how.
Suddenly I remembered learning
the "dead man's float" in Boy Scout
swimming lessons and a light went off.
That's what I'll do to rest up,
the dead man's float without water.

I got in bed and conjured the feeling
of floating and recalled my last
dead man's float about a mile
out in the ocean east of Key West
when I tired from too much swimming ambition.
Big waves kept drowning my nose.
I gave up floating and swam desperately to shore.
I dozed in the hot sand and a pretty girl
stopped and asked, "Are you okay?"
"I'll never be okay," I said, and she left.
I saw her later but she wouldn't talk
to this goofy. A poet blows a chance with
a dumb witticism.

If you need me now
I'm here along the Mexican border
dead-man floating.

BAREBACKED WRITER

When I say I'm a barebacked writer
people will start talking about horses.
I say I did that too on broad-backed June.
Her flesh hid her painful backbone so that
we could lope in the pasture in comfort.
I mean I write half-naked, shirt off,
after two years of shingles, "post-herpetic neuralgia"
where the pain is always present but can be
unbearable in a shirt, even soft cotton.
So I keep the heat high enough to go bareback
through my prose and poetry when it's snowing
outside. What is the effect except the poetry
and prose are also barebacked? Shorn of
ornament with adjectives cast in a snowbank.
Someday again I'll wear a shirt when I write
if the gods will it. For now I'm barebacked
trotting through the universe like everyone else.

FEEDER

All the men grouped along the bar
like birds at the feeder at home.
The seeds of alcohol provide
a little hope and a smile or two.
These are hard times so they're sipping beer
rather than the more expensive drinks.
Sometimes I buy a round of the top stuff and
they're happy like the birds when the feeder is replenished.
Do these men live as well as birds?
It's not for me to say. They're certainly not as pretty.
They are as ordinary as house finches.
This is a story that doesn't end very well.

THE GIRLS OF WINTER

Out the window of the bar I'm watching
a circle of girls stretching and yawning
across the street. It's late January and 74
degrees. They love the heat because
they *are* a moist heat. Heat loves
heat and today's a tease for what comes
with spring around here when the glorious birds
funnel back up from Mexico. The girls
don't care about birds because they *are* birds.
I recall in high school a half-dozen
cheerleaders resting on a wrestling mat
in short shorts in the gym, me beside them
with a silly groin ache. What were they?
Living, lovely, warm meat as we all are
reaching out of our bodies for someone else.

WEEKS

The weeks rush past headed
for the infinity of the past, twelve billion years
ago before they had the job of being weeks.
They're tired of it and want to go back home
to a pillowed galaxy, the homeland
in the spheres with no people around
to bother them with multifoliate appointments.
Odin is welcome to stand there indefinitely
with ravens perched on his shoulders
and Vallejo to die on a rainy Thursday
in Paris after collecting discarded wine bottles
to buy bread. Bread alone only makes you
hungrier, he said. Thursday is a good day to die
especially if there's a cold rain on Montparnasse.
Vallejo wanted to go home to Peru but couldn't
with an empty wallet and a heavy heart,
seeing his soul rise over Paris up into the rain.

TIME AGAIN (2)

Time stopped at eleven a.m. Monday morning.
The fire in the mountains froze to the eye.
The Beethoven quartet on the radio continues.
Where did its sound go to become lost?
My skin tingled then stopped as it must.
Fair Catherine in the distance walks in the wheat
field, the tassels almost to her chest.
She stops and so do the sandhill cranes well ahead.
Both were adrift in this huge world,
they drifted as clouds, graceful animals,
something telling us where we're going
like migrating birds, flying into the future.

TIME

Time sinks slowly to the deepest part
of the ocean, the Mariana Trench.
She's tired of light and there it's pure black.
She's also fatigued with the carcasses
of civilizations, the fleas of little lives.
She cares for children to whom she gives
more of herself willingly—their dance steps
do not drag. The very old are also
indulged with a few more days. She feels
abused by clocks. They were never meant
to be. She preferred us drifting through
our lives like clouds, without dials,
machinery, alarms, riding her
like the gentlest of horses.
Now she wants the ocean's bottom
to greet the unimaginable creatures who ignore her.

TETHERED

Blacky, half Catahoula wild hog dog
and half blue heeler cow dog
has been tethered for years.
What kind of life is this?
When loose he runs into the surrounding mountains
for days on end eating what he kills.
What a choice: tethered or run away.
His girlfriend Lola, tethered across the yard,
died last week and he seems mystified.
There are rare times when
he's asked to help herd cattle in the mountains.
He becomes angry and bites the tails of calves.
His mother Lisa tore off the horn of a big bull. Tough girl.
The bull wouldn't go in the corral but swung and flung
her. They were head-to-head but she won
and carried her horn trophy around for days.
So the choice is to run into the mountains
or hang around for dinner like ordinary humans.
Some poets would run for it while most locked themselves
in universities and stayed home for dinner.
Lisa got exiled to a big ranch in Mexico.
The rancher said, "She's too much dog."

RIDING THE WOLF'S NOSE

I have the mask of a wolf's head
from Mexico. On his nose is perched
a naked, virginal girl who looks unhappy.
I imagine them running through the night
with her balanced there. The wolf
isn't reflective and doesn't know what the girl
is doing there. She had been bathing
in a pond in the forest when he picked
her up. He had to keep running or she
would get away. He doesn't know whether
to eat her or take her home to her parents.
He's heard the whole town calling for her
in the forest night and day. At dawn he dumps
her off his nose in the town's shallow fountain.
She screams at the cold water.
No one will ever believe her.

WHIMSY

All I wanted when I returned from the war in China was a red-haired woman to fix me a hamburger. It was just me against twenty-five million troops. I walk through many doors that aren't there. You can't stop the molten lava coming down the mountain. Why try? Life presents us with so many impossibilities. The country boy in Kansas is in love with an actress he'll never see in *real life*. The severely crippled girl I met has never been kissed yet writes love poems. I am the bar-tailed godwit of poets. I fly 7,000 miles from the Aleutians to New Zealand without stopping. Unknown to the ornithologists I pause in China for a bowl of noodles. I can't help it. I'm full of noodle love. The same old woman puts out the bowl on her porch each year. She told me that she was once beautiful and perhaps I am a dream lover from the past. I lie back in her arms. We kiss.

THE GREEN MAN

Since early childhood I believed
in a door in the forest. I looked for it
for more than a half a century
and it evaded me. The Green Man
lived there, part tree and part human.
Keeping his distance he told me a lot.
Walk mostly sideways in the wilderness
to confuse those who would track you.
When outside, sleep with your eyes open
and see the coyote pup approach out
of curiosity, the small bear resting
against a stump a hundred yards away,
a warbler standing on your toe singing.
When I was lost he howled at me from a tree, "Wrong way."
I dreamed where he lived, high on the steep
bank of the river concealed under a thick drapery
of tree roots but I skidded on my tummy
down into the river, a sign to give up.
There was a stinking wolf den close by so my dog
wouldn't stay with me. The Green Man alone, forever.

INCIDENTALS

Many bugs bite us.
Some snakes bite.
Birds bite bugs and seeds.
Men bite off ears in fistfights.
At dawn peeking out a cracked
window: the profusion of yellow roses
flowed over the beige stucco wall
like water. Roses bite with thorns.

PAIN (2)

Pain is at the steering wheel
swerving left and right for a year now.
It costs a fortune, which I don't have,
to try to get rid of pain. Maybe a girl
could help or more vodka but I doubt it.
Or a trip to the tropics where the pain would boil away
like the hot cabin last summer where you awoke
and thought you were a corned beef boiling in a pot.
You want to give up, throw in the towel but you
can't give up because you're all you have.
Maybe they should put you down like an old dog
like our beloved cocker spaniel Mary who is nearing
the end with paralysis. Unlike me
she's happy much of the time. On walks
she keeps falling down and I pick her up
to get her started again. She seems to smile.
Neither of us wants to die
when there's work to be done,
other creatures to be snuck up on,
food to be eaten, a creek to wade,
though I hope to eventually ask God to fully
explain the meaning of Verdun where 300,000 died.

MAN DOG

I envied the dog lying in the yard
so I did it. But there was a pebble
under my flank so I got up and looked
for the pebble, brushed it away
and lay back down. My dog thus far
overlooked the pebble. I guess it's her thick
Lab fur. With my head downhill the blood gorged
me with ideas. Not good. Got up. Turned around. Now I
see hundreds of infinitesimal ants. I'm on an
ant home. I get up and move five feet.
The dog hasn't moved from her serene place.
Now I'm rather too near a thicket where
I saw a big black snake last week that might decide
to join me. I moved near the actual dog this time
but she got up and went under the porch. She doesn't like
it when I'm acting weird. I'm failing as a dog
when my own kind rejects me, but doing better
than when I envied birds, the creature the least
like us, therefore utterly enviable. To be sure
I cheeped a lot but didn't try to fly.
We humans can take off but are no good at landing.

THE DOG AND TOBACCO ROOM

I am the old man alone in a hotel
waiting for a ride north to Mayo Pain Clinic.
Loneliness is only a theory when we have
the past, which is a vast tumble of events.
Sort and re-sort and never win.
We live with our memories, a backpack
of mostly trash we can barely carry.
A motel in Utah gives me
the "dog and tobacco" room.
Zilpha and my cigarettes are proud.
On television I see hundreds
of cage-free piglets romping.
Things are getting better for some of us.

NOTES ON THE SACRED ART OF LOG SITTING

To give the surgeon a better view of my interior carcass I was slashed from neck to tailbone. Recovery was slow and the chief neurologist told me, "You can walk your way out of this." I began walking out by shuffling down a long hallway. It was very hard on my tender empathy to see so many hopeless cases, especially the truly beautiful girl who was paralyzed for life.

I want to walk in the morning with Zilpha again. I want to walk in the morning with Zilpha again. I want to walk in the morning with Zilpha again. I want to walk in the morning with Zilpha again. I want to walk in the morning with Zilpha again. Amen.

And I want to bird hunt, which I've done with intensity for forty years in a row. Is this even possible? The answer, come to find out, was that I couldn't keep up. Zilpha would flush some birds then look to me wondering why I hadn't shot. I was far behind, sitting on an Emory oak log and staring hard at the landscape.

My shuffling mood was always corrected by sitting on an oak log, so I decided to make some notes on the sacred art of log sitting:

> Approach the log cautiously with proper reverence as if you were entering a French cathedral or the bedroom of your lover.

> If it's over 60 degrees, inspect the lower sides of the log for Mohave rattlesnakes.

> Now examine the log closely for the most comfortable place to sit, usually away from the sun.

> Sit down.

> Empty your mind of everything except what is in front of you—the natural landscape of the canyon.

> Dismiss or allow to slide away any aspect of your grand or pathetic life.

> Breathe softly.

Avoid a doze.

Internalize what you see in the canyon: the oaks and mesquites, the rumpled and grassy earth, hawks flying by, a few songbirds.

Stay put for forty-five minutes to an hour.

When you get up bow nine times to the log.

Three logs a day is generally my maximum.

When you get in your car it will seem as wretched as it is. A horse would be far better. For hours your mind will still be absorbed in the glory of what you saw rather than mail, e-mails, cell phones, TV, etc. Hopefully log sitting will allow you to change the contents of your life. You will introduce yourself as a "log sitter" rather than a novelist, detective, or mortician. You will walk more slowly and perhaps your feet will shuffle like mine. I can readily imagine buying a small ranch I'd call "The Log Ranch." I'd truck in thirty-three logs and arrange them on the property like the Stations of the Cross. This could soothe me during my limited time in the twenty-first century, which has been very coarse indeed. Especially after Zilpha died.

THE FUTURE (2)

Lorca was raised on his father's large
farm as a gentleman. He didn't work in the fields.
He dressed nicely and sat near ponds,
creeks, a river. In his youth he couldn't
figure out whether he liked boys or girls but boys won.
He loved birds and inevitably dreamed
of the gunshots that would kill him on the mountain,
men he knew pulling the trigger over and over.

Many of us can see our ends coming
as in a dream. Under a tree in a meadow,
or more likely, a car in the night,
balling in the bathtub when drunk,
sitting in a chair at the window
and the world slowly disappears
to music you've never heard before.
The twenty-three maenads in your life pass slowly,
some real, some imagined, of great beauty.
We never got close but they kept me alive.
They live on the mantel in my mind,
austere women shining above the fire.

LORCA AGAIN

When Lorca was murdered
they had him turn around and look down
the steep mountainside at Granada far below.
Goodbye hometown. They shot him in the back as always,
also in the butt because he was gay. The powerful
rifles splintered him and later the family
picked up the pieces on the slope for burial.
What a rare bird. It was like shooting
the last blue heron on earth. There's a sundial
there now. We drank a bottle Christine made
called *Memoire*. I choked on the wine
and tears. At some ages he was my favorite
poet who would make me moonstruck.
I walked along the Guadalquivir in Seville
and saw his perpetual shadow in the moving
water, the local *gitano* music constricting
and exploding the heart. Water kept carrying
this burden of musical shadow to the ocean.
In the Mediterranean I heard his voice on the water.

WINTER CREEK

Creeks find their destiny according to the slant,
the tilt of the earth. None ever can turn around and go the other
way, at least none that I've heard of. The weight of water
and gravity are the tools. Dams are the fatal enemy
of water. You'd think the mighty Mississippi
with its trillions of tons of water would simply plummet
forward off the earth in its downhill race from Minnesota
to New Orleans. It might still happen or maybe
the Nile will fall backward and make an immense garden
of the Sahara. I sit around waiting for these things
to happen, real big thrilling things, not the greasy
soil of rotten politics but mighty bodies of water
going amok. Rain doesn't fall up but down,
the great rapids show water trying to rid
itself of earth and go back to the sky. I still
swim in rivers at night to frighten myself.
I just walked my dog to the creek where on a cold
morning she flounders and rolls happily in the mighty
mystery of moving water.

FEBRUARY

Warm enough here in Patagonia AZ to read
the new Mandelstam outside in my underpants
which is to say he was never warm enough
except in summer and he was without paper to write
and his belly was mostly empty most of the time
like that Mexican girl I picked up on a mountain road
the other day who couldn't stop weeping. She had slept
out two nights in a sweater in below-freezing weather.
She had been headed to Los Angeles but the *coyote*
took her money and abandoned her in the wilderness.
Her shoes were in pieces and her feet bleeding.
I took her to town and bought her food. She got a ride
to Nogales. She told us in Spanish that she just wanted
to go home and sleep in her own bed. That's what Mandelstam
wanted with mother in the kitchen fixing dinner. Everyone
wants this. Mandelstam said, "To be alone is to be alive."
"Lost and looked in the sky's asylum eye." "What of
her nights?" Maybe she was watched by some of the fifty
or so birds I have in the yard now. When they want to
they just fly away. I gave them my yard and lots of food.
They smile strange bird smiles. She couldn't fly away.
Neither can I though I've tried a lot lately to migrate
to the Camargue on my own wings. When they are married,
Mandelstam and the Mexican girl, in heaven they'll tell
long stories of the horrors of life on earth ending each session
by chanting his beautiful poems that we did not deserve.

DECEMBER BUTTERFLIES

Close after dawn walking the dog,
the first yellow shafts of light shone
in the woods, and on the trail. Stand
in them and you warm up ever so little,
temperature at freezing. Saw frost on the car
windows in the driveway. Now I see
three yellow butterflies fluttering this way
so as to catch sun through the trees and
still-green willow bushes. The first hard frost kicked
the cottonwoods and now I see some of
their yellow leaves floating down the creek,
flouncing in the current. Back in Montana
it's zero and 80 mph winds.
That's why I'm here on the Mexican border.
One night here below freezing, the next day 70
degrees. This morning I feel afloat
on the creek with these leaves. Down here
the birds seem happy in winter. So am I
compared to the howling-snow-blasted north
though it's not easy to be a leaf floating in a creek.

POOL OF LIGHT

On our small front patio in this jagged landscape
there's a pool of warm light every
morning while it's still cold in the shadows
beneath a rock cliff twenty feet away.
I sit in the light for a few minutes after walking
the dog to the creek where her mind doesn't
say "creek" but mine does. I can't help it.
It occurs to me that this beloved pool of warm sun
won't last forever. It's the nature
of our nature to bid goodbye to warmth and light.
Like everything else it works for the time being,
the same as the dormant rose staring back at me.
Mind you, I'm in no rush for this to end.
I learned that after death I'll be a Chinese poet
on a ten-square-foot island and don't want to go there.
I salvaged a barrel and a piece of canvas
from the shipwreck. With lots of rain
I have sixty gallons of warm water. Migrant crabs
covered me one night and I tried to cook
them on hot rocks. Not good. I have a hook and line
but no fire so I'm eating my own brand of sushi.
If you don't love it find another universe.

POETRY NOW

Poetry stinks with ten thousand poets
pissing in the same overflowing bowl.
We must go it alone, swimming at night
down the River of No Return.
At dawn we'll see unknown animals
on the bank, and unknown women, some
without faces. We're now sure that we
have both leprosy and gangrene, outcasts. After
a few nights the sight begins to fail but by now
we've earned an inner light that blossoms
in our heads. We'll talk to old Rumi
and become one with the Great Tao. We get
out on a bank and walk blindly into a forest
with our sight slowly returning. We are
now in western China and read the local old
poems. We're back in the T'ang dynasty
and it takes a couple of centuries to walk
slowly to Europe reading all the way. We
stop in France and read another century
in all these great poems of Europe. When we
get home to the Midwest nobody recognizes
us but we have learned the cosmos of poetry.

CRITICISM

Like a bird dog my blood is a dictator.
I've had no choice in this matter. They put
me down in a grand field and I was off and running
for the unruly birds, poems, looking in a dozen nearly
impenetrable thickets. I'm also a hangman
for my bad poems. String them up, dammit,
from the old clothesline where the wind
will whip them to shreds. Our local wind
tips over trucks with its fury. It can easily
shred bad poems to tiny chicken feathers.

MONEY

The 8,000 isn't coming now and won't ever.
I had counted on those birds in the bush.
This mud bath doesn't smear the landscape,
but it is a huge pothole in my road—
it can break an axle or cause a blowout—
deep with sharp edges.
On my hands and knees I stared
into this pothole thinking
of the black holes in outer space—
then one was on the ground right in front of me.
The money hole I called it, like
the willow shadows of late October,
dark and cold and then a few feet away
you can walk into morning sunlight
where the frost is melting, and up to
my bench in the pasture
where money doesn't exist.
The mountains on the moon
were so bright last night.

Money on the moon? I don't think so.
Money is listless and lives in total dark.
Money can be slightly soiled and disrupting.
Money can buy valuable things such as macaroni and wine.
Money is the major pothole of my life.

BIRD NIGHTMARES

The worst dream ever that all the birds in the world died overnight. Science couldn't figure it out but then a humble graduate student from Caltech said that a prodigious number of quasar particles were speeding toward earth at 5,000 miles per second. These particles supposedly pass through us harmlessly from a galaxy that had a black hole the equal in power to five billion suns. Is God thinking too big? I wondered. So the birds were destroyed by this surge in cosmic power. Bird-watching groups committed suicide en masse. They were in a medieval hell without birds. It was soon discovered that the quasars were reducing human intelligence by a fatal half. Minor wars broke out everywhere in the world. Luckily no one was bright enough to press the red button. Dogs ate dogs. Married couples murdered each other in great numbers to no surprise. Animals went berserk, unlike us they couldn't adjust to being stupid. People were reduced to reading poetry because it was shorter. A raven on the verge of death said to me, "Why did you do this to us?" The same question they always ask us. A few swallows were found in Brazil deep in a cove behind a giant waterfall. Brazil kept these for themselves, wanting to be the only country with birds. There was money in it. Thousands died trying to visit the birds. The waterfall made Niagara look like a trickle. Many stayed with the birds until they starved to death.

HE DOG

I'm a very old dog,
much older than most dogs.
I can't give out my wisdom
because I bark loudly and virtually
no one understands this barking except
a few other dogs of my peculiar species.
I don't bark at cars. They're beneath contempt.
I bark at the rising sun when it rises
red out of a forest fire.
I bark at thunder out of pure envy,
the mighty noise this sky dog makes.
I growl at myself when I sleep too much
and don't run to the far field in the morning
where I saw the bear bigger than me and ran home.
I don't bark at the night. I love its black music.
I sleep under the porch, inside during winter.
Once I had a girlfriend for the day.
I have puppies but I don't know where.

TREE CORONER

When we have rare big winds down here
trees blow over, almost always the cottonwoods
which are huge but short-rooted, while mesquite
taproots go down seventy-five feet, and
the Emory oaks are also solid. I wander around
examining the fallen trees for causes.
Most often like people there is rot
inside. The other day one was rotted six feet
through the trunk, which was utterly ripped
and twisted with the roots above ground, the torsion
force incredible and you wouldn't want
to be there to get driven like a nail into the ground.
Tree coroner isn't an elected office
where my dark past would confuse voters like Joyce Kilmer,
who thought a poem couldn't be as lovely as a tree.
Grow up, Joyce, you're comparing apples to oranges.
This is one of those things you've got to know.

BOOKS

Looking around this casita and the house
in Montana I see I must have bought
thousands of books. Of course many came
free from people to irritate me with guilt
for not reading so many galleys and manuscripts.
It's plain as day that I've vastly overfed
my brain. At this age it's a dense jungle
and I can't write ten points of wisdom
for you to grease your skids on the way
to our mutual doom. A few years ago
my living motto was "Eat or Die" but now
that's worn out, too tired to guide my clumsy
way from pillar to post to pit of despond.
I must sell these books, some quite rare,
or exchange them for good food and the wine
I can no longer afford. I used to look
at pages 33, 77, 153 for the secrets of the world
and never find them but still continue trying.

PATAGONIA AZ

A little rain at dawn after months
of drought. The dust holds
the smell of rain tight to its chest.
In the rocks I hear the voice
of a girl from fifty years ago.
Down here you listen to mountains.

MELROSE (2)

A long freight train is parked out front.
A thunderstorm comes across the mountains,
not a huge one just a regular thunderstorm.
I'd like to have rain on this tin roof,
an early memory that soothed my blind eye,
hot and raw in my head at our little cabin
on a lake. That and catching so many fish
for the family to eat. I was only seven and proud
to catch dinner. Many pans full of bluegills
and perch all brown and tasty. "Watch out, the bones
can kill you," I'd say, having heard it from adults
over and over. The splendor of hard rain falling,
which is now. Me and my young-boy hard-on
wondering what I'd do on earth because that's all
I had. Maybe be a hero, or if that's difficult, a farmer.

DARK

By miracle night arrived
along with the liquid dark.
I like it best while camping
at first you see the dimming lake
and then you can't see ten feet
past the fire. At dawn you're reassured
by the first trickle of light
from the east. I love its paleness
though the day becomes blazing
the tent too hot for a nap. I sit in the shade
of a cliff, watch a big rattler come
out of its hole, wait a few minutes,
go back in the hole, too hot for a rattler.
I drink all my water on the three-mile
way back to the car, drive a couple of hours
to Tucson from this wretched desert, an outdoorsman
with a credit card. I check in at the Ramada
and sleep all day in the air-conditioning,
the TV said it was 107 today. All night
I heard yodeling angels, likely a pack of coyotes
crisscrossing the dark. I carry a gun
because I'm a fearful human. A thousand
times I awoke to think of a beautiful girl
who died in Flint, Michigan. A disease quickly ate
her up. If she had been with me I couldn't have
stopped death. We would have sung songs of mourning
all night long. Also laughter in the dark. At dawn
as a dog breathes, so breathe I.

SUNDAY

On a Sunday morning walk I carry a pistol
having seen a big rattler on the path yesterday.
I don't want to lose my beloved dog, Zil.
I lost my setter Rose to them, a fang in the eye
and one in the cheek. She suffered horribly.
I therefore declared jihad against them
when they're close to the house
in favor of grandchildren and dogs.
They are so startling as if our blood
understands the rattle. I have teased
them with my walking stick and am amazed
how far they can strike with their fat, curled bodies.
At heart I don't want to kill on the Lord's day.

CATTLE NAP

How lovely the sleeping Black Angus cows
in the green, green pasture. They start
eating at dawn in the first pale light,
then when the heat gathers midmorning
they all flop down, sprawling in naps
except a few calves who don't want
a nap and wander around bothering everyone
but they are ignored and finally sleep.
The bull calves wake up first, spar and butt heads
in imitation of future sexual wars,
"I'm biggest and strongest I want all the females,"
but now all becomes peaceful on a somnolent
summer day, lumps of black in the green
pasture, a hundred or so, large and small
and then as if on signal they get up and start eating.
Why does this so please me? Like ourselves
it's important that these doomed creatures are
ignorant of the future and remain peacefully
with nature eating the thick green grass.

LIFE

I'm not so good at life anymore.
Sometimes I wake up and don't recognize it.
Houses, cars, furniture, books are a blur
while trees, birds, and horses are fine
and clear. I also understand music
of an ancient variety—pre-nineteenth century.
Where have I been?
Recounting flowers from the train window
between Seville and Granada, also bulls and olive trees.
I couldn't sleep in Lorca's room because it was haunted.
Even the wine I carried was haunted.
Spain has never recovered from this murder.
Her nights are full of the red teeth of death.
There were many who joined him. You can't count,
up and down, birds and flowers at the same time.

UNIVERSE

The landscape above confuses me.
Only twice have I seen Venus drowning
in the cup of the new moon.
I want to read it like a sky-
high book and know what's beyond.
Seeing is believing.
I'm told there's no last page.
It's just black and lasts forever. At church
they said that each year is a single grain
of sand and when the beaches of the world
are used up eternity is just getting started
so you don't want to spend that time in hell.
Machado said that the indifferent water holds
the stars in its heart. Precisely. I can only
study the universe on the surface
of a calm lake way back in the forest,
where the speed of light comes to a dead stop.
Buried in water the stars move very slowly.

HERRING

I'm sitting at the window eating pickled herring
and watching the existence of earth.
A small brown bird flies in from the left,
a fellow creature. We are each other
though he's more closely related
to dinosaurs. Lucky for us
this existence doesn't include
the future, which at this point is questionable.
Israel and Iran bomb each other at the same
split second. Thousands
of small brown birds will die in what
the media call *conflagration,* temporarily the world's
biggest double bonfire. I won't attend the party.
It's far too small for God to see
in a universe with ninety billion galaxies
small brown birds and herring.

THINGS UNSEEN

When I was a child they'd sing at church, "I love to tell the story of unseen things above." The Lord sat on a throne of pearl, gold, diamonds but my dad said take this with a grain of salt. The Lord spent forty days in the wilderness, that's what he liked. After church out in the yard I'd stare straight up in hopes of seeing these unseen things above. You couldn't stand out in the parking lot because big Christians were swerving out headed for the Pancake House. This was an after-church ritual. A huge plate of pancakes drowning in syrup to compensate for a boring sermon. I knew the son of the owners of the Pancake House who said that these sugar-freak Christians go through expensive gallons of syrup on Sunday mornings. My family never went because of the expense. When we got home we'd change clothes and my father would stand at the stove to make his favorite buckwheat pancakes and a pan of sausage. We'd have homemade maple syrup made from thirty maples in the yard. This was good enough for us. He said those people knock themselves out and can't work in the garden until late afternoon. Drink a quart of syrup and see what happens to you. I still stare at the sky for signs of heavens but without the help of syrup.

CIGARETTE

With earth you wonder whether God lit
the wrong end of the cigarette, tossed it aside.
But no, we were magnificent once.
Now we humans are vile machines of attrition.
Nothing escapes our notice, even the butterflies
in the Amazon that must get their salt
from the tears of turtles are a possible profit
for window displays, salt ads,
a fortune in butterflies drinking tears.

NUTHATCH GIRL

The gods lost footing and rolled down
the mountain into a heap at the bottom.

We have to do thus and so to keep
them alive.

Everyone forgot their assignment
except a young girl from Missouri
who danced down a cliff bare naked.

She's part bird so it was cheating a little.

Gods encourage supernatural cheating.

Meanwhile the girl climbed up a tree
like a nuthatch to read Rumi aloud
in his original language.

It's up to poets to revive the gods.

BIG ISSUES

All these planted flowers
I stare at every day have become
part of my brain. Outside the studio door
twelve poppies, seven peonies.
The numbers change nearly every day.
Are they doing damage
keeping me from all the big issues?
Of course, but the big issues don't need me.
The surrounding mountains are a real big
issue. To them my steps are soft as a moth's.
There are too many people for me to be a big
issue. I'm more on the level of a crow.
The sixteen poppies and eight peonies are getting in the way
of the United Nations, existentialism, and masculinity.
These big issues all fade in the face of beauty.

APPLE

I just picked and ate the first apple
of the year, slightly sour, from a low-hanging
branch. There was a deep peck hole
from a magpie I ate around. Me and the birds,
deer, the apple herself, are lucky to have apples in our world.
The biggest branch broke off in a storm and we lost
a third of the harvest, like the dog eating rabbits
and duck eggs. Nature gets bruised, injured,
murdered in bed. But now staring into the greenery
there are hundreds of apples slowly turning rose.
We are saved from apple hunger.

SUNDIAL

Startled by the earth at dawn.
It was far too green.
The horse was a wet gray.
The birds were too loud.
I touched a veronica flower
with my eyelash.
The snake tested the air
with its tongue.
The mountain across the river
is in flames, a week now.
This isn't a dream.
I heard the sounds of all doors
of earth opening and closing.
You can't close a door on the river.
We drank wine on the mountainside
next to Lorca's memorial sundial.
A house was burning in Granada.
The train went north toward Seville
where the Guadalquivir waited for it to cross.
Someone dropped an olive in the grass.
A boy played a guitar on a rooftop,
which made me weep tears
the exact temperature of life.

WINTER, SPRING

Winter is black and beige down here
from drought. Suddenly in March
there's a good rain and in a couple
of weeks we are enveloped in green.
Green everywhere in the mesquites, oaks,
cottonwoods, the bowers of thick
willow bushes the warblers love
for reasons of food or the branches,
the tiny aphids they eat with relish.

Each year it is a surprise
that the world can turn green again.
It is the grandest surprise in life,
the birds coming back from the south to my open
arms, which they fly past, aiming at the feeders.

APRIL

Still April though the last day.
So many days are somber here with darkish
clouds floating through the mountains. At night
cold rain falls turning to snow in the mountains,
which crawls down to the valley bringing a taste
of winter again. People say "Oh no" having had
a rough winter. The grizzly bears have emerged
from their dens wondering, "What's there to eat,"
which they haven't done in five months.
Down here it's green under the slight
blanket of snow. I brush it off my peonies.

TINY BIRD

The urge to be a tiny bird
upon a tiny limb, maybe
a bridled titmouse
standing on its spidery feet,
not a big guy who falls
with a resounding thump
and bruises sidewalks and pastures,
sinks in river mud to the waist.
If my feet were spears I would have descended
to one of the tumultuous underground rivers which are
everywhere, earthborn by the black current.
When young I thought I'd die in my thirties
like so many of my favorite poets.
At seventy-five I see this hasn't happened.
Still, I am faithful to my poems and birds.
Birds are poems I haven't caught yet.

APPLE TREE

Sitting under the apple tree on a hot
June day harassed by blackbirds
and a house wren who have nests there.
I'm thinking of the future and the past,
and how the past at my age has become
obviously so much longer than the future.
This feeling always precedes my sense
that severe weather is coming. I don't believe
in doom or destiny—I believe in turmoil,
thunderstorms in the head, rolling lightning
coming down my brain's road. As an artist
you follow the girl in the white tennis dress
for 25,000 miles and never close the deal.

GALACTIC

Sitting out in my chair near Linda's garden.
A mixture of flowers and vegetables, pink iris,
wild poppies, roses, blue salvia and veronica
among tomatoes, green beans, eggplant and onion.
I think that I sense the far-flung galaxies
and hear a tinge of the solar winds.
Where is my dead brother? I want to know.
With so many infirmities I await the miraculous.
Galaxies are grand thickets of stars
in which we may hide forever.

THE RIVER

Yes, we'll gather by the river,
the beautiful, the beautiful river.
They say it runs by the throne of God.
This is where God invented fish.
Wherever, but then God's throne is as wide
as the universe. If you're attentive you'll
see the throne's borders in the stars. We're on this side
and when you get to the other side we don't know
what will happen if anything. If nothing happens
we won't know it, I said once. Is that cynical?
No, nothing is nothing, not upsetting just
nothing. Then again maybe we'll be cast
at the speed of light through the universe
to God's throne. His hair is bounteous.
All the 5,000 birds on earth were created there.
The firstborn cranes, herons, hawks, at the back
so as not to frighten the little ones.
Even now they remember this divine habitat.
Shall we gather at the river, this beautiful river?
We'll sing with the warblers perched on his eyelashes.

DAYLIGHT

Did you notice the daylight today?
These days are short in December.
It comes before dark. Sometimes it passes
in a hurry to get someplace else
more friendly, perhaps. Fiji, maybe.
We become forgetful and miss it some days.
In March there were six different warblers
in one willow bush. What else could
you possibly want from daylight?

WARBLER

This year we have two gorgeous
yellow warblers nesting in the honeysuckle bush.
The other day I stuck my head in the bush.
The nestlings weigh one-twentieth of an ounce,
about the size of a honeybee. We stared at
each other, startled by our existence.
In a month or so, when they reach the size
of bumblebees they'll fly to Costa Rica without a map.

THE FINAL LIST

They want to operate on me again.
They took away my driver's license.
I can go nowhere to get food and wine.
Thousands of buds fell to the grass
from the apple and crabapple trees.
The apple buds are white against green grass.
The crabapple buds are bright pink.
They see it coming. It happens every year.
They are happily enough flowers for the void.

A DOG IN HEAVEN

An ancient problem never solved until this moment.
Did Jesus have a dog with him
during the forty days in the wilderness?
Yes. In the village the dog was called Cain
in jest. He would eat anything he could get
in his mouth. He would try to make love to chickens
to the laughter of the children who threw stones
at him, a great sin to throw stones at poor
stray dogs. So when Jesus left the village
at dawn with a loaf of bread and a bedroll
Cain followed and Jesus didn't have the heart
to yell "Go away" to the woe-begotten Cain.
So Cain trailed happily along and at the end
of the first hot day he stopped, sniffed the air.
He turned left and waited for Jesus to follow.
Cain led the way down a gorge to a spring he knew.
The spring emerged from a tiny cave in the cliff.
Cain and Jesus drank deeply and he filled his container.
Then they bathed in the cool water. At twilight they
were next to the north shore of the Sea of Galilee.
Jesus caught a fine fish with a hook and line he had packed
cooking it on a flat rock where they had built a fire.
He picked a bone out of the dog's gum. A few years later
he told Cain to stay home because he had to be crucified
in Jerusalem. He actually put Cain in the tomb
with a chunk of camel meat and said he'd come back to get
him. On the third day Jesus's tomb was empty.
Cain had been invited along for the Resurrection ride.

QUARANTINE

I've been quarantined by the gods.
Do no harm, they said.
Tell no secrets. I had stored
my spirit in the big willow tree to the west
of my study on the advice of Rumi.
It was getting badly bruised every day
and my spirit needed a resting place.
I forgot where I put it when you
should check it every morning.
I sank lower and lower until one day
I called it back from the tree
then wrote a pretty good poem.
There is no time to fool around, the gods said.
They blew my poem with the wind to
the top of Antelope Butte. I can't walk there
with my cane. Some gods have been dead
a thousand years and need our magic
and music to come back to life.
We owe it to them. They got us started.

MOON SUITE

The moon came to the forge
with her skirt of white, fragrant flowers.
The young boy watches her, watches.
The boy is watching her.

                     Federico García Lorca

The full moon is rising from her nest
high in the Absaroka mountains—
a miraculous cliché
shining down, glistening,
on thousands of acres of hay.

      —

The new moon, how I loved it
out over the still lake in childhood.
It meant a fresh start whirring
in from the sky with the nightjars,
bullbats, and ten thousand swallows
to eat the mosquitoes you were breathing.

      —

Seeing the moon the loon began to call
and a few stars seemed to hiss.
When we were young on the lake the night
was alive, bobcat yowl, buck deer snort,
a thousand irritable birds, the hum of night
herself holding her weight of stars and moon.
Dawn only came when the night was exhausted.

      —

Brother said the moon was a mushroom
feeding on light until it got white and fat.
Astronomers say this is true.

—

The moon was sitting on the hill
behind the house
so I walked right into it—
cold and soft and not bright white
as you might think, more cream-colored
with a warm wind.
I thought I might see John Keats.

—

The big moon rose
through the forest fire across the river.
I had a primitive fear she was aflame.
An older man was caught camping up there
and had to hike with his old dog Brownie
across the divide ahead of the chasing fire.
They made it in the burning moonlight.

—

"Walking in Jerusalem just like John"
but farther east in the desert.
In the moonlight you could see mating vipers.
They were everywhere in old Bible pictures
at the feet of the saints but didn't strike them.

—

In the Far East we worried about immense tigers
eating the moon, its pieces falling from their jaws.

—

You can't rearrange the heavens to suit
yourself. Even the gods are powerless
with sun, moon, and planets. Wildflowers
listen carefully to the gods and also to sea lions.

Perhaps the gods want us to be wildflowers.
Surprises on earth, these wildflowers.
We can't seem to change anything anywhere.

—

The stars have been getting too large lately,
big white loose splotches in a liquid sky.
Can I handle this jigsaw puzzle
of the universe? I'll need a thousand
dog teams and very long ropes.
There'll be no seating for the audience
they must stand in the nation's backyards.
Earth will be at peace again through dog power.
The International Dog Church will be founded.
The moon will be called Holy Dog Moon,
the sun called Sun Dog.
The gods are now called dogs and are much happier.
Marching is permanently banished in favor of trotting.

—

The bear broke free from his constellation
and loped through the cosmos thinking
he scented a female in a distant world.

—

Our difficult selves are cast in iron.
Only the most extreme heat makes us malleable.

—

All my life I've been a night bird.
Thousands of evenings looking at thousands
of acres of black windows. What's out there?
Everything from murderers to ghosts
and gods who are safe from us in the dark.

The gulley is full of big green willow bushes
waiting patiently for the tiny migrant warblers
due in a few weeks. The stars don't
know who we are. The slim new moon
rising strains to capture Venus in her
curve. Sometimes I'm inside and
outside at the same time. Blackness is a friend
concealing my disfigurement from private wars.

—

Last night the big moon carved me up
with her invisible white knives. In the dark
yard I chanted and flopped. Where is my
straitjacket when I need it? I held on to
a willow so as not to be taken up in the air.
I can't leave earth tonight, I pleaded.
We always say *not yet* to the gods,
who get irritable when they can't kill us.

—

A new moon with Venus nearby
though not in the moon cup as I'd prefer her.
So hard to organize these things.
Yahweh is the God of galaxies
while the moon rolls freely to help the oceans
and to haunt us with our life before birth,
in a different kingdom far away.

—

We swam at night
under the moon's reflection
and tried to catch her.
She slipped through our fingers.

—

The moon stares at me impolitely
through the fir trees and the willow and window.
She's like that. Staring back
you can trip in the yard.

—

The full moon caught herself in the contorted rose vines
beyond the window. The rose is called Madame Alfred Carrière,
bred for climbing castle walls. We only have
a little casita, a gatehouse, but the huge rose
is here just the same for peasants.
I am not strong enough to disentangle the moon.

Nobody is.

—

We were frightened last October when a big wind
from the north scudded the moon back south
where it was prayed for, needed by Día de Muertos.
What fun to dance, get drunk in a cemetery.
An immense angel died, fell draped over the mountains
imagining snow. We missed the full moon.

—

Once I heard wolves in full moonlight.
A huge storm visited the cabin, also green northern lights.
The sky split open in the west, and beyond the storm
the wolves were howling within the thunder.
The earth was forcing me to not forget her.
I never recovered from that night.
This all would never happen again.

—

The last moon will be black in the red sky.
The last girl will weigh two sparrow feathers.
At my age you don't think about the future
because you don't have one.

—

Up close
the moon
fills the world.

BRIDGE

Most of my life was spent
building a bridge out over the sea
though the sea was too wide.
I'm proud of the bridge
hanging in the pure sea air. Machado
came for a visit and we sat on the
end of the bridge, which was his idea.

Now that I'm old the work goes slowly.
Ever nearer death, I like it out here
high above the sea bundled
up for the arctic storms of late fall,
the resounding crash and moan of the sea,
the hundred-foot depth of the green troughs.
Sometimes the sea roars and howls like
the animal it is, a continent wide and alive.
What beauty in this the darkest music
over which you can hear the lightest music of human
behavior, the tender connection between men and galaxies.

So I sit on the edge, wagging my feet above
the abyss. Tonight the moon will be in my lap.
This is my job, to study the universe
from my bridge. I have the sky, the sea, the faint
green streak of Canadian forest on the far shore.

LAST POEMS

2014–2016

These poems were written after the manuscript for *Dead Man's Float* was completed. They are presented in chronological order, with publications noted.

MINER POETS

I am melancholy with fraudulence
of language. It is coal and we are miners
down in the blackness with weak lanterns,
a big chisel and sledge, some dynamite,
a baloney sandwich. We squash fingers
chipping off poems that silhouetted we hope will burn
spontaneously giving us a little light to live
by while remembering spring far above us,
the new lilacs the memory of which follows
us underground. The crystal pond that had
brook trout now clouded by mine tailings.
We disemboweled the earth and die without lungs.

MOTH CONSCIENCE

In the bathroom sink I inadvertently
flushed down a small moth.
What unforgiveable inattention!
Now the moth is dying in the septic tank,
dark as a dungeon, when it loves
to flutter at lamps as if they were the sun.
I turn on the mirror light. Maybe the moth
will see light and crawl upward.
Near tears I wait a half hour thinking
I could have called the excavator from town,
dug up the septic tank, but surely the moth is dead
in the toxic liquid as if the tank were full of rotting
politicians who poison the air we breathe.
I say this without rancor because it's true.
This was a bad death for a winged creature.

BUSTER

The old black dog named Buster
tethered to his dog house near the clothesline
the other night when it was thirty below zero
forgotten by everyone watching *Creature Feature*.
The boy carried his hard body in putting him on a blanket
near the stove praying he'd come back to life.
In the morning the dog smelled, his father
was angry saying "nothing dead ever comes back to life."
The roughest thing I have learned.

HAND

Because of death my phone book
is shrinking. Elvis, who I didn't know,
pitched forward off the toilet dead as a toad
in the road. Many who died
were much younger than me. I offered
them a handshake for disappearing gracefully
but they wouldn't let go of my hand.

WEAK WINTER SUN

I have been enshrouded for months
by the weak winter sun, so weak
you can stare into the face of it
without hurting your eyes and see the fire
veins in its body. It is stupidly
human to rush the season. The boy
cleans up his trout equipment. Only two
more months to the fishing opener
and the dry flies and streamers
are impatiently waiting. Seventy-seven
years of weak winter sun, the lake
froze over with several feet of ice. The moon
glowing once without a trace of heat.
The bulbs in the flower garden ache
from the last inches of snow. Under the bridge
the trout feed on snow flies, so tiny hardly a bite.
The moon behind the skein of clouds freezes
me and advises patience. It says "be the moon with me."

Narrative, 2015

DOG IN THE TOMB

My seventy-seventh Easter.
What luck. I dreamt I was in the tomb
with Jesus. He was very cold because he was
dead. But not for long. Christ the Lord
is risen today. Hallelujah. I was in a
corner wrapped in a robe. I called for Cain
the little dog that had spent forty days
in the wilderness with Jesus. He came over
for a few minutes to warm me up
and then faithfully went back to the Savior.
I wondered if I'd be here until I was bones.
Suddenly there was a clap of thunder and a blinding
flash of light. Jesus and the dog were gone
and I was sitting on the bank of the River Jordan.
This is not scripture it's a dream,
a dream, the stuff our life is made of.

Alta, 2021

CAT PRAYER

In at least half the homes on earth
prayers emerge from the chimney with the smoke.
It is better not to ask God for something
in particular and get a thunderous, silent "no."
Out the window beyond the pyracantha tree
does the cat pray to catch the raven who teases it?
Does the raven pray to avoid the cat, or
neither? Each day they play it as it lays.
Their spirits don't quite crave life like
we do. Alive is something they merely do
each morning when they wake. Breakfast
is simply another creature dead or alive.
Yesterday evening the cat caught and ate
five mice in the weeds, taking number six
out to a hiding place I once found by the
bad smell, a little pyramidal stack of dead
mice behind a stack of white pine boards and shingles.
When the cat sleeps in a ragweed the raven
will often dive bomb it with a shriek. The cat
seems to sense it and jumps twisting high
and once caught a tail feather but nothing to eat.
Afterwards the raven spent more time teasing
the three cow dogs during their long naps.

WEEPING BIRDS

Mid-morning in mid-March.
The mournful doves everywhere
singing desire or sadness I don't know which,
and the even more doleful gray hawk
at which all birds fall silent because of fear.
It chases away vultures, ravens, red-tail hawks.
The gray hawk wants all of the creek
land to sing the deaths of a hundred Irish poets
all by itself, this spring dirge
that haunts us humans by daylight.
So endlessly dolorous, this sweet death.

Alta, 2021

GHOSTS

Friends are helping me on my slow path to the grave.
Three beat me there last summer.
Matthiessen, Bowden, Torrey. Now I'm taking their ghosts
on a walk up the pasture hill to my bench
to celebrate the Solstice. Another friend
is on the lip. One still living friend
thinks that we live too long. He's the only
one I know who thinks this. He says
how long do you want to continue doing
what you're doing? We think something new
might be coming along, a girl, a big check
that will take us back to France
for a better life of wandering and poetry.
It was time to leave the bench but I was helpless,
the ghosts refused to leave saying why
go any place else now that we've been here.
You can't move recalcitrant ghosts
but unlike ghosts I still eat dinner
and went home while they sang a medieval chant.
At dawn I returned with Folly our dog
who was frightened. The ghosts were dozing
with the birth of God coming with the light
caught and held safely by the mountains in their cradle
of stone. The philosopher said, "The miracle
is that the world exists." We bathe in the beauty at dawn.

Alta, 2021

THE SPEED OF DARK

I have studied and become intimate
with the speed of darkness. It's so fast
it's always here. When the light withdraws
the dark comes from no place. It always lives
with us. Your heart and brain are black.
They never see the true light except in violence
or autopsy. Of course the brain can cast
its own blinding light that we wait for in a poem,
at least blinding to us. In our trances, the loves
of long ago enter the room unescorted, silent
perhaps from the black bottom of the ocean
where we all die in perfect darkness, a sense
of whirling that recedes back to the time
the ocean swallowed the smallest stars
then heated us into our early life.
Darkness is always there, it only stands revealed.

Alta, 2021

MY NEW CONTRACT

I can no longer believe in the world of quantities,
time, measured substance, distance, silence.
What are the contraries of destiny?
My body has abandoned me in the world.
My parents are dead and a brother and sister.
I lost my principles at night at sea.
My wife and children keep me alive.
I walk slowly across the surfaces of maps
trying to see underneath them. I haven't
heard the WORD or anything or anybody.
Nature has crowded me into the far field.
I filled myself with the clutter of all ages.
All of our little pieces don't go together.
Maybe when I give up the world will be lighter.
I can't even find the gangplank to the void.
I have to take a year off to figure this out.
I can't quite believe that this is what I get.
I haven't caught up to my life to see what it is.

SHE

My wife died in the autumn.
Now on Saturday morning down here
on the Mexican border my housekeeper,
an Apache Tarahumara woman, sings me a lament
in Spanish of love and death. We were
married fifty-six years, fell in love two years before
that. My soul knows this song she sings.
This so far is a haunting, the bleeding heart
we used to hear about. I've been told the heart
will run out of blood but I doubt it.
Lover, come back to me.

Alta, 2021

THE WHISPER

I'm learning the difficult terrain
of the heart of darkness. No maps
are available. Light never enters
there. The brain is helpless
which is fine. I depended on it
too much to no avail. The brain
is what I am or so they say but I sense
another element, perhaps the soul
I've never written about. When my wife
died I lost the motive for life and fell back
on the cushion of the soul which is everything
I can't account for in life. The moon whispers tonight
the sun in leaden gravitas doesn't want to rise
in a world of beheaded children.
We have been abandoned with what we see.
Our lives aren't good but passable,
our mortgages and cancer loom. But birds
lead us outside where we belong.
Around here all the gods live in trees.

Alta, 2021

Jim Harrison died at his writing desk. His body was found on the Saturday morning before Easter, notebook opened to a handwritten draft of an untitled poem—the last words of a writer who took his vows as an artist at age nineteen.

Jim's notebooks—like his beloved rivers and thickets—were sacred places. We extend our deep gratitude to the Harrison family for allowing us to share the last page of Jim's final notebook as a coda to *Complete Poems*. As Jim said in a poem, "Death steals everything except our stories."

In a case the earth turned clockwise and
before when its gravity failed all who
fell off the earth. I was in Africa
at the time and fell near an elephant
I made my way to her and stretched
out on her stomach for protection
from the polar cold of the high atmosphere
I caught a couple of passing
tomatoes to eat and a bottle of whiskey.
The earth used to be God's toilet
but he took so many we ran and abandoned it
he left us with the husk we made
of her body like a wasp's nest
I am what his parts and trees of God's body

In unease the earth turned itself inside
out when its gravity fled. All of us
fell off the earth. I was in Africa
at the time and fell near an elephant.
I made my way to her and stretched
out on her stomach for protection
from the polar cold of the high atmosphere.
I caught a couple of passing
tomatoes to eat and a bottle of whiskey.
The earth used to be God's body
but he took too many wounds and abandoned it.
He left us with the husk we made
of his body like a wasp's nest.
Man shits his pants and trashed God's body

THE SHAPE OF THE JOURNEY: INTRODUCTION

1998

It is a laborious and brain-peeling process to edit one's collected poems. You drift and jerk back and forth between wanting to keep it all intact, and the possibility of pitching out the whole work in favor of a fresh start.

But then there are no fresh starts at age sixty and this book is the portion of my life that means the most to me. I've written a goodly number of novels and novellas but they sometimes strike me as extra, burly flesh on the true bones of my life though a few of them approach some of the conditions of poetry. There is the additional, often shattering notion gotten from reading a great deal in anthropology, that in poetry our motives are utterly similar to those who made cave paintings or petroglyphs, so that studying your own work of the past is to ruminate over artifacts, each one a signal, a remnant of a knot of perceptions that brings back to life who and what you were at the time, the past texture of what has to be termed as your "soul life."

I fear that somewhat improperly, humility arrived rather late in life. I don't mean self-doubt which is quite another thing. The Romantic "I" with all of its inherent stormy bombast, its fungoid elevation of the most questionable aspects of personality, its totally self-referential regard of life, has tended to disappear. I recall that Bill Monroe, the bluegrass musician, said that he didn't write songs but "discovered them in the air." If you add Wallace Stevens's contention that "technique is the proof of seriousness," we come closer to the warm, red heart of the matter. Of course you come to realize that your Romantic "I" never had much to do with your poems in the first place but was mostly a fuel tank for public postures.

Another good source of humility is the dozen or so famous poets I can enumerate whose work has apparently vaporized since I published my first book, *Plain Song,* back in 1965. It's been years since I went on one, but a reasonably well-attended reading tour can give you an unjustified sense of permanence. More desirable memories are those of picking potato bugs for a dollar a day at age ten, or living in a windowless seven-dollar-a-week room in Greenwich Village with photos of Rimbaud and Lorca taped to the wall above one's pillow. A good sidebar on impermanence at the time was the arrival, every few days at the bookstore where I worked, of the eminent anthologist Oscar Williams who would carefully check the racks to make sure his work was well-displayed. In his anthologies Oscar would add an appendix with lists of the twenty-five "Chief Poets of America," and perhaps fifty "Chief Poets of the World," featuring photos, which invariably included Oscar and his girlfriend, Gene Derwood. This added a tinge of cynicism about literary life to a nineteen-year-old. But then we have always had our Colley Cibbers, our Oscar Williamses, our Casey Kasems trying to establish an infantile worth with premature canons. By nature a poet is permanently inconsolable, but there is a balm in the idea that in geological terms we all own the same measure of immortality, though our beloved Shakespeare and a few others will live until the planet dies.

Of course any concerns over what has actually happened in American poetry in the last thirty-five years or so are inevitably fragile if you're not a scholar. There was obviously a healthy diaspora during which there were Pyrrhic wars, the exfoliation into the MFA "creative writing" period, and now apparently lapsing into a new faux-sincere Victorianism. If there is health it is in the biodiversity of the product. I suppose I was too overexposed as a graduate student in comparative literature to both the wretchedness of xenophobia and the repetitive vagaries of literary history, to maintain interest. If after a few days I can't mentally summon the essence of the work I've been reading I simply don't care who says it's good and why. The impulse to choose up sides is better abandoned in grade school. I recall how startled I was in my early twenties in Boston when I discovered I was not allowed to like Roethke, the Lowell of *Life Studies,* and also Duncan, Snyder, and Olson, the latter three whom I came to know. Not that I was above the frays, just that I was unequal to maintaining interest in them. I remember that in my brief time in academia, in our rather shabby rental in Stony Brook, we had gatherings of poets as diverse as Denise Levertov, Louis Simpson, James Wright, and Robert Duncan who all rather effortlessly got along. But then, the poem is the thing and most of the rest are variations on the theme of gossip.

If I attempt to slip rather lightly over my own volumes, distinctly visual images arise with each book, emerging from what job I had at the time to support my family, what studio or kitchen table I used to write the work, where we lived at the time, and my usual obsession with what kind of cheap wine I was drinking. Other images include what dog or dogs were our beloved companions, and what cats tormented or loved the dogs. This is what I meant by cave paintings or petroglyphs: cooking our lives down we don't really cook away our Pleistocene ingredients. I am reminded that in the splendid history of Icelandic culture everyone is expected to at least try to turn a hand to poetry. I am also reminded of Heidegger's contention that poetry is not elevated common language but that common language is reduced, banalized poetry.

1. *Plain Song.* My first book, published through the efforts of Denise Levertov, who had become a consulting editor at W.W. Norton. Nothing equals, of course, the first book, which is at the very least a tenuous justification of what you insisted was your calling. I had been eating the contents of world poetry since I was fifteen and without any idea of what to spit out. I collected *Botteghe Oscure,* but also Bly's magazines *The Fifties* and *The Sixties.* I was obsessed with Lorca, W.C. Williams, Apollinaire, Rimbaud, and Walt Whitman but none of it much shows in the book, which is mostly poems out of my rural past. It was primarily written in Boston where I was a road man for a book wholesaler; but I had my first real exposure to other poets, most of whom hung out in Gordon Cairnie's Grolier Book Shop, in Cambridge. I also spent some time with Charles Olson in Gloucester but was too bent on my own obsessions to digest any of his gospel.

2. *Locations.* Quite a different book. I couldn't endure the city so we moved back to rural northern Michigan, where I worked as a common construction laborer and studied Pound and Rilke at night, also T'ang Dynasty poets. Rilke can be viewed as some sort of ornate European shaman who devours his imperiled readers who must wonder if they

are ever going to emerge. I was also drawn to Stravinsky at the time, whom I endlessly played on our thirty-dollar record player in the living room of our thirty-dollar-a-month house that never got warm. I think this fascination with classical music lead me to the "suite" form.

3. *Outlyer & Ghazals.* An old professor and friend, Herbert Weisinger, engineered my getting a long-abandoned master's degree and dragged us out of northern Michigan to Stony Brook, Long Island. This was likely a good thing with an exposure to hundreds of poets and to New York City, where in my late teens I had been a solitary buffoon. I began writing ghazals as a reaction to being terribly overstuffed with culture.

4. *Letters to Yesenin.* An utterly desperate period with multiple clinical depressions. I was still in high school when I discovered a Yarmolinsky anthology of Russian poetry and became fascinated with it, aided later by the splendor of the New York Public Library. I was temperamentally unfit for academic life and we had moved back to northern Michigan, aided by two deceptive grants from the National Endowment, and the Guggenheim Foundation; "deceptive" because I did not see the dzay of reckoning when I'd somehow have to make a living again. I went to Russia with Dan Gerber in 1972 and followed the tracks of Yesenin, Dostoyevsky, Voznesensky and Akhmatova, poets we loved. I tried everything to make a living, including journalism and novel-writing, neither of which quite supported us. For nearly a decade we averaged ten grand a year. *Letters to Yesenin* was an act of desperation and survival.

5. *Returning to Earth.* More from this occasionally grim period, leavened by the fact that we lived in a relatively poor area and our condition was scarcely unique. This long poem was, I suspect, both a conscious and unconscious attempt to internalize the natural world I had been so strongly drawn to after a childhood injury that had blinded my left eye.

6. *Selected & New Poems.* Probably premature but then I had finally had a financial success with a book of novellas, *Legends of the Fall,* and my publisher was quite willing to collect my poetry.

7. *The Theory & Practice of Rivers.* Written at a remote cabin nestled by a river in Michigan's Upper Peninsula, and at our farm in Leelanau County. It was an attempt to render what could keep one alive in a progressively more unpleasant world with some of the difficulties of my own doing in the world of script writing in New York and Hollywood. It is certainly not my *métier* but it was a well-paid option to teaching, at which I was a failure. I used to think it was virtuous to stay distant from academia but gradually I realized that any way a "serious writer" can get a living is fine. The problem with both town and gown is the temptation to write for one's peers rather than from the heart. The same is true of the multifoliate forms of regionalism.

8. *After Ikkyū.* A largely misunderstood book. Dan Wakefield has noted that in our *haute* culture books thought to have any religious content are largely ignored. I have practiced a profoundly inept sort of Zen for twenty-five years and this book is an attempt to return to the more elemental facts of life, unsuffocated by habituation, conditioning, or learning.

9. "Geo-Bestiary." The new work included in these *New and Collected Poems.* A rather wild-eyed effort to resume contact with reality after writing a long novel that had drawn me far from the world I like to call home.

Jim Harrison
Grand Marais, Michigan
May 7, 1998

INDEX OF TITLES

INDEX OF FIRST LINES

Awake in Paris all night listening to rain, 471
A wave lasts only moments, 551
A welcome mat of moonlight, 478
A whiff of that dead bird along the trail, 426
A winter dawn in New York City, 755

Back in the blue chair in front of the green studio, 602
Back on the blue chair before the green studio, 763
Bear died standing up, 386
Because of death my phone book, 878
Because of the late, cold wet spring the fruit of greenness, 651
Before I was born I was water, 483
Behind my back I have returned to life with much more surprise, 215
Between the four pads, 462
Beware, o wanderer, the road is walking too, 369
Birds and bugs, 464
Birds know us as "the people of the feet, 652
Black dog on white snow, 468
Blacky, half Catahoula wild hog dog, 817
Bought a broken pocket watch, 458
Bucket in the rain, 468
Buddhists say everything is led by mind, 470
Bullfrog groans, 478
But the seventeen-year cicada, 443
By accident my heart lifted with a rush, 622
By miracle night arrived, 842

"Charred beyond recognition" is bad news, 459
Christ rose so long ago but the air, 780
Clear summer dawn, 442
Close after dawn walking the dog, 831
Come close to death, 477
Come down to earth! Get your head out of your ass, 368
Come to think of it, 471
Coming home from the tavern, 474
Coming home late from the tavern, 452
Coming out of anesthesia I believed, 557
Concha is perhaps seven. No one knows this cow dog's age, 419
Coyote's bloody face makes me, 432
Creeks find their destiny according to the slant, 829
Crow with a red beak, 461
Cuando ella cantó su canción, 540

For my horse, Brotherinlaw, who had no character, 159
For my new part I'm in makeup, 563
For sixty-three years I've ground myself, 440
For the first time, 388
For the first time, 511
For the first time the wind, 282
For years I've believed the world should speak Spanish, 561
Fresh snow standing deep, 464
Friends are helping me on my slow path to the grave, 883
From the roof the night's the color, 86
Fruit and butter. She smelled like the skin of an apple, 204

Gentle readers, feel your naked belly button where, 485
Gentle readers, tomorrow I undergo, 451
Getting older I'm much better at watching, 451
Ghazal in fear there might not be another, 173
Giselle gave me a primitive statuette, 523
Giselle me dio una estatuilla primitiva, 522
Go, my songs, 35
God I am cold and want to go to sleep for a long time, 186
God's hand is cupped, 458
God throws us out the back door, 806
God wears orange and black, 579
Going in the bar last Sunday night I noticed that they were having, 224
Go to sleep. Night is a coal pit, 82
Great-uncle Wilhelm, Mennonite, patriarch, 25

Hammering & drifting. Sea wrack. Cast upon & cast out, 294
Hear this touch: grass parts, 9
He climbed the ladder looking over the wall at the party, 192
He contends with the other only to find, 94
He fell off the cliff of a seven-inch *zafu,* 769
He Halts. He Haw. Plummets, 113
He is young. The father is dead, 8
Here along the Mexican border, 737
Here I am at the gateless gate again hoping, 672
Here in the first morning sunlight I'm trying, 526
Her voice had a deep resonance, 472
He said the grizzly sat eating the sheep and when the bullet, 139
He sings from the bottom of a well but she can hear him up, 151
He thinks of the dead. But they, 30
He waits to happen with the clear, 38
He went to sea, 704

His voice cracks on tremolo notes, 611
His wife has asthma, 542
Home again. It looked different for a moment, 370
Hotei didn't need a *zafu,* 326
Hot, hungry, eighteen and reading, 795
How attentive the big bear resting his chin, 460
How can I be alone when these brain cells, 429
How can I disappoint myself, 457
How can it be, 460
How can Lorca say he's only the pulse, 454
How can this dog on the cushion, 723
How evil all priesthoods, 475
How exhausted we can become, 524
How foolish the houseplant looks, 447
How heavy I am. My feet sink into the ground and my knees, 406
How is it the rich always know, 475
How long, stone, did it take, 49
How lovely the sleeping Black Angus cows, 844
How lucky in one life to see, 459
How much better these actual dreams, 429
How one old tire leans up against, 439
How restlessly the Buddha sleeps, 486
How sharp must be the fletcher's knife, 467
How tall would I be, 458
How the love of Tarzan in Africa haunted my childhood, 431

I am four years older than you but scarcely an unwobbling, 202
I am melancholy with fraudulence, 875
I am the old man alone in a hotel, 824
I am uniquely privileged to be alive, 701
I am walked on a leash by my dog and am water, 160
I am wherever I find myself to be, 450
I believe in steep drop-offs, the thunderstorm across the lake, 601
I can hear the cow dogs sleeping, 413
I can no longer believe in the world of quantities, 885
I can't be seventy-four, 792
I cleaned the granary dust off your photo with my shirtsleeve, 206
I confess that here and there in my life, 367
I couldn't walk across that bridge in Hannibal, 161
I don't have any medals. I feel their lack, 200
I don't know what happens after death, 742
I don't know what. I don't know what, 562
I don't weigh an hour, 16

I love these raw moist dawns with, 777
I'm a brownish American who wonders, 575
Imagine a gallery, 471
Imagine being a dog and never knowing what you're doing. You're, 212
I'm a very old dog, 837
I'm drawing blood the night of the full moon, 531
I'm greedy for the pack rat to make, 753
I'm hoping to be astonished tomorrow, 605
I might have been a welder, 452
I'm learning the difficult terrain, 887
I'm making a movie about my life, 496
I'm not so good at life anymore, 845
I'm sitting at the window eating pickled herring, 847
I'm sitting on the lip of this black hole, a well, 781
I'm sixty-two and can drop dead, 471
I'm so pleased that Yeats, 463
I'm the pet dog of a family of gods, 527
I'm trying to create an option for all, 752
I'm trying to open a window in this very old house, 586
In 1947 a single gold nugget was found, 462
In an egg yolk, 459
In a pasture, wild turkeys, 460
In at least half the homes on earth, 881
In Brazil I leapt, 471
In deer season, 461
In each of my cells Dad and Mom, 451
In Mexico the big, lovely, 455
In Montana the badger looks at me in fear, 427
In my garden, 462
In my "Memoir of an Unsuccessful Prostitute, 495
In my recent studies I have discovered cancer, 725
In New York, 446
I no longer lead my life. I'm led, 670
In our farthest field, 467
In our October windfall time red, 479
Inside people fear the outside; outside, the in, 370
In the bathroom sink I inadvertently, 876
In the best sense, 342
In the Cabeza Prieta from a hillock I saw no human sign, 424
In the electric chair's harness, 473
In the end you are tired of those places, 102
In the far back room of the school, 521
In the hotel room (far above the city) I said I bet you, 158

It rained so hard the sky became water, 478
"It rains most in the ocean off Trinidad, 739
It's better to start walking before you're born, 702
It's criminal to claim you've earned, 798
It's harder, 572
It's hard to believe there's a skeleton, 463
It's nice to think that when, 467
It's the date that gets me, 571
It's the Devil's, 474
It was Monday morning for most of the world, 372
It wasn't until the sixth century that the Christians, 369
It was one of those mornings utterly distorted by the night's dreams, 565
It was one of those mornings when my feet seemed unaware, 646
It would surely be known for years after as the day I shot, 208
I used to have time by the ass, 445
I've been apart too long, 537
I've been married since birth, 477
I've been quarantined by the gods, 864
I've been translating the language with which creatures, 592
I've emerged from the seven-going-on-eight divorces, 374
I've had enough tonight, 19
I've known her too long, 10
I've never learned from experience, 456
I've wasted too much moonlight, 361
I walked the same circular path today, 413
I want a sign, a heraldic bird, or even an angel at midnight, 157
I wanted to feel exalted so I picked up, 201
I wanted to play a song for you, 709
I want to be worthy of this waking dream, 236
I want to bother you with some recent nonsense; a classmate dropped, 221
I want to describe my life in hushed tones, 443
I want to die in the saddle. An enemy of civilization, 124
I want to go back to that wretched old farm, 751
I was born a baby, 479
I was chest-high in the wheat field with wind blowing, 770
I was commanded, in a dream naturally, 421
I was commissioned in a dream by Imanja, 337
I was hoping to travel the world, 417
I was lucky enough to have invented a liquid heart, 182
I was paralyzed from the waist up, 450
I was proud at four that my father called me Little Turd of Misery, 210
I was sent far from my land of bears, 421
I was there in a room in a village, 729

I was thinking that weather might be the reason, 671
I was walking because I wasn't upstairs sitting, 295
I was without Christmas spirit, 713
I went to Tucson and it gave, 364
I will walk down to a marina, 327
I woke up as nothing. Now start piling, 464
I won my wings! I got all A's! We bought fresh fruit! The toilet, 225
I worry much about the suffering, 796

Jesus wants me for a sunbeam, I sang in Sunday, 372
John in the desert, 40
July, and fat black flies, 462
Just another plane trip, 567
Just before dark, 377
Just before I fly out of myself, 479
Just before World War II I was smuggled into America on a tramp, 649
Just like today eternity is accomplished, 365
Just seven weeks ago in Paris, 378

Last year the snake, 470
Late-night herring binge causes sour, 754
Late November (full moon last night), 548
Lazed on the floor like an old baby, 466
Leaving on an exciting journey, 764
Let go of the mind, the thousand blue, 447
Let's not get romantic or dismal about death, 766
Letters from beautiful women, 455
Life has always yelled at me, 464
"Life's too short to be a whore anymore, 424
Li Ho of the province of Honan, 53
Like a bird dog my blood is a dictator, 834
Like Afghanistan I'm full of corruption, 750
Like a fist, the toad, 451
Like an old dog, 476
Limp with night fears: hellebore, wolfsbane, 126
Lin-chi says, having thrown away your head so long, 367
Look again: that's not, 465
Looking around this casita and the house, 839
Looking at a big moon too long, 391
Lorca was raised on his father's large, 827
Lost: Ambition, 442
Lost for a while, 454
Love is raw as freshly cut meat, 746

Nine days of dark, cold rain, 520
No poems about copious blood in the urine, 609
Not a new poem for Helen, 78
Not casida, canzone, 48
Not here and now but now and here, 363
Nothing is as it appears to be, 745
Nothing is the same to anyone, 300
Nothing quite so wrenches, 552
Nothing to console the morning but the dried grasshopper, 743
Nothing to do, 444
Not how many different birds I've seen, 433
No tranquil pills this year wanting to live peeled as they, 209
No trips to Egypt this week, 125
Not those who have lived here and gone, 90
November cold. Hey, grasshopper, 464
Now an outlander, once a poet in NY, 447
Now changed. None come to Carthage. No cauldrons, all love, 136
Nowhere is it the same place as yesterday, 536
Now in the dog days of summer Sirius is making a dawn peek, 643
Now it's the body's dog, pain, 456
Now that I'm older I perfectly, 473
Now this paste of ash and water, 88

O Atlanta, roseate dawn, the clodhoppers, hillbillies, rednecks, 147
O BLM, BLM, and NFS, 415
Of course we're born in the long shadow, 620
Of late I've been afflicted by too many hummingbirds, 667
Often I travel at night and am surprised, 477
Of the hundred swans in West Bay, 87
Oh, to be in love, 466
Oh, to write just one poem, 467
O happy day! Said *overpowered,* had by it all and transfixed, 155
Oh the dark, rank, brackish rut, 448
Oh what dew, 441
Old centipede, 445
Old friend, 439
Old white soup bowl, 445
Old willow, 450
On a Sunday morning walk I carry a pistol, 843
Once and for all there's no genetic virtue, 373
Once and for all to hear, I'm not going to shoot anybody, 168
Once I saw a wolf tread a circle in his cage, 29
Once I stood all night, 20

That the housefly is guided in flight by a fly brain diminishes, 194
That winter the night fell seven, 465
The 8,000 isn't coming now and won't ever, 835
The alfalfa was sweet and damp in fields where shepherds, 133
The ambulance driver told me in a bar, 785
The big fat garter snake, 440
The biomass of ants, 443
The birds, / confused by rain clouds, 453
The birds and beard turn gray, 657
The birds are flying around frantically, 773
The black sleeve falls back, 454
The blind man navigates, 479
The blond girl, 345
The boots were on the couch and had, 123
The boy stood in the burning house. Set it up, 239
The brain opens the hand which touches that spot, clinically, 141
The brown stumps, 446
The butterfly, 460
The butterfly's brain, 469
The child crawls in widening circles, backs to the wall, 185
The clock stopped at 5:30 for three months, 460
The clouds are unmoving near Cambria, 804
The clouds swirling low past the house and, 177
The colder the raindrops, 471
The color of a poppy and bruised, the subalpine green that, 138
The cow dogs caught their first jackrabbit, 459
The crow comes from, 447
The crumpled candy wrapper, 457
The cups of the tulips, 449
The dawn of the day we arrived, Abel Murrietta, 371
The deer hung flapping, 448
The drunken man, 453
The earth is almost round. The seas, 89
The face you look out of, 457
The fat snake's gone this year, 450
The firefly's one word, 458
The four seasons, the ten oaths, the nine colors, three vowels, 367
The full moon dark orange from another forest, 621
The full moon is rising from her nest, 865
The full moon often rises, 478
The girl ran across the cemetery, 787
The girl's bottom is beautiful as Peacock's dancing bear, 372
The girl thought that the sky was God's, 805

The girl with blue shorts and brown legs, 453
The gods lost footing and rolled down, 850
The goofy young bald eagle, 448
The Great Gourmand rows his boat, 459
The handle of its neck, 475
The hay in the loft, 456
"The horses run around, their feet, 715
The hound I've known for three years, 363
The imagination's kisses, 467
Their balls were so swollen they collided, 467
The landscape above confuses me, 846
The last and I'm shrinking from the coldness of your spirit: that, 228
The last trip to the river this year. Tonight I think, 735
The lettuce pushed up through the cold, cold ground, 790
The little bull calf gets his soft pink, 415
The low ceiling grazes, 470
The mad have black roots in their brains, 83
The man eating lamb's tongue salad, 757
The man sitting on the cold stone hearth, 578
The masques of dream—monk in his, 288
The mirror, backed in black, 449
The mirror tastes him, 22
The monk is eighty-seven. There's no fat, 366
The moon, all lordly white, 466
The moon comes up, 659
The moon is under suspicion, 686
The moon put her hand, 472
The moon put her white hands, 452
The mushrooms helped again: walking hangdoggedly to the granary, 218
The night is thin and watery; fish in the air, 143
The nightmare we waken from, 457
The ninth time I screwed Ophelia, 459
The nuthatch is in business, 440
The old black dog named Buster, 877
The old Finn (85) walks, 465
The old Finn hadn't washed his cup, 789
The old hen scratches, 467
The old man's angleworm stares, 674
The old rancher of seventy-nine years, 576
The one-eyed man must be fearful, 455
The other boot doesn't drop from heaven, 606
The other day at the green dumpsters, 728
The owl is a bronze urn of ashes, 461

The tree also died the exact, 475
The urge to be a tiny bird, 856
The wallet is as big as earth, 428
The wars: we're drawn to them, 74
The wasp, 464
The water spider, 470
The way a springer spaniel, 455
The weeks rush past headed, 814
The well pit is beneath where the pump shed burned, 361
The wind came up so strongly at midnight, 741
The wit of the corpse, 441
The world is wrenched on her pivot, shivering. Politicians, 371
The worst dream ever that all the birds in the world died overnight, 836
They're amputating the head of the poor girl, 619
They're putting a new green tin roof, 478
They say the years are layers, laminae, 700
They used to say we're living on borrowed, 748
They want to operate on me again, 862
Things I didn't know about until today, 591
Things to paint, 285
Thinking of those Russian schoolchildren, 518
This adobe is no protection against the flossy, 367
This amber light floating strangely upward in the woods—nearly, 154
This bronze ring punctures, 46
This is all it is, 234
This is cold salt, 41
This is the county fair, 473
This matted and glossy photo of Yesenin, 199
This moment says no to the next, 658
This morning, 463
This morning I felt strong and jaunty in my mail-order, 374
This morning I seem to hear the nearly inaudible, 608
This nadir: the wet hole, 96
This other speaks of bones, blood-wet, 21
This slender blue thread, 459
This small liquid mouth in the forest, 612
This song stays, 95
This year we have two gorgeous, 861
Three teeth pulled including, 478
Through the blinds, 34
Throw out the anchor, 441
Thunder before dawn, 783
Thus the poet is a beached gypsy, the first porpoise to whom it, 216

ABOUT THE AUTHOR

Over a fifty-year writing career, Jim Harrison (1937–2016) published nearly forty books of poetry, fiction, and nonfiction, all of which remain in print. His work has been translated into two dozen languages. Harrison is widely credited with reviving the novella form with the publication of the trilogy *Legends of the Fall*. The success of *Legends* led to his work in Hollywood writing screenplays. Known also for his deep appreciation for food and drink, Harrison wrote popular food columns for several journals and magazines, notably *Brick* and *Esquire*. In 2007 he was elected to the Academy of American Arts and Letters, and his extensive literary archive is housed at Grand Valley State University.

Jim Harrison was fiercely loyal to independent publishers, and two independent publishers are particularly loyal to his work: Grove Atlantic is dedicated to publishing Harrison's fiction and nonfiction, and Copper Canyon Press is committed to his poetry.

As the *Sunday Times* (London) wrote, "Jim Harrison is a writer with immortality in him."

ABOUT THE EDITOR

Joseph Bednarik is the co-publisher of Copper Canyon Press and served as Jim Harrison's poetry editor since the late 1990s.

ABOUT THE CONTRIBUTOR

Terry Tempest Williams is the author of numerous books of nonfiction, including *Leap, Red,* and the environmental classic *Refuge*. She is a fierce advocate for freedom of speech and environmental justice, and her writings appear frequently in journals and newspapers worldwide.

THE HEART'S WORK:
JIM HARRISON'S POETIC LEGACY

Jim Harrison: Complete Poems is the work of a lifetime by a single poet.

The book you hold became a tangible reality through the philanthropic support of hundreds of readers who sought to help secure and advance Jim Harrison's legacy as a poet. We are especially grateful to Bruce S. Kahn, whose spirit of generosity and genuine enthusiasm for Jim's work is deeply inspiring.

Copper Canyon Press is grateful to the following donors and supporters for their foundational investment in The Heart's Work and the publication of *Jim Harrison: Complete Poems:*

Joyce Harrington Bahle
Will Blythe
Denver Butson
David Caligiuri
Michael Cashin
Lea Chatham
Russell Chatham
Dr. Mary Lee Coffey
Susann Craig
Michael Croy
Todd Davis
Guy de la Valdene
Michael Delp
Chris Dombrowski
Mary and John ("Nick") Dumsch
Austin Evans
John Evans
Saramel Evans
John Freeman
Dan and Debbie Gerber
David and Cynthia Harrison
William Hearst, III

Amy Reynolds and Victor Herman
Anna Harrison Hjortsberg
Judy Hottensen
Lisa and Richard C. Howorth
Amy Hundley and Kristabelle Munson
James T. Harrison Trust
Dana Jennings
David Johnson
Bruce S. Kahn
Garrison Keillor
George Knotek
Ted Kooser
Peter Lewis and Johnna Turiano
Larry Mawby and Lois Bahle
Colum McCann
Terry McDonell and Stacey Hadash
Liesel and Hank Meijer

Rebecca Newth Harrison
Jack Nicholson
Gregg Orr
Molly Phinny
Peter Phinny
Red Pine
Jamie Harrison Potenberg
Nancy Richard
Randy Riley, Library of Michigan
Joseph Roberts
Paul and Jennifer Saffo
Bud Schulz
J. Stephen Sheppard
Liesl Slabaugh and Joseph Bednarik
Stephen Spencer
Joy Williams
Terry Tempest Williams
Joan Woods
Ray Zepeda

Copper Canyon Press extends profound thanks to the following supporters of The Heart's Work, and for their passionate advocacy for Jim's poetry. Each and all have helped bring this monumental book to life:

Anonymous (5)
Porter Abbott
Conrad Addison
In Memory of Dean
    Ahearn
Sean Akerman
Rudy Altergott
Don and Theresa
    Alverson
Kirby Ancona
Michael Patrick
    Anderson
Jon Andrew
Colman Andrews
Paul Assey
Loretta Libby Atkins
Glenn L. Bailey
Ryan W. Bailey
Robert Milo Baldwin
In memory of John
    Bancroft
Yves CL Barbeau
Teresa Barillas
Bart's Books
Mike and Susan
    Barzacchini
Joseph Cleeland
    Baufield
Carol Bawden and Scott
    Craig
John Baynes
Henry J.S. Benes
Susan Bergholz and Bert
    Snyder
Bob and Gayle Bergier
Dave and Ashley Bessom
Beth Bigler
Peter David Birt
Zackry Bodine
Amy Bolmer
Sally and Maurice Bolmer
Annabelle Bonebrake
Greg Boone
Tom Booth

Dan Born
Conner Bouchard-
    Roberts
Nick Bozanic
Brant Brechbiel
David Brewster and
    Mary Kay Sneeringer
Wickes Brewster
Charles W. Brice
Hannibal Bronson
Brett Brunmeier
Bryan Burns
Dan and Lorraine Burns
Robert L. Bussard
Michael Butler
Nickolas Butler
Steve Byrne
Bruce Campbell
Timothy James Campbell
Elise M. Cannon
Emily Capehart
David L. Capers
David V. Carner, Jr.
Gary Case
Catherine
Christopher Chaffee
The Charles Bowden
    Literary Trust
In memory of Russell
    Chatham
Justin Chimka
Katie Chriest
Trent Christensen
Jonathan Clark
C. Shelby Coffey, III
Charles Shelby Coffey, IV
Dr. Mary Lee Coffey
In memory of Wayne J.
    Colahan, Jr.
Karen Wilson Collins
Morris Collins
Kati, Coley, and Mike
    Conklin
Thomas Ford Conlan

Paul Copp
Irene and Mike Cotter
Robert W. Counseller
Keith Richard Courtad
Brent Cox
Connor B. Crawford
James K. Cribb
Dave Crowley
Aaron Dargis
Bill Davie
Jerry Davis
Gary DeCoker
Dan DeGusta
Jo DeLay-Kopp
Robert DeMott and
    Kathryn Fox
Ian Demsky
Lorraine Diaz
Max Dickinson
Ron Domen
Andy Dracup
Martin Dudley
Linda Dufelmeier
Drew Dumsch and Lisa
    Farago
David J. Edney
John Albert Ehrenfried
Ann Ehringhaus
Larry Eickstaedt
Elk River Books
Benny Emery
Craig Eslinger
Nancy M. Faaren
Deborah and Neal
    Fellows
Ross A. Field
Jay Fier
Rob Firchau
Michael Fountain
Bob Francis
Mo Frechette
Mark Galus
Lea Gamble
Gaudefroy-Demombynes

Corine Susan Geldhof
Alexandra Guequierre
    Giardino
Todd Goddard
"George Gordon"
Pamela and David Grath
Robert Murray Greene
Bob and Glee
    Greenwood
Kim L. Greenwood
Mike Groenewold
In memory of Miles
    Dean Grussing
Michael Guthrie
Kirby Hammel
Jim Hanlen
Art Hanlon
Albert Bryce Hanner
Kimberly Harrington and
    Rick Somarriba
Buck and Jackie Harrison
LuAnn and Klaus
    Heinert
Jordan Heinrich
Carlton Wayne
    Henderson
Dinah Henderson
Jason Henderson
Matt Henriksen
Mark D. Hicks
Jack D. Hill
Stephen D. Hill
Dave Himber
Capt. Steve Holbrook SC
    USN
Steven Hopkins
Steven Howard
Tom Huggler
Chris Huntington
William Quinton Hurley
Ninon Jamet
David Jannard and
    Autumn Rhodes
C. Randolph Jones
Hans Peter Jorgensen
Lyle S. Kearns
Shawn Kenney
Jill King

Jim Kirk
Erik Koik
Rick Kosinski
Daniel Kraft
Kevin and Sharon
    Krause
James Krepps
Andy Kristensen
Joel Kuipers
Denise LaFarr
Tom Lakin
Thomas W. Lambert
John Lane
Steven Lane and
    Cassandra McClintock
Alida and Christopher
    Latham
Jonathan Lax
Arthur Layton
Matthias Layton
David Le Mentec
Brian and Mindy Lee
Denis Lépée
Dan Lepo
Laurie Lisuk
Margrethe Löhrke
Ralph J. Long Jr.
P.W. Longhurst
Suzanne Lopez
Brett Lovelace
Jared Lowery
Ryan Ludlow
Conrad Lumm
Thomas Lynch
Sandra and Robert Lyon
Maggie C. Macdonald
Douglas MacHugh
Jillian MacLellan
Mitch Malecho
d.l.marfurt...
    makeshiftpoet
Ann Marshall
Jan Martenson
Christopher W. Martin
Henry Matthews
Ronald Mawby
Gary D. Maxwell
David Ira Mayberg

Erik Ira Philip Jordan
    Mayberg
Barry and Grace Mazur
Meredith Parsons
    McComb
Greg McCord
Shannon E. Price
    McGrath
Jamie McGraw
Conor J. McGuinness
Lawrence McKay
Brian Menges
Hans-Karl Meyer
David Mihalyov
Harry Miller and Barbara
    McNeil
Rebecca Elizabeth Miller
John Monczka
Shawn Monitor
Jerry D. Moore
Selena Moore
Ichiryu John Moran
    (一粒瑞海)
Chatham Morgan
Jennifer and Jamie
    Newton
Milo Newton
Eugene O'Brien
Kevin Emmett O'Brien
Shawn O'Dell
Jason O'Grady
Deb Ochs
Carissa Lee O'Connell
Reef "The Wonder Dog"
    OConnell
Rick Bear OConnell
Garrett Okenka
James Olson
Anne-Marie Oomen
Priscilla Oppenheimer
Gil Ott
W.I. Owen
Rachel Papadopoulos
Greg Pape
Patric A. Parker
Edward C. Parks
Juliet Patterson
Ben J. Peacock

Buddy Peacock
Brian and Leanne Perry
Eva and John Petoskey
Alan J. Pettingill
Ron Pihl
Chris Pinto
Ellen W. Pisor
Richard S. Posey
Ameer Qalbani
Mickey Ranalli
Julia Reed
R. Scott Richter
José Rico, Jr.
Tod F. Roach
Cindy and Dean Robb
Beth Rodenhuis
JBK Roditi
Maria de los Angeles
    Rodriguez
E. David Rollert
Marc Rosen
Jeffery David Ross
Hal Rowe
Gabriel N. Salazar
samfiftyfour
Pamela Jean Sampel
The Samuelson Family
    of Vermont
Scott Samuelson
David C. Sanderson
Anthony Sasso
SB
Bob Schleicher

Wilfried Schubert and
    Family
Nic Schuck
Eric Claude Schulte
Scott Thomas Schutte
Jesse Sensibar
Kelley and Philip
    Swanstrom Shaw
Matthew Shoemaker
Sibling Rivalry Press
Rebecca Siegel
Richard Silver
Sue A. Simon
Paul Sizemore
Madeleine Morlet Smith
M.L. Smoker
John Smolens
In Memory of Edith
    Snyder
Thomas Keener Spruth
Tait Stamp
Clemens Starck
Isaac Watson Stephenson
Kevin Stock
Joseph Stroud
Daryle Sturino
David and Alison Swan
Yolanda Danyi Szuch
Rana Tahir
G. Keith Taylor
Mary and Arthur Tomes
Ryan Topham
Ron Trendler
Sherry Tuminaro

Frederick Turner
Daniel Urban-Brown
The Van Emst Family
Robert van Vliet
Jan Vodicka
Kevin Votel
David A. Wade
Greg Wahl
Nicki Louise Walker
Jimmy Watts
For Wayne
Amber Wessel
Mimi and Norm Wheeler
J.D. Whitney
Doug Wick and Lucy
    Fisher
George E. Wilber, Jr.
Wm Willemstyn
Devin Spencer Wilson
Fred J. Wilson
Laura Wilson
John Winkelman
Benjamin Woodbeck
Don Woodruff
Stephen Wyatt
Jay Yencich
Glen Young
Jeff Zillgitt
Guy and Mary
    Zimmerman
Timothy R. Zuellig

Poetry is vital to language and living. Since 1972, Copper Canyon Press has published extraordinary poetry from around the world to engage the imaginations and intellects of readers, writers, booksellers, librarians, teachers, students, and donors.

WE ARE GRATEFUL FOR THE MAJOR SUPPORT PROVIDED BY:

THE PAUL G. ALLEN
FAMILY FOUNDATION

Anonymous
Jill Baker and Jeffrey Bishop
Anne and Geoffrey Barker
In honor of Ida Bauer, Betsy Gifford, and Beverly Sachar
Donna and Matthew Bellew
Will Blythe
John Branch
Diana Broze
John R. Cahill
Sarah Cavanaugh
The Beatrice R. and Joseph A. Coleman Foundation Inc.
The Currie Family Fund
Stephanie Ellis-Smith and Douglas Smith
Austin Evans
Saramel Evans
Mimi Gardner Gates
Gull Industries Inc. on behalf of William True
The Trust of Warren A. Gummow
William R. Hearst, III
Carolyn and Robert Hedin
Bruce Kahn
Phil Kovacevich and Eric Wechsler

TO LEARN MORE ABOUT UNDERWRITING
COPPER CANYON PRESS TITLES,
PLEASE CALL 360-385-4925 EXT. 103

WE ARE GRATEFUL FOR THE MAJOR SUPPORT PROVIDED BY:

Lakeside Industries Inc. on behalf of Jeanne Marie Lee
Maureen Lee and Mark Busto
Peter Lewis and Johnna Turiano
Ellie Mathews and Carl Youngmann as The North Press
Larry Mawby and Lois Bahle
Hank and Liesel Meijer
Jack Nicholson
Gregg Orr
Petunia Charitable Fund and adviser Elizabeth Hebert
Suzanne Rapp and Mark Hamilton
Adam and Lynn Rauch
Emily and Dan Raymond
Joseph C. Roberts
Jill and Bill Ruckelshaus
Cynthia Sears
Kim and Jeff Seely
Joan F. Woods
Barbara and Charles Wright
Caleb Young as C. Young Creative
The dedicated interns and faithful volunteers
of Copper Canyon Press

This book is set in Monotype Garamond Pro.
Display type set in LTC Deepdene.
Book design by Gopa & Ted2, Inc. and John Miller.
Printed on archival-quality paper.